FRANCIS PAUDRAS was born in 1935. He began playing classical piano at the age of five and continued to perform as an amateur throughout his life. After studying graphic arts at the Ecole Estienne in Paris, he set up his own studio and pursued a career as an illustrator. Paudras was the author and editor of *To Bird With Love*, an iconographic book in homage to Charlie Parker; *The Eye of Jazz*, a book of jazz photographs dedicated to the photographer Herman Leonard; a historical essay "Jazz and Ravel—Ravel and Jazz"; and a study of Lili Boulanger's work on jazz, "Lili Our Love." He also wrote jazz reviews and articles, contributed to radio and television programs dedicated to jazz, and developed multi-media programs that introduced students to jazz.

Paudras first saw Bud Powell—for him the most important musician in the universe—in 1956 and met him personally in 1957. Alarmed by rumors concerning Powell's well-being, Paudras further investigated the situation and discovered the jazz pianist's great distress and loneliness. Despite the pressures of a racist society, a profound friendship was born between these two men, reinforced by their musical affinity. He helped Powell cope with the crises of an ill-fated life and cared for him in his home. Francis Paudras's privileged relationship with one of the great jazz masters, and the extraordinary events experienced at his side, gave substance and spirit to this book, which was the inspiration for Bertrand Tavernier's film *'Round Midnight*.

Francis Paudras committed suicide on November 27, 1997 in his home in Antigny, France.

Bud Powell and Francis Paudras, Paris 1959
(Photo by Mic)

FRANCIS PAUDRAS

DANCE
OF THE
INFIDELS

A Portrait of Bud Powell

Translated from the original French by Rubye Monet
English translation edited by Warren Bernhardt

Foreword by Bill Evans

DA CAPO PRESS • NEW YORK

Library of Congress Cataloging-in-Publication Data

Paudras, Francis.
  [Danse des infidèles. English]
  Dance of the infidels: a portrait of Bud Powell / Francis Paudras; translated from the original French by Rubye Monet; English translation edited by Warren Bernhardt; foreword by Bill Evans.
    p.   cm.
  ISBN 0-306-80816-1
  1. Powell, Bud. 2. Jazz musicians—United States—Biography. I. Title.
ML417.P73P413   1998
786.2'165'092—dc21
[B]   97-51909
                                                       CIP
                                                       MN

First Da Capo Press edition 1998

This Da Capo Press paperback edition of *Dance of the Infidels* is an English translation of the edition first published in France in 1986, under the title *La Danse des Infidèles*, with minor editorial emendations and new photo inserts. It is published by arrangement with the author.

Published by Da Capo Press, Inc.
A Subsidiary of Plenum Publishing Corporation
233 Spring Street, New York, N.Y. 10013

DEDICATION

To another genius, the pianist and composer
Bill Evans

After many years of reflection and research, I am very proud to have succeeded in completing this work. I wanted it to be substantial, sincere, and without restrictions. But most of all, worthy of the man and the artist to whom it is dedicated. Realizing this homage to Bud Powell has been the greatest privilege life has had to offer me.

The humility and love which inspired me all the way through this venture should be the first message to be understood by the reader.

ACKNOWLEDGMENTS

I would like to thank:

Yuval Taylor, my editor at Da Capo Press, for his enthusiasm and help in the realization of this work.

Francis Dreyfus, who kindly financed the translation of this book; without his generosity *Dance of the Infidels* would not be here today.

Rubye Monet, the translator, for her incomparable talent and extreme sensitivity.

Warren Bernhardt, the great pianist who contributed tirelessly to the shaping and editing of this book into the jazz idiom.

Frances Barnes and Cecilia Powell, for their invaluable cooperation and for permission to reprint letters and poetry from Bud Powell's archives.

Anita Huguet, for her valuable help and support all the way on this crusade for Bud.

Randi Hultin, Kirsten and Skip Malone, as well as Margareta Lundström, for their exceptionally important evidence, immense contribution, and permission to include their stories and letters in this book.

Dizzy Reece, the great trumpeter who guided me in my difficult research, especially in Harlem.

Maxwell T. Cohen, Bud Powell's lawyer, for having given me access to his archives, which allowed certain obscure points in Bud's life to be clarified.

Alain Chevrier, Nils Edström, Jorgen Leth, Mic, Jan Persson, and Don Schlitten, my photographer friends, who generously offered their marvelous photos.

Sara Rowland, who kindly translated the introductory passages.

Marylène Boisdin, Michel Laurier, and Stéphane Paudras, for their help at all times.

Toshiko Akiyoshi, Rozeland Allen, Baroness Nica de Kœnigswarter, Charles Bellonzi, Mildred Berg, Jane Bernhardt, Andy Browne, Kenny Clarke, Ornette Coleman, Maurice Cullaz, Carolyn, Mary and Bud Dean, Charles Delaunay, Gil and Anita Evans, Leonard Gaskin, Dizzy Gillespie, Ira Gitler, Babs Gonzales, Jimmy Gourley, Jenny Gregory, Johnny and Myriam Griffin, Fred Harris, Jacques Hess, Bertha Hope, Richard "Prophet" Jennings, Freddy Jones, Doctor Joussaume, Jackie McLean, Marian McPartland, Pierre Michelot, Kurt Mohr, François Postif, Peter Pullman, Henri Renaud, Max Roach, Russell Rockman, Marcel Romano, Jean-Thierry Roussillon, Steve Schein, Dolly Schmidt, the Schomburg Library, Claude Sclouch, Carl Smith, Art Taylor, Doctors Mr. and Mme. Teboul, Franck Tenot, Jean Tronchot, René Urtréger, and Jean Wagner, all of whom generously shared their stories with me in personal interviews, and/or whom granted permission to print their stories in this book, and all the friends devoted to the memory of Bud, who helped us.

Editors Note: Every effort has been made to acknowledge and identify all sources, including publication date, where possible.

CONTENTS

FOREWORD

Of all the musicians I ever loved—Bird and Stan Getz and Miles and lots of others that no one even knows I listened to—it was Bud who influenced me the most.

I was fifteen when I first heard Dexter's recordings with Bud. Then came Bird and Dizzy and the big bands . . . they all influenced me, but Bud more than anyone else.

He was so expressive, such emotion flowed out of him! There are different kinds of emotion: there is the easy, superficial kind, and there is another kind, that doesn't make you laugh or cry, that doesn't make you feel anything but a sense of sheer perfection. That's what I felt with Bud. It's a feeling we sometimes get from Beethoven. . . . It's not that it's beautiful in the sense of pretty or brilliant, it's something else, something much deeper. When people talk about the giants— Bird, Bud, Dizzy, and Miles—I think they underestimate Bud. They're always putting him down, saying he was this or that. . . . But I never felt that way about him.

Bill Evans
From an interview with Randi Hultin,
Oslo, 1964

If I had to choose one single musician for his artistic integrity, for the incomparable originality of his creation and the grandeur of his work, it would be Bud Powell. He was in a class by himself.

Bill Evans
Comments made after his concert at Cardin Hall,
Paris, November 26, 1979

INTRODUCTION

Everybody wants to be in the image of God.
That's why I play jazz.

JOHN LEWIS

Before I could write this book there were such obstacles to overcome that at times I was afraid I would never do it. To begin with, there was something almost indecent in talking about Bud. How would I ever find the right words to express the intensity of my feelings, both for him as a person and for his music? I dreaded that my judgments might be deemed too absolute, my enthusiasm too excessive, and my deep emotions nothing more than blind passion. But now these fears have dissipated, leaving in their place only a serene determination.

The words that follow come straight from the heart. But they are also the fruit of a conscious decision: to stick as close as possible to my personal reflections, the thoughts I have hitherto kept entirely to myself. Rather than an anecdotal account, this book is an outgrowth of a long meditation beginning in 1956, the year I saw Bud for the first time.

I make no claim to reveal all the facets of Bud's interior world. The complexity of his genius is such that his personality, however likable and endearing, will probably always remain shrouded in mystery. Yet how dreadful it would be to let his vast contributions fall into oblivion.

If this great exponent of black American culture inspired me, a white European, to devote a book to his work, it is simply because I think his music is of universal scope. The work of Bud Powell is not only a message of love of a black artist for black people, it is also a message of great beauty, hope, and peace for all the peoples of the world.

My utter certainty of this has provided the impetus to take on the task, all the more so as Bud Powell's life and work seem thus far to have inspired no more from commentators than shopworn anecdotes and trivia. My passion springs not from some romantic infatuation, but from thirty consecutive years of deep and painstaking study of his music, a body of work I consider one of the most compelling in the history of music.

I should also add that I am quite aware of how most American jazz writers regard European amateurs. It has been said repeatedly that we have a romanticized vision of jazz and a false idea of the jazz world.

Such comments and criticisms have in no way made me want to modify my own point of view. The French may have less first-hand knowledge than those Americans who lived through these musical events, but apparently all of their combined knowledge has not enabled the American writers to produce the kinds of genuine studies that we, such true lovers of jazz, so yearn for.

Furthermore, after a lifetime devoted to this music, I still believe it's no accident that so many of the great American musicians found their ultimate consecration in France or elsewhere in Europe, where many of them came to spend their lives. From my own experience and that of other well-placed observers, I can affirm that they found our vision and ideas, not to mention our welcome, to their liking.

Many musicians felt out of place as the United States became increasingly commercial. A society where the opportunistic pursuit of immediate profits outweighed all other considerations was completely ill-suited to their artistic demands. Musicians like Billie Holiday, Lester Young, Kenny Clarke, Thelonious Monk, Fats Navarro, Charlie Parker, Bud Powell, and Bill Evans, to mention only a few, never totally accepted integration into a system that was antithetical to their personal artistic endeavors.

In their categorical refusal to compromise, they were following in the footsteps of the classical masters of the old world. It is easy to see how they might be more at home with Europe and its romantic spirit. Many American musicians have felt a deep nostalgia for the roots of a certain European music. Thelonious Monk, for example, once said in an interview, "We loved Ravel, Stravinsky, Debussy, Prokofiev, Schoenberg, so I guess we had to be influenced by them." If Africa is largely responsible for the rhythms and the pulse of jazz, its structure, melodies, and harmonic conceptions more often than not hark back to earlier European creators. During a lecture in Houston, Texas in April 1928, Maurice Ravel said, "American folklore? But just what is your folklore? Indian melodies? Are they American? Negro spirituals? Blues? Are they what is meant by American?"

Ravel seems not to rule out the development of a new European school that would be the continuation of classical music. He probably never imagined that the only ones to lay claim to the advances of the great classicists would be the American school represented by Art Tatum, Charlie Parker, Bud Powell, Bill Evans, and the like. After Frédéric Chopin, Claude Debussy, Gabriel Fauré, Maurice Ravel, and Lili Boulanger, after Richard Wagner, Alexander Scriabin, and Sergei Rachmaninoff, Europe was seeking the continuity of its romantic impulse. We were to find it in the American music called jazz, the classical music of tomorrow.

Readers of this book will soon become aware of a gulf between reality and fiction, between the facts about the period when Bud lived with me and the accounts of other writers who took it upon themselves to recount this period of time. The discrepancies are so glaring as to cast doubt on these writers' reliability in other matters and to make one realize how cautious one must be when reading their accounts of his earlier life as well. They could very easily have checked their facts by asking those directly concerned, but of course it's simpler to repeat whatever gossip comes quickly and easily to mind. In so doing, they kept alive a legend that did only harm to Bud. None of them ever bothered to take a long, hard look at his music, which is the only subject really worth our interest.

If I sometimes seem less than charitable to certain persons, I make no apologies. My only aim is to do justice to a man who, in his lifetime, was rarely treated with any of the consideration he deserved. All I care about today is to show as best I can the arbitrary quirks of misfortune and the downright ill-will he came up against time after time throughout his tragic life. In the conspiracy of silence that always surrounded Bud, there were many who shamelessly and constantly took advantage of him.

Last of all, I gladly omit those musicians who pillaged and parodied him, and the others—those who deliberately deserted his work and today feign ignorance of his very name, the better to claim the fatherhood of musical forms of which he was the true innovator.

WILLOW GROVE

(Recorded in New York, April 25, 1955 [Verve])

I n the early hours of a chill wintry morning, on January 21, 1945, the smoke-filled bar on the outskirts of Philadelphia was slowly closing up for the night. At the piano sat a young man named Thelonious Sphere Monk, solid as a rock, yet somehow mysterious, surreal. All night, he had played like a god on the club's old out-of-tune upright. The last customers—the most faithful fans—were using any excuse to linger on, to get one more look at the man who had once again confounded musical tradition. Some were put off by the incredible boldness of his music, others were deeply awed.

The drummer, Max Roach, a trim, slender young man whose glasses gave him the look of a college boy, was patiently putting away his gear. Drummers are always the last to leave a club. You really have to love your instrument to be willing to take it apart piece by piece and lug it back and forth every day. The only things you can ever afford to leave in place are the bass drum and the larger tom-toms, which are pretty hard to steal without being noticed.

Thelonious sat listening to the comments of the inebriated patrons with a skeptical little smile. The scent of marijuana hung in the air, wafting around the room with every gust of cold air as the door opened to let another customer out into the chilly night.

All at once there was a commotion in the club. A squad of police officers burst in, stormed past the clients slumped at the bar, and headed straight for Monk.

"Let's see your ID!"

"Nope," came the firm but laconic reply.

One cop, built like a football lineman, grabbed Thelonious by the arm and started frisking him, none too gently. With a violent movement Thelonious wrenched out of the iron grip, only to find himself seized from behind by another cop, expertly positioned just in back of him. In seconds he was being propelled roughly toward the exit. Just then, a shadowy figure stepped out and stood between Thelonious and the cops.

"Cut it out! What do you think you're doing?"

"Where'd this guy come from? Keep outta this, you! Nobody asked you nothin'!"

"Stop that, man! You don't know what you're doing! The guy you're pushing around just happens to be the world's greatest pianist!"

A hand shot up, that of the cop who seemed to be the leader, and a short, stout club came down squarely on the interloper's head. His skull gave way with the awful sound of a cracking nutshell.

Thelonious, immobilized by the hands gripping his arms, watched in stunned silence as his friend slumped to the floor. It was his best friend, practically his brother: Earl Powell, Bud to his friends, and to all those who knew him well enough to talk with him.

Earl Powell was a brilliant young pianist, just turned twenty and already appreciated within the closed circle of modernists who were beginning to revolutionize music. No one knew very much about him. He was quiet, reserved, proud sometimes to the point of arrogance, and always dressed to perfection.

Thelonious himself admired him greatly, and, after Duke Ellington and Art Tatum, whom he adulated, he considered Bud to be the most promising pianist in the world. A classic artist, a virtuoso pianist, inventive and visionary, young Earl was quite introspective where beauty was concerned, almost excessively steadfast and uncompromising.

Before they even knew what was going on, the last few patrons, much the worse for liquor, saw the police van driving off into the early morning, taking the two musicians to some fearful destination.

Thelonious was held briefly for questioning and then released to return to the streets of Harlem. As for Bud Powell, he was recuperating slowly, but suffering from terrible headaches. After the hospital had superficially treated his head wound, the police, who had not welcomed his intervention, had him transferred to a prison cell, where he was given ammonia showers to calm him down whenever he protested. Then Bud went home to Willow Grove, to be cared for by his mother Pearl and by Frances Barnes, a charming eighteen-year-old he had met two years before. They tried to treat his headaches, but nothing stopped the pain: neither the compresses of Pearl and Frances, nor the liquor he had started drinking in search of relief. He went back to his music with enthusiasm but the persistent headaches forced him to seek treatment. He went to Bellevue, where they kept him for observation and then sent him to Creedmoor State Hospital where, drowned in the state bureaucracy, he was to remain for months without a hearing.

Behind the locked gates of Creedmoor, caged behind barred and wire-covered windows, beyond the dirty red brick walls and the impenetrable hedge of barbed wire, who was this young black man, lost in an anonymous crowd? Surrounded by alcoholics and drug addicts, chronic mental patients left to themselves in solitude and indifference, he was one individual crushed by despair, no different from the others, nothing else but a man with a number, rejected by society as undesirable, and even considered by some as dangerous.

He grew used to this desolate little world and took refuge in its anonymity. The premises of Creedmoor have since been put to other uses and are closed to the public, but I talked my way in, camera in hand, thanks to the complicity of some black guards on duty one Sunday morning in the sixties, impressed, no doubt, by my determination. They allowed me to film.

Within the four walls of his cell, what was he *now*? A musician? Or a forgotten man? Without his piano, was he still a pianist? A few friends still remembered that he was a genius and that the world of music couldn't do without him: his soul brother Thelonious Monk, his spiritual twin Elmo Hope, and his unconditional friend Marian McPartland. They came to Creedmoor to see him, braved the gates of shame to bring him a little of the affection he needed for survival.

In a sign of derision—or was it despair?—Bud had drawn a keyboard on the wall of his cell. When Elmo came to visit, Bud walked up to the drawing, placed his hands on the imaginary keys and played a soundless chord. His eyes filled with distress, he asked, "How do you think that sounds?"

At each of his visits, Elmo noticed with growing concern that Bud was deteriorating physically although no logical explanation was offered by the nurses on the ward. With much difficulty, he managed to attract the attention of a youthful doctor, himself a jazz-lover, who had not realized that the hospital harbored so prestigious an inmate as Bud Powell. The young doctor quickly took charge and ordered a series of tests to determine the reasons for the patient's physical decline. Placed in the care of an older doctor with whom he had problems getting along, Bud had received treatment of the most expeditious nature, including many doses of medication—tranquilizers, sleeping pills, and injections of another (unidentified) substance. In short, in the guise of prescribed medical treatment, he was slowly but surely being poisoned. Worst of all were the electroshocks, administered systematically and mercilessly. Each time, his cries of terror rang through the hospital walls: "Help, help, they're trying to kill me!"

This dreadful period, described to me by Elmo Hope in 1964, was thankfully brought to a close through his vigilance and the sympathy of the young doctor, whose first action was to send for a piano and allow Bud to play once a week.

(In 1964 Thelonious also told me that Bud's courageous intervention in the club that night, though disastrous to himself, had undoubtedly saved Monk from a lot of trouble.)

In his unpublished collection of musicians' memoirs, Maxwell T. Cohen (Bud's attorney) reports the testimony of Marian McPartland about her visits to Creedmoor to see Bud:

> It was a large room. There were a number of patients and their visitors having lunch and talking. There was an old decrepit piano with a number of defective keys. I tried to persuade Bud to play but he declined. He asked me to play "A Nightingale Sang In Berkeley Square." I did so. After a while Bud did play the piano. Notwithstanding the defective keys he seemed to get wonderful tonality out of the piano and seemed to be able to play around the defective keys. As I left Bud turned to me and plaintively inquired, "Marian, has everybody forgotten me? Do they still remember me?"

Earl Powell's life had begun with a mistake. On his birth certificate is a clerical error, not in the day or the month, but in the year of his birth. Bud Powell was born on September 27, 1924, and not in 1922 as written. When this was pointed out to the authorities at the Records Office, the reply was, "Unbelievable. That's never happened before and you can be sure it'll never happen again."

The "Earl Bud Powell" file, kept at his lawyer's office, is a pile of papers three feet high and easily three feet wide. Each paper bears the mention: "subject presumed incompetent." Bear in mind that this is the man who revolutionized piano playing in terms of harmony, melody, and rhythm.

The young doctor who had decided to help Bud finally suggested that a concert be held in order to prove to the hospital authorities that their patient was fit to work. The announcement of the concert and the return of the great pianist attracted a considerable crowd. His friends were afraid that after such a long interruption, Bud would have lost the legendary speed and drive that had made his reputation. Of all the guests invited to the concert, not the least worried were Max Roach and Curly Russell, who had been booked to accompany

Bud. With the first measures, Max Roach later told me, Bud's fingers let loose sparks. Strange as it may seem, he played as never before, with speed more stupefying than it had ever been. His ideas were limpid, dazzling, with a beauty and originality that were positively breathtaking.

At the end of the concert, the crowd went wild with applause and shouts of admiration. Bud was released to the care of his mother, who tried in vain to soothe the terrible headaches that would, from that time on, give him no peace. But at least the "amazing Bud Powell" was back on the jazz scene. Alas, it was not to be for long . . .

ALL GOD'S CHILLUN GOT RHYTHM

(Recorded at Carnegie Hall, New York, December 25, 1949 [IAJRC 20])

T he story thus far I have gathered from the accounts of several musicians. I cannot swear to its accuracy; I was not there. To make clear where *I* come into this picture, I should say a few words about my own musical background and the events that shaped my personality.

My father knew nothing about music. My mother was fond of it, although she'd had no musical education. Her taste was the fruit of mere chance and her musical world was quite a limited one. But as long as she lived, she took an interest in any form of music I brought home, whatever conflicts it may have created. She had become aware very early of the joys she had missed and had sworn to give her children music lessons. My father went along with her wishes, never realizing the consequences it would have.

So at age five I started piano lessons, as my sister Noëlle, five years younger, was to do later on. It was my mother's favorite instrument. My first piano was of dismal quality. Its touch was awful and its wooden frame made it impossible to keep it decently tuned. Nevertheless, thanks to a lively imagination, my interest in music grew. In the tinny sounds that came from this inferior instrument, I could hear the possibilities hidden in the pieces I played.

I would be an ingrate not to be thankful to my parents, for in the unlikely surroundings of their home I first acquired the passion for music that would eventually brighten my life. The year I began my music lessons, 1940, was hardly favorable to artistic pursuits. The war had just broken out. We lived very modestly, money was scarce, and my father gave up his job as a journalist to throw himself heart and soul into the Resistance.

For the first time in my life, music became my shield, protecting my inner world from the terrible conflict that raged outside. My father came from an old Breton family. He was one of those staunch, upstanding men who, when it comes to freedom, is afraid of no one and stops at nothing. He had joined the Resistance from the first moments and, flouting the most basic rules of security, had set up the headquarters of his network in our house, thus involving his whole family in a most dangerous adventure.

The four years during which we lived in this whirlwind atmosphere were both frightening and uplifting, and in my childhood memory, music is inseparable from the rest. In the hardest moments, it worked on me like a magic balm. My piano was my means of escape, my symbol of freedom. It was my confidante and the only witness of my childish questions in an adult world I couldn't understand. I learned to equate the struggle going on around me with my own struggle for inner peace and truth.

There were thirteen in my father's Resistance group, all exceptional men. This was no wonder, for only exceptional men with great personal affinities and a similar vision of the world were able to make such a commitment. Most of them were ordinary workers, market porters who unloaded produce at Les Halles, then the main wholesale food market in Paris, and lived in our little town of Saulx-les-Chartreux, outside the city. One was different, however. He was the village priest. It was a strange partnership, to say the least, for my father was a freethinker and never went to church. For that matter, our family's relation with the church was limited to the weddings and funerals that propriety dictated we had to attend. For this priest, all that mattered was the common combat. He never talked religion with the other members of the group and if anyone looked questioningly at his cassock, he would reply, "You know, I'm a priest only as far as the belt!" (He never made clear whether the priestly part was above or below the belt.)

My father had a wonderful sense of humor and the vivid language of the old Parisian working class. I still remember how he would refer to the Jews whom we helped escape into the Unoccupied Zone as the "gentlemen of the altered organ." The black Americans who parachuted into our woods he called the "Owens," a reference to Jesse Owens, the famous 1936 Olympics champion. Both groups were treated with good humor and no trace of the racial prejudices of the time. And this humor never cast any doubt on their courage and suffering. Some German Army deserters, called "les fridolins," whom my father no longer viewed as enemies, also came in for the same light-hearted treatment despite the gravity of their situation. After all, a deserter might have been a fake, planted there to spy on us. The priest decided that liquor was the universal truth serum, and all the suspects were plied with our local brew, in the course of "interrogations" that left the entire crew reeling, not to mention rocking with laughter.

Thus, from my earliest childhood, I received an incomparable lesson in anti-racism. These people we were helping to escape represented our only link with the free world. My father always spoke of respect for the individual, so I learned that loving your neighbor was something you did regardless of religion or color.

In a secret closet we had hidden an ancient radio that my father used to receive word from the front, as well as the coded personal messages sent to the Resistance by London. Most of the messages were either instructions or confirmations that someone we sent had safely arrived in the Free Zone. I remember one American paratrooper who was so tall we nicknamed him the Basketball Player. The message we received about him was: "The Basketball Player scored four points, twice." Another message was: "Adolph isn't bike-riding any more." That meant that a German deserter, nicknamed Adolph, who had arrived at our house by bike, had reached his destination. "Maple Leaf meets fish and chips" meant that our Canadian had reached England. Each message received was greeted with an explosion of joy. The Germans tried to jam transmissions and the resulting static meant that we really had to listen closely. My father tried to improve reception with a complicated and mysterious device he had put together, a sort of antenna shaped like a large cobweb that he would carefully adjust, trying to bring in London as clearly as possible.

We waited impatiently for these personal messages and for the news broadcasts, but we also listened to the Voice of America. I remember how the sound would intermittently surge and fade. This was how I heard for the first time a new kind of music, an extraordinary, incomparable music coming from another universe whose existence I had never suspected. It was the sound of hope, of a free world. I could hardly identify the instruments. The music sounded almost abstract and arrived in waves. It would grow, swell, then just as a melody began to take shape, it faded again, mysterious and unapproachable. I was shocked and at the same time frustrated to be unable to catch the rest of these melodies and to keep them for myself. In these floating wisps I was hearing for the first time, with strange premonitions, the music that would change my life.

In this very special atmosphere, my father endeavored to bring me up according to rigorous principles of the sort that are not so common any more. For him there were two above all: a sense of honor and a devotion to duty. He taught me the importance of total commitment, of giving oneself for an ideal through an existential choice, of humility before the accomplishment of one's duty. Perhaps this will explain to uncomprehending rationalists why it was easy for me to make such a commitment to Bud Powell, who was first of all just another human being in trouble.

After the war a series of piano teachers trooped through our house, each as much a dilettante as the others; but no matter, the virus of music had infected my system. Gradually a strange sort of music, unknown and inconceivable on the piano, began to overcome me. I had received no outside influence: we had no record player and my father's radio emitted only the most confused sounds. My musical training went on assiduously but in great disorder. In my search for new sounds, I had what my teachers considered an unfortunate tendency to modify the harmonies of certain pieces. This attraction for modulations outside of the traditional repertoire would soon find its justification in a boarding school near Le Mans, some two hundred miles from Paris.

My parents thought that after the hard years of war in the Paris suburbs, the fresh air and tranquility of the provinces would do me good. The political situation was not very stable and education was not yet well organized. So I was sent to boarding school, far from my family and friends. It was a hard separation, particularly as I could only go home every three months, but music made it easier to bear. This somewhat monastic life was to have a decisive influence on my character.

For enjoyment, and to forget my loneliness, I threw myself into my musical studies. I had been given permission to leave the school to take lessons with a private teacher and to practice daily in a house next door, which belonged to a family of musicians and music teachers. This family had a son, Michel Ganeau, two years older than me, who was also student at the school and who played, as I did, on the basketball team. At fifteen, Michel was already a virtuoso violinist. Because he was so young, he had been refused the first prize of the Conservatory (which he won the following year) as well as the Ginette Neveu prize. I was impressed by Michel's brilliance and sensitivity as well as his casual simplicity. He would often come to hear me practice on the family piano. At the time, I was playing Bach, Schumann, Brahms, and Beethoven, but also Chopin, for whom I had a marked preference. Chopin's Slavic sensibility touched me more than the German composers. My tastes are unchanged to this day, and the great interest I had in Bill Evans, who was of Russian origin through his mother, confirms the attraction I have always felt for the cradle of this music. There are even some genealogists who say my own name is of Slavic origin.

Sometimes, as he listened to me play, Michel would have an amused grin. One day he made this remark, astonishing but at the time meaningless to me: "It's funny, when you play Bach or Chopin, it sounds like jazz."

"Jazz? What's that?" I didn't even know the word. He had to remedy my appalling ignorance. First he made sure his parents were out, then he took me to his room, where he had an old beat-up gramophone.

"What? You've never heard of jazz? Just listen to this!"

The revelation was such that the moment is engraved forever in my memory. I was hearing Fats Waller for the first time. It felt like a punch square in the chest. I was bowled over, but at the same time troubled with a feeling of familiarity, an indefinable feeling that I had heard it somewhere before. Michel was overjoyed by my look of ecstasy. From that day on, unbeknownst to his parents, who were fervent classical musicians, I had a daily session with his jazz records: James P. Johnson, Jelly Roll Morton, Earl Hines, until the apotheosis, the epitome—Art Tatum. The instant I heard Tatum I knew I was marked for life.

After two years at boarding school, the time had come to decide what I was going to do with my life. As I had some talent for drawing, my parents and my teachers agreed that I should pursue this path. Music, which was clearly my principal concern, was never envisaged as a possible profession. At the time, piano playing was seen as a frivolous occupation, akin to that of tumblers and clowns.

I was accepted at the Ecole Estienne in Paris and embarked on a course in graphic arts. Fascinated by all forms of drawing and painting, I was particularly attracted to engraving. Four years later I graduated, having obtained a number of diplomas but without having lost my interest in music. During this period I met some people who shared my passion for jazz and with them began to discover the jazz clubs and cellars of the capital—sordid places, some of them, left over from the Occupation years of clandestineness. Here we heard Django Reinhardt, Sidney Bechet, Bernard Peiffer, Raymond le Sénéchal, Maurice Moufflard, Michel de Villers, etc. I went regularly to the cinema Le Rex where Charles Delaunay's program *Jazz Varieties* was presented every Sunday morning and broadcast live on the radio. I had a wire recorder at home and when I wasn't there, I got my mother to record programs for me. During these years I came to know the picturesque denizens of Paris nightlife and completed my education in the world of jazz. After Tatum, Nat King Cole made his entry into my life. His music prepared me for Erroll Garner's, whose energy and harmonies bowled me over. Garner was said to adore Rachmaninoff and vice versa. To my great satisfaction, Bill Evans later confirmed the importance of this great artist, stupidly denigrated because he was more successful commercially than most jazz musicians. A "real" jazz musician, as we all know, in order to be authentic, has to be poor, miserable, and preferably unknown! While I was listening to all this music, I was also pursuing my own research, which didn't get much approval from my peers. But my new piano teacher, Colette Ourisson de Bosredon (who had taught at the London Conservatory), was first intrigued by my research, and then deeply interested. "Your music is courageous," she said one day.

At the time little of this music was written down and most of my work was done by ear. She was extremely helpful in giving me my first notions of harmony. During frequent auditions to which students and their parents were invited, I had the opportunity to try out my first attempts at improvisation before an audience that was skeptical, to say the least. I was pleased to have made the leap. But I kept in my repertoire some select pieces by Bach, Chopin, and Debussy that my teacher said I played with a certain brio, just to show that to my mind jazz was inseparable from the great classics.

I listened to all the jazz broadcasts on the radio and recorded many of them on tape. It was there that I heard for the first time a man who some thought was a promising young pianist while others said that what he played was not jazz. It was Bud Powell. The experience was like a lightning bolt, a sublime and blinding revelation. I was filled with bliss. Bud played "All God's Chillun Got Rhythm" in a trio with Ray Brown and Max Roach. I couldn't explain why, but I knew at once that for me this music was the most important in the universe. As this certainty grew, the course of my life was transformed. The power of this music became a part of my everyday gestures, my everyday acts.

I was fifteen when Bud invaded my inner world. I scoured the pages of *Jazz News* (the magazine of Nicole and Eddie Barclay) and *Jazz Hot*, on the lookout for news of my "master." I read and reread the article by Ralph Schecroun in *Jazz News* of April 1949, whose comments warmed my heart and confirmed my personal feelings, feelings I could share with no one.

Bud's left hand gives his playing a fullness and sureness that no other be-bop pianist has. Bud is also the only be-bop pianist sufficiently independent from the tempo to be able to improvise fast, complicated phrases in the manner of Charlie Parker, phrases that always land on their feet with amazing precision.

Let me add that Bud Powell has enormous inspiration: in all his solos we recognize the sound of a great musician and the true class of someone who has something to say and says it well. . . . Bud Powell, the "madman of bop," heats up the combo like nobody else and brings in the solos with his dazzling entries.

When I heard Ralph in the swing sessions recorded by Charles Delaunay, I realized that he had not written those words lightly. And when I listen to them today, I have no doubt that at the time he understood Bud's lesson better than anyone.

Also in *Jazz News* (October 1949), Nicole Barclay, who knew all the bop musicians and was deeply involved in their music, wrote a piece after her return from the United States that made my heart beat faster:

The extraordinary pianist Bud Powell, also playing at Birdland, gave us the strongest emotional experience of the entire trip.

Bud is quite simply astounding. He has taken Art Tatum's style and adapted it to bop while adding his own winning personality and innumerable ideas.

Charlie Parker says Bud is a genius. Bud says the same thing about Parker and we think they're both right.

UPS 'N' DOWNS

(Recorded in Paris? 1960? [Mainstream])

But alas, the first ominous notes of something deeply wrong began to trickle in from the United States. They were tiny bits of information and their vagueness made them all the more disturbing. The May 1951 issue of *Jazz Hot* carried this note in Larry Quillingham's "News from America" column: "Bud Powell, back in New York after his last 'nervous breakdown,' is making a brief appearance at Birdland, no more than a week, with Dizzy and Bird."

In France in the early 1950s, traditional jazz was still the ruling force. Dizzy Gillespie had come to Paris the first time in 1947, and returned with his big band in 1948. Charlie Parker had come in 1949. On the radio Maurice Cullaz presented their music as "the most advanced type of jazz," but so far it had few followers. All it managed to do was stir up polemics, with critics and journalists on opposing sides attacking each other for all they were worth. Charles Delaunay, the founder of *Jazz Hot* and the main supporter of the new musical trend (in France intimately linked with the name of Boris Vian), was in pitched battle with Hugues Panassié, for whom jazz had stopped in the 1930s. Raymond le Sénéchal, Bernard Peiffer, and Martial Solal were already playing the new music with real conviction. Henri Renaud, pianist, journalist, and enlightened fan, introduced for the first time on radio a young pianist named René Urtréger. (If I only mention pianists, it is partly, of course, because I followed them more carefully, but also that I've always felt the piano is the main current for developing styles.) Henri gave some further impressions in *Jazz Hot*, "Fresh from New York" (July-August 1951), when he reviewed Bud's latest record. This stupendous album, with Curly Russell and Max Roach, had come out on the Roost label in January 1947, and had just been released in France. Now, for the first time, I learned a little about the life of this man who had so captured my attention. I was so stirred by the article that I practically knew it by heart.

> Everyone knows that a pianist's toughest test is a solo record. Only the great masters have managed it. Bud is undoubtedly the only bop pianist with the necessary qualities to record so many solo sides: stunning technique, a brilliant left hand, strong swing, boundless imagination. Many

have spoken of the influence on Bud Powell of Art Tatum and Thelonious Monk. At the start of his career he may have been inspired by Tatum, as were most young pianists. But whereas this influence is noticeable in other boppers like Hank Jones, for Bud it is only the manner of racing along the keyboard, the dizzying speed that evokes Art Tatum. As for Monk, it is common knowledge that Bud Powell admires him greatly and likes to play his compositions. But Bud's playing is not like Monk's, at least not in the phrasing and sonority . . .

Throughout these sides, Bud gives us a left hand that is utterly amazing. He has perfected a most peculiar left-hand style that is "always light and always in action, whether in chords in counterpoint to the right hand or a bass line right out of Count Basie" (as Ralph Schecroun said in *Jazz News* no. 4).

If anyone was my unwitting initiator, it was Henri Renaud, and I still have a special fondness for him, in the name of the boundless passion we both share to this day.

Then came more bad news about Bud, still without details, like a drop of poison eating away at my imagination. *Jazz Hot* (October 1951) reported: "If you believe what you hear, two news items in rapid succession have caused a wind of panic among modern pianists—Thelonious Monk has been arrested for drug dealing and Bud Powell is hospitalized in a rest home."

WEBB CITY
(Recorded in New York, September 6, 1945 [Savoy])

After this news came a long period of silence broken only by vague rumors of Bud's transfer from one hospital to another.

In January 1953 I was relieved to read in the "News from America" column of *Jazz Hot:* "Bud Powell will soon be back at work. He played Birdland on December 11 with Max Roach and Curly Russell, replacing George Shearing, who was off that night conducting a symphony orchestra."

Mary Lou Williams had also entered my musical universe and I was intrigued to find her in the camp of the boppers. The interview she gave to Charles Delaunay (*Jazz Hot*, February 1953) dispelled any possible doubt as to her tastes: "I really appreciate musicians like Bud Powell or Thelonious Monk, who are always on the lookout for new ideas. All modern musicians owe them a lot. What I can't understand is why musicians and critics never give them their due, yet go on praising instrumentalists who 'borrowed' all they know from others."

But these odd tidbits always left me hungry for more. They told me nothing concrete. I felt that Bud's confused situation had made the columnists wary. They didn't elaborate on the nature of his problems and were even less explicit about his work.

I continued to glean brief isolated bits of news: Bud had played at Birdland with Dizzy Gillespie for a nearly all-black audience; he had just signed with the Gale agency (which handled Lester Young and Charlie Parker), and he had played at George Wein's Storyville in Boston.

In *Jazz Hot* of February 1954, Henri Renaud, back from the States, reported some more encouraging information:

> Bud Powell has started a 20-week engagement at the Haig in Los Angeles after a long gig at Birdland with Curly Russell and Arthur Taylor. . . . Bud is a strange man. He barely speaks and between pieces seems lost in a dream from which he emerges only when one of his sidemen reminds him he has to play. . . . After each set he sits alone in a corner of the room looking exceedingly sad. Mr. Goodstein, his manager and Birdland's owner, told us Bud thinks he's not playing well at the moment. As the bandstand is too small for the Count's sixteen-piece band, they've moved the piano

down to the floor. If you can manage to get a seat up front, your eyes are about eight inches from Bud Powell's hands. Those hands are unforgettable! They are beautiful, with long slim fingers that Bud holds in a surprising way, flat on the keyboard, almost arched backwards from the normal position.

My happiness at reading this kind of news would then be tempered by a succession of grim announcements from the American correspondents of *Jazz Hot*. My spirits alternately rose and fell. Bud's California tour was interrupted for a week but they didn't say why. Then, quoting an article from *Jazz Journal*, they said Bud's name had been linked to drugs.

At that point in my life, Bud had become my main center of interest. Not that I had abandoned the others: Fats Waller, Tatum, King Cole, Garner—they are all in my pantheon to this day. But Bud had given rise to other needs. He had opened up the vision of what would forever be my music: bebop, a word that had no particular resonance for me at the time. It was only later that I pondered at this strange label pinned onto a type of music. All I saw then in this new conception was the synthesis and the logical outgrowth of all musical knowledge, classical and modern combined.

Perhaps this is as good a time as any to say what I think about the label "bebop." Between 1930 and 1950 there had been an extraordinary explosion of musical creativity. Every school, every style, overflowed with invention. It was a musical revolution comparable to the one that had taken place in Europe at the turn of the century.

There was one important difference, however. In the United States, critics are often a bit too quick to categorize, to lump musicians together under a single label, and the European critics simply follow suit. In classical music, on the other hand, each composer is positioned by his own personality. It is at best useless and probably harmful to have assembled under one label a group of artists as diverse as Charlie Parker, Thelonious Monk, Dizzy Gillespie, and Bud Powell. And to use so restrictive and tendentious a label as "bebop" showed that insufficient attention had been paid to the originality and density of their works. The enormity of their creation should have earned them the right, like the great classical masters, to "splendid isolation."

Interviewed by Sharon Pease in *Down Beat* in 1951, Bud Powell said about his music, "I wish it had been given a name more in keeping with its seriousness of purpose."

The journalist Kurt Mohr, after a conversation with Bud in 1957, added, "He couldn't understand that the critics always apply certain labels to musicians, and that he, by chance, carried the same label as Charlie Parker, the label 'bop' . . ."

Jay McShann states in an interview in *Jazz Magazine* in September 1976: "No, Bird has never played bebop. Bebop is only a term that they stuck onto his music. Bird was playing the blues, all of his music is based on the blues. Even when he played 'Night and Day,' he was playing the blues. But you know, people like to give a name to everything. . . ."

As for Miles Davis, he announced to all who wish to hear: "Bebop? That's a word invented by white people."

A pretty state of confusion! In time, later generations of listeners and musicologists will put things in proper perspective. Can we imagine Wagner, Debussy, Fauré, and Ravel lumped together as a single school? Each of these creative spirits has given us a unique and incomparable universe. The same is true for the masters of the "bebop" era. Their only "error" was to have been contemporaries. Though they may have shared their discoveries when working together, each nonetheless preserved his individuality. What they had in common was their great generosity and a profound honesty before their art. It would be very easy to put the writing of Charlie Parker and Bud Powell side by side and show how different their phrasing is, even though some critics contend that Bud is no more than a pianistic replica of Bird's melodic line. It would be just as easy to show the unfeasibility of combining the melody of the one with the harmonic changes of the other, each conception being too completely thought out to tolerate the slightest amalgamation with the other.

Another idea that has always shocked me is the preposterous notion, advanced by many critics, that Bud plays Thelonious Monk's work better than Monk himself. As if anything could be more beautiful than Thelonious played by Thelonious! As if anyone else knew better than he how to make his music live, with modesty, asceticism, and a personal dose of the silences and rests proper to his style and to his incomparable personality.

When Bud plays Monk, he does so with deep affection and respect for his best friend. But is that enough to attain the perfection of execution of the creator playing his own work? When I listen to Thelonious I know it's that way and no other that his music reaches the sublime.

For the same reason, Bud's theme song, "Dance of the Infidels," becomes Parkeresque when played by Charlie Parker. Bird never has the same pulse as Bud any more than they share the same basic vision.

Formed as I was in the classic tradition and pressed by all my background into a conformist mold, I found it nearly impossible to express my convictions without creating conflicts at home. Each day brought more arguments with my parents and teachers over jazz, which to them was the antithesis of "real music." I couldn't communicate my emotion and at the time I had no solid arguments that could convince this hostile audience. Any reference to the Afro-American origin of this music made my words even more suspect. Gradually I retreated ever deeper into my private musical world and my research on the piano was done in secret to preserve an already unstable peace. I was bored playing a piece exactly as written with no place for any creative fantasy. Only my ventures into jazz opened my horizons and made me feel free.

In Europe, jazz was enjoying an extraordinary growth. Charlie Parker came back in 1951 but unfortunately didn't play in France, as the conditions of his previous contract had not been respected. During this tour his music was better received. Among its adepts were Hubert Fol in France and Jacques Pelzer in Belgium. Dizzy Gillespie came regularly and the French trumpeter Roger Guérin was often mistaken for his master. René Urtréger, possessed by Bud, created a sensation among pianists. Martial Solal, with his stunning technique, was developing an original body of music and attracting attention even from the Americans. Raymond Fol, too, was mad about Bud. In a word, modern jazz was alive and well in France. Many young musicians like myself felt they had found the most important music in the universe.

The readers' poll in *Jazz Hot* (February 1955) confirmed I wasn't the only one who loved Bud Powell. French fans had ranked him as their favorite pianist, ahead of Oscar Peterson, Art Tatum, Thelonious Monk, John Lewis, Erroll Garner, and all others. Their lucidity was a fitting tribute, at last, to America's most creative musician, who was also the most contested in his own country.

Here again was an American artist, consecrated in France, who had received no honor or recognition in the United States despite his stature and his influence on a whole generation of pianists since the early forties. Bud wasn't even mentioned in the *Down Beat* charts! How could the American public remain indifferent to such recordings as the fabulous Savoy sessions like *Long Tall Dexter* with Dexter Gordon (January 1946), *Be-boppers Mad Bebop* with J. J. Johnson, *The Bebop Boys* by Sonny Stitt's quintet, or those sessions recorded with Fats Navarro? With the number of masterpieces Bud had recorded since 1944, it just goes to show the level of the American fans of this period! If anyone is still in doubt, I suggest they go back and have another listen to all the work of that period.

The jazz world was still mourning Fats Navarro, who had died in June 1950, when the news of Charlie Parker's death on March 13, 1955 hit us like a bombshell. We were crushed, and it took the musicians a long time to get over it. Bird was their guiding light, their model. It was as if something in their world had snapped. Just before the end, he had played two nights at Birdland with his old friend Bud Powell, a final get-together before the last farewell.

Shortly afterward, a young trumpeter named Clifford Brown came to Paris. Some members of his band, like Max Roach (an old friend of both Bud and his kid brother Richie) were already known to Parisian audiences. But two of the greatest musicians of all time, Art Tatum and Bud Powell, had never come to France and were mythical figures to us. Their records were practically impossible to find but still I devoured the press for any mention of their names.

In the April 1955 issue of a new publication called *Jazz Magazine*, founded by Frank Ténot and Daniel Filipacchi, two impassioned fans, the journalist Yetty Lee related a disturbing story that shed an ominous light on Bud's troubled character.

> One night at Birdland, Bud Powell was at the piano, in great form. Art Tatum was in the audience. Tatum, known for being stingy with his compliments, said he thought Bud's left hand was a little weak. When someone repeated the comment to Bud, he took out a pocketknife, cut his own hand, then crudely bandaged it up and went on playing with the self-inflicted handicap. He showed such virtuosity in both hands that Tatum was dumbfounded. Some say he never forgave Bud . . .

When I saw Bud's manager, Oscar Goodstein, in 1964, he confirmed this story, adding that he still had horrible memories of that night. He had tried to call off the next set but Bud had insisted on playing. A journalist later said that Art Tatum had been very upset by the incident.

That summer I read that Bud had cut a record for Verve with George Duvivier and Art Taylor. In October, Nat Hentoff's "News from New York" column in *Jazz Hot* related Bud's return to the jazz scene: "He played a week in Cleveland accompanied by Charlie Mingus and the drummer Elvin Jones. The reviews were all favorable and he's had offers from other clubs. A European tour may also be coming up."

With the hope of seeing the master in Paris, I followed the magazines even more closely, watching for the momentous announcement. Bud was playing the clubs regularly. He was back at Birdland where Leonard Feather went to hear him one evening: "Bud seemed better than I had seen or heard him for a long time. Clearly he had put on some weight and was less frenetic. Mentally, too, he seemed in better shape. But I very much fear that the spark Bud Powell had a few years ago will never come back again. He has merely improved enough to resemble a good imitation of Bud Powell."

This comment was offset by some favorable echoes from Nat Hentoff who announced Bud's sensational return to the New York scene. It didn't last long. In March 1956 *Jazz Magazine* reported his arrest in Newark, New Jersey:

> A paternity suit has been brought by Elivia Edwards [this was in fact Altivia, who was also known as Buttercup], who claims [Bud Powell] is the father of her child. Bud, performing at a Newark theater, was arrested on this charge, then released on $5,000 bail. He denies the accusation and Oscar Goodstein, his manager, states that as a result of treatment during his hospitalization for mental illness, Bud Powell has become sterile and cannot therefore be guilty of the charge.

I found it revolting that music magazines should print this kind of gossip. They had nothing to report beyond some vague allusions to mental illness and it seemed to me terribly out of place. I agreed completely with Demètre Ioakimidis, a journalist for *Jazz Hot*, who wrote: "For some jazz critics who are short of material, Bud Powell is a godsend. It's a lot easier to talk about Bud as a misfit, secluded in his thoughts, a prey to internal dramas, etc., rather than to have to discuss his music."

One comment gave me back a little optimism—that of John Lewis, reported in *Jazz Magazine*: "All pianists sound like Bud, or like someone else, but Bud doesn't sound like anyone."

Three months later Bud was hit by another catastrophe. On a road near Philadelphia, Clifford Brown and Bud's younger brother, Richie Powell, were killed in a terrible car accident. Clifford was 26 years old, Richie 24. I could only imagine Bud's pain.

In September, the newspapers announced that Bud's contract with Verve was up.

   Apart from a few more allusions to a nervous breakdown, the jazz magazines said nothing about Bud Powell or his music. But by listening assiduously to his records and with the help of the few photos I could find, I ended up creating for myself a fairly concrete image of my hero. In my dreams I was transported to Minton's, to the Royal Roost, then to Birdland and Carnegie Hall, under the magic spell of Bud's music.

PARISIAN THOROUGHFARE

(Recorded in Paris, February 1953 [Reprise])

At last came the long-awaited announcement! Bud Powell was scheduled to play in Paris, as part of a series of European concerts, the 1956 Birdland Tour. The program also featured Lester Young, Miles Davis, Sarah Vaughan, and the Modern Jazz Quartet.

I had just been drafted into the army and was pining away in a barracks not far from Paris. On November 2, I went AWOL for the first time and, with beating heart, rushed to the concert hall, Salle Pleyel, where Bud was to appear. From my seat at the back of the hall I heard his name announced and was overcome with emotion. Until the very last second, after the introduction by Marcel Romano, I could scarcely believe I was about to see him in the flesh. It seemed unreal as he walked out hesitantly to thunderous applause. My heart skipped a beat and my mind was racing. He looked so human in his light gray checked suit, a bit self-conscious before the fervent ovation of the Parisian audience.

From afar, he looked small and a little pudgy. His elegant air added some reality to the physical presence that I was finally forced to accept. But not until he played the first phrases was the revelation complete. The doubt that held me in tense expectation vanished completely with the first notes that flew from his fingers. The magical sounds that poured forth were indeed the music that had become so familiar to me, that of the only genius capable of creating it. The mere thought of that moment moves me deeply to this day.

His performance was brief. He played "Strictly Confidential," "Parisian Thoroughfare," "Dance of the Infidels," and "Bouncing with Bud" as solos, then left the stage quickly. Recalled tumultuously by the audience, he came out a few minutes later and took a timid bow.

The public clapped and called for an encore, but he didn't come out again. The music he had played was elusive but so appealing, and in it I thought I felt his suffering. But no matter, I had seen him at last. I had heard the sounds of his genius, sounds that only he could have imagined.

As I left the hall my head was spinning. I intended to follow the events closely but I had a long wait. Bud left Paris the next day for a three-week European tour, for which the reviews were mixed.

The press never tried to find out the causes of Bud's illness, the reasons that had led him from one mental institution to another until at last he was declared legally incompetent by the New York State Supreme Court in 1953. Only in 1956 were his civil rights restored so that he could take part in the Birdland Tour. Nor did they mention the painful events that had wounded him.

After the brutal death of his brother Richie Powell, the piano world was saddened by the loss of Art Tatum (in November 1956), who had been Bud's spiritual father. René Urtréger, who played with Miles Davis during the tour, remembers the day: "We heard about Tatum's death just before going on. I was with Bud when Buttercup [the woman who had come with him and called herself his wife] broke the news to him, saying, 'He's dead. You see, Bud, that's what comes from drinkin' too much beer.' Bud didn't say a word. He never talked much. But I could feel how upset he was."

This latest shock to his already shaky emotional state was disregarded by the press during the Birdland Tour.

René Urtréger told me in an interview how unforgettable the tour was:

> Every night I played with Lester Young and Miles Davis. Then I'd go listen to Bud Powell, whom I'd never met before.
>
> I was crazy about Charlie Parker. I was always trying to capture his music on my piano. One day I heard a record of Bird in a quintet with Bud. It was "Chasin' the Bird" and Bud played a sixteen-bar solo. He did on the piano what I had dreamed of hearing! When I met him I felt I was in front of God. The love and respect I felt for him were infinite. There were nights he approached genius and others when I had to admit it wasn't up to scratch. But I knew he'd been ill, had an alcohol problem, that he'd been treated with drugs, and was on some kind of tranquilizer. Everyone loved and respected him. One night, his playing was something else!! We were all there, Lester, Miles, Milt Jackson, John Lewis, Connie Kay, etc., behind the curtain, listening. . . .
>
> That reminds me of another story. It was in Holland. We were all hungry after the concert, Connie Kay, Miles, Bud, and me. It was late and all the restaurants were already closed. We made one last try at an elegant place that was just closing up. It didn't look promising. The maître d' told us the cooks had gone home, and the only thing he could offer us was oysters but he had no one to open them. We offered to do it ourselves! The waiters got a real kick out of seeing us in shirtsleeves, prying open oysters

and preparing the sauce. They quickly set a table for us and we passed the platters of oysters from the kitchen out to the table. We were getting hungrier by the minute and somebody went to check if there were enough oysters. There on the table was a pile of empty shells. Bud was sitting calmly at the head of the table, polishing off the oysters as quick as they came out of the kitchen. He must have eaten five or six dozen! Man, were we mad!

There were all kind of legends about Bud. In the month I spent with him I wasn't disappointed. He was picturesque, all right! His reactions were unpredictable but completely natural at the same time. I remember one day the two of us were having lunch in a fancy restaurant. At a nearby table was a woman wearing one of those ridiculous hats—you know, the kind that are covered with flowers, cherries, strawberries . . . All at once, I heard someone laughing hysterically. It was Bud! I paid the bill and we beat it out in a hurry. In fact, everybody felt like laughing—only Bud did it out loud!

It was also during this tour that Pierre Michelot (another sideman with René Urtréger for Lester Young and Miles Davis) met Bud for the first time. He told me it was his "first shock":

> We had been told that Bud Powell would play solo. We were relieved to know we wouldn't have to accompany him because people said he was hard to get along with, a little crazy, that he would sometimes do a number and forget the bridge, etc. To this day, I don't see the problem. We could've accompanied him just fine.
>
> My first impression was Bud coming onstage at Salle Pleyel. We had rehearsed with Miles and Lester. I watched this man come out, sit down at the piano and start to play. It was magical, something miraculous, after what I'd been told and what I'd heard on records. All we'd had to go by was the records. But seeing him wiped out anything I'd ever heard. There he was, a guy like me, with arms, legs, an instrument . . . expressing himself in a system I knew perfectly well; but the music that was coming out of his soul, that he was inventing, was like nothing I'd ever heard.
>
> What was fascinating was the amount of creation. Bud was a creator, one of the greatest.
>
> Bud was with Buttercup and they kept a little apart. There were practically no relations between Lester and Bud. But I do remember one funny story. Lester always had a pint bottle of whiskey that he kept in the pocket of his saxophone case. Each time he took it out, Bud popped up and asked for a swig. Lester realized he was doing it on purpose and started hiding the bottle. We had a long flight to Sweden. In the plane, we were sitting up front and Bud was in the back with Buttercup. Lester had his hat on—I think he never took it off except to sleep. I've seen him in pajamas with that hat on his head! Lester turned around furtively. Bud

was in his seat and seemed to be drowsing. Thinking the time was right, Lester slipped down in his seat and discreetly took out the bottle. Just as he was about to drink, a hand reached out and snatched the bottle. It was Bud, who had come out of nowhere and was about to polish off the whiskey. Lester grabbed the bottle back just in time. He was furious! . . .

I had hoped Bud would play in Paris again before the end of the European tour, but he went straight back to New York.

I had just met Jean-Claude Casadessus, a young musician from the famous artistic family who later went on to a great career as an orchestral conductor. He too was depressed by military life. In his privileged family circle, he had received a solid classical training but had also fallen under the spell of jazz. He had formed a small group and I was its pianist. Whenever we could wangle a furlough, we would rehearse at his family home on the Rue de Steinkerque in Montmartre, in a room he had fixed up on the top floor. His mother, Gisèle, a well-known actress, would drop in to listen, but she was constantly worried about the reactions of the neighbors, particularly the woman in the apartment just below. Eventually, the poor woman decided to move.

Thanks to the army's "excellent" medical care I soon developed severe bronchitis. I took advantage of this, making it last as long as possible and reporting in at one army hospital after another, playing the perfect malingerer. Each hospital had a rec room and each rec room had a piano. . . .

Then suddenly the fun was over. We were shipping out, heading into a conflict I wanted no part of—the Algerian War. I left for Algiers in March 1957 and there lived through some pretty nasty events. In general, my feelings about the military coincide with those of the eminent philosopher who said: "For those who take pleasure at the sound of military music, I have nothing but contempt. That they have a brain at all is pure accident—a spinal cord would have been enough!"

I got through this trying time with the help of music—especially Bud's. As always, music was my mainstay, perhaps my crutch (to borrow an image from Salvador Dali). At night in my bunk before falling asleep, I imagined a keyboard on the edge of my blanket and practiced my fingering in the cover of darkness. On guard duty, too, I tried to do the same exercises, but after a few months I had to admit I had lost touch and no longer had any decent idea of the intervals on the imaginary keyboard.

Our camp was perched on a high peak, from which we could see a broad expanse of lifeless desert. At night, however, it came terrifyingly to life, in the form of violent surprise attacks by an unseen enemy.

Through the long and sleepless nights on guard duty, I crouched down at my post and peered into the darkness. In reverie I took myself to the lights of Paris, to music and to Bud. It was this ability to escape in thought that helped me overcome my unhappiness and get through the horror of everyday life. By saving my spirit, music probably saved my life.

After six months of hell, I was granted a leave. When I hit Paris, I heard that Bud was due to play at the Club Saint Germain. The French concert organizer Marcel Romano had just come back from New York with a signed contract for the first three weeks of November 1957. Romano later told me that Bud, whom he'd met at Pleyel the year before, had been very happy to see him in New York at the Alvin Hotel where he was staying during his Basin Street gig. They were together constantly. Bud even invited him home one night and greeted his arrival with a rendition of "La Marseillaise." Marcel Romano related his trip in the October issue of *Jazz Hot*: "Bud is in great shape. I thought so before but hearing him is always a surprise. As Urtréger says, he is *the* Bud Powell, always and forever. Half an hour after the set is over I'm still as breathless from what I've heard as he is when he leaves the stage. He hasn't played this well for years."

So I impatiently awaited November 1. This news helped to dispel the nightmare of Algeria. While waiting I listened over and over again to my record of Bud, trying to get over my "army blues." After the long months without practicing, my piano was like a stranger to me and it filled me with a deep sadness.

My military service was not up yet. At the end of my leave I started making the rounds of military hospitals once again. Building on past experience, I got myself admitted for a range of symptoms, most of them simulated, with the aim, of course, of not being sent back to Algeria. At night, I would sneak out of bed, put on civilian clothes and head for the clubs. I even started playing regularly at a small club called Le Caducée, on Rue Champollion, in the Latin Quarter. I found my old friends, all West Indians and all piano players, the only people I could talk to. There was Bernard, the Tatum specialist and ex-classical pianist; Roger Megi, a disciple of Garner and a good imitation of his master; Ken Kelly, who swore by King Cole; Jacques Berthelot, an enlightened initiate in our music; Michel Sardaby, who adored Oscar Peterson; and Gilbert Alexis, who worshiped Monk. Monk's harmonies were still very surprising at the time and few had mastered their syntax. Gilbert was one of the best, along with Jacky Knudde.

Some journalists expressed reservations about Bud's upcoming return to Paris. During his brief passage at Pleyel, all they seemed to have noticed was his tortured appearance, when in fact, even well below his usual level, Bud was still unique, still brilliant and absolutely incomparable.

STRICTLY CONFIDENTIAL
(Recorded in Paris, 1962/1964 [Black Lion])

The second time I saw Bud was as unforgettable as the first. On opening night at the Club Saint Germain he was welcomed like a diva, with bouquets of flowers and thunderous applause. His face was radiant and he looked relaxed. At home, he had probably never had such a welcome, but in our little community he was a giant, revered and admired. For the first few days he played in a trio with Kenny Clarke and Pierre Michelot. I never missed a performance. Those nights were for me like something out of my boyhood dreams—the atmosphere, the sound, the inspiration . . . I was in the presence of the gods. The performances of this exceptional trio were to my mind a high point in Bud's career. The films and tapes I made at that time, and which I still have today, are indisputable evidence. Their unity was remarkable. Pierre Michelot found the ideal sound and a driving pulse, and the third partner and accomplice, Kenny Clarke, was as discreet as he was efficient.

I listened with rapture to the enthusiastic comments buzzing all around the club. The faces in the audience were filled with emotion, wreathed in ecstatic smiles. So I wasn't the only one elated by Bud's music!

He seemed to me a sort of alchemist, blending matchless craftsmanship with unbounded inspiration, and topping it off with impeccable taste. The combination of dizzying power and heartrending tenderness transported us straight to heaven. Calm, spare, with no excessive gesture, he nevertheless allowed his creation to explode past the limits of physical resistance. Now I understood better why some judged him abnormal while others, the more discerning and more fortunate, felt he belonged to the sphere of the paranormal. The intensity of his playing was such that he had trouble breathing between phrases. At times it was unbearable. Bud punctuated each syncopation by a sound that was closer to moaning than singing. This constant moan that accompanied his playing would often leave him breathless at the end of a long uninterrupted phrase. At last his breath returned, in a conclusion drawn out of his very depths. He gulped down a little air and his eyes rolled upward with the worried look of someone about to plunge into the unknown for an indefinite time and come up at the limits of asphyxiation.

His fingers seemed unaware of the constant struggle. At the high point of his playing, submerged in a tumult of ideas, Bud took every pianistic risk. His hands, barely mobile, had a disconcerting nonchalance. His long, well-shaped fingers moved with such apparent slowness that it was incomprehensible to the public and even more incredible to the pianists in the audience. As if by magic, his fingers always found the notes he wanted. Despite the endless chances he took, his fingering was perfect. Never before had I seen a pianist with such fantastic technique.

Besides the esthetic experience, this was the most audacious music I had ever had the privilege to hear. Esthetic is the right word, for the movements of his fingers were spellbinding in their perfection, like the movements of an acrobat. Each tune seemed to tear its way straight from his heart and when it was over he looked exhausted, but serene and liberated, like someone who faces overwhelming odds and always comes out the winner. Each set seemed incredibly short. I wanted the enchanting music to go on forever, in perpetual motion. I left each evening happy and exhausted, but also troubled. The fans in the audience always tried to retain Bud after the last set, but in his reluctance to play again, I could see his fear of the physical ordeal, the fear of bringing face to face on the one hand his own genius and, on the other, his fear of not attaining the absolute that he demanded of himself. Never had any artist or musician given me the impression of such concentration, such a headlong rush toward perfection. At times he seemed stunned or even bewildered by the depth and the profundity of the emotion he had just expressed. In fact, it almost seemed that he was scared at times by the very phenomenon of himself. He had become his own listener, in much the same position as the attentive fan in the audience.

Then Barney Wilen came to join the trio. He looked like a teenager, a clean-cut kid from a good family, but his playing knocked us out. I remember once Bud stopped right in the middle of Barney's chorus, turned to him with arms crossed and gave him a smile of approval mixed with amazement. Barney was only twenty and already the music held no secrets for him. Each evening was an awed communion, like a religious experience.

At the club, I stood amid the excited crowd, always making sure I was in line with the keyboard. At the end of each set, Bud hastily left the stage and made a beeline for the bar. One evening I placed myself right in his path and so managed to see him close-up for a few seconds. He glanced at me as he brushed my shoulder and this fleeting contact was enough to make my blood stand still, as if touched by a magic wand. I felt electrified and full of an indescribable strength. I wanted time to stop but it went on as it always does, and in the end, I was not to regret it. During the breaks, I watched Bud out of the corner of my eye. The rule at the bar was to refuse him any alcoholic beverage. He would try half-heartedly to negotiate a few drinks, then give up in exasperation, push his way through the crowd and disappear up the staircase. I can still see Marcel Romano frantically searching for Bud, who had vanished during the break. I went with him, feeling I was on a mission of greatest importance. After combing the neighborhood and all its bars, we found him at last on the little square of Place Furstenberg, laughing up at the starry sky.

René Urtréger was another fervent disciple who never missed an evening. He shared a few memories with me: "The audience was not always ideal at the Club Saint Germain. Some were there to listen, others came just to have a good time. But some nights, when Bud started a ballad like 'It Never Entered My Mind,' he imposed a religious silence. It was unbelievable to see people like that, so thick-skinned, so badly prepared or ill-disposed to listen, forced to pay attention because they could feel that something extraordinary was taking place."

Now at last the press had some positive things to say—after a dazzling display like that, how could they do otherwise? But there were still hints of reservation—preconceived ideas die hard.

I later learned from Marcel Romano that the engagement, initially scheduled for three weeks, was cut to two by the club's management. The Saint Germain was a place people came to have fun. But the jazz buffs wouldn't tolerate dancing to Bud's music and that created tensions. So for the third week, Bud's trio was replaced by a larger and less "intellectual" band. To make up for it, Marcel booked Bud for a concert at the Fontainebleau Conservatory, accompanied by the group that played the club Saturday and Sunday afternoons: Barney Wilen on tenor sax, Paul Rovère on bass, and Al Levitt on drums. Levitt, an American expatriate living in Paris, had known Bud in New York and remembered him warmly. He told me: "Birdland was playing his latest record, and Bud said to Curly Russell: 'Hey, listen to that!' He was real happy with what he did on 'Indiana.' "

Despite his triumph in Paris, Bud came in only eighth in the *Down Beat* readers' poll, behind such pianists as Oscar Peterson, Dave

Brubeck, and André Previn. It goes to show once again—"no man is a prophet in his own land."

Bud's records began to get a wider circulation in France, but one of the finest was inexplicably panned by Martial Solal, an excellent pianist who had once followed Bud closely and brilliantly reproduced his style. The review appeared in *Jazz Magazine* of July 1958. I found it mortifying at the time and it still baffles me. As a result, the record sold poorly in France and the fans missed out on a major phase of Bud's style. He wrote:

> It is sad to see a record like this from a man who was one of the finest, perhaps the finest, of jazz pianists. On both sides of the 12-inch record, there are maybe five minutes that recall the Bud Powell of several years ago. The rest is a succession of wrong notes, flubbed arpeggios, and other errors painful for anyone who admired Bud Powell as I did. "Buttercup" and "Fantasy in Blue" are the best pieces, where we find the Bud we love. These two cuts are the only ones worth listening to on the whole LP.

Happily, not everyone was of the same opinion: witness the review by Kurt Mohr in the summer 1955 issue of *Jazz Hot*.

> One extraordinary interpretation dominates this record: "It Never Entered My Mind." Bud is in complete mastery of his means and expresses himself with frightful lucidity. In the sparest language, he plays a sort of pensive hymn, heavy, marked by utter resignation. Not a single lapse of taste mars the impeccable execution. . . . I was happy to learn that he in no way disavows this piece. . . . In art, the end justifies the means, and here, by dissolving the harmonies and metrics of the theme, Bud has created a masterpiece.

How is it possible that Martial Solal didn't notice the sublime interpretation of the standard "Moonlight in Vermont," which ranks with Debussy's "Clair de Lune"? The deep chords with their perfect harmonies, the long phrases with their sumptuous changes in the high notes are breathtakingly beautiful. Its calm and serenity, echoed also in "My Funny Valentine," make it, to my mind, one of his all-time masterpieces. The sound here illustrates, if more proof is needed, the extent to which Bud was a descendant of the great romantics and impressionists. The execution is faultless. As "Moonlight in Vermont" dies away, the sun rises with incomparable freshness on "Spring is Here."

Throughout this record, in the medium tempos ("Buttercup," "Foggy Day," "I Get a Kick Out of You") Bud's swing is unbelievable on phrases whose impact is equal to their originality. In the fast tempos ("Fantasy in Blue" and "The Best") he sticks to the bare essentials, without any frills, showing that he, at least (unlike some pianists regarded as virtuosos because they play fast), never mistakes haste for speed.

And last of all, the ballad "It Never Entered My Mind," painful and disconcerting, reveals Bud's vision of a heartbreaking universe unheard of at the time (it was done in the same spirit by Miles Davis in a Blue Note album some years later). Bud's interpretation comes across like the first approach to a sound, both confidential and dramatic, that Miles was later to soak up and adopt as his own. What was startling, even shocking, when Bud did it, was widely admired in Miles. But when Miles started out, wasn't he too, like so many others, a pupil of Bud's?

All those who expected nothing more from Bud Powell than a certain continuity (attributed to what they saw as "his language") were always disturbed by the constant shifting in his art. For Bud it was no more than a transient vision. His changing styles, perceived by some as a permanent imbalance in his musical expression, were in fact, to my mind, signs of the anxiety of a self-demanding artist in the process of continual renewal.

In June 1957, François Postif pointed out in *Jazz Hot* Bud's obvious importance:

> In the history of jazz piano, two clear landmarks stand out: Earl Hines and Bud Powell. Earl Hines, from 1926 on, blazed a new trail for pianists of the period by creating an intelligent phrasing different from that of Louis Armstrong. Twenty years later, Bud Powell, with the fire of his 24 years, drew on his own strength as a "puncher" and the full range of the piano's rhythmic possibilities and brought about a complete renewal by taking Tatum's phrasing and ridding it both of its classical aspects and its superfluous arabesques.
>
> What was true in 1949 is still true today, nearly ten years later, even though Bud's manner has changed. The younger generation of pianists haven't really broken with Bud Powell's style. Each with his own personality is only following the path that Bud opened in 1948, a path that to this day still seems the only valid conception for the piano.
>
> Taking Bud Powell as a starting point, we can imagine a reasonable classification for the pianists of the future. Even now, without having the necessary perspective of time, we can already define three groups that are developing simultaneously:
> those who follow Art Tatum through Bud Powell,
> those who follow Thelonious Monk through Bud Powell,
> those who are looking for themselves through Bud Powell.

Bud may still be too recent for us to see clearly the importance of his contribution to the evolution of music on a universal scale.

EMBRACEABLE YOU
(Recorded in Toronto, May 15, 1953 [Début])

My frequent trips to England as a child, in addition to what I learned at school, had made me fairly comfortable with the English language. Later, when I began to hang out with musicians, I added some slang to my vocabulary, including some rather colorful (and off-color) expressions. Babs Gonzales, during his visits to France, made an excellent teacher and he found me an apt pupil. But my true initiator had been Lester Young, a master in the art, and I owe him the tribute of a respectful word or two.

Lester was one of those people who couldn't pronounce ten words without interjecting two or three juicy curses. People from the south of France have a reputation for swearing a lot, but even they are no match for Lester. In situations where decency compelled him to avoid such words, he would express himself by savory turns of phrase that bordered on the surreal. For example, he liked to feminize things and people. His saxophone he fondly called "Lady Saxophone" or "Lady Violet," the same word he used for wine. Johnny Griffin became "Lady Griffin," etc. Ben Benjamin, the owner of the Blue Note, was nicknamed "The Great White Father" and his wife Itla "Madame Queen." Shaking hands with his friends, he accompanied the gesture with a sonorous "doom ... m ... m" like a tolling bell. Ray Brown relates that during a bus trip with Jazz at the Philharmonic, some prankster had hidden the bottle of whiskey that Lester always kept in the overhead baggage rack. When he noticed the disappearance of his precious brew, Lester went through all the racks with a fine-tooth comb. Then he sat down without a word and after a minute announced in a quiet voice: "Whoever it is who swiped my bottle, I want him to know I am an intimate friend of his mother's!"

That was Lester, a genius in music, language and humor.

Later Johnny Griffin served as my finishing school, adding some indispensable subtleties to my knowledge of English.

So by the time I met Bud, I had no trouble speaking to him in his native tongue. More than once I was to surprise him by my use of some colloquial American expressions.

Riding in the Métro one afternoon in November 1957, I looked up and saw Bud on the platform with Kurt Mohr. Bud was just leaving, as Kurt waved goodbye and boarded the train. I jumped off, seized by a desperate desire to speak to him. Without thinking about what I was doing, I planted myself in front of him, speechless with emotion. He must have vaguely recognized me from attending his concerts, for without a word he took my arm and we found ourselves as if by magic at a café counter over a couple of beers. The conversation was quite solemn. Bud only wanted to know if I had the wherewithal to buy him another drink. My reply being affirmative, his face lit up in a grin. I have no idea how long we were together, but it seemed an eternity when I realized it was time to say goodbye. I was miserable because Bud had told me he was going back to New York. Because of my shock, I can remember nothing at all about our parting.

TIME WAITS

(Recorded in Hackensack, May 28, 1958 [Blue Note])

His departure left a hole in my life, and my morale plummeted. I had finally been discharged from my nasty military obligations and with no small difficulty I started to work. This was the beginning of a long period of lean times. Still, I managed to buy an American upright piano, a Stek-Pianola that probably still remembers the beatings I gave it trying to drag out of its entrails some of the magic that Bud had so generously dispensed each night at the club. I practiced furiously. Naturally, Bud's compositions formed the core of my program. I would scarcely have chosen anything else, for what I heard in his work was the very heart of my musical aspirations. Through this identification I was applying to the letter the recommendations of Maurice Ravel: "One should never fear to imitate ceaselessly. If you have nothing to say, you might just as well (while waiting to fall silent for good) repeat what has been said well. If you do have something to say, that something will never appear more clearly than in your unintentional infidelity to your model."

As I played Bud's themes and tried to improvise freely in his language, I never thought of it as servile imitation. This fear of imitation is just a bugaboo in people's minds. It never occurred to me to reproduce Bud's improvisations note for note, which would have been ridiculous. Quite the contrary, improvising on the rich and complex structure of his tunes, I felt sure I was stimulating my creativity at a very high level. It was always an exciting adventure and one of the great joys of my life.

I was surprised to see that, except for René Urtréger, no one was playing the works of Bud, Parker, or Monk. Jimmy Gourley once told me the story of the fan talking to Bud during a break at the Blue Note, asking him for a "recipe" for playing like him, or at least for playing well in the bebop idiom. Bud must have found the question interesting for, contrary to his usual habit, he answered spontaneously: "If you can just manage to play all the tunes without making a mistake, you'll be doing pretty good." This was a clear answer and one that corroborated Ravel's advice. When a question seemed worthy of interest, Bud could indeed abandon his legendary muteness.

In *Jazz Hot* (February 1959) Kurt Mohr gave some impressions that confirmed my deepest sentiments. He entitled his article "The Great Bud." "Bud doesn't like being guided or pushed. Asked on one occasion to make a recording in homage to Charlie Parker, his first reaction was to say: 'I'm a pianist. Why not make it "Homage to Art Tatum"?' "

Now Bud was gone. While I waited patiently for him to return I consoled myself by going to see Billie Holiday and Lester Young. Despite my exclusive passion for Bud, it was a pretty exciting way to bide my time.

Accompanied on the bass by Michel Gaudry, Billie Holiday was singing at the Mars Club, where we sometimes saw our friend Yves Chamberland, the sound engineer known by all the musicians, playing with brushes on a newspaper. I didn't know Billie well, but she looked downhearted in those wretched surroundings. The musicians had a tiny dressing room and the owner's dog, who didn't like to stay alone, had gotten in the habit of sleeping there. Billie showed up one evening in a fur coat and the dog, who had never reacted before, suddenly began to growl. Maybe it was the coat! When Michel expressed his surprise, Billie brushed it aside with a bitter, "Ah, forget it! Nobody loves me any more, anyway."

As for Lester, I just hope he was able to take his last days in Paris philosophically, because if not, the sad spectacle of the empty Blue Note must have wrecked his morale. On one of the last nights, René Urtréger and I went to see him together. Besides the two of us there was one other customer lost in the middle of the room. When Lester started to play, René stood up and said, in a voice tight with emotion, "Ladies and Gentlemen. This is an historic moment. The great Lester Young is playing the Blue Note in Paris and three people have come to listen to him, two of whom are musicians!"

Lester was heartbroken. He drowned his troubles in the innumerable bottles that innocent well-wishers brought him. Every day Lester did the cooking in the little kitchen adjoining his room at the hotel. He enjoyed preparing nice down-home dishes for his friends and visitors, but he hardly ever ate any himself. He preferred to drink, consuming vast quantities of sticky apéritifs and sickeningly sweet dessert wines.

Meanwhile, I combed the press for any news of Bud, but there was too little even to fuel my imagination. One brief note in *Jazz Magazine* (April 1958) mentioned simply that after Sonny Rollins and

Maynard Ferguson, Bud would play at Birdland until March 5, with no further comment.

In the States, the critics were still reserved, if not frankly hostile. Bud was in tenth place in the *Down Beat* ratings and in their listeners' poll he came in eleventh.

However, since September of 1956 Bud had recorded the remarkable album *Blues in the Closet* with Ray Brown and Osie Johnson, a fine recording of an exceptional trio with a wonderful swing. Bud was in an extremely lyrical mode and the new coloration of his music in these tracks disturbed the American critics. This time, however, they were not evasive but pretentious enough to want to explain themselves. First in *Metronome*, May 1958, signed simply Jack: ". . . The music still has that oddly lugubrious quality in the choice of chords, and there are moments of dissolution, but you will also hear a more confident and secure Bud than you've heard for some time. This confidence seems to have been born out of a quality of violence and impatience. . . . For some reason, Bud smashes in with chords that almost destroy the continuity of Ray's solos."

Then in *Down Beat*, May 29, 1958:

> Here, frankly, is the way it is (and the way it often is nowadays, alas): there is bad time and bad fingering at up tempos ("I Know," "Be-Bop," etc.) and sometimes at medium as well ("Heart," "Swingin'," etc.). There is a kind of pounded Tatum on "Care"; and it and "Fall in Love" contain some of those flowery keyboardisms that have always been disconcerting in Powell's work. . . .
>
> . . . It would be exceptional, to say the least, for an artist to have worked more surely, on the whole, without his having discovered what technical resources he could utilize, but I cannot help feeling that may be the case with Powell. . . .

Critics of this ilk also ignored other major sessions, including those of Bud's trio with George Duvivier and Art Taylor, who had also done some brilliant work together in 1952. This was one of Bud's finest trios and the fire and originality they showed in their New York reunion in 1956–1957 was so startling that their work of this period was greeted with a deafening silence. Hard to believe, when there were such sides as "There'll Never Be Another You" (Victor, October 1956) and the mind-blowing Birdland sessions on the Queen Disc label (January 1957).

We, the devoted little band of French fans, were in rapture over these sessions, but apparently they left the American experts cold.

Last of all, how could one remain indifferent to the masterpiece re-corded by this stupendous trio on February 11, 1957, on RCA Victor? Were they simply afraid of this album, afraid of the tumult? The stunning interpretations of "Oblivion," "Midway," "Get It," "Shaw-nuff," and "Another Dozen," all in a racing tempo, are of a quality and perfection rarely attained. For me, this was one of the high points in Bud Powell's career, though most observers saw only the last gasps of a man who was once a genius but who was now only a dim memory for blasé fans and columnists alike.

This is one of the very rare discs I would take with me to the pro-verbial desert island. It has energy, perfect equilibrium, sheer beauty, maybe the kind of beauty vibraphonist Bobby Hutcherson meant when he said, "Beauty carries Death in its arms."

Perhaps this indifference to the revolutionary genius of his work can help us to understand why the artist, perfectly conscious of his worth, we can be sure, slowly retreated into a protective universe from which he could ignore the all-powerful "intelligentsia" that per-sisted in snubbing him, whatever he might do.

Yet without the approval of dull-witted "experts," the beauty of Bud's constantly renewed work would continue to influence the mu-sical conceptions of a whole new generation of musicians. Fortunately, some of them later set the record straight.

Keith Jarrett, for example, took a blindfold test (*Jazz Magazine* no. 176) on another record ignored in the United States, a Paris-made homage to Thelonious Monk with Pierre Michelot and Kenny Clarke:

> I give it five big stars. Bud is not in top form here, but I'm crazy about this record because it's so full of love. In the jazz world today nobody thinks of forming phrases any more.
>
> If musicians talked the way they played, they'd be impossible to listen to—boring, with no feeling.
>
> In his time, the musicians had more spirit than now, because they were closer to the origins. . . . Bud, Monk and the others, Scott Joplin for in-stance, they played with love. . . .

There it is—clear, honest, to the point, and so true.

The comments in our magazines were still as ambiguous as ever. Without trying to demolish Bud, they managed to find some faint praise for his music, but one way or another they undermined the reputation of all his new albums.

Each time Bud explored new and ever more daring modulations, in unconventional phrasings from his boundless imagination, I realized that the critics, once again nonplussed, took them for errors and weaknesses. Talk vanishes but the written word remains. Today, when pianists accustomed to far more daring harmonic complexities exploit these very modulations that once so jarred the unaccustomed ear, it's time to face facts—some critics would have been wiser to keep their ideas to themselves. One need only listen carefully to the early recordings of great pianists like Bill Evans, McCoy Tyner, Chick Corea, Keith Jarrett, and Herbie Hancock to realize that they all built their research on Bud's discoveries. It just goes to show the lucidity of these musicians who went on to make such brilliant careers. Take, for example, the way Bill Evans uses dissonances, harmonic frictions, and textures of pure beauty, and expresses them all with his fine-tuned sensibility; Herbie Hancock's sinuous phrases, positively abstract on first hearing; Chick's startling rhythmic constructions, so magical in their perfect geometry; the fire and mathematic power of McCoy, always ready to burst into flame; and finally Keith, whose heart-rending romanticism is wrenched from lovely phrases with a total commitment. Bud's shadow hovers over them all.

Listening recently to some recordings which Bud made in the early fifties, Herbie Hancock said, "It's incredible that he could have done that at that time. I only realize it today. In those days I was listening to other pianists—Bill Evans, in particular. It's clear now that Bud had already mastered things that sound modern to us today."

Bud's problems recall the misadventures of Ravel, who never won a Prix de Rome due to successive refusals by Théodore Dubois, Conservatory director, jury member, and, of course, "source of all truth," who had nothing better to say about Ravel's harmonies than "Monsieur Ravel is mocking us!" Today, when the world hails the genius of Ravel, who still remembers Théodore Dubois?

All this led me to reflect on the profession of music critic. What is a critic? With what right can *he* decide the career of a record or even of an artist? Where does *he* get this vast authority? Is *he* a musician himself? Is *his* technical level high enough to attack the work of artists who, apart from their genius and talent, devote their lives and their entire souls to art?

In the end, aren't some critics merely frustrated writers more eager to enhance their own reputations than to serve the musician who needs the publicity to attract the attention of the public or to help the reader by giving him relevant information?

Jacques Reda, commenting on a review of Bud's *The Lonely One* (Verve 511106) that appeared in *Jazz Magazine* no. 41, may help provide a lucid explanation of this disturbing aspect of criticism: "If we have the time and energy we could ponder why it is that a semi-successful recording by Bud Powell still seems more interesting than a totally satisfactory album by a pianist who doesn't bear the stigmata of genius. It would bring into clearer focus a certain notion of the artist latent in our understanding of jazz from its beginnings." The remark is well-taken. But why then, in the next breath, does he forget his own reasoning and go on to give this genius a grade of 70 percent? What a responsibility!

What then is the vocation of the critic? To educate the ignorant reader—or is he as ignorant as they? To guide the public in the purchase of their records—or to receive free records from the press service and free admission to the nightclubs? I have no answers to give, but I know these questions are continually asked by all musicians who have just cut a record or played a concert and are waiting for the "verdict."

Aside from the traditional reviews, there's always the technique of praising one rising young musician to the detriment of another. What better way to launch a new talent than to compare him to his master? Bud was not spared this indignity, as shown by this remark in a biographical essay on the young pianist Horace Silver (*Jazz Magazine* no. 34): "His playing is spare, not tortured like Bud Powell or Monk. He never plays a note too many and shows perfect regularity." What a pointless swipe at Bud and Monk!

A year later, Horace Silver was quoted in *Jazz Hot* (March 1959): "My greatest influence, naturally, was Bud Powell, but I must say Monk fascinates me, too." Then he made things even worse by adding, "At that time [1951] there was a lot of Bud Powell in my playing and I think even now he's the one who influenced me the most."

Out of sight (or rather hearing), out of mind. In the readers' poll of *Jazz Hot* (February 1959), Bud Powell came in only third.

Marcel Romano, who for two years now had been handling programming for the Club Saint Germain, was thinking of bringing Bud back to Paris. Fourteen months after his departure it was announced that he had been signed to play at the Blue Note in March 1959, together with Pierre Michelot and Kenny Clarke.

It had been a long wait. Now I felt my spirits revive, only to be dashed again by the death of Lester Young on March 15. He had become a legendary figure for us and, shortly after he left Paris, he left our world forever.

But I wiped that out of my thoughts. Bud was coming back.

DEEP NIGHT

(Recorded in New York, December 16, 1954 [Verve])

Bud's opening night at the Blue Note is engraved forever in my memory. I had come very early and for the first time I had the opportunity to observe the club's owners. Ben Benjamin, the manager, seemed at first glance a jovial person. A large heavy man, with a bulging paunch squeezed into trousers symbolically held up by suspenders, he stood in the doorway and eagerly awaited the customers.

He was aided by a staff of servile waiters who bullied the prospective customers into the club. Before they had a chance to read the program, they were relieved of their coats, hustled to a table, given a menu and rushed into placing their orders.

Ben favored dark, curly-haired boys, and his waiters, recruited from Paris's Italian colony, were all devoted to him.

Itla, his wife, was short, chubby, and quite unattractive. It was she who really owned the club and Ben's status was that of an employee. For her part, she preferred women. In retrospect, they were a good match. She knew how to snap her whip and, with her cold steely eyes, she ran her little world like a martinet.

On the other hand, her brother Jacques seemed to have no feeling for anyone. He looked like the headmaster of a Jesuit boys' school and to know his deepest thoughts, assuming he had any, you'd have to be clairvoyant. A tiny figure in skimpy suits that made him seem even smaller, his one important responsibility was running the bar. He reigned in absolute sovereignty behind the counter, which he hardly ever left, keeping an expert eye on the waiters, tossing out well-aimed nasty remarks, and always on the lookout for customers who might try to sneak in without paying. I doubt that he ever realized he was in a place where music was made and where people came to enjoy themselves. He was too busy being a watchdog.

For the great occasion, I had miraculously managed to find a seat from which I had a good view of Bud's fingers. When Bud first showed up on the bandstand, I noticed that he had put on some weight and seemed in good shape. His face was fuller and wore a luminous smile.

Although the music was uneven during this period at the Blue Note, I remember the first evenings as prodigious. Unlike other observers I can have no reservations where Bud is concerned. I loved every aspect of his playing and all his moods. Even if there were less exalted moments, he always seemed to me more exciting than anything else one could hear on the piano in this style.

Bud was never boring. Quite the contrary, his playing brought a constant questioning, a ceaseless succession of surprises, all in his inherent good taste. Having the time now to closely observe his technique, I realized once more how deceptive my imagination had been. Nothing in his fingering corresponded to the traditional norms I was still accustomed to. My professors had all taught the "Cortot method": hands held rather high over the keyboard, fingers pointing downward with respect to the palm. The other classical techniques also called for rounded fingers, whether the palm was high or low. It was nothing like that with Bud. His palm and fingers were on the same plane, so you couldn't even see the fingers bend. How he could strike the keys so hard was a mystery to me, for the finger movement that produced the sound was all but invisible. Between punctuations, he would rest his cupped hand on the edge of the keyboard for a moment's rest. The figures and transitions of the right hand looked so easy and relaxed that the gestures seemed to be in slow motion. Sometimes I had to shut my eyes to forget this fascinating vision and come back to the pure sound. Just as he did with his left hand, Bud rested the right hand as often as he could between each phrase. In that way, he could relax his hands and arms. I began to understand how, with these energy-saving techniques, he could play chorus after chorus at a raging tempo and never miss a beat. Like many black pianists, he played with his fingers fully extended, hitting the key with the flat of the last phalanx. Certain notes he attacked with the side of his right hand, with the outer edge of his little finger, like a percussionist, giving him those strong accents in the perfect structure of his phrasing.

But the most admirable part of his playing was the perfection of his fingering and the placing of his hands. His long, slightly plump fingers were always at the note he wanted and they pressed down deep into the keys as if looking for more intimate contact. There were never any jerky thumb movements or difficult contortions to reach a needed note at the last minute, never any reckless precipitation, just the calm, majestic assurance of being in exactly the right place at precisely the right moment.

He punctuated his phrases with movements of his head, but the rest of his body remained motionless. He'd sit with his left foot on the right pedal and his right leg extending outward, never marking time. In his posture at the piano he had everything down pat, well-balanced, judiciously dosed.

His deep concentration and physical commitment sometimes caused feelings of anxiety and exhaustion in spectators who were really involved. As he strained toward his unknowable visions, I felt he was completely engrossed, painfully suspended, in his own sounds and profoundly moved by them.

During this whole period at the Blue Note, I observed Bud with an unchanging passion. I noticed the amazing preparation he imposed on himself before starting to play, which sometimes meant a long silence that the audience didn't always appreciate. Their impatience would be expressed by noise and shuffling, but these had no effect on Bud. The less knowledgeable members of the audience could not be aware of the seriousness of the phenomenon that we insiders knew well. We reveled in the suspense as we waited for Bud to get going. All at once, he would come to with a start, take a deep breath, throw his shoulders back, and attack the first notes without the slightest indication to his partners. At that instant a fantastic energy surged forth, and from the very first bars the audience could feel that everything was perfectly in order: the tempo, the beat and the syncopation. The spirit and the coloration he gave to a tune were perfectly in tune with his mood of the moment. It made me think of the long, deep concentration of an athlete before a decisive effort. Bud had the same need for preparation before playing and he took the time he needed. He was exceptional in this respect. I'm not sure musicians have always understood the need for this "conditioning" and the vast preparations necessary to reach the highest level.

Pierre Michelot spoke to me of his impressions during that period, when he saw Bud daily:

> Contact with Bud was difficult, first because he didn't talk and then my English wasn't very good, though it improved later on. But there was never any problem on a musical level. It all went very smoothly. As soon as it was our turn to play, Bud would sit down at the piano and attack a piece. It was up to me to figure out what it was!
>
> We never rehearsed. We kind of got "broken in" over the months, playing every evening. From the first day I played with him till the last, he never hesitated on the tempo.

Sometimes he looked absent. His mind seemed elsewhere. A distraction in the room, perhaps. . . . He was certainly sensitive to things ordinary people didn't feel.

Anyway, he wasn't crazy. He drank, but I never saw him stagger. Drugs? No, except for medication. He took something to calm him down. I don't know if he needed to be calmed down. I'm no doctor, but he always struck me as a totally kind and gentle soul.

At that time I had heard things, but I had no idea that Bud had been under medication in the past, sometimes under medications so severe that those near to him had been quite concerned about their strength and their effect on Bud. Later on, Maxwell T. Cohen, Bud's attorney in the States, gave me a letter which he had received from Oscar Goodstein, written by Bud's mother showing her concern over these very medications:

Dec. 7/53

Mr. Goodstein,

Mr. Goodstein. I am scared to death about this medicine you told me was given Bud by the doctor. I don't think anyone like Bud with such weakness should be given any medicine like that. If he dies wouldn't your conscience whip you the rest of your life! If Bud is so bad I will ask you to let him come with me. You handle all his money and will you arrange to give him so much each week. So I can nurse him back to health.

I am so worried about Bud. I don't want him to die that way. I will do all I can for him. I wish it was like it used to be. I don't advise the medicine Dr. Fox is giving him. My nerves go to pieces when I think of it. At least let me hear from you.

Yours truly,
Mrs. P. Powell

One evening at the Blue Note, I overheard a conversation between some musicians to the effect that Bud was planning to settle permanently in Paris. My heart skipped a beat. If it were true, I was ready to bring a cot and move into the Blue Note. Nothing seemed more important to me than listening to Bud Powell. But he did leave the Blue Note for a few weeks, which gave me a chance to catch up on my sleep and to get back in touch with the real world.

We had just gotten used to the idea that Lester was gone forever when another tragedy shook the jazz world: Sidney Bechet, French by adoption, who had made jazz popular in our country, had the singular bad taste to abandon us and join the other vanished angels in May.

Then we all mourned Boris Vian's premature death. Jazz had lost one of its most clear-sighted defenders. In his Press Review in *Jazz Hot* (July-August 1954), Boris had cited a remark made by the critic Mike Neward, who had said he detested the "emotionless deluge of Bud Powell." His answer was the following: "Dear Mike Neward, Are you sure your powers of perception are up to the level of a Bud Powell? Or could it be that he has gone much too far and much too fast for you to follow? Science teaches, dear friend, that one cannot measure bacteria with a wooden yardstick. So if you want to hear, and appreciate Bud, maybe you'd better sharpen up your ears!"

BOUNCING WITH BUD
(Recorded in Copenhagen, April 26, 1962 [Sonet])

After the Blue Note, Bud appeared a few times as guest star at the Caméléon, with René Thomas on guitar and Allan Eager on saxophone, regularly accompanied by the Dutch pianist Nico Bunink.

In July 1959 he started playing at Le Chat Qui Pêche, a damp, uncomfortable, smoke-filled cellar in the best Parisian tradition, a hangout for diehard jazz freaks. The tiny stools were more like instruments of torture than seats, but the joint was full of soul. So here I was back in the Latin Quarter that I had deserted for the Right Bank since the Blue Note opened on Rue d'Artois. My repeated visits had exhausted my meager savings and I was so broke I couldn't afford the admission to Le Chat Qui Pêche. But the cellar club had a little window just at street level, and here I would crouch and listen to the music coming through the bars. It was hardly comfortable, but at least I didn't miss a note, for my makeshift "loudspeaker" was very clear.

At the end of each set, I watched the door, hoping to see Bud come out. One evening he saw me and came up to me with a determined step. Without a word, he took my arm and led me across the street to a bar called Storyville. I was too overcome to speak and I followed without thinking.

"Can you buy me a beer?"

"Sure, Bud."

Storyville was run by the father of the clarinettist Maxime Saury. He soon got used to our nightly visits because the same thing happened every evening. The clients of the bar were mainly musicians and jazz buffs and you could listen to the record of your choice.

With Monsieur Saury, the beer was on the house, which was a lucky break for my finances. I also got to hear a lot of new music at his place, for he had all the latest recordings and each night he'd put one of Bud's records on the phonograph.

"You know," he'd say to me, "Bud is one helluva guy!"

Bud would always ask, "Who's playing?"

"It's you, of course, Bud. Nobody else can play like that."

"Nah, that's not me," he'd say, incredulous, watching for a smile that would tell him if we were kidding.

Our conversations rarely went beyond this kind of talk. After this break, Bud would take me firmly in tow and lead me into Le Chat Qui Pêche, undeterred by the cashier's disapproving glare.

How could all this have happened to me? I still wonder about it. Perhaps it was a miracle, the sign of my inescapable destiny as a passionate disciple.

Bud was playing with Chuck Israels and J. T. Hogan. The trio pulsated like a red-hot locomotive. The tension was enormous, the density of sound unbelievable. Bud's fingers set off thunderbolts. During these electrifying evenings, there were hardly any ballads and one tune followed another in a relentless tempo.

J. T. Hogan played very loud, using only the sticks, a little like Elvin Jones did later on with John Coltrane. I could feel the effort Bud was making every night to keep up the infernal pace. He would enter an almost hypnotic trance, his body motionless, facing the audience like Nat King Cole, his face, contorted and running with sweat, raised toward the smoky ceiling, totally detached from the keyboard as if trying to create some distance between his head and his fingertips.

With its vaulted ceiling and bare stone walls, the club resembled a chapel. A spectator who was the slightest bit attentive succumbed to the fascination. From the opening bars, Bud was under pressure. He kept a careful ear on his partners' preparations and then the magic began. The irresistible beat and the faultless logic of the melodic structures gave a wonderful feeling of security. The phrases arrived in waves, with a haunting ebb and flow. Bud punctuated the syncopation with jerks of his head and little movements of his upper body. He was in a trance, like some sort of medium, and his eyes seemed to decipher the perfect writing of an invisible score. I watched in awe, knowing that he was a genius, and happy to be aware of the fact.

I lived these tumultuous nights feeling like I'd been sucked into a whirlwind. Bud played all summer at Le Chat Qui Pêche and sometimes Barney Wilen came to sit in with the trio.

Now that I was hearing Bud every night, I came to realize that the same tunes he played several nights in a row changed so much as to be unrecognizable from night to night. Each new interpretation was perfect, a miracle of originality and equilibrium. Bud had within him the perfection and the magic of an ideal architecture. He took great risks but he always won, and this was the only way he could conceive of music.

Listening to the same compositions on records, one might think that they followed one ideal, predetermined conception, and they remained fixed and unchanging once and for all in the listener's mind. Hearing him live over and over again, it was clear how limited and subjective this was, and that the compositional reality of his nightly output was far more impressive.

The syncopation was built on an ingenious mathematical system which was, within itself, in perfect osmosis with the geometry of the phrase. The spaces between sound and silence seemed balanced to perfection. The proportion of the elements, be they harmonic, melodic or rhythmic, created a perfect universe. Hearing Bud endlessly develop his own compositions, I came to understand that all his playing was based on risk. It was the most concrete illustration of the phenomenon of free jazz, at least as I had always conceived of it, for to me freedom has never meant anarchy. Certainly Bud played fast, but he must have thought even faster, to be able to foresee so beautifully what was coming next.

In those years Paris was the jazz hub of Europe and I grow nostalgic now as I look at the yellowed programs and old ticket stubs. But 1959 was another sad year, for Billie Holiday died on July 17, taking her final bow, just like Lester, shortly after leaving Paris.

"La Capitale" was losing all its giants. Alone with Bud at the Storyville bar, I would avoid talking about this. He seemed sad enough as it was.

So many had died since 1955; I felt myself aging too quickly. Musicians probably never imagine how deeply they enter the emotional lives of their admirers, to what extent they become their "spiritual family." Bird, Billie, Tatum, Clifford, and Lester were an intimate part of my sentimental life. Each loss left an empty space in my world. I couldn't get it out of my mind. Their image obsessed me like a permanent reproach, a condemnation to the whole world to have permitted such injustice, to have deprived us of these beings we needed so much and who could never be replaced. Each death was like a wound that wouldn't heal.

BUTTERCUP

(Recorded in Paris, October 14, 1960 [Vogue])

After Le Chat Qui Pêche, Bud toured all over Europe, returning to Paris after each tour. He had moved into the Hotel Louisiane, together with a monumental and voluminous creature named Buttercup, who called herself Mrs. Powell. A three-year-old child, Johnny, completed the family portrait. I would often see them strolling along the Boulevard Saint Germain, Bud walking in front with Buttercup ten yards behind, the little boy beside her. Several times he noticed me and, taking advantage of a momentary inattention, he slipped away with surprising agility to join me. As usual, he'd ask me to buy him a drink and we found ourselves at a bar somewhere over a glass of "vin rouge." Bud could pronounce "vin rouge" with a perfect accent, though his French never went much further than that.

I took to meeting him around the Rue de Seine, at one of the bistros near the hotel. His face would light up when he saw me. He spoke very little and our conversations were really monologues to which he responded with vague sounds I had to interpret according to his expression. The only times he really reacted were when I mentioned Art Tatum or when he thought it time to order another drink. To fill the silence, I would run down the list of all the people we knew in common and occasionally succeed in getting a comment from him.

Marcel Romano, who was still in charge of programming at the Club Saint Germain, was living at the Hotel Saint André des Arts, and he also would run into Bud in the neighborhood. Sometimes he'd go back to the hotel with Bud, where they would drink and play Monk's records. During one of these visits, Bud leaned toward him and asked, "Marcel, do you know Francis?"

"I assumed he meant André Francis, the jazz critic," Marcel said to me, "so I said of course I did. It wasn't till much later that I realized the Francis he meant was you!"

A concert of the Jazz Messengers was scheduled for December 18 at the Théâtre des Champs-Elysées. The composition of the group changed each year and I was interested to see who would be their pianist. Art Blakey always had flair and a sure taste for picking his rhythm section. I had always suspected him of being secretly in love with the piano. Despite the power that marks his style, he is a light drummer par excellence, and one of the most sensitive and attentive to the pianist. Making a superhuman effort to overcome my shyness, I asked Bud if he'd come to the concert with me. I couldn't get over it when he accepted my invitation without a moment's hesitation. Sitting beside him that evening, I was as proud as could be. We were in the middle of the hall and no one seemed to notice him. Bundled up in a winter coat and wearing the beret he wouldn't take off, he kept giving me playful looks like a child who's been taken to a show for the first time.

During the concert, Blakey came up to the mike to introduce his musicians: Walter Davis, Wayne Shorter, Lee Morgan, Jimmy Merritt, and a guest, Barney Wilen. Then, to my great surprise, I heard, "Ladies and gentlemen, we are honored to have with us this evening the great pianist Bud Powell."

Apparently, Blakey had known of Bud's presence all along. He had never really been incognito. In the audience, all heads turned looking for Bud as he slipped further down into his seat trying to hide under his beret. Art called him several times, while Bud pretended not to notice. But as the audience insisted and began calling out his name, he finally stood, to a thunder of applause. I managed to get him out of his coat and grab his beret, as he slowly and timidly made his way to the stage and Walter Davis left the piano to greet him.

Walter was the first to shake his hand, then wouldn't let go and tried to haul him up on stage with the help of the spectators in the front row. Bud looked reluctant, but in the face of unanimous encouragement, he resigned himself and sat down to play. It turned into a Bud Powell festival, with "Dance of the Infidels" and "Bouncing with Bud." He took long choruses, leading the rhythm section into a hard yet supple pulsation as only he could do.

This concert was released on a record called *Art Blakey on the Champs-Elysées*. Only later, reading the columns in the jazz magazines, did I realize that Bud's participation in the concert had been announced beforehand. He had never said a word to me about it! Judging from his attitude when Art Blakey had called him up, he didn't seem too hot on the idea and I concluded that the whole thing had probably been set up by Buttercup.

To close a wonderful evening, we went backstage to meet the musicians. Buttercup was there too. She struck the first wrong note of the evening by berating Bud for refusing to stay with her or speak to her. Fortunately, Jean-Louis Viale was there to cheer him up. He had been a drummer for Lester Young at the Club Saint Germain. Sometimes, in order to calm his furious, excitable drumming, and get him to soften up a little, Lester would say to him, "Make me some of those sweet eyes, big bomber." Bud remembered, and in no time at all he was transformed. He exploded in unstoppable laughter, repeating over and over, "Big bomber, big bomber . . ." Bud and Jean-Louis understood each other without words. Obviously, they were reliving hilarious memories. They didn't need to talk, their knowing looks were enough.

Buttercup enjoyed a good laugh as long as she was the center of attention. But apparently the musicians didn't wait for her to begin celebrating. They were chatting happily in little groups: Wayne Shorter with Barney Wilen, Walter Davis, Jimmy Merritt, and Art Blakey with Lee Morgan, who cracked them all up by announcing that Santa Claus had arrived! Buttercup, whom no one had invited, looked peeved. Then, with astounding speed for a woman of her size, she waltzed out and returned triumphantly ten minutes later with the police. Bud, Wayne, Lee, and a few hangers-on were invited to end the night at the police station where they were relieved of their clothes, strip-searched, and made to sit around naked as jaybirds till morning. Nice way to end a concert and a party!

A few days later, I did my first radio program with Frank Ténot and Daniel Filipacchi, in a series entitled *For Those Who Love Jazz*. The week before, Frank Ténot, giving a rundown of the best living pianists, had left out Bud. I had phoned the show to protest the glaring omission. He accepted my remarks with great courtesy and, to make amends, invited me to present a program devoted entirely to Bud. That day, the studio was jumping when I played the records I had brought, on-air people and technicians all equally excited. I let Bud know about the broadcast, but the next day he told me Buttercup wouldn't let him turn on the radio.

Bud was back at the Blue Note, playing with Jimmy Gourley and Lucky Thompson. They shared the bill with a young pianist named Alice McCloud, who was to be the future Mrs. John Coltrane. She had come to Paris to work with the master, Bud Powell. Jimmy, returning from the States, had met Bud in Chicago at a concert in March 1951. Playing with him was, he told me, one of the great privileges of his life:

He was playing in a trio with Max Roach and a bassist whose name I've forgotten. It was in the great days, and he played . . . oh my God! At that time, Bud was out of this world! I met him again in Paris. Bud was the perfect accompanist. He had everything: rhythm, harmonies, swing. He played for us. It was easy to play with him. There were a few details you had to respect. For me, it was perfect, I felt supported. Musically, it was stupendous!

Buttercup kept watch over him. To keep him from leaving the hotel she would take away his pants and he'd be left in his undershorts. He was always trying to get a drink and Buttercup never gave him any money. When he came up to see us, he was looking for a drink. It was the first thing he talked about. That reminds me, one night at the Blue Note, Bud asked for a cognac and Jacques put the bottle on the counter and told him to help himself. Before we knew what was happening, Bud reached out and started drinking straight out of the bottle. By the time we stopped him, the bottle was three-quarters empty.

We lived in the same hotel and I had a car so sometimes I'd take him home, driving past the Place de l'Etoile with the gigantic Arch of Triumph. One night as we circled the Arch, he looked out the window and said, in an admiring tone: "Yeah! You see that in history books."

That oversized arch, like a monstrous stone wedding cake, always appeals to foreign visitors. Lester Young was another one who wanted to see it as soon as he hit Paris. He looked at the flickering flame and the tombstone on which was written, "Soldat Inconnu—1914–1918."

"What is it?" asked Lester. "Who's buried there?" Told it was the Tomb of the Unknown Soldier, his expression went from curiosity to one of profound consternation and he exclaimed, "It's bad enough to be unknown, but to die so young!"

'ROUND MIDNIGHT

(Recorded in Paris, 1962 [Cyl])

In December 1959, I spent my first Christmas Eve with Bud at the home of Hazel Scott, who was one of the faithful fans. Her Right Bank-apartment on the Rue de Miromesnil was a permanent hangout for musicians. She always kept the shutters closed, so you could never tell if it was day or night. Hazel was truly devoted to Bud and he was very fond of her. Her piano teacher had been none other than Art Tatum. She could go on endlessly about Tatum and her stories would plunge Bud into a state bordering on beatitude. Everyone knew that Hazel's and Bud's families were very close. Bud would listen with rapt attention and make her repeat the same stories over and over again. She told us that Tatum called her "little stuff" when she was a kid and that he urged her to go to Birdland to hear a young pianist who, in his own words, "plays faster than me." "And that young pianist" she would announce, "was none other than Bud Powell!"

Bud's face would light up like a kid's, so moved and so moving. Nothing made him happier. Hazel had to patiently retell the tale all night long, searching her memory to flesh it out with more details. Each time, Bud would feign surprise and then dissolve in absolute bliss. The esteem of Tatum, his master, seemed to him the supreme confirmation. He never expressed the slightest doubt as to the reality of this compliment. Bud knew what he was worth.

But in his childlike way he could be more proud of a new tie than of any consideration of his genius, a genius that he never doubted, that was as natural for him as breathing and that was better not to talk about too much, except in a serious way. Such matters were therefore relegated to the strictest intimacy. If ever a privilege was granted to me, it was that of seeing Bud listen with real interest to my comments about him. He would listen gravely to my impassioned words, taking them to heart and seeming to draw some comfort from them.

Hazel often spoke of her friend Billie Holiday, whom she had seen again in Paris the year before. Hazel had a photo of Billie facing the piano, and the day Billie died, Hazel lit a lamp next to the photo—a little lamp left burning day and night.

For our Christmas Eve party, we did the shopping, then locked ourselves behind the closed shutters for an indefinite time. Hazel had in-
herited a fabulous Steinway grand that was considered one of the
three finest pianos in the world. Our festivities were glorified by the
superb sounds from the magical instrument. May Mezzrow, the wife
of Mezz, an old friend of Hazel's, was also there. Despite her reserved
looks, she was the life of the party, never melancholy. Santa Claus had
brought a little grass (he brought it from pretty far away, judging
from its quality!) and the party went on for several days. Hazel was a
fine cook and we had meal after meal, to the great satisfaction of Bud,
who was blessed with a hearty appetite.

When we decided to go out, it was still night, but I had no idea
which night it was. We headed for the Blue Note. When we arrived
the party was in full swing. Hazel was wearing a lavish mink coat, a
present from her husband, Congressman Adam Clayton Powell, and
with it she had put on a pair of sneakers. The effect was startling.
When Ben Benjamin dared make a remark about her shoes, she responded with an avalanche of curses about him and his club. "What
shit is that with your fucking club, where you exploit the musicians!
This joint oughtta be burnt to the ground!"

"Hazel, calm down," begged Ben. "It's Christmas!"

"Yeah, you bunch of tightwads, you slavedrivers!" Hazel always
had the knack of creating a delicate situation. Ben's wife, Itla, knew
enough to keep out of it. Her brother Jacques stayed behind his bar,
staring intently at his shoes. In the end, Hazel kissed everybody all
around, except for Itla, and the incident ended in general laughter.
During this time, Bud strolled casually from table to table, finishing
off people's drinks, pretending not to know what was going on. That
evening he played with Jean-Marie Ingrand and Jean-Louis Viale. It
was a great event and for me a wonderful Christmas present.

Bud continued to be a big hit at the Blue Note with the same trio.
Sometimes, out of kindness, Jean-Louis would give up his place to a
young drummer named Jean Guérin, who never missed a night. He
used to sit down just behind the piano and not budge till closing time.

Without my fully understanding how it happened, Bud had become a part of my life. I saw him regularly—evenings at the club and
daytime as well—but it all seemed more and more unreal. In addition,
I was putting in long hours as a graphic designer, working days for an
advertising agency and often freelancing at night. When everybody
else went home to bed, I would stay up to work and listen to Bud's
music playing softly through the night.

BLUES IN THE CLOSET
(Recorded in New York, September 13, 1956 [Verve])

Around this time I moved into a new apartment. It was a one-flight walkup in a northern section of Paris, at 65, rue Boursault. Nicole moved in with me. We shared the same passion for jazz in general and Bud in particular. That was what had first brought us together. She spoke English fluently, even though she didn't say "motherfucker" as naturally as I did.

In all my friendships and acquaintances, music always played a prime role. It would have been foolhardy to attempt a relationship with someone who didn't share my enthusiasm in that respect.

The apartment was in two parts: on one side a kitchen and a bathroom; on the other, a single studio room, small but facing a garden with a handsome tree whose branches came up to our window railing. The whole thing was miniscule and getting everything in its place was a miracle.

I managed to replace my old Stek-Pianola with an Erard baby grand. My other possessions consisted of an English Ferrograph tape recorder bought from a cocaine addict in need of cash, a bed, a drawing table, a small phonograph, and mountains of records, tapes, and jazz magazines.

When the piano and the table were moved in, I had to admit the obvious—no one could sit at the piano because it was up against a large built-in wall closet with double doors. There was only one thing to do. When we removed its doors, the closet became a cosy alcove, large and deep enough to accommodate the piano stool and the pianist. While I was at it, I also installed my phonograph and tape-recorder there. That way I had everything at hand. I have never yet found a better way to work at the piano.

I covered the walls of my new space with beige canvas and put up my favorite photos: Bud, of course, and Tatum and Bird and Billie, but also Yves Tanguy and Salvador Dali, my favorite painters. I still painted a little at the time but after a while I gave it up. Attempting to paint in such cramped quarters was an acrobatic feat.

Bud had left the Blue Note and I missed him terribly. I had gotten too used to seeing him in recent months. But I heard about him from a musician friend who lived in the Latin Quarter and who knew I was interested in him. He told me Bud still lived at the Louisiane and he often saw him wandering aimlessly through the streets. Then, shamefaced, he added that he'd seen Bud panhandling on the Boulevard Saint Germain.

The news left me terribly depressed. I had a lot of work and couldn't take time off to check out his story, but all week long I was obsessed by the image of Bud asking for handouts. Saturday morning I took the car and left with Nicole to search for Bud in Saint Germain des Prés. Luck was with us, for no sooner had we reached the boulevard when a familiar silhouette caught our eye. It was indeed Bud, thin and haggard, shuffling miserably down the street gazing at the people around him.

I was heartbroken and at the same time filled with a violent feeling of revolt. In so short a time, he had lost weight and his trousers, now too large at the waist, were held up by suspenders. In an unbuttoned raincoat, with his hands in his pockets and a cap pulled down over his ears, he looked like a weary traveler waiting somewhere for a train that will never come. With his searching eyes and despondent expression, he was the image of loneliness.

His immense solitude emptied the space around him like an infectious disease. This image of despair clung to him as he vanished into the nameless throng along the boulevard. He was misery incarnate.

When he recognized me, he gave me an embarrassed little smile. He was quickly persuaded there was a better place to go and on a quiet café terrace I ordered the inevitable *vin rouge* and a sandwich and tried in vain to talk to him. He seemed sunk in the depths of desolation. We spent the day together and as night fell I offered to take him home.

Buttercup was waiting for him and there was nothing welcoming in her inquisitorial stare. I was struck by the attitude of submission that Bud adopted with this woman. When she saw he wasn't in too bad a state, Buttercup quickly regained her jovial manner, talking loud and laughing at her own jokes. Despite that, the atmosphere was tense and Bud looked utterly miserable the whole time.

LULLABY FOR A BELIEVER

(Recorded in New York, October 5, 1956 [Victor, unreleased])

Nicole and I had already made up our minds to invite him for lunch the next day. Cautiously, we announced this plan to the lady of the house, who thought it over and, to our astonishment, seemed to find nothing wrong with the idea. Bud was transformed! Over and over, at least ten times, he made me repeat what time I would be coming to pick him up. Nicole, hoping to pamper him a little by preparing his favorite food, asked him what he liked to eat.

"Oysters," he said, spontaneously, his voice betraying a hint of hesitation. His face shone when I answered that that would be no problem at all.

My mind was racing so much I had trouble falling asleep that night. What a guest we were going to have! In a twinkling, without any thought or preparation, here I was living the dream that had filled my adolescence as a young pianist in love with jazz. The idol of my life was about to dine at my table just as simply as that! I had detected in Bud's look a need for friendship, for boundless and unconditional love. I felt I could provide it, in return for what Bud had already given me through his music.

After a restless night, I drove to the Louisiane at the appointed time to pick up my precious guest. I ran up the stairs four at a time praying fervently that nothing had come up to interfere with our plans. When I reached the door I knocked timidly. The door opened before I had even finished knocking, and Bud sprang out at me, bundled into his coat, his beret pulled down onto his head, impatient to get going. Before I had a chance to greet Buttercup, he was pushing me firmly toward the staircase. We had reached the next landing by the time Buttercup came out to shout her superfluous instructions to bring him home on time and not give him any alcohol. I had already formulated my own ideas about the way to handle that delicate problem.

Sitting in my little sports car, a Triumph TR3, Bud looked over at me, surprise and delight on his face. As for myself, I can't imagine how I must have looked, contemplating *him*, Mr. Bud Powell! I was in seventh heaven. I remember I drove more carefully that day than I ever had before, so conscious was I of my enormous responsibility. I was aware of every gesture, every possibility of error. I would have liked the trip to last forever as I savored every minute of it, repeating to myself: "That's *the* Bud Powell sitting there next to you in your car! Incredible, incredible! . . ."

Nicole was as awed as I was. She had lovingly prepared the meal and wanted it to be worthy of him. The moment we came in, Bud's eyes were drawn irresistibly to the platter of oysters in the middle of the table. We had barely finished our greetings when he asked eagerly if we could start eating. We were thrilled. There was no talk during the meal. Bud chuckled with pleasure like a child. His looks and smiles filled the silence better than words. Nicole served a specialty from her native Périgord, followed by much appreciated French pastries. When he had finished, Bud got up and started looking around the room. He noticed on a shelf a little book on jazz, an exhaustive dictionary put together by a French journalist, one of our self-styled experts. He sat down on the bed to flip through it and we saw him frown and look more and more worried as he noticed his name wasn't mentioned. I managed to convince him that it was only the first volume and that the second would surely carry a long article on him.

As soon as we arrived, Bud had suggested we put on Art Tatum. He continued to ask only for Tatum and, naturally, I was all for it. It took a great deal of pleading by Nicole to get him to sit down at the piano. The suspense grew as he sat in deep concentration. Then he played "April in Paris," at length, and with a romantic lyricism that I had never heard. From my good old piano came the familiar sounds mingled with another music, a music he would henceforth offer us in the privacy of our apartment. A music full of serenity—tremendous, definitive—that my trusty Ferrograph would record again and again.

The afternoon passed as if in a marvelous dream and the awakening was brutal. The time had come—like the hated bugle call in the army. I dragged out the return trip by taking the scenic route, to stave off the painful moment of separation. The Rue de Seine seemed to me as gloomy as a railroad platform, and my passenger was heading not for a train but for a prison, judging from his miserable expression as he climbed the stairs.

Buttercup was waiting for us on the landing, a questioning look on her face. She gave Bud a quick once-over, then recovered her gaiety, reassured that her "meal ticket" was none the worse for wear. We had passed our exam. She added that Bud would be delighted to accept any future invitations and, without wasting a second, he asked me to set the next date. I would have gladly given him every day of the week, but at that stage of my career I really had to keep my nose to the grindstone.

For some time I had been working as an advertising illustrator at home. My few attempts to work in an agency had been disappointing. First of all, I missed having my music during working hours, and then my contacts with the members of the advertising profession were none too rewarding. Freelancing was tough but encouraging and my music and my piano kept me company and kept me happy.

When Bud had been to our apartment several times and talked enthusiastically about his visits, Buttercup, intrigued, asked if she could come too, in order, as she said, to get to know us better. We arranged a dinner for her and Bud and she brought along another lady friend. As soon as they came in, I noticed that both women seemed over-excited and Bud kept looking at us in embarrassment. The evening was pleasant all the same and, with Buttercup's constant prodding, Bud gave in to all her whims. She started reminiscing about his early days and wanted him to tell me his youthful adventures. Bud had played a little earlier and the tape recorder was still on, so I can reconstitute the conversation verbatim:

BUTTERCUP (to Bud): You know what I'd like to hear?
NICOLE: "Sweet and Lovely!"
BUTTERCUP: No, do the "Click Clock Song." I wrote to your Daddy today—and I thought about that tune.
BUD (suddenly tender): You wrote to my father?
BUTTERCUP: Yes.
BUD (with a lump in his throat): You wrote to my father? . . . (Then to Buttercup in the third person) She wrote to my father? (Thoughtfully) Hum . . . m . . . m . . . m. (Brusquely) She wrote to my father? What'd she say?
BUTTERCUP: I told him you're alright. I sent some pictures to your Dad, some other things. . . . I always write.
BUD (more and more tenderly, almost languidly): Oh yeah . . .
BUTTERCUP: I told him you're okay. I always write, you know . . .
BUD (dreamily): You wrote to my father . . .
BUTTERCUP: You wrote to your mother before she . . . you remember?
BUD: I don't know . . .

BUTTERCUP: Come on, Bud, play something for us.

BUD (in a timid voice): You want me to play "Click Clock Song"?

BUTTERCUP: Ha ha! His daddy wrote this tune.

BUD (in a very convincing tone, to himself): The best . . . Yes. He was the best in town . . . he is the best. (suddenly, now very excited by a resurgence of memory) But . . . wait, when I was a kid, my father took me with my mother, someplace where he was playing . . . No . . . I was out with my mother and she took me to a vaudeville theater to see him play. I don't remember where it was, but I was there, ha ha ha!!! (He laughs like a happy little kid.)

BUTTERCUP: His father played the piano. Bud was very impressed because his father was in a tux with a conductor's baton . . .

BUD (happily and decidedly): Listen, I'm gonna play the song.

(He attacks his father's tune in a joyous tempo, using a ragtime beat in his left hand. Laughter explodes all around. Everyone applauds.)

BUTTERCUP (rhythmically, nostalgically): Those were the good times, weren't they, Bud?

BUD: Oh yeah. That was a great time.

BUTTERCUP: Oh yeah, of course. You remember, Bud, that night when your father came on Christmas Eve? You stayed up all night . . . you all played together . . . no way to get you off the piano . . .

FRANCIS: You remember, Bud—"Bud on Bach"?

BUTTERCUP: Oh yes, Bud, play "Bud on Bach"!

BUD: No, no, no. No play no more. (Laughs)

BUTTERCUP: Play me a ballad. And I don't ask you no more.

EVERYBODY (in unison): Oh yes, Bud, a ballad. Please, be nice.

BUD: You promise?

BUTTERCUP: Promise.

BUD: You promised. What kind of ballad?

NICOLE: "It Could Happen To Me."

BUD: "It Could Happen To You"!

(Laughter . . . Bud announces the tune again, and after an interminable introduction, he plays "Everything Happens To Me" in the midst of wild applause.)

BUTTERCUP: You just played "Everything Happens To Me."

BUD: You wanted "It Could Happen To You"?

BUTTERCUP: Yeah—and sing it!

(Bud begins the tune majestically, with really profound chords connected together by incredibly long phrases, like Tatum.)

BUTTERCUP: Sing it to me! Sing it for me!

BUD: No, Butter, no.

BUTTERCUP (a light bulb goes on—has a brilliant idea): Oh I know, listen . . . that's it, I'll tell you (she starts singing) . . . you know I love it.

(Bud picks up the tune, the most beautiful song I've ever heard, and then, after eight bars, Bud sings the lyrics, followed by Buttercup. The bridge connects heartbreaking harmonies together one after another, so unexpectedly, with incomparable beauty. I get goose bumps all over my body.)

BUTTERCUP: That's the most beautiful song I ever heard in my life.

NICOLE: Bud, play "Thelonious."

BUD: No more.

BUTTERCUP: He wants a glass of wine, then he'll play "Thelonious."

BUD: Okay, gimme another glass of wine . . .

NICOLE: And then you'll play "Thelonious"?

BUD: Sure, okay.

NICOLE: So, play "Thelonious" first.

(A general explosion of laughter)

BUD: We're going to eat now?

NICOLE: Yes. It'll be ready in a minute.

BUD (suddenly dreamily): What could I sing now?

BUTTERCUP: "You Go To My Head"?

(Bud plays the intro, with emphasis, and Buttercup sings along with him. She has a very warm voice, excellent pitch, and a beautiful vibrato, and Bud helps along with some great counter-melodies. She has a memory lapse, but she sings with a lot of sensibility. She reproaches Bud for trying to help with the words, but he goes on anyway without bending. Suddenly his voice bursts out imperiously with the song. Buttercup punctuates the ending with "Jingle Bells, Jingle Bells," etc. and Bud leaves the piano.)

NICOLE: Oh Bud, you're finished?

BUTTERCUP: Francis, you play. Play some.

BUD: Francis is going to play!

(Buttercup begins to start "Just You, Just Me," and I accompany her, but she stops right away because she forgets the lyrics and so we both stop at once.)

BUTTERCUP: I forget everything! All the words, all the time . . .

(During that time Bud is making a tour of the kitchen to have a look at what's simmering on the stove, then he comes back to the piano.)

BUTTERCUP: Bud, do you remember "It Never Entered My Mind"?

BUD: Never entered my mind . . .

BUTTERCUP (and her friend, in chorus together): Yeah, you know it . . . you know it!

BUD: Nope.

(Without playing, he starts singing the tune in a very strong voice, punctuating all of the modulations. Buttercup lets out a huge scream.)

BUTTERCUP: Oh, I love the way you play that! Go on . . . play it, I love it!

(Bud continues, singing and laughing at the same time, altering the song drastically with this strange mixture. Then he sits at the piano and simply plays the song. I am knocked out to hear the exact same interpretation as on the record. And this confirms to me that this version of the tune, so hotly contested by all the critics of the time, was no accident, and was not connected in any way to any momentary weakness, but, on the contrary, it had been perfectly thought out and was totally masterful in its dramatic context.)

(Laughter and bravos)

FRANCIS: And "I Remember Clifford"?

BUD: I'll get something to eat . . . I'll get something to eat!

(He keeps repeating this, at least ten times, making a game of it.)

(Dinner is served. . . . end of the recording.)

The general excitement cooled down as the evening progressed. Buttercup's friend fell asleep on my bed, much to Bud's consternation. By the time they left, Buttercup was exhausted and I practically had to carry her to the taxi—no easy task, given her weight. It was like holding up a solid oak chest. What an evening!

OBLIVION

(Recorded in New York, February 11, 1957 [Victor])

In the months that followed, Bud got in the habit of spending his afternoons in my quiet little apartment at 65, rue Boursault. He would watch me draw, with the rapt attention of a child discovering one thing after another, and we listened tirelessly to Tatum. These moments have left me a memory of pure bliss. Sometimes, Bud would go to the piano and sit with a dreamy air, not playing but contemplating the keyboard. For a long time, no real talk was possible. In answer to my questions, he would only smile. But the atmosphere was never heavy and the good vibrations that flowed between us were conversation enough. I felt sure that this serenity was helping my creative work and was teaching me a new way to be in life.

Bud passed his time in contemplation. He would stare out the window watching the foliage sway and the birds hopping about. Tatum worked his magic on the ivories and the entire universe was in harmony.

Naturally reserved, Bud found it hard to make contact with strangers, so I avoided encounters that would have made him feel ill at ease. I did my best to make sure that his moments of escape from the Hotel Louisiane were peaceful and soothing. We didn't entertain that much at the time and the close friends we did see were all jazz fans who shared our devotion to Bud.

At the time I had left home, my sister Noëlle, also a pianist, was still quite young. Our conversations about the music I loved and the creators I admired had never succeeded in convincing her of its validity, partly due to the influence of our parents, but mainly through her own lack of experience. One day she dropped in while Bud was there. They had never met before and as I made the introductions, she seemed so ill at ease that I knew Bud would clam up and no contact would be possible. Bud had an uncanny way of sensing people's feelings. He immediately disappeared into the kitchen and nothing I did could make him come out until she had left. He never explained, but the message was clear. Fortunately, like so many others who were at first indifferent, she too eventually succumbed to the charms of Bud and his music, and later on they became quite fond of each other.

In the early evening I would take Bud home, as Buttercup liked to check him out before he left for the club. Bud asked if I'd come and hear him that evening. It was like asking a blind man if he wanted to see! I would have gladly spent my life at the Blue Note.

I usually showed up early, before the first set, and took a seat on the podium, behind the piano, whose place had been changed. Thus I was close to him and could watch him play. Those evenings revealed to me even more about the soul of this man I thought I knew so well. After finishing a tune, he would sometimes give me a worried look, as if unsure that he had achieved his goal. I hoped that the few words I managed to utter were able to express all the emotion I felt.

Bud was not in top form during those evenings and I watched his physical condition gradually decline. His music wasn't the same, though to my mind it was still of great interest. It was slower, but despite a labored articulation the magic was still there and the ideas were still brilliantly original. Bud seemed to be struggling to stay awake and I realized that something was wrong. I knew he wasn't drinking, because I had been with him all day and there had to be another cause of this state he was in. The public and the other musicians assumed it was alcohol or drugs, but obviously there were other origins for this, and their suspicions made me furious.

I couldn't bear Bud's sadness when it was time to go back to the hotel, and to lighten his sorrow, I always tried to confirm the date and time of our next encounter. Buttercup never stopped harping on the dangers of alcohol, which was totally superfluous as we had no trouble curbing Bud's desire to drink. Our affection and deep respect made him amenable to all our suggestions.

Along with her instructions, Buttercup gave me three little pink pills that Bud was supposed to take in mid-afternoon. At first, I had attached no particular importance to these pills. But seeing the effect they had on him, I finally came to realize their significance. He would fall into a sort of lethargy, his movements became slower, and he lost interest in everything around him. He seemed to make a superhuman effort to respond to my questions and his speech became at first labored, then impossible to understand.

The work I was doing at the time on advertising campaigns for pharmaceutical companies put me in contact with laboratories and doctors. I decided to keep one of the pills to find out what it was. It turned out to be an extremely strong tranquilizing medication called Largactyl.

Later on, Dr. Teboul, a psychiatrist whom we saw socially with his wife, gave me his opinion about this drug:

> Largactyl, which was discovered by Professor Henri Laborit, is a good medication for schizophrenia. Naturally, it should be administered under medical supervision, including electrocardiograms, blood tests, and neurological examinations.
>
> It was through you, Francis, that I got to know Bud Powell and his music. I think he liked me. During several talks I had with him, I got the feeling that his problems were . . . I don't know if psychiatric is the proper word. Bud talked about himself when I saw him, but there was never really a dialogue.
>
> I think the treatment he was getting was simply crazy, the dose was far too strong. I still wonder how that woman could have obtained the drug so easily.
>
> Largactyl numbs the patient and can cause impotence. Furthermore, neuroleptics can produce suggestibility, and after the treatment there can be memory loss for up to three months.

Marcel Romano told me that he too had once been on Largactyl. "During that period, I heard what people were saying, but I didn't want to answer—it was just too tiring. Any response seemed pointless. That experience helped me to better understand Bud."

I too was beginning to understand. This powerful medication was curbing Bud's every faculty. The doctor who knew the drug and the patient who had once taken it told me the same thing: it killed initiative, dampened the will, and made the patient submissive and indifferent.

Suddenly, it all became clear—all the attacks, all the misconceptions. Poor Bud! He had been accused of every vice when in fact it was his "benefactress" who was responsible for his sorry state. And on top of it, she was the one people felt sorry for! To make her own life easier, it seemed, she had found nothing better than to destroy Bud's mind and body. I thought of his struggle to stay awake at the piano and his pain-filled eyes under the public's disdainful gaze.

In those eventful years we had many jazz programs on the radio and also some on television. French TV had one channel at the time but there were broadcasts of Bud Powell live from the Saint Germain or the Blue Note, as well as Miles Davis, Barney Wilen, Lucky Thompson, Jimmy Gourley, Kenny Clarke, René Urtréger, and Martial Solal. Sim Copans presided, with his excellent taste. Raymond Mouly also had several series, mostly filmed by Jean-Christophe Averty. (Ah, Jean-Christophe, why won't you show us the treasures you had the good fortune to shoot?) When I think of all the documents filed away in the archives of the National Audiovisual Institute that we may never see! Today France has six TV channels and innumerable local radio stations so close together that their frequencies overlap, and if only their quality matched their quantity, we'd be sitting pretty.

During one of my visits to the Louisiane to pick up Bud, I also invited a friend of his who was at that time vacationing in Paris. Her name was Anita and she later married Gil Evans. It was no accident that she was in that hotel. The Louisiane had become a place of pilgrimage for jazz fans and musicians. Lester and Billie had stayed there, to mention only two of its famous guests. Anita had a lot of musician friends and she was particularly fond of Bud. She was trying her luck as a singer and we all made some nice music together, along with two of my friends, Franck Nizery and Mic, both fervent fans.

In this relaxed atmosphere, Bud seemed to revive. He was eager to play and we listened in awe. Our evenings always followed the same pattern. We would dine by candlelight and then play music just for fun. Bud loved it. Sometimes I would play a tune that gave him an idea. He would go to the piano with a mischievous smile and repeat it with the most unbelievable harmonies. One night, he had a surprise for us. While playing "When I Fall in Love," he started imitating the sound of a horn through closed lips. Then his voice took on the moving intonation of a child's, frail but determined, with an exceptional sense of timing. The modulations and holds gave a striking effect of surprise and his singing gave forth an astounding emotional charge. We sat transfixed as the tears rolled down our cheeks in the candlelight.

Bill Coleman, who was an old friend, often came to join us. Our tiny apartment seemed to grow to accommodate all our friends. I still wonder how it was possible, but everyone found a place, somehow. One spot, and not the worst by far, was under the piano. Bill often got out his trumpet, and he sang too, very well.

He would talk about his early days with Louis Armstrong, Teddy Wilson, Billie, and the Duke, then Bud would go on about Tatum and Monk. One night, he said, while Tatum was playing at a club, he came up behind him and stood watching him play over his shoulder. After a few minutes, Tatum stopped and without turning around, said, "Is that you, Bud?"

Still intrigued by the incident, Bud asked, "Do you think he's really blind, Francis? How did he know I was there?" Then with a pensive air, "But I guess he is. He had a big blue Lincoln but he didn't drive it himself, he had a chauffeur. He took me for a ride, sometimes . . . Those were the good old days. . . ." And he went back to his thoughts, a sad little smile on his lips.

Bill Coleman went off for a concert tour and left us his cat for a couple of days. It was then I discovered that Bud hated cats, though he had no idea why. The cat, however, was deeply attracted to him, and whatever he did to chase it away, the beast would persist in winding itself around his legs or jumping into his lap without warning. Bud was absolutely terrified.

Bud took very little interest in the outside world, though occasionally an insignificant situation could disturb him immensely. A dispute in the street could fill him with anxiety for hours afterward. He would be terrorized and filled with anguish. One night we had dinner at Lili and Bill Coleman's and while we were there our car was stolen. We were both upset, but Bud kept repeating, as if to himself, "They stole the car! They stole the car!" We loved the little Triumph TR3 in which we had taken so many nice rides. Bud loved riding through the Paris streets at night and we changed our route all the time so we could explore the different neighborhoods of the city. Now we stood there on the sidewalk, feeling helpless. We were both shaken, but it was Bud who brought me back to reality. "Francis, we have to go to the police, right away!"

He was right, of course. There was nothing else to be done. He took my arm and we headed for the nearest police station.

I made my declaration while Bud stood by glaring at the police officer. He couldn't say a word but his look was perfectly eloquent.

Luckily, the car was found a week later, undamaged, and Bud was relieved of the worry that had obsessed him all week long.

A few days later, Buttercup phoned in a panic. Bud had been missing for two days. Assuming he had gotten drunk, I started calling the police and the hospitals, but with no luck. Buttercup had all his papers and he had no ID on him that could enable rapid identification. I gave a precise description and we finally located him. He was under observation at a large Paris hospital, the Hôtel-Dieu. Later, when we had been through the same horrible scenario a number of times, it occurred to me that never before had I had so much contact with cops and hospitals.

At the Hôtel-Dieu, I waited patiently and was finally seen by a young doctor who was a jazz fan and had recognized him. He was pleased to have such a prestigious patient and while he was reassuring me about Bud's health, I suddenly felt a slap on the back and heard a cheery "Hello, Francis!" I couldn't believe my eyes. There was Bud, in a magnificent red bathrobe and matching slippers. He seemed relaxed and gave the doctor a knowing smile. He was delighted to hear that he could leave the hospital right away.

I called Buttercup to give her the good news and at Bud's insistence we went out to eat at a nearby restaurant. We ended the day at home, where Bud spontaneously sat down to play with genuine pleasure. I had the feeling that he was communicating with me, that the notes were like words, the first significant words that passed between us. We were about to become close friends.

Going back to the hotel always darkened his mood. To delay the dreaded moment, he used every pretext possible. It was obvious to me that Bud was afraid of Buttercup. It was also obvious to me that her friendliness was all an act. I had often felt she was irritated by Bud's desire for my company and his eagerness to get out of the hotel room on any pretext whatsoever. When I was there, her attitude toward him was one of forced cordiality. Bud wasn't fooled and kept looking at me to see how I was taking it. He would give me an ironic look and stare at her wordlessly. The atmosphere would grow heavy and in the end she stopped trying to put up a front. At first she was suspicious toward me, then openly hostile.

I had never tried to talk to Bud about Buttercup. Though the situation was ambiguous, I took it at face value: she was his wife and the little boy Johnny was their son. The constant presence of a young Austrian named Henri made things look even murkier, as his behavior with Buttercup left no doubt as to the nature of their relations. Cautious at first when I was around, his attitude later gave way to one of open provocation. Bud seemed more and more filled with consternation and I grew more and more upset by his silence and his resignation.

I did my best to get him away from there as often as I could, but I wasn't always available. Then I would hear that he had left on his own and found a way to get drunk. He would wind up either collapsing in the street or falling into the hands of the police. The morning after, I would be the powerless witness to Buttercup's angry scolding, each time more vicious than the last, and see his humiliation at being mocked in front of the child, the sneering Austrian, and the neighbors down the hall, who found the whole thing pretty funny.

Buttercup now doubled Bud's daily dose of Largactyl. This medicine was her strongest ally, for it kept him in complete submission. It was like a huge eraser, wiping out any outside interest he might have had. The spectators at the Blue Note who saw Bud under its influence, struggling to stay awake, whispered to one another that he was on drugs. In fact, he was drugged in spite of himself, just to keep him in line.

From that point on I saw Bud, more depressed than ever, in his dismal room. All around him were the incessant comings and goings of those who hung out at the hotel. This life had been familiar to him and he had learned to live with it. He never spoke of his anguish except to ask indirect questions, looking in a roundabout way for some answer, some explanation that would give him peace. Quietly, timidly, he revealed in these conversations a part of his soul that he could never reveal to more casual observers.

JOHN'S ABBEY
(Recorded in Paris, 1959 [Xanadu])

One day, when Nicole and I arrived at the hotel, we found Bud with one foot tied to the table leg. Johnny was dancing wildly around him and Bud was begging in a plaintive voice to be untied, which of course I immediately did. The child threw me a dirty look and ran out of the room, slamming the door angrily. Bud jumped up and locked it. A few minutes later Johnny was back and, finding the door locked, he started pounding on it and yelling. Alerted by the din, Buttercup arrived and I hurried to open the door for her. Johnny leaped into the room and, with a virulence surprising for a five-year-old child, started telling his mother, "Hit him, Ma, hit him!"

Bud retreated to a chair and raised his arm over his face to protect himself, like a child about to receive a blow. "What did you do to him now?" she screeched, her eyes shooting daggers.

"Nothing, Butter, I swear I didn't do nothing," he replied in a broken voice, never taking his eyes off her face.

Johnny screamed even louder, "Hit him! Go on, ma, hit him."

The atmosphere bordered on hysteria. Buttercup looked furiously from Bud to Nicole to me. She must not have seen much sympathy in my gaze, for her anger grew. I felt like an intruder and didn't dare intervene. But I couldn't leave either as I knew that if not for our presence, she would probably have hauled off and hit Bud. I explained what had happened and she calmed down. Johnny, still in a rage, walked up to Bud, spit in his face, then stormed out, slamming the door. Nicole was pale. We didn't dare make a move to leave but we knew we couldn't stay much longer. Bud came to our rescue by offering to walk downstairs with us. Now he confided in us for the first time.

"Francis, Buttercup's not my wife, she never was. And Johnny's not my son."

I suddenly thought of the item in *Jazz Magazine* about Bud's arrest in Newark. "What does this all mean, Bud?"

"Buttercup made me recognize Johnny as my son."

It was hard for me to talk about this problem with my musician friends. Most of them were very discreet about what they knew and I wasn't close enough with them yet. The only one with whom I could bring up the subject was Kenny Clarke. I had known him for a long time and noticed he was very cool to Buttercup and never spoke to her. His reply to my question was straightforward, but with his customary discretion he refused to go into the details. He seemed to find the whole situation distasteful. "I can tell you one thing, Francis. Buttercup is not his wife and never was, and Johnny is not his son."

I was stunned. "Then why are they together?"

"Don't ask me any more about it," he said. "It's awful and I don't want to stir up trouble. All I can say is I know what I'm talking about. It's an ugly story. I know how it all began and I'm sure of one thing—Bud had a physical incapacity and could not have been his father at that time."

Obviously, I would have liked to know more. This unexpected news aroused my worst fears but also increased my desire to help Bud. I didn't want to bother Kenny. He alluded to certain treatments Bud had had and their dire consequences, but the mere mention of it seemed to revolt him.

Things became clearer in my mind and I began to understand Bud's behavior. By passing herself off as his wife, Buttercup could live off Bud's earnings. Bud, numbed by tranquilizers and in constant fear of reprisals, had long ago become resigned. He had been thoroughly conditioned by his successive hospitalizations, his time in jail, and his run-ins with all kinds of people who had power over him, as a man and as a musician. With his past raked over and spotlighted by the press, he didn't stand a chance in case of conflict. He was caught in a vicious circle and his withdrawal into himself was a desperate means of self-protection in order to avoid any embarrassing indiscretions. But I sensed that he had kept his lucidity. This lucidity came out in his music, where each note was a cry for help. He struggled against the injustice of a life he didn't deserve, against ignorance and lack of understanding. He wanted to justify himself but was afraid to try. He fought against the disastrous effects of Largactyl combined with alcohol. He fought to preserve the one thing that mattered: his music. But it was an unequal battle. His physical and emotional state worsened every day. To express himself in music, as in life, all his powers were failing him. To overcome this debilitating state, he found another music, excessively slow but even more poignant than the familiar one. He played within self-imposed restrictions, with a great economy of means, his message stripped of all artifice, reduced to raw sentiment. His pain engendered a cruel beauty. As always, Bud seemed to disconnect from the music as soon as he'd finished playing it, and more than ever he wanted my opinion. It's true that only the most attentive listening could draw the depths of meaning from this music. The answers I gave were always comforting, but of course, because of the circumstances, I could never share my true feelings with him.

Many times I left the Blue Note shattered and unable to sleep. I would play one of Bud's records and feel a little energy return, conscious that his music was surely a solution. I could then go back to my drawing with new enthusiasm. In the silence between two records, my spirits flagged again. The music was my nourishment, the source of my resistance, my ability to keep up my long nights of work. The most boring tasks became pleasant to the strains of "I'll Keep Loving You," "Oblivion," and "Hallucinations." This music fired my imagination and electrified my pens and brushes. Bud never knew it, but he brought out the best in my life.

In February of 1960 he left on a tour with Oscar Pettiford and Kenny Clarke, first to Italy, where the trio performed in the San Remo festival on the 21st. In the monthly magazine *Jazz* (Easter 1960), Hubert Pastorelly wrote: "Then came a trio that could be considered one of the best in the world, made up of Bud Powell, Oscar Pettiford and Kenny Clarke. Playing with them enabled Barney Wilen to enter the ranks of the greatest jazzmen. No one name can be singled out—the trio literally 'blew the room away.'"

When the tour hit the south of France, bastion of modern jazz fans, the local press echoed this opinion. The daily *Le Méridional*, among others, announced the coming concert at the Alhambra on March 8 in the following terms: ". . . We will have the opportunity to hear Bud Powell, the greatest of jazz pianists. . . . To all the young pianists for whom he was a prime source of inspiration, Bud Powell is still a god. This concert is the greatest jazz event to hit France since the famous Charlie Parker concert of 1949."

After Marseilles, the trio, under the auspices of the French state radio-TV network, went on to play from Lyons to Bordeaux, crossing over to Basel, Zurich, and Lausanne, then Nantes, Angers, and Toulouse before returning to Paris.

Buttercup was living it up with her pack of hangers-on in the crowded little hotel room. She looked happy as a lark. The Austrian, now a permanent member of the family, acted as head of the household. Bud seemed left out of the general merriment and I came to get him as often as I could, to spend quiet days in my apartment. Then he left for Essen, where he played with Oscar Pettiford and Kenny Clarke, joined by Coleman Hawkins. The concert was later released by Fontana, and after that on a pirated Italian label. The days we had spent together seemed to have revitalized him and the recording shows all the fire he was capable of when he had his self-confidence back.

That summer Bud was invited to the Antibes Jazz Festival to play solo, and then with the Mingus sextet with Eric Dolphy, Booker Ervin, Dannie Richmond, and Ted Curson. The recorded concerts were issued by Verve. With Mingus and Dannie Richmond, Bud does a long improvisation on the harmonies of "I'll Remember April," then stops, as Dolphy and Booker Ervin trade fours in a wild contest.

While researching this book, I came across the films of those sessions. They show Bud bravely struggling to fight off the effects of Largactyl. I never did find out how Buttercup got a permanent prescription for this drug, which is usually administered for a limited time and under strict psychiatric control.

DUSKY 'N' SANDY

(Recorded in New York, February 1951 [Verve])

With Bud away on tour, there was nothing to keep me in Paris, so Nicole and I decided to take a holiday in Spain. We had already loaded our bags into the Triumph when the postman showed up with a parcel that incited us to head straight back up the stairs two-at-a-time.

Modern jazz records were poorly distributed in France and some of them had to be specially ordered. I had completely forgotten the order I had placed a few months earlier with Doléjal in Switzerland and so it was a great surprise when I opened the parcel and found Bud's record. It was *The Genius of Bud Powell*, on Verve, one of his finest ever. He played only his own compositions and the solo side convinced me once and for all of his incomparable genius. Without wasting a minute, I put the record on the phonograph and was promptly overwhelmed by the tune "Dusky 'n' Sandy." It was like an explosion in my mind. I played it again, moved to my very soul. Nicole felt the same way. Each time the piece ended, it left an emptiness, an unbearable melancholy. I felt I would never break away from its melodic spell. Never before had I heard anything so poignant, so upsetting. This music evoked in me unknown images and endless horizons, like in a painting by Yves Tanguy. There was nothing to do but stay, and we dragged our suitcases back into the house. We didn't leave for Spain till three days later. Tape cassettes had not yet been invented and the thought of leaving the disc behind, of breaking the charm of this music, would have ruined my vacation. All summer long, "Dusky 'n' Sandy" went around and around in my head. The mystery of that tune, the sublime beauty that inspired Bud, still baffles me today. It is surely what I would take along to that mythical deserted isle. One day, maybe . . .

Bud was working on and off, but as he was living in Paris I could be sure to see him during his idle hours. Our meetings with Bud and our disputes with Buttercup became an invariable pattern. Oscar Pettiford died suddenly and Bud lost a faithful companion with whom he had played a lot in recent months. A concert was held in his memory and Bud took part. Then he went back to the Blue Note, which had become his base. He played in alternation with Stan Getz, who was accompanied by Maurice Vander, a French pianist who had played with Django Reinhardt. A brilliant musician, Maurice had grown up in the school of Art Tatum and was therefore indirectly influenced by Bud. He was the epitome of a typically white trend in the jazz of that time. Fascinated by speed, he used sophisticated harmonic systems long before the generation of "intellectual" pianists would put performance above emotional expression. In the weeks that followed, the Blue Note's other performers were Jimmy Gourley, Rita Peys, Pim Jacob, and the great Carmen McRae, who sang with Bud and the trio.

In December, René Urtréger won a well-deserved award, the Django Reinhardt Prize, for his work in nightclubs, radio, and television. The prize was presented by Georges Auric in the presence of other celebrated prize winners, Louis Armstrong and Duke Ellington. The reception was held in an unusual setting, a barge on the Seine, and during the evening, tribute was also paid to an excellent ten-inch LP René had recently made, called *René Urtréger Plays Bud Powell*. In a tune called "A la Bud," René had used Bud's intro to "Tea for Two," an idea already suggested in Art Tatum's performance of the same piece. This continuity of research and embellishment is in no way surprising, as Bud always recognized Tatum as his master. For me, René's daring intro opened great new horizons in harmonics. I listened endlessly to "Tea for Two." In the careful arrangement and reharmonization of simple tunes, I saw the constant need for the writing of more original compositions. We can easily suppose that with more freedom and fewer professional constraints, Bud might have created musical treasures that were much closer to his inner songs. In a more understanding milieu and with some financial subsidies from public authorities or cultural bodies in the United States, he might have left behind masterpieces which, instead, remained imprisoned in his mind.

An advertising agency I worked for at the time had asked me to arrange a cocktail party for six hundred guests, members of the advertising profession. The agency logo was a trumpet and, knowing my interest in jazz, they asked me to find a famous trumpet player to host the evening. I first thought of my old friend Bill Coleman but he, with his legendary modesty, suggested I ask Louis Armstrong, who just happened to be in Paris making a film called *Paris Blues*. They were shooting at the Boulogne studios, and Duke Ellington and a host of musicians were also there. Practically every jazz musician in Paris had been asked to take part in the film.

Bill introduced me to Armstrong, who found the idea amusing and accepted right away. I also met Duke Ellington, who eagerly asked for news of Bud. I was surprised. I never suspected he was so fond of Bud or so concerned about his health.

The next day I went to see one of the last of the great master glass makers of Paris and ordered hand blown glass trumpets. I had them filled with cognac and delivered to Satchmo and all the other musicians. I also gave one to Bud, but replaced the cognac with wine, thinking it would be less dangerous for him.

The party was scheduled for the period of Epiphany, which the French celebrate with a traditional pastry, the *galette des rois*, a round, flat cake in honor of the three kings. The "king" of our evening was the Duke, so to honor our enormous star, I had the idea of making an enormous *galette*. The famous Parisian pastry chef Cadot agreed to bake a *galette* 25 feet long. It had to be delivered by special convoy, and a smiling Louis Armstrong gallantly cut it up with a sword. The crowd was thick with celebrities and I was happy that Frank Ténot had come, at my invitation. But the highlight of the evening for me was the moving reunion between Duke and Bud. I was touched by Duke's kindness and his obvious respect for Bud, who was much younger than himself. I had become too accustomed to the offhand manner of so many musicians toward him.

After the party, we headed for the Blue Note, where Bud was playing with his trio. Pierre Michelot and Kenny Clarke sometimes yielded their places to Jean-Marie Ingrand and Jean Guérin. Bud kept aloof during the breaks but despite this he was often surrounded by good-looking women. I don't know what attracted them, as he barely spoke to them. At most, he would hold hands with them, a mischievous leer on his lips.

I caught him one night holding hands with the wife of a big industrialist from the provinces. She was "slumming" in a Parisian jazz club. All at once, he turned to her and, in a voice that was calm but firm, said, "Hey, give me some pussy!" The poor woman knew no English and asked her husband to translate!

Bud later told me he had once made a similar suggestion to Ella Fitzgerald. In a stern tone that brooked no refusal, he ordered, "Come on, Ella, let's make it!"

Then, laughing until he nearly cried, he recounted Ella's response, "Wha-a-a-t?" and imitated the incredulous look on her face.

This joke set everyone laughing uncontrollably, and if the hilarity died down, the mere evocation of Ella's face was enough to start it up again, until our sides ached with laughter.

Lots of celebrities came to the Blue Note to hear Bud. One night, the Duke and Duchess of Windsor showed up. The club was always full of faithful fans, musicians passing through town, well-known actors and even, to my surprise, classical musicians like Samson François.

Bud still struggled against the numbing effects of the Largactyl. His blank moments and fatigue were still misunderstood by the press in general and gave rise to nasty notices like this one by Henri Gault on January 12, 1961, from a paper called *Paris-Presse l'Intransigeant* (which may have been "intransigent" but was certainly not very astute):

> At the Blue Note, Bud Powell's long black fingers seem to imitate those of a jazz pianist. But as for me, I didn't hear a thing. This deafness I experienced makes clear the unfortunate failure of a certain jazz. The music is physically unbearable. The drummer completely covers the melody section. . . . So I heard nothing of Bud Powell's playing. As for how he looked, his eyes, fixed and hazy at the same time, show he's still pursuing the dream that has led him to psychiatric hospitals before, and if he hears himself play at all, it's from the inside. He doesn't hear the trio, doesn't feel them, communicates only with himself. And we, the audience, remain on the outside looking in, nursing our gin-fizz. . . . The Bud Powell trio serves us a lullaby that might as well be a mattress.

After a period of indecision, Bud left Paris at the end of April 1961 for a series of concerts in Italy with a trio consisting of Jacques Hess on bass and his old friend from New York, Art Taylor, on drums. On the same program was a quartet with Thelonious Monk.

They played the Teatro Lirico in Milan on the 21st, the Teatro Duse in Bologna on the 22nd, and finally the Teatro Sistino in Rome. The Italian press was lukewarm, compared to the reception he'd had at San Remo the year before.

Bud and Monk hadn't seen each other for a long time. Their reunion made a big impression on Jacques Hess, who later shared with me:

> During the whole train ride, Bud and Monk sat facing each other. Buttercup was there and so was Thelonious's wife Nelly. I asked Buttercup, "How's Bud? Not too tired, I hope?"

"No, he's fine," she said, with a nod in the direction of the two men. "You can see how happy they are to be together again." They didn't say a word to each other during the whole trip!

I also remember during the Milan concert, Bud would have these blanks, like he didn't remember where he was. Suddenly, in the middle of a piece, he would stop playing at the end of a chorus. I would take a chorus, then two or three, Art Taylor would take a couple and Bud was still absent. He'd be looking at his watch that he'd put on the piano, as if he didn't know he was on stage. People began to realize and there was a stir in the audience. I'd say, "Wake up, Bud, we're on stage!" And after a while, he'd start playing again, coming in on the 21st measure, at exactly the right note!

I had some photos from the tour, and when it was over I asked him to autograph one for me. He wrote, "To Jack from Bud." I asked him to write his last name, too, and he added Powell, saying it out loud, and the way he said it I could tell he knew what his name meant to people, he knew what he was worth.

In June, Monk came to Paris for a concert, and Bud and I went. It was then that I realized the deep friendship that existed between them. From then on, Bud often chose Monk during our record-playing sessions, whereas before it had been almost exclusively Tatum.

The next month Bud took part in the festival of Comblain-la-Tour along with Benoît Quersin and J. Bourguignon. But his morale was low. Things went from bad to worse with Buttercup, and when he wasn't working his life was hell. His only purpose was to bring home the bacon, and the bacon went to feed a growing number of parasites hanging around their hotel room, which was beginning to look like a railroad station.

With all the noise and the people coming and going, Bud could never get any rest. Meals were potluck or sometimes just a miserable sandwich at the Café de Seine next to the hotel.

Sometimes Buttercup did the cooking. They were short on plates and she served on anything that could hold a portion of rice and a sausage. When the meal was over, she'd toss it all into the bidet. Most Americans never know quite what to make of a bidet, but at least she had found a practical use for it—washing the dishes!

Bud looked on in silence, but his eyes expressed all the pain he felt. Buttercup taunted him for the amusement of the guests. Once again, I admired his unflagging patience. His philosophical acceptance would have made a Zen master look high-strung. No one seemed to care about his appalling condition, and some treated it like one vast joke.

DANCE OF THE INFIDELS
(Recorded in New York, August 8, 1949 [Blue Note])

When I criticized people for their passive attitude about Bud and Buttercup's relationship, they would answer, first, it was none of their business, and second, Bud never talked to them. Obviously such reasoning could only lead to indifference. Granted, it wouldn't have been easy to intervene, but the most basic human reaction would have been to help a person in danger—for Bud was indeed in danger.

In the perennial state of conflict that poisoned their relations, Bud and Buttercup were opposites, physically and psychologically. Buttercup's loud voice and cackling laughter were the antithesis of Bud's muteness and his hangdog look. He grew thinner as she got fatter. He was the butt of jokes for the whole merry crew and no one hesitated to tease him or provoke him openly. Henri, the Austrian, had put on weight, both literally and figuratively. For some time Buttercup had been praising his talent as a bassist, but Bud remained skeptical. Bloated and permanently apoplectic, Henri looked like a pudgy, red-faced baby, with mocking little eyes and a forced, congealed giggle. Sprawling over the table littered with dirty dishes, along with the drummer Kansas Field and some other neighbors, he would endlessly sip unidentified beverages as Bud looked on with longing. Kansas Field rarely left the squalid room, which had become his permanent headquarters. It was by now a place of passage and looked more and more like an oriental bazaar.

On the overloaded shelves, a collection of heterogeneous objects accentuated the impression of total negligence. Side by side were tattered books and empty bottles, a row of records, an old jam jar holding a few spoons, and an expensive lizard-skin Hermes handbag. Bowls that were part ashtray and part sewing kit served as paperweights for mounds of papers that half covered the dusty record player. Through the nearly opaque windows that faced a filthy back courtyard, one could just make out some assorted underwear hanging on a makeshift clothesline.

Kansas Field presided over mysterious transactions with several individuals who were always in a hurry and who made furtive appearances in the room, which had by now become the bureau of complaint. Their conspiratorial air and coded talk left no doubt as to the nature of these dealings.

Johnny, usually dressed in leather shorts with wide suspenders, was constantly clowning and carrying on around Bud.

Completely cut off in the midst of this environment, lost in the blue swirls of smoke from the cigarettes he chain-smoked with his usual elegant gestures, Bud seemed to have been dropped there as if by accident. His princely look clashed with the sordid surroundings, the strangeness of his being there reinforced by his surreal expression and look of utter indifference.

The minute he was out of work, Bud was treated as less than useless. He was berated for not supporting his family, while Henri, who worked occasionally as a messenger, was held up as an example of the devoted family provider. It was a nightmare. Bud was still wearing the same suit and the only regular meals he had were those we fed him. He had worked like a dog since his arrival in Europe and he was treated like a dog. Yet he remained a man for all that. And if one mark of manhood is having money problems, those he certainly had.

Tender was the last word one would use for Buttercup. She was ponderous, violent, extremely loud, and quite vulgar. And I choose my adjectives gently. Every day she found new ways to hurt Bud and praise the talentless Henri. Every day it became more chaotic. Johnny was only six and obviously influenced by his mother. Besides the harm she did to Bud, she turned Johnny against a man he could and should have been taught to respect.

During one of those painful conversations in which Bud was the object of endless criticism, Buttercup suddenly announced, "Bud's gettin' just what he deserves. After all, he sold me to Henri for one franc."

The whole room rocked with laughter. It amused me too, but for other reasons. I thought of my friends from Les Halles who used to say of someone worthless that he was wasn't worth "a swig of cider." Bud had exchanged Buttercup for the equivalent of a swig of wine, a small glass of the "vin rouge" he loved so much.

By the end of autumn, Bud still had no club dates. He recorded two discs that year, one called *Tribute to Cannonball*, with Don Byas, Idrees Sulieman, Pierre Michelot, and Kenny Clarke, the other produced by CBS, entitled *A Portrait of Thelonious*, with a painting on the jacket by Nica de Koenigswarter. Canned applause was added to each track to make it sound live. One intro played by Pierre Michelot was recorded twice, a mistake that gave one critic a field day. Apart from that, Bud was excellent in his original compositions. He played Thelonious's tunes with respect and humility, but surprisingly, he usually didn't play many, though they were all in his repertoire.

With winter coming I was worried about Bud's wardrobe. It seemed that some of his suitcases were stuck in customs and Buttercup hadn't picked them up because there were charges to be paid. Naturally, the unclaimed suitcases were the ones with Bud's things. So he always wore the same black suit, which by now looked more gray than black.

After long hassles with the customs officers, we managed to get the missing suitcases. The staff of the French Customs Service is largely made up of people from the former colonies, Martinique, Guadeloupe, Indochina, etc., who, as often as not, have chips on their shoulders. The chief, none too bright, saw himself as a high priest and not a civil servant, and ordained that Bud had to sign the papers in person. Bud, seeing the uniform, thought he was at the police station and his terrified air aroused the suspicions of the overzealous officer. But all ended well, after several hours of negotiations. Bud was delighted to get his clothes back. He liked to dress well, though in all the months of wearing the same old threadbare suit he had never complained. It was just in time, as the weather had turned cold. Enveloped in his warm overcoat, Bud looked like his legendary self again. He became bolder and now told me that if I wanted to help, there were other suitcases that could probably be recovered from several hotels around Saint Germain. Buttercup confirmed that they had been left behind in two hotels as security when they couldn't pay the bills. I paid up immediately and the bags were found safe and sound in the cellar of one hotel and in the attic of the other.

There were several distinctive features that made Bud unmistakable in a crowd. His calm silence and slowness of movement gave him a Buddha-like quality. His face was fleshy and well-formed, his mustache wide but sparse. His shirt collars always seemed too tight and the collar pin he wore heightened the impression that he was choking. A white pocket handkerchief completed the classic look. He rarely removed his beret, which he wore French style, pulled well down on his forehead. The cops in the Latin Quarter all knew him and the minute they spotted him, they would stop traffic to let him pass, knowing he was always in the clouds, oblivious to cars and traffic lights.

Bud could seem alone in the midst of any crowd, under any circumstances. One day he went with me by Métro to see one of my clients. I was carrying my portfolio and a number of magazines and, to give me a hand, he carried one of my sketchbooks. As we waited on the platform for the crowd to disperse, I looked up and there was Bud, right in the middle of the crowd, writing music furtively in my sketchbook. He had drawn a staff and was hastily jotting down notes, indifferent to the noise around him, following his own inner path.

Shortly thereafter, he left with Buttercup for a concert tour in Switzerland. Alarming rumors appeared in the press. They spoke of hospitalizations and electroshock treatments. Nevertheless the tour went on to Sweden, where Bud played for four weeks at the Golden Circle Club in Stockholm. Five discs commemorate this tour, all on the Steeple Chase label. He then went to Copenhagen where he recorded a session for Sonet with Niels Henning Oersted Pedersen and William Schioppfe.

In Copenhagen, he ran into Jorgen Leth, a filmmaker he had met in Paris. It was a significant encounter, for Jorgen filmed a portrait of Bud in a short that marked the beginning of a promising career. Jorgen liked Bud and his music. With a minuscule budget and few technical means he managed, with his talent and sensitivity, to capture images of great beauty that packed a massive charge of emotion. All the feelings that Bud projected, tenderness and pain, resignation and hope, were expressed completely in their harrowing pathos.

After the shooting, Bud returned to the Blue Note, then left for a long tour that took him first to the Whiskey Club in Madrid, then to the Montmartre in Copenhagen. Here he met again the bassist Niels H. O. Pedersen, for whom he had great esteem since their first meeting at the Sonet sessions some months before.

Years later, on his way through Paris, Niels reminisced with me:

> The Montmartre had just opened and the audience was enthusiastic, as Bud was the first major pianist to perform there. The audience was in awe, very quiet, all eyes fixed on him. I was fifteen at the time and hardly spoke English. The audience regarded me as a kid and I was really scared. Some musicians I played with (I won't name names) were not very kind. A wrong note (and at fifteen there are plenty of them) was a whole to-do. There was even one who made remarks on stage!
>
> It was the first time I ever played with a musician of such renown and I was scared to death. But with Bud the fear subsided as soon as I saw his smile. My mother came one night and she commented how warm and gentle he looked. He was always kind, never frightening. Everything I did he took with a smile, and it gave me confidence.

We had no real relationship. I was very shy and at the time I was at school all day so I only saw him in the evening, from 8:45 to midnight. Besides, Buttercup or someone else was always there and he didn't say a word. He never spoke. I was sure he was shy too. We communicated only by looks, but in his eyes I saw he was my friend. Buttercup gave him some pills to take with a glass of water. I remember before his arrival people were saying he was ill and we shouldn't hope for too much. I thought: if he plays like that when he's ill, what must he have been like when he was in good health!

Thanks to the filmmaker Henrik Iversen, one of the evenings at the Montmartre was filmed for Danish television. In this document, Bud looks exceptionally relaxed and smiling. Maybe a beautiful blonde was hovering nearby. These comforting and well-filmed images will be included in a film I am working on.

Another account comes from poet, writer, and radio journalist Skip Malone and his wife Kirsten, a photographer, who met Bud at this time and became his friends. Skip told me:

> . . . When Bud first came here, the old Montmartre had just opened up, and it had had local musicians. It was the end of the winter in 1962. The public was very critical and aware, but they were pretty hip and they were really hungry. Bud was the event. Bud was the fire. He was playing with Niels H. O. Pedersen and William Schioppfe. William always used to play with a cigarette dangling from his mouth. One night Bud smashed down a chord and said to him, "Man, if you'd forget about that cigarette in your mouth, maybe we could play something!"

I never saw Bud smoke while he was playing, though he chain-smoked the rest of the time, and I never saw him put a glass or a cigarette butt on the piano as so many others do. For me, it showed the deep respect he had for the instrument.

Skip continued:

> From that time on, the Montmartre became an international jazz club—as opposed to a local one. All the musicians who came in town heard that Bud Powell was playing at the club. They all used to come and jam with him. There were jam sessions happening all the time. . . .
>
> This one night, the Adderly brothers—when they first came to Copenhagen—showed up. They were really up to play with Bud. They showed him great respect. But Bud was real blasé. He wouldn't even play. He just sat there at the piano. But after a little while, he started playing with them.
>
> Then Brew Moore came, and the MJQ and Art Blakey. It was quite obvious that Art had a lot of respect for Bud. The tone that he used with other

people was quite different from the tone that he had when speaking with Bud. He had a very humble tone. A party was organized one night in a studio with Art and Bud. But Buttercup hauled Bud back to the hotel to go to bed, like she used to do quite often, saying that he was tired and pretending that he couldn't stay up. . . . Sometimes during the day, whenever she wanted to free herself, she would hide his pants so he couldn't go out of the hotel. . . . It was like he was in jail. . . . I remember a time when she locked him up in the hotel. Mingus was in town, persistently asking for Bud, who was locked up, and Mingus couldn't get to him. . . . Once in a while I was able to grab Bud away from Buttercup for a while, just for a walk in town and a couple of beers. But at that time I didn't know that he had a drinking problem. . . .

One evening, Buttercup allowed us to go out. I did not have to steal him as usual. We went to a bar and the waiter offered us a bottle of schnapps. We ended up drinking it and got pretty drunk. Then we went to the Club de Paris where people recognized him and they announced that Bud was there. I went to the bathroom for a minute, and when I came back, Bud was sitting at the piano. He just sat there and didn't play. . . . We came back to the hotel and in his room were seven bottles of beer. This was his ration for special occasions when Buttercup wanted to go out by herself. . . . She bought light beers, saying that it was okay for him to have those. . . .

One day my wife Kirsten and I were in a bar-restaurant owned by Oscar Pettiford's widow where we had an appointment with Buttercup and Bud. I remember that Bud walked in by himself and came straight to Kirsten and I and said very clearly, "Listen. It's all over between me and Buttercup. I'm on my own now. I'm tired of her. . . . I'm taking care of my own business by myself from now on." It was kind of surprising. It was that way for a few days, then Buttercup got her hands back on him and Bud gave up grudgingly.

I accompanied Bud once to see Thelonious when he came to Copenhagen during a tour. They stared at each other and held hands. It was a warm moment. Nobody could come into their world except those who knew their cryptic language. I did not try to come into that space, and that's probably why Bud loved me. He was always relaxed with me. Every time he came to our home he was always comfortable. We talked a lot, and everybody was astonished. He used to ask me a lot of questions. . . . He seemed to have a respect for physical strength. He was impressed by the fact that I could have gone through the army. And I was impressed that he could have avoided the army! . . . He told me about the shock treatments and consequently about his sexual problems, because he knew that those treatments had made it so that he couldn't get a hard-on. . . .

When Buttercup and Bud came back to Copenhagen, they rented a house with a garden on the edge of the city. This was a pretty good time for him. He was working pretty well in Copenhagen. I wish he could have stayed. . . .

Bud went on to Oslo to play at the Metropole, where he met Randi Hultin, the newspaperwoman and photographer who was to become a close friend. She befriended all the musicians and they always dropped in to see her on their Scandinavian tours. Her name was synonymous with kindness and her house a symbol of hospitality. She was responsible for putting jazz on the map in Norway, making the rounds of clubs and concerts and writing them up in the press. I met her in 1964 and we became great friends. But it was only much later, in a recorded interview, that she told me about her meeting with Bud and about certain significant events that show once again Buttercup's obnoxious behavior:

When he came to Norway for the first time, it was from September 27 to October 7, 1962. It was fantastic to hear him live at the Metropole Jazz Club. He was only there four days, but he stayed in Oslo until October 7 because he didn't have any other gig. Then he went back to Paris. But that first evening it was crowded. I was standing close to the piano with my camera, but he was playing so well that I forgot to take any pictures! In fact, I never wanted to disturb him with my flash. All of a sudden, he turned to me and demanded, "Aren't you going to take any photos of me?" It was like he had eyes in the back of his head. At the end of the set, after looking around, he came to me and took my hand. He said, "Would you come and sit with me?" He kept my hand the entire evening. After that day, he held my hand every day, and the very first thing he'd do each time he saw me was to take hold of my hand.

We were still together one night and Buttercup showed up. She was the one who decided of course what Bud should do all the time. I invited them to my house, but she said he had to go to bed, that he couldn't make it. Bud said, "I want to go to her house! Why can't we go there?" So Buttercup said that I could go to their hotel room to visit. They were at the Standard Hotel. Once we got to the room, Bud asked if we could have some sandwiches and she ordered one apiece. After eating one, Bud said that he wanted another sandwich. But she said, "You eat too much. You're not going to have another sandwich."

"But I'm hungry," he said. "I'm not asking for a beer, I want a sandwich!"

"No!" she said.

"But I can have a sandwich, I'm hungry," he said. "Isn't it me who earns the money, Buttercup?"

"No, no, you'll get too fat."

"But I'm hungry. Do you think I don't know that you're sending money to Henri? It's my money. I asked for a sandwich!"

I felt sorry for him, so I said, "Bud, you can have the rest of mine."

Buttercup said, "No. No, Randi. He can have my sandwich."

And she took her sandwich and she spit on it, and she was laughing and laughing and she gave it to Bud. And I was crying inside. I thought it was so horrible. I can't understand that mean sense of humor, and I couldn't sleep that night. I thought about it all the time the day after. I can't understand how she could behave that way with him. So I went to their hotel every day to try to be with him.

I stayed amicable and cool with Buttercup until the end of their stay in Oslo, because if I'd protested her behavior, she wouldn't have let me be with Bud at all. As far as I was able, I tried to support Buttercup, because I knew it would be the only possibility for me to help Bud, who really needed some help. During their fourteen-day stay in Oslo, Bud had been trapped between those four walls in that horrible place. Everytime I showed up, his eyes lit up when he saw me. The only thing I could do was to cry when I went back home. Bud was bored. He wanted to go out. One day I came with my daughter and we found the boy Johnny by himself in the hotel room. I asked him where Bud and Buttercup were. He screamed, "My daddy is in jail! My daddy is in jail!" I said, "In jail? Why?" "We came home and he had been out drinking with some people from the hotel, so my mother called the police. And we tried to keep him still, but he was angry. And now he is in jail. And my mom will be here soon."

I waited and waited, but then I had to leave, and I felt it was so strange. I felt so sorry for Bud. I left a note for Buttercup and she called me to ask if she could come to my house, and was it okay if she brought over some musicians. Now it was okay for her to come to my house, since Bud was in jail! But she was laughing because she said he couldn't even find his way home without her. Even when he got out of jail the next day, no one was there to meet him. But he found his way back eventually.

Once I came to the hotel and I brought a lot of pictures because I wanted to entertain Bud. She grabbed the pictures and wanted to see them first. Buttercup didn't like me to talk with him because she wanted to talk herself. She asked me to call Oscar Goodstein in New York to tell him that she was sick, and it was necessary for him to send her some money right away, that they were ready to come back soon but that she was sick right then. I got Goodstein on the phone, but I didn't tell him she was sick because that was not the truth. So she got terribly, terribly angry with me.

To come back to those photos, Bud saw one of Count Basie and asked me who I liked the best, him or Count Basie. So I asked him, "As a pianist, or as a person?" He did not answer. He never answered any questions.

So I went on by saying that as a person it was probably him, because he was the more genuine.

Every day when I came to the hotel, Bud was sitting outside, begging for money so that he could raise enough money to buy half a bottle of beer. I can't understand how she could let him do that. He was famous, for some people at least, in the jazz world, and I thought it was so sad to see this.

Another day when I came, he was sitting outside on the steps and I said, "Bud. Are you coming out with us tonight to listen to Ines Cavanaugh?" He replied, "Oh sure." And when we arrived in the room, he said, "Buttercup. Randi says that tonight we're going . . ." Buttercup interjected, "We are going, but you're not. You are going to bed!"

She gave him sleeping pills every day. In fact, the day I brought those photos, Bud fell asleep because of them. But I remember that before he went to bed, he very carefully laid his clothes over a chair. Then he fell asleep while Buttercup bullshitted about him. All of a sudden, Bud woke up and began to scat-sing, then asked, "Buttercup. Do you know the name of that tune?"

"Go back to sleep."

"No. No. Don't you remember?"

"Why are you asking me that?"

"I was dreaming. I dreamt I was playing with Count Basie's big band."

"That's stupid. Basie's a piano player."

"Yeah, but this time I was playing drums!"

Talking about drums, one day we were invited to a guy's place, named Fitzpatrick, who was working at the American Embassy. . . . While Buttercup was telling a story, Bud was sneaking in and out of the kitchen and he was getting more and more drunk, and happier after each trip. Fitzpatrick had a drum set and Johnny started to play them. Bud, listening to Johnny, who was playing along with a Miles Davis record, said, "He's playing! Buttercup? What do you want him to be? If he becomes a musician . . . what do you want him to play?"

"Shut up! I'm talking. Don't disturb me."

"But I'm asking you a question, Buttercup. What do you think he should play?" A slight pause, and then Bud announced, "Oh, I think he should be a drummer."

Suddenly Buttercup rolled from the chair and walked furiously to Johnny, stopped him and took away the drumsticks, and she sat down and began to show him how to play. But then Bud came over to them and said, "No, Buttercup. Let me show him because, after all, I started as a drummer."

Johnny said, "Yes, Mommy, let Daddy show me. He knows better than you."

It was the first time I ever saw Johnny show some respect for Bud, and I was very happy to see that, because the kid was young and quite wild. It probably wasn't so easy for him to live between those four walls in that little hotel room. Buttercup had taught him to hate Bud, telling him that Bud was crazy. Johnny was very violent with Bud. In the elevator, for example, Johnny constantly stepped on Bud's feet.

"Stop, Johnny, don't do that," Bud would say, "Randi, what's wrong with this kid? He won't behave."

I told Bud that Johnny started to fight with me once when I came to the hotel with my daughter that time Bud was in jail.

"Did you hear that, Buttercup?" Bud said. "He's even been fighting with Randi. We have to talk to him."

And Buttercup answered, "He's learned everything from you, because you're crazy!"

And Bud looked at Buttercup resignedly, like he was giving up.

Oh, I forgot to tell you about one day when I went with them to a radio station and Bud was holding my hands all the time. Buttercup let me walk with him because she knew that this would be the best way to get him to do his best on the radio show. In the studio he still held my hands all the time. While we waited for the drummer and bass player, he was studying my hand.

Bud asked me, "Randi, why are your hands so hard?"

"It's from working so much with them, Bud," I said.

"Buttercup. We must buy some gloves for Randi. . . . Randi, are we going back to your place after the show?"

"Yes, Bud," I said.

"You want me to write in your guest book?"

"How could you know that I have a guest book?" I asked in surprise. That was so strange since he had never been over to my place.

On the day of their departure, I went with them to the train station. Bud wanted to drink a final beer before he got on the train. First we checked the bags. I'd love you to see, Francis, how he was driving this enormous baggage cart with all the suitcases piled on top of it. He was running, running fast thinking about this half-bottle of beer I had promised to buy him earlier. Before they got on the train he kissed me and asked, "Will I ever see you again, Randi?"

"Sure, Bud," I said. "I will come visit you in Paris, I promise."

There are many anecdotes about Bud's habit of cadging drinks and money. Some called him "Mr. Buy-Me-a-Drink." As amusing as they may be, the stories reflect pitiful circumstances, for they show a man reduced to the extreme dependence of a child. This dependence was constant in his life except, of course, when it came to working, where he was expected to produce like an adult.

Bud's pleading for a couple of coins put all his friends in a delicate position. My friend, the bassist Luigi Trussardi, a great admirer of his, was aware of the problem and tried to be careful. One afternoon he saw Bud walking along Boulevard Saint Germain looking intently at all the passersby. He realized what Bud was looking for and prudently hid behind a tree until he had passed. Once out of danger, he went on in the opposite direction. All at once he heard a plaintive voice behind him. "Hey, Luigi, can you give me a couple of francs?"

There were lots of similar stories. Jimmy Gourley tells one where the stakes were higher. "Jimmy, let me have one hundred francs."

Startled, Jimmy could think of no other answer than, "I haven't got that much on me, Bud."

"Well, how much have you got?"

Jimmy, trying to squirm out of it, gave the first answer that came to mind. "I don't know, thirty or forty francs."

"That's okay," answered Bud, "That'll be enough."

On another occasion, Bud was with a musician obviously impressed at being in his presence and asked him for fifty francs.

Without thinking, he replied, "But Bud I'm broke. I only got seventy francs to my name."

He thought he had found a perfect argument. But with his disconcerting logic, Bud countered, "Well there's no problem then. All I need is fifty!"

Or, finally, this story from the journalist Marc Crawford, a longtime fan who related his meeting with Bud in Paris in *Down Beat* (November 1962):

> It had been almost seven years to a September afternoon in Paris since last I had seen Bud. That was in Detroit when I was a forty-dollar-a-week reporter for a small weekly newspaper. I had remarked to a brilliant French writer, Allen Albert, that I very much wanted to see Bud, and we had sat there at a sidewalk table of the Deux Magots, drinking Ricards, right across the street from the Cathedral St. Germain des Prés. Allen's finger had just fallen from pointing out the apartment of Jean-Paul Sartre, a block down the Rue Bonaparte, when he shrugged a shoulder up Boulevard St. Germain and announced, "There comes Bud now."
>
> Bud's gait suggested that he had never awakened to the new day that it was. My eyes had picked him up coming our way as he passed between the church and the public urinal. A bear of a man he had become, in contrast with the slender one of times past. Under that blue beret it seemed as if he had forgotten to turn the lights on in his eyes or as if the switch had been broken long ago. His mustache was long, heavy, and wildly flow-

ing. As he mounted the near curb, I ran to greet him. "Bud! Hey, Bud! Over here, Bud!"

My hand shot out to take his, and his fat fingers came out to meet it, his palm up, and then he said, "Buy me a red wine, please. Buy me a red wine."

"Sure," I said, "but how are you, Bud?"

"Buy me a red wine, please?"

And as he repeated the refrain, I knew that the him of him [*sic*] was protecting him from my intrusion, or anyone else's, and so I gave him my last five-franc note. Without a word, he disappeared into the passing throng, perhaps to find a quiet walnut bar where a blue beret and a glass of red wine could coexist in peace.

FOR MY FRIENDS

(Recorded in New York, 1964 [Mythic Sound])

Like Randi Hultin, all our close friends had a boundless passion for jazz. Most of us played an instrument, as amateurs. I was introduced to the whole group by an old school friend, Michel Vincent. Michel was a slim young man, always calm and measured except at the dinner table, where he could put away quantities of food that amazed us all. Michel worshipped Monk. He immediately adopted Bud and would often invite us for weekends to his house in the Paris suburbs. He always had a knack for being around, as if by magic, any time I needed him.

It was the same for another of the cronies, Roger Guerrier. He played bass and a little piano. He was rock-solid, with a taste for brawling and no patience for those who didn't live up to his idea of "honor." Most conflicts were settled in the most expeditious manner with the help of his strong-arm buddy Ranci.

Ranci looked like a heavyweight and could hit like one too. He didn't seem to know his own strength, but those he tangled with never forgot it. A sometimes guitarist, he would weep listening to Django Reinhardt or Wes Montgomery.

When I wasn't around, Roger and Ranci acted as Bud's bodyguards. He loved them both and reveled in their permanent protection.

Another inseparable friend was Mic, who lived in the neighborhood and worked as an illustrator in an advertising agency. He was small, round, quick-tempered, and wore his heart on his sleeve. Despite his name, he was the prototype of the average Frenchman. He had always liked Bud's music and, once he met him, was devoted to him with all his soul. Bud liked his simple, straightforward manner, and few others became as affectionate with Bud.

Lastly there was Franck Nizery, a childhood friend who had lived through all my musical tribulations. For him, meeting Bud was a dream come true. Tall, svelte, and kindly, Franck was a true and loyal friend. Every evening he too was part of our little community. We adopted a private language of our own, based on the market slang taught us by Roger and Ranci, who worked in Les Halles. As it excluded outsiders, it enhanced our feeling of togetherness. We initiated Bud, and some of the images made him laugh till he cried. In this private slang, hands were called ladles, a nose an eggplant, hair was weeds, ears were clams, legs guitars and fingers hot-dogs . . .

Babs Gonzales learned our language too, very fitting for someone whose own language was filled with a similar earthy poetry, just like the grand master of that style, Lester Young.

WAIL

(Recorded in New York, August 8, 1949 [Blue Note])

Bud returned from Oslo and I was happy to see him although he had lost more weight and looked extremely tired. His teeth were in terrible shape from neglect and poor nutrition. I had noticed this the previous year but now it seemed serious. When I mentioned it to Buttercup she instantly became defensive, shouting at me that it wasn't her fault if Bud refused to go to the dentist. Her unspoken meaning was, "Why can't this guy mind his own business?" The atmosphere at the Louisiane was worse than ever and Bud seized every possible occasion to escape.

A few days later I went to pick him up as usual, feeling strangely apprehensive. I knocked at his room but no one answered. Then I heard a call for help coming from another room. He was locked in. At the desk they told me that was Bud's new room, as Buttercup now occupied the old room with Henri and Johnny. The receptionist had no key, so I had to content myself with talking to Bud through the door. It was heartbreaking.

I came again each day to learn that Bud was always kept locked in now. It was all I could do to persuade Buttercup to open the door and let me spend some time with him. It was a horrendous spectacle. The squalid little room was strewn with dirty plates, the floor littered with cigarette butts. Seated on the unmade bed, Bud hung his head and avoided my eyes. Who would have believed that the great Bud Powell could be treated with such contempt, kept prisoner in these ugly surroundings, and that no one around him seemed to care?

Jacques Hess, who lived a long time at the Louisiane, said to me, "I was very upset to see him like that. He was the great Bud Powell, but I couldn't help pitying him. The others were deep into drugs. They hung out in little groups according to what they were on: coke, heroin, or whatever. They had so many problems of their own there was no way they could think of anyone else. You could watch someone killing himself with complete indifference. It was part 'mind your own business' and part cowardice."

Of all the people who talked to me about Bud, it's surprising how few of them were musicians. But this was a true reflection of reality. Aside from fleeting encounters backstage at the clubs, no one in this little world cared about Bud's problems. I suppose one could say in their defense that they had problems of their own.

In 1961, Jackie McLean made a European tour. He played at Le Chat Qui Pêche with René Urtréger. Jean-François Jenny Clarke, a young virtuoso on the bass, would go on to a great career, as would Daniel Humair, the drummer who completed the group. Daniel spent his time at the Blue Note and also hung out with the lodgers of the Louisiane.

On one occasion, as Jackie told me later, he met his childhood friend Bud:

> When I was young—this was in 1948—I was working in a record store, selling records, and I used to play records all day long. One day, a young kid came into the store just as we were listening to one of Bud's records. The kid paid for his, and just as he was leaving, he said, "You're listening to Bud, huh? He's my brother." Of course I didn't believe him for a minute. I told him, "Aw, get out of here, you're not Bud's brother."
>
> "Yeah. That's my brother, and he's getting out of the hospital [Creedmoor, September 1948] on Sunday. Just because you don't believe me, I'm gonna bring him here. You'll see."
>
> A few days later he came back with someone I didn't recognize, because at that time, I'd never set eyes on Bud. Since they saw I was still in doubt, they invited me to come with them after the shop closed up. When we got to their apartment, the bigger brother immediately sat down at the piano. After sixteen incredible bars I had no doubt whatsoever about his identity. This was the real Bud. And the kid was none other than Richie, of course. Nobody could play like Bud! I had just met the man who became my teacher, my friend, and my idol. . . .
>
> Long after that, I saw Bud in Paris, in 1959 or 1960. I found then that he had changed a lot. Right away he started complaining to me, "I'm so unhappy, Jackie. Buttercup treats me like a dog. Why, Jackie, why?"
>
> I was destroyed, so sad to see Bud looking so pitiful. Bud, the one we all respected so much, the one we all loved so much. . . .

Bud had no choice but to submit to her authority and I could do nothing to help. Buttercup was now openly hostile and all our conversations ended up as shouting matches, with Henri butting in as well. According to them, I was unconscious of Bud's real problems and therefore I couldn't see the necessity for the new arrangements. Bud was mentally deranged, possibly even retarded, and had to be treated as such. As I didn't see things quite that way, our relations degenerated from day to day.

I had begun to despair of any improvement when I suddenly had a call from Buttercup. All her arrogance was gone. Her voice broke as she announced that Bud had been arrested, and he was due to play that very night. The inevitable had finally happened. He had gotten sick of being locked up and had escaped through the window onto the roof of the next building. He went from roof to roof till he saw an open window, climbed in and found himself in the living room of the butcher on the Rue de Seine, where the butcher's wife was in the middle of her housework. Terrified by the apparition, she let out a shriek, her husband came running, butcher knife in hand, and grabbed Bud while she called the police. Buttercup came down to the police station but her explanation was neither clear nor convincing and the affair had gotten off to a bad start.

The police chief was not a bad sort. I did my best to clarify the rather peculiar situation and tried to impress him with my description of the great star who was now in his custody. He seemed touched by my arguments and after listening attentively he felt impelled to show me that he too was a music lover and therefore inclined to be indulgent. To show off his knowledge of jazz, he began talking about "Duck" Ellington, "Cob" Calloway, "Lewis Astrog" and "Dizly Gilplexy." I breathed a sigh of relief. It was as if I had found an old army buddy and we were talking over old times. The cloud had a silver lining after all!

Back on the Rue de Seine, Bud walked straight ahead, holding tightly to my arm. He kept giving me frightened looks as if to ask if we were being followed, and I did my best to reassure him. Back at the hotel after this painful interlude, Buttercup greeted us with open arms, her unusual warmth doubtless caused by her relief at seeing her means of livelihood return. As for Bud, he regarded me as a magician. With this accomplishment to my credit, I got Buttercup to agree to let Bud out of the room whenever I would visit. And on this promise, Bud went back to his "cell" for the night.

On one of my next visits, the key was at the desk but Buttercup had confiscated Bud's pants. He stood there in his undershorts, barefoot amid the cigarette butts on the dirty floor. The air was thick with smoke. Poor Bud was caught in a trap and there seemed to be no way out. My anger grew with each visit.

Locked in his room, Bud could hear the sounds of merriment coming from next door, a non-stop party that his work paid for. All my attempts to talk to Buttercup ended in furious screaming and I feared I would lose my temper with Henri, who grew more arrogant by the day.

Bud was given his pants back only when he had to go to work. That he could make music at all in such circumstances seemed miraculous. Kept in line by the Largactyl, Bud continued to obey.

The writer Chester Himes, who was living at the Louisiane at the time, described the situation to Michel Fabre in *Jazz Magazine*: "Bud would show up to play each night completely potted. It's true he could get drunk on one beer. In fact, he was a very sick man. His wife, the famous Buttercup, didn't let him out of the hotel all day. She would double-lock the door and keep the key. The boss of the Blue Note would send a car to pick him up, he'd play—like a god most of the time—then they'd drive him back and lock him in again until the next day."

But somehow, he managed to escape again one night at the Blue Note, and this time he seemed to have vanished for good. Three days later I had still found no trace of him.

IT NEVER ENTERED MY MIND

(Recorded in New York, June 4, 1954 [Verve])

I had searched all of the hospitals and police stations to no avail, leaving my phone number with each of them—and growing more frantic with every passing hour—when at last I received a phone call from Laënnec Hospital. They had just admitted a patient for observation who said his name was Earl Rudolph and who matched the description I had given them.

I rushed to the hospital and there was Bud, looking ashen and vacant, with a three-day beard, but to my great relief, still alive. In my moments of despair I had feared the worst. Decidedly, things were going downhill. No dialogue was possible, nor even any contact. I couldn't capture his attention or make him smile. I felt paralyzed, a powerless observer to his inexorable decline . . .

He remained in observation for three days in a large ward for infectious diseases, filled mainly with poor North African immigrants. I visited every day to try to cheer him up. Each time I would find him slumped on the edge of the bed, looking despondent. He would brighten up a little when I came, only to sink back into gloom when I had to leave. One day the faithful friends, Roger, Michel, and Ranci, came with me. Knowing how Bud loved oysters, they brought him a phenomenal platter of them, the biggest I had ever seen. We maneuvered our cumbersome load past the astonished eyes of the staff. Bud laughed out loud when he saw us, making us feel it had been worth all the trouble. He dug in and started consuming oysters at an alarming rate, but given the quantity, even he couldn't get through them all so he invited his roommates to share in the feast. That evening I returned home with a lighter heart, knowing that we had brought Bud some small comfort.

The next day I wasn't too busy working so I decided to go and see him in the early afternoon. I arrived in the ward to find him gone and his bed unmade. No one—the other patients, the nurses or the staff doctor—could tell me what had become of him. At the office there was no record of his release but they had no information as to his whereabouts.

Laënnec Hospital is an old-fashioned hospital complex, built like a village with different buildings containing the various wards. For two full hours I searched through its labyrinthine alleys and corridors, becoming more and more anxious by the minute, and exasperated by the offhand manner with which the staff answered my questions. I was ready to give up when an African cleaning woman who had been scrubbing the floor stood up and came over to me. She had overheard my questions and whispered softly, "I think I saw a colored man this morning. They were taking him to the psychiatric ward, down there, at the end of that path."

All at once, everything was clear. I understood the significance of all the cautious replies. Of course, I was not related to Bud and therefore had no right to any confidential information. My anxiety turned to anger as I wondered what had caused this transfer and in what state of mind Bud would be when I found him. I thanked the cleaning woman and rushed off in the direction she indicated, my heart in my mouth.

At the entrance, as always, I was greeted with the question, "Are you a family member, maybe?"

We were indeed part of the same family, the great family of music, but I didn't think I could explain that to the keeper of the gate, so I evaded the question. When I insisted on entering all the same, he called the ward supervisor, who listened to my plea with a bored look on his face. My patience was wearing thin and the tone of our discussion was rising dangerously. When I shouted that I had seen more hospitality in a police station than in this establishment, he lost his temper, grabbed me by the arm, dragged me down a hallway to a door with a peephole in it, and motioned for me to take a look inside.

My heart sank. There in a tiny cell, in the pallid light of a small dim bulb, sat Bud, huddled up alone, overwhelmed, staring at the locked door with terror in his eyes. After all he had lived through in the United States, here it was happening all over again. I started protesting once more and our shouting brought a number of colleagues running. One of the male nurses opened the door and the other shoved me inside, locked it behind me, sneering, and I heard, "You wanted to get in? Well, now you're in!"

Before I knew what had happened, Bud had leapt up and was clutching me with all the strength of total desperation, begging, "Francis, get me out of here! Please, get me out of here!"

The world reeled around me. Once again, Bud had touched bottom and I was powerless to change it. At that instant, I felt I would willingly give my life for him and with that realization came a newfound calm and a strange determination. I knew I wouldn't abandon him, that I would calmly put an end to this tragic situation once and for all. "I swear to you, Bud," I said, "I will not leave this place without you."

The room we were in was a padded cell traditionally used in psychiatric wards for agitated patients. It contained only a bed and a table. There were no sharp angles, no loose objects, the light bulb and window were protected by heavy grating. The only thing missing was a straitjacket. Bud knew such places well from his previous internments, and I could feel his fear.

After a while, the door opened and a young doctor came in. He held out his hand with a cordial smile and asked in a tone both curious and conciliatory, "So, what's going on? What was all the hullaballoo?"

"It's scandalous, doctor," I began, "to think of an artist like Mr. Powell locked up in these conditions. . . ."

He explained that the hospital had received Bud's record from the American Embassy, and because of his psychiatric history they had placed him in the disturbed ward, just to be on the safe side.

In a matter of seconds, I launched into an explanation of Bud's life, his misfortunes and suffering, but also his immense talent, his musical genius. The doctor listened, apparently fascinated. I wondered, was I winning over a new fan? He said I could stay with Bud and told me that the chief doctor would be along presently and would certainly find a suitable solution.

"Don't worry," he said to Bud. "It'll all work out."

A few minutes later, I repeated my plea to the chief doctor, who also listened with great interest. He admitted that things had been a bit brutal and he proposed to examine Bud right away.

The most I had dared hope for was that he would be put back in observation. Now the doctor was going to interview Bud. He seemed well-disposed toward me and offered to let me listen in, unseen of course. He thought it might help me better understand this person I was obviously so attached to. To this day, I am grateful to the doctor for this initiative, and for his trust.

Behind the open door, I listened to the interview. First he examined Bud from head to toe, then began to ask questions of a psychological nature. Questioned about his sleep, Bud answered that he never got a good night's sleep, that he awoke exhausted every morning. Asked if he had dreams, he blurted out, "Oh yes, doctor, I never stop playing the piano."

He complained of the immense fatigue caused by playing in his sleep. The doctor tried to determine whether he was satisfied with the music he made, but his only memories were of painful work, devouring his strength and his intellect. At last, in response to ever more pointed questions, Bud hesitantly admitted there were voices in his dreams, and that he heard them also when he was awake. He wouldn't or couldn't give any more details about the voices, but he knew it was a strange perception and it seemed to worry him. Questioned about his sex life, Bud told of the total degradation of his natural reflexes, which had not been normal since the treatments inflicted on him in psychiatric hospitals in the United States. He spoke of his horror of the electroshock treatments, saying they had ruined not only his sex life but his creative powers. "I'm a pianist and a composer, doctor. Those treatments destroyed me."

I listened in agony, holding on to my chair. The psychiatrist was asking Bud the last time he had had sexual relations. The answer came out slowly, in a miserable and absent voice, filled with sorrow, "I don't know, doctor. It was so long ago. . . ."

The conversation went on. You could feel the current of sympathy between the two men. Bud, usually so silent, was doing his best to answer the doctor's questions.

I have no other noteworthy memory of their talk. I know they checked his reflexes and did some other neurological tests. Bud's words had upset me and I dreaded the doctor's decision. But he came out with a reassuring smile and said in a friendly voice, "My dear young man, you must not worry. Your friend is not doing badly. I'm sure we can work things out." He asked me for further details about Bud's life and daily activities. "You seem to know him very well indeed. Do I understand correctly, that you've even been taking care of him?"

"Well, uh . . . yes, I have." I made it clear that for me, he was like a member of my family.

"Well, then listen to me, young man. With a friend like you, I see no problem. You may take him home. Just go on looking after him and everything will be all right."

I couldn't believe my ears. I could have kissed him. Realizing that I must be showing my amazement, I tried to regain my composure and to look as if the decision was quite natural. The doctor handed me a signed release form. I winked at Bud to let him know we'd made it.

It was nearly nightfall as we made our way toward the hospital gates, walking as fast as our legs would carry us, Bud hanging on to my arm for dear life. With some trepidation, I presented the paper at the exit, was handed Bud's overcoat and beret, and the next thing we knew, we were out on the street and hailing the first passing taxi.

Bundled into the taxi on the way home, Bud didn't say a word. He held my hands tightly in his, and looked at me with an intensity I will never forget. Without thinking it over, I heard myself saying, as if it were the most natural thing in the world, "Bud, if you like, you can come and live with us from now on."

His reply was instantaneous. His face broke into a wide grin as he pressed my hands and uttered two words, "Oh, yes!"

So there it was. The decision had been made, as simply as that. After the long days of anguish, I felt suddenly euphoric. I could read the newfound hope in Bud's eyes.

We arrived at Rue Boursault, raced up the stairs to the apartment. Nicole, who worked as a translator for UNESCO, was not home yet. Without even taking off his coat or beret, Bud made a bee line for the piano and a swell of music poured out, majestic, generous, and so revealing. It was a message coming from the depths of his soul, and I ran to turn on the tape recorder.

I have always had mixed feelings about this contraption, torn between the impertinence of daring to record such moments and the regret of seeing them vanish forever. Today I have no regrets, content that I was able to preserve unique and priceless messages for future generations.

I told Bud he should phone Buttercup right away to tell her he was out and mainly to let her know of our decision. The recorder went on turning and later on I found this historic and amusing conversation on the tape:

"Hello Buttercup? It's Bud. . . . Yeah, I'm out of the hospital. . . . Yeah, everything's okay. . . . I'm fine. . . . Can I stay with Francis and Nicole? . . . I can? . . . Oh thank you, Buttercup. . . . Thank you. Yeah, sure. . . . Thanks, Buttercup. Yeah . . . Okay, here's Francis."

"Yes, hello Buttercup. No problem, Bud's fine. . . . Yes, he can stay with us, there's no problem. . . . Of course, I'll take care of everything. . . . Sure, right, yes, Buttercup. See you soon. . . . Yes, of course I'll keep in touch. . . . Right, see you soon."

Although I was pleased she had agreed so easily, I was pained by Bud's attitude of complete submission. He thanked her as if she had granted him some royal privilege whereas I knew he had just relieved her of a burden.

Bud was hardly working any more and for her he was merely a source of worries. So it was all settled quickly and amicably, and I made arrangements for Bud to visit regularly with Buttercup and Johnny. He refused at first but I insisted that we keep on good terms with them.

It was impossible to put Bud up at our little studio, so we got him a room in a small hotel just next door at 22, rue Boursault. The room was pleasant and comfortable with a private bath, but it was still a hotel, with all the loneliness that implied. Every evening he tried to delay the hour of his return as we attempted to convince him that he really had to get some sleep. As I walked him to the hotel, he would use any pretext to detain me for as long as possible. Each night I returned home heartsick at having left him alone once more. Each morning he would appear around ten o'clock, a changed man, delighted to take his place in the tight but cozy little apartment that had become his home. Thus our days went peacefully by.

My immediate aim was to bring Bud the calm and security he so needed to recover his peace of mind and long-lost *joie de vivre*. With the boundless energy he expended at the piano, I knew that peace was vital to him.

Our daily routine was simple. Generally I worked late into the night and was just getting up when he arrived. Nicole had already left for work. I prepared him a substantial breakfast of ham and eggs with a big glass of milk. Then I went back to my drawings as he watched me with an amused eye. Every so often, I would have a flash of realization—here was my master, next to me, observing my modest work, watching my every gesture.

He could remain silent for hours, in a Buddha-like calm, lost in his inner world. Sometimes the silence would be broken by a burst of unforeseeable laughter that brought tears to his eyes. I never received any explanation concerning these moments of mysterious euphoria which seemed to emerge so irresistibly. He was also prone to sudden depressive states during which his behavior showed nervousness and apparently uncontrollable impatience. I tried asking him what he felt at such moments of anguish, but he was incapable of giving me the slightest explanation.

No real dialogue was yet established between us. The best I could do was to pull him out of his nightmare. He would come to all at once and look at me in astonishment as if wondering what had happened. He would grab on to my arm with desperation like someone trying to regain his balance. When he noticed my own anxiety, he would smile at me, a sad little smile he hoped would reassure me.

One of the major problems to be negotiated each day was wine. As if playing a game, he would repeat insistently those two words he pronounced so well, *"vin rouge."* I would launch into long lectures on the ravages of alcohol, reminding him that he had to keep fit for the sake of his music. He listened gravely and with total concentration and at the end of each monologue, he would lean forward, his voice filled with emotion and say, as if broaching a new subject, "Okay Francis, now how about a glass of *vin rouge?"*

I never gave up, but the result was the same every day.

On the advice of a doctor friend, I had gradually reduced the dose of Largactyl. The change in him was slow but significant. Instead of collapsing at the end of the day as he used to, he now remained lively and our evenings ended joyfully. He began asking questions about us, and we told him our lives. Nicole, with her southern French humor, was a born storyteller and could turn the simplest anecdote into a hilarious tall-tale that had Bud rocking with laughter. As the days went on, we discovered a new Bud who, as the effects of the drug wore off, was good-humored and fond of fun.

As for the *vin rouge*, we remained vigilant—no easy task for us, as we were *bons vivants* ourselves, but there was no question of our drinking when Bud couldn't. So we hid away our bottles and limited ourselves to the dose we had determined Bud could tolerate, sipping slowly to make the pleasure last. As for Bud himself, he always drank "bottoms up." At one point, I thought I had found a way to solve his drinking problem. I had heard of a substance, a colorless, odorless powder which, when slipped into someone's drink, was supposed to disgust him with alcohol. I tried it on Bud, but he downed the drink in one gulp, with no ill effects whatsoever. In any case, Bud drank everything in one gulp, whether it was water, milk, or orange juice. He had an enormous need for liquids.

Bud had lost a lot of weight and could now wear my clothes. My shirts and some jackets suited him well and he thought it fun to exchange ties and cufflinks. Sonny Stitt had given him a pair of silver cufflinks that my friend Vincent had engraved with his initials. But Bud preferred a gold pair I had received as a birthday present and he suggested we swap for keeps. I agreed willingly and still have the precious keepsake, which I have worn just once since his death, at the memorial concert in his honor at New York's Town Hall on June 24, 1985.

During the long, slow days spent together, I asked Bud a host of questions about his life and his childhood. I wanted to enlighten myself about his past. I had heard different stories about the origin of his nickname, Bud, and he gave me his version which, of course, I take to be the real one.

When they were children, Bud and his brother Richie, eight years younger, used to play in the streets near their home at St. Nicholas Avenue and 149th Street in Harlem. They often saw a panhandler who asked them for change. One day as they were out shopping for groceries, he stopped them and asked for a few coins. Bud hesitated, while Richie tried to persuade him. He had lost his front teeth at the time and his pronunciation was unclear. He used to call his brother "broth'" but in his mouth it came out closer to "Bud." "Come on, Bud," echoed the beggar. "Lemme have a little something." As they saw the panhandler daily, Richie began to adopt the nickname too and pretty soon everyone was calling him Bud.

In all the years I spent with Bud, my emotion never diminished and I never managed to take the situation for granted. His presence always seemed unreal, although we became like family. We no longer shook hands to say good night, but kissed each other warmly on the cheek. Nicole pampered him like a child and, with his childlike ways and immense need for affection, he lapped it up. Occasionally I would be struck by the difference between his utter humility and his gigantic stature in the world of music, and I would remain stunned, meditating on it.

Modern jazz had arrived clandestinely in France, like a breath of fresh air during a period of frustration, terror, and suffocation. For those battling for freedom it was like a promise of escape and eventual peace. Those who discovered it later, of course, couldn't feel it the same way. Too subjective? I don't think so. We mustn't forget that bop grew between 1940 and 1946 in a world ravaged by war. For those who remembered the era when the goose-step had replaced the foxtrot, the pulse of jazz would outlive the thud of the jackboots.

At the same time in the United States blacks were fighting for their rights and their freedom, and the cultural revolution that grew out of these struggles gave rise to the bop era. A group of young "aristocrats of the spirit" tried to push back the frontiers of music. Uncompromising, fighting against facility and vulgarity, they made their mark on those who quested after beauty with a strength and conviction perhaps unique in the history of music. For me, this aesthetic revolution will be the deepest and most long-lasting of all. In the space of a few years black musicians forged a new era that is still at its beginnings. The slogan "Black is Beautiful" was not born until many years later.

For that matter, the giants of the "official" music of the time were not mistaken. Debussy, Ravel, Rachmaninoff, Stravinsky, and Bartók took an interest in the new musical current. Speaking of his first concerto, also called *Concerto Américain,* composed after a trip to the States, Ravel stated in an interview in the *Daily Telegraph*: "In some respects, my concerto, not unlike my Violin Sonata, contains elements borrowed from jazz. . . ." And concerning *Concerto pour la Main Gauche,* he described it as ". . . different in character and all in one movement, with lots of jazz effects, and the writing is not as simple."

Taken to the American jazz clubs by such musicians as Horowitz or Gershwin, Ravel sometimes took notes. He gave these notes to his conductor, Manuel Rosenthal, who, some time later, alluded to the technical difficulty of the pieces by remarking, "But Maestro, this is unplayable!" To which Ravel retorted with a biting, "Really? Do you think I made a mistake in notation?"

My mind teemed with thoughts like these. Here was Bud Powell, a quiet, unassuming man who held the sum of musical knowledge of his time. He was at the very forefront of a school whose adepts often didn't even know his name.

SOME SOUL
(Recorded in Hackensack, May 28, 1958 [Blue Note])

B
ud had lost his job at the Blue Note and, in our little studio on
the Rue Boursault, he found the peace he had so long been
seeking. I explained my work and he sat quietly watching me. When
he recognized a drawing all at once he would give me a quick smile of
complicity and then go back into his dreams.

Sometimes he asked for a little money and went off for a walk. I
knew he never went further than the corner cafe. Then he would return and take his place beside me.

I often spoke to him of Salvador Dali and his influence on my own
work and showed him reproductions of Dali paintings in my art
books. The summer before I had paid the master a visit in his house
at Port Lligat. Next to my meeting with Bud, this was the high point
of my life. The kindness with which he received Nicole and me and
the extraordinary simplicity with which he spoke of his painting made
me once again reflect on the difference between the public image and
the true personality of those who are too quickly catalogued by the
media. Dali was often in the news, like Bud, but in listening to him,
all I heard was a man passionate about drawing, in love with art, surrounding himself with a surreal and wonderful universe, like a setting
for his spirit thirsting for the Absolute. Quite unlike his reputation, he
was humble in the face of art, and spoke of beauty with both passion
and an unfailing sense of humor.

Bud would listen with interest as he looked gravely at the pictures.
He would sink into long meditations, fascinated by these images of an
extra-terrestrial world in which everything looked so present. I never
knew what Dali's surrealist world meant to Bud. His attitude seemed
to correspond so well to the vision of this school of painting. Bud's
music often transported me to unknown and incredible worlds that
recalled the vast landscapes of Yves Tanguy's *The Light of Shadow* or
Dali's *The Phantom of Vermeer.* "Moonlight in Vermont," "Dusk in
Sandi," and "It Never Entered My Mind," as interpreted by Bud, also
belonged to this eerie and impalpable world. I'd tell him these impressions and each time he seemed touched. We would listen again to
these tunes that seemed to come from another dimension: "Glass En-

closure," "I'll Keep Loving You," "Tempus Fugue-it," and "Mediocre."
I had listened to this music so often, it was as familiar to me as my
own breathing. Listening with Bud was positively surreal, for he too
listened with great intensity. I felt sometimes that he had become a
stranger to his own music and was then caught in its magic just as I
was. When Bud played, he seemed to me more and more like an unconscious medium, a prey to irresistible forces, his face expressing the
state of grace he had entered.

I recorded regularly and several days later, without saying a word,
I would play the tapes. He emerged instantly from his meditations
and, sitting up with a start, would ask, in an urgent voice, "Who's
playing, Francis? Who is it?"

He never recognized his own playing and I was amazed by such
apparent detachment. His creations certainly startled him, dredged up
as they were from his secret world and arising at moments of great
emotional urgency. For some people this surprising phenomenon was
just another symptom of a deranged psyche, but for me it was further
confirmation of his ability to seize a message of rare beauty that an instant later returned to the unknown world whence it had come. The
music was as overpowering for him as it was for us and it captured
his interest just as if it had been another's creation. To my mind he
belonged to another dimension, in contact with some higher power
that nourished his creative force. By his reverence and his intense as-
piration to beauty, he was in a state of osmosis with a perfect world, a
world that he alone could envision. For me, Bud's fingertips touched
the mystery of the beyond.

Only late at night did he sit down at the piano. Those moments
made me very nervous for I felt that he was suddenly inhabited by
mysterious compulsions. He seemed beset by internal stimuli that he
could only check by great force of will. From the first notes, his face
would be covered with sweat. I had never before witnessed such a
phenomenon of trance. The music was of a gravity and majesty approaching the unbearable.

But these moments of ecstasy were not without some small draw-
backs, for our neighbors soon began to protest. On the floor above us
lived a young pianist just out of the Conservatory who couldn't bear
Bud's music even at decent hours. Whenever Bud played, he knocked
on the floor in time, though alas never in the proper time.

After the complaints came petitions demanding that we vacate the
premises. One morning as I was working, the doorbell rang and Bud
went to answer. This time it was the lady from the apartment below

us, 75 years old, who wanted to know who it was who played every evening. Dreading what was coming, I cautiously explained how Bud had gotten in the habit of playing at night . . . She cut me off and turned to him with a cry: "Ah, Monsieur! So it is you who play like that? How beautiful it is!" She looked at him in wonderment.

"What'd she say?" asked Bud.

"She loves your music and listens to you every night."

A sweet smile lit his face. The old woman went on talking. Without understanding a word, he drank in her compliments, then raised his hand and gave her a soft pinch on the cheek as one would in praising a small child. We had found an ally in a hostile world. In fact, she was the only one in the building who hadn't signed the petitions against us.

Later on, we invited her for lunch and after the meal she begged Bud to play. He went to the piano without coaxing and played with frank and open pleasure.

In this period of convalescence, we didn't go out much. We had stopped going to places where Bud's presence would have aroused unhealthy curiosity. He himself gave no sign of wanting any contact with the jazz world. Sometimes we spent the weekend with Michel, in the outskirts of Paris. Bud loved these outings and the company of these old friends, whose simple and genuine friendship he appreciated. It didn't matter that they spoke no English. His sensitivity quickly found their individual qualities. We spent the days feasting and listening to old records of Bud. I would sometimes try to talk to him but he remained silent and completely possessed by the music, lost in his own world. The only communication was an exchange of knowing looks after some fabulous modulation that had bowled us over.

When he was eating, Bud became so intent he heard nothing that was said to him. His innate behavior bore a similarity to Zen. I told him that one day, provoking hilarious laughter. "You think I'm like that, Francis? Do you really think so?"

I told him I had studied Zen philosophy for many years while I was doing judo. This seemed to fascinate him and he looked at me with admiration. Suddenly he said, "I have a friend who does judo. The pianist Walter Davis. He's very good, you know." Then, with a worried tone, he added, "Do you think I could learn judo, Francis?"

"Of course, Bud. Anyone can learn it."

"Show me a hold."

He was as excited as a child and wouldn't rest until I'd demonstrated a movement. He caught on immediately. As I thought he would enjoy it, I took him to my old judo club. He was delighted.

But this tranquil life couldn't last. There were the problems with the neighbors, which we realized could only be settled by soundproofing our apartment. This was far too expensive and we could only dream of doing it in a place that we owned. There were also the nightly separations, when Bud had to go back and sleep at the hotel. It had been going on for a long time now, but none of us had ever gotten used to it. All these factors pushed us into thinking about moving.

Still, in his new surroundings where Bud slowly reorganized his life, he revealed to us ever more likable sides of his personality. For his daily walk, I continued giving him a few francs, knowing all the while I was doing him more harm than good. The ambiguities of this situation caused me great pain. I was torn between treating him like a brother and like a child who has to be constantly reasoned with. I had to struggle not to give up and take the easy way out. Giving in to his whims would have simplified our relations but would have shown neither affection nor respect. I was in perpetual conflict with myself.

One afternoon as I sat at my drawing table, I heard Bud putting on his raincoat to go out, when all at once he stopped moving. I was puzzled. My back was to him but a shiny chrome lamp on my table reflected the image of the room behind me. Bud was standing still staring at something on the closed piano lid. After a few moments I saw him reach out carefully and pick up a hundred-franc bill that Nicole had left for me before going off to work. He turned it over in his hands while staring at the back of my head. I held my breath and went on smearing my brush mindlessly across the paper. My heart was beating wildly. With a final glance in my direction, he put back the bill, pushing it decisively toward the far end of the piano. I hadn't budged the whole time. As usual Bud asked me for a few francs and as usual I gave it to him with a sinking heart, fully aware of the contradictions.

We paid our regular visits to Buttercup but now Bud refused categorically to go up to her room so we met in a small café nearby. I was treated to Buttercup's tirades. She would start off with some reserve, but slowly all her resentment came out. She accused Bud of indifference and showered him in reproach. Gradually, his patience wore thin. He would start fidgeting in his seat and without looking at her or answering her, he would say, "Can we go yet, Francis?" It had been about five minutes. "A little longer, Bud."

He saw no point in these visits, as Buttercup only spouted nonsense. I tried to change the topic of conversation but there was no stopping her. So Bud sat patiently, impassive, turning more and more away from her to stare at the rooftops across the street. In her whining voice, Buttercup continued her litany of reprimands until Bud asked again, "Now can we go, Francis?" "Okay, Bud, let's go." And failing to calm her, we would get up and walk out.

Back at the studio, we avoided talking about it. I felt ashamed to have once more subjected Bud to a useless flood of words, to risk throwing him back into a depression.

Occasionally I would take Bud to the Square des Batignolles, a small park behind a church only a stone's throw from the house. The Batignolles quarter was then like a village and we knew nearly all the inhabitants. The shopkeepers were as curious and gossipy as in any country village and soon everyone knew who this strange new character was as they saw him strolling tranquilly through the neighborhood.

We had been obliged to tell the various café owners about his case and explain the precautions they had to take. Without exception, they took our words to heart. Bud was always cordially received as well as protected. The owner would treat him to a last *vin rouge*, prudently cut with water. Bud was probably never fooled by their watering his wine, but he was touched by their kind attentions. He would hold up his glass to the light and ask with a wry little smile, "Is there water in this wine?"

"Not at all. It's a light wine, that's all."

A playful question got a playful answer. But it got harder to convince him. We would offer intricate explanations full of scientific details about lighter or heavier wines as he looked suspiciously at the glass. He would carefully taste the wine, look dubious, then toss it back in one gulp as always.

Bud truly venerated wine, but it was a false god who brought him only harm. The great vintages were his patron saints: Saint Emilion, pray for me; Saint Estèphe, pray for me; Cinzano, pray for me . . . But his prayers were never answered. He would have done better to make his devotions to Saint Yorrhe, the deity of the famous mineral spring in France.

GET HAPPY

(Recorded in New York, January/February 1950 [Verve])

We spent hours in the Square des Batignolles sitting in the shade, feeding the ducks in the large pond and throwing crumbs to the sparrows and pigeons that gathered around. Bud loved nature and found its quiet soothing. He was as happy as a child. If I suggested any other sort of outing, he systematically refused. One evening, though, he surprised us both, and had a change of heart. It was his first sign of interest in returning to the outside world.

"Francis, could we go out tonight?"

"Sure, Bud. With pleasure." With great curiosity, I asked him what he'd like to do.

"We could go have some fun."

"Where would you like to go? Do you have an idea?"

"A club or some place that I don't know."

"With music?"

"Yeah! You know a place like that?"

It was clear that he didn't want to see his familiar haunts. We were not far from Pigalle and I suddenly thought of the café La Cigale, where there was a fine group of musicians from the French West Indies: Emilien Antille, a dead ringer for Charlie Parker, who played alto in the same idiom; Michel Sardaby or Jean-Louis, both excellent, who accompanied on piano; Jack Butler on trumpet and Benny Waters on tenor. I suggested we go there and Bud accepted enthusiastically. It was our first visit to a club and I was glad the suggestion had come from him.

When we arrived the band was playing and no one noticed Bud. There was a table free near the piano. Jean-Louis, the pianist, turned his head and recognized Bud instantly. When the piece was over, he leaned down to greet us and asked Bud if he wanted to sit in. Bud only smiled. Jean-Louis whispered to Benny Waters who took the microphone, and announced triumphantly, "Ladies and gentlemen! We are honored to have with us tonight the great pianist Bud Powell!"

Then, turning to Bud, he said, "Good evening Bud. How about playing something for us?"

The drinks we had ordered were just being brought to our table, but Bud had already grabbed my arm and was pulling me out the door. There we were on the sidewalk! I was stunned but there seemed nothing to do but go home. Our first outing had been a short one.

The next evening, Bud again proposed we should go out. I was trying to think of another place to suggest, when he said with an innocent look, "We could go to La Cigale, Francis. What do you think?" I was meditating on the incident the night before, but he went on, impatiently, "Come on, let's go right now."

Nicole got her coat, and, somewhat nonplussed, we headed for La Cigale. Benny Waters was surprised to see us walk in, but this time he didn't introduce Bud. Like the night before, we ordered three strawberry milks and Bud drank his down in one gulp as always. Again we had a table near the piano and the pianist gave us a puzzled look. The set was going strong and Jean-Louis kept giving Bud questioning glances, but he sat there expressionless. Jean-Louis looked more nervous by the minute. All at once, I asked, trying to sound casual, "Hey Bud, do you think you feel like playing something?"

He looked at me like a child who's been offered a second helping of cake. His eyes were shining and he nodded timidly. Jean-Louis understood. He gave a discreet signal and the tune ended as if by magic. The last note had barely died away when Bud was at the bandstand. In a whirlwind, he sat down at the piano, counted out the beat and without a word to the rhythm section, attacked "Get Happy" in a furious tempo. The drummer's expression went from surprise to bewilderment. The bassist came in on the fourth measure and, after a few false starts, the show got going. In any case, Bud gave no quarter. You had to jump in head first and it always seemed to work out in the end. I had seen it happen before. Bud could carry in his wake the most recalcitrant of partners.

With his eyes on the ceiling, he accompanied each syncopation with a characteristic grunt. By the fiftieth chorus, the drummer was looking beat. The minutes ran on and we held on to our chairs as if we were in a rocket to the moon. It seemed that nothing would stop this infernal machine! Benny shrugged in response to the pleading eyes of the drummer who seemed more and more panicked. The bassist held his head pressed down on his chest as if to draw a last ounce of energy.

Bud often entered this kind of creative trance during which his inspiration was boundless. One chorus led to another, as if he had discovered the secret of perpetual motion. I cannot honestly recall how many choruses Bud took that night, when finally Benny came up behind him and quietly recalled the first notes of the tune. Bud was dripping with sweat and a beatific smile lit his face. It was like a séance with a medium. When he heard the saxophone he began to come out of his dream, his eyelids fluttered and he looked around himself in surprise. At the end of the last chorus the band took the theme with him. Bud ended with a flourish, then stood up and rushed through the room and out the door, reaching the curb just in time to lean over and vomit up his strawberry milk. By the time I got outside it was all over.

It was an unforgettable evening, a moment of grace. I only regret that no recorder was present to capture the beauty and perfection we had all experienced and which had just vanished into thin air.

The next thing we heard was that Johnny Griffin was coming to Paris. He had recently played with Thelonious Monk and I was looking forward to meeting him and hearing him live. His first Paris date was at the Blue Note, with Georges Arvanitas, Michel Gaudry, and Art Taylor. Fans and musicians alike were quivering with impatience.

Meanwhile, without the Largactyl, Bud grew stronger and his morale got better all the time. His appetite was a pleasure to see, and he began to play his old tunes on the piano again, significantly bringing something new to each one. I thought he might enjoy playing in public again and I suggested we go see Ben Benjamin at the Blue Note.

Not so long before, Bud was all the rage at the club, not to mention making them a fortune. Now, he entered timidly, like a shamefaced schoolboy returning after a suspension for misconduct.

I gently broached the subject of Bud's coming back to the club, but Ben refused categorically.

"No," he said. "Bud can't play any more. He falls asleep at the keyboard. Once he even threw up on the piano. It's out of the question!"

"But Ben, Bud is a new man. Everything is different. He plays magnificently."

"It's just not possible. Anyway, the program is all booked. The musicians have been announced and Griffin is starting tomorrow."

Bud didn't bat an eyelash, as if he were unconcerned. I was disappointed, but decided not to let it go at that. We returned to the Blue Note the next day to catch Johnny Griffin's opening.

The club was packed. As soon as we entered I could hear Griffin playing backstage while the other musicians were out front getting their instruments prepared. Then he came out, to wild applause. He hadn't seen Bud, but all over the audience people were whispering, "Bud is here! Maybe he'll play with Griffin."

When George Arvanitas heard, he looked questioningly in our direction. At that very moment, Ben Benjamin, undoubtedly urged by his patrons, walked up to our table, leaned over and feigning indifference, asked, "Would you like to play, Bud?"

His eyes shining, Bud looked at me for approval.

"Go on, Bud. Johnny hasn't seen you yet. Surprise him."

Bud stood, crossed the room like a whirlwind, knocking into everything in his way. You could've heard a pin drop. Johnny had his back turned, when a confident voice rang out behind him,

"Move. One, two. One, two, three, four. . . ."

He jumped, let out a shout when he recognized Bud, and in three seconds the red-hot locomotive was off and flying at top speed. Johnny played the theme with Bud, at a terrifying tempo. At the break, he let out a huge laugh, leapt off the stand and sat himself down at a front row table with his head in his hands. Bud kept up the tempo for chorus after chorus. The audience, some of them standing, gradually fell into a trance, completely enthralled by this unexpected event. The tune ended to thundering applause, led most of all by Johnny. But Bud had already swung into " 'Round Midnight," inviting Johnny to come back and play. It was, after all, Johnny's opening night in Paris, and his tactful retreat, a remarkable homage to Bud, had also given Bud the opportunity to make a glorious comeback at the Blue Note.

When the set ended, Ben Benjamin walked up to me and, without looking at me, asked in a casual voice, "Do you think Bud would like to come back here to play?"

And so it was that Bud came back to the Blue Note for a long time to come.

The fans who had the good fortune to live through this period all have wonderful memories of it. He had recovered his enthusiasm and his incredible energy. Kenny Drew or Lou Bennet shared the bill, and on some nights the music reached exceptional heights. In the little world of musicians, Bud was the main subject of conversation.

Buttercup heard about his return to the club and lost no time in showing up. We came to a very simple and mutually satisfactory agreement: she could have Bud's pay and in exchange she would leave him alone.

She was as good as her word. Every night she came and picked up what was left of his meager pay, fifty francs, from which they deducted his pack of cigarettes and Coca-Cola. She never stayed to listen. She would show up after the last set, collect the envelope without a word and without an ounce of shame, and then get back into the taxi that waited outside the door.

A concert was set up for January 3, 1963 in Coblentz that would bring together a number of American musicians living in Europe. Bud needed some new clothes and before leaving we did some shopping for him, buying a navy blue blazer and a nice pair of gray flannel slacks in which Bud felt comfortable. At the piano he had the habit of pulling up the right leg of his trousers with a quick movement. The flannel was so supple that when he pulled it, on the day of the concert, it went up above his knee. It was a funny sight and a photographer caught it for posterity. It was used on the cover of the record commemorating the concert, *Americans in Europe*. Bud played a stirring version of " 'Round Midnight." He played with the trio of Jimmy Woode, Joe Harris, and Idrees Sulieman (alias L. Graham for the occasion). Don Byas also joined the group for the same concert.

The Jamaican writer Lebert Bethure had plans for making a film on Bud, a short that was to be called *The Amazing Bud Powell.* Unfortunately, Buttercup handled the negotiations and her demands were such that the project never got off the ground.

Life went on quietly in our little studio. The window looked out onto the garden and Bud liked to stretch out on the bed and gaze through it. He listened endlessly to Tatum and laughed out loud at each flourish. Sometimes he'd pick up the newspaper Nicole bought and stare for hours at the same page. As he read no French, I took this to be his way of seeking solitude and I respected these moments of escape. One evening, when he had been staring a very long time at one page, I tried asking him, "Bud, do you read French now?"

His only reply was the usual grunt, which could have been taken as an affirmation.

"Are you sure you can read French?"

He looked up, puzzled.

"It might be easier if you held the page right side up," I said, laughing.

He quickly turned the paper around, embarrassed at having been caught, then with a shamefaced little smile, he returned to his meditation.

The rule at home was never to ask anything of him in exchange for what we gave him. Both of us were trying to give him back some of the joy and hope his music had given us in the past. When people

Bud Powell
(Francis Paudras Collection)

(Courtesy of Celia Powell)

Thelonious Monk, Bud's "soul brother"
(Photo by Alain Chevrier)

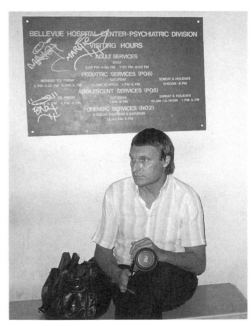

(Francis Paudras Collection)

Francis Paudras
(Photo Anita)

Elmo Hope, Bud's "spiritual twin" *(Courtesy of Celia Powell)*
(Courtesy of Bertha Hope)

Creedmoor Psychiatric Center, where Bud was a patient in 1945.
(Photo by Francis Paudras)

Bud with Marian McPartland, his unconditional friend.
(Courtesy of Marian McPartland)

Bud with his mother Pearl Powell
(Courtesy of Celia Powell)

The legendary Clud Minton's Playhouse
(Francis Paudras Collection)

(Francis Paudras Collection)

Art Tatum, Bud's "spiritual father"
(Francis Paudras Collection)

(Courtesy of the Schomburg Library)

Bud with his girlfriend Frances Barnes and his family
(Courtesy of Celia Powell)

Frances, mother of Bud's daughter Celia
(Courtesy of Celia Powell)

Pearl Powell, Bud's mother
(Courtesy of Celia Powell)

Bud with his family
(Courtesy of Celia Powell)

Charlie Parker, Sidney Bechet, and Kenny Clarke
(Francis Paudras Collection)

Art Taylor, Henri and Ny Renaud, and Bud
(Courtesy of Henri Renaud)

Entrance to Creedmoor Psychiatric Center
(Photo by Francis Paudras)

(Photo by Ira Gitler)

Creedmoor Psychiatric Center
(Photo by Francis Paudras)

Bud with Oscar Goodstein, his guardian
and manager of Birdland
(Courtesy of the Schomburg Library)

(Courtesy of Henri Renaud)

(Francis Paudras Collection)   *(Francis Paudras Collection)*

Winston Greg, Leonard Gaskin, J. J. Johnson, Bud Powell, Allan Eager, and Max Roach
(Courtesy of Leonard Gaskin)

Henri Renaud
(Photo by Alain Chevrier)

René Utréger
(Photo by Alain Chevrier)

Nicole Barclay
(Francis Paudras Collection)

Charles Delaunay
(Photo by Alain Chevrier)

(Francis Paudras Collection)

Boris Vian
(Photo by Roussillon)

Charlie Parker and Maurice Cullaz
(Francis Paudras Collection)

Dizzy Gillespie big band
(Francis Paudras Collection)

(Photo by Alain Chevrier)

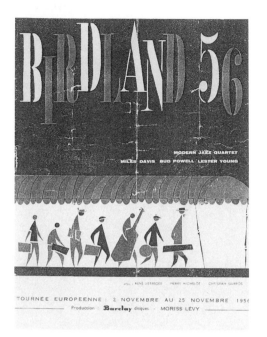

Birdland program
(Francis Paudras Collection)

Miles Davis and Bud
(Photo by Alain Chevrier)

Bud in 1956
(Photo by Alain Chevrier)

Lester Young
(Photo by Alain Chevrier)

Richie Powell, Bud's younger brother
(Francis Paudras Collection)

Pierre Michelot and Clifford Brown
(Francis Paudras Collection)

Marcel Romano, Stan Getz, Bud, and Paul Chambers
(Courtesy of Marcel Romano)

Façade of Club Saint Germain
(Photo by Francis Paudras)

(Photo by Alain Chevrier)

(Photo by Nils Edström)

Pierre Michelot
(Photo by Alain Chevrier)

Kenny Clarke
(Photo by Alain Chevrier)

Barney Wilen
(Photo by Alain Chevrier)

Bud Powell at the Place Furstenberg in 1957
*(Photo by **Alain Chevrier**)*

(Photo by Francis Paudras)   *(Photo by Francis Paudras)*

Bud Powell's amazing hands
(Courtesy of Liliane Rovère)

Dexter Gordon and Charles Bellonzi outside the Blue Note
(Courtesy of Charles Bellonzi)

Inside the Blue Note
(Photo by Francis Paudras)

Ben Benjamin, owner of the Blue Note
(Francis Paudras Collection)

Kenny Clarke, Bud, and Pierre Michelot
(Francis Paudras Collection)

(Photo by Jan Persson)

(Photo by Nils Edström)

Jimmy Gourley
(Photo by Alain Chevrier)

Kenny Clarke
(Photo by Alain Chevrier)

Bud Powell and Francis Paudras in Francis's apartment on the Rue Boursault, 1959
(Photo by Mic)

Bud and Francis
(Photo by Mic)

(Photo by Francis Paudras)

(Photo by Francis Paudras)

Hotel La Louisiane
(Photo by Francis Paudras)

(Photo by Francis Paudras)

Johnny, Buttercup, Kansas Field, and Henri, the Austrian staying with them
(Photo by Randi Hultin)

(Photo by Francis Paudras)

(Photo by Jorgen Leth)

Bud, Nicole, and Francis in the Triumph TR3

Francis and Bud in Francis's apartment
(Photo by Mic)

Nicole and Bud
(Photo by Francis Paudras)

Mic and Bud
(Photo by Francis Paudras)

(Photo by Francis Paudras)

Francis and Bud
(Photo by Mic)

(Photo by Francis Paudras)

(Photo by Francis Paudras)

(Photo by Nils Edström)

(Photo by Nils Edström)

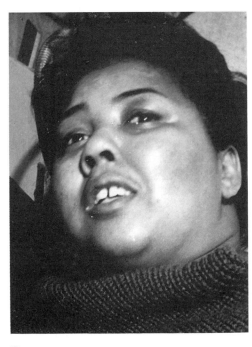

Nicole, Bud, and Francis
(Photo by Mic)

Buttercup
(Photo by Francis Paudras)

wondered at what we were doing for him, we could only explain that, in our view, it was we who were eternally in his debt.

Nicole was never at home for lunch so I prepared the midday meal. Bud loved French cuisine and enjoyed all the dishes we prepared, with the single exception of the sausage *boudin*, which he looked at indignantly. I soon learned that he had periodic cravings, often lasting three or four weeks, when he would demand a particular dish again and again. There were, for example, the *pâté* period, the sardines period, the ham-and-cheese period, the tuna-eggs-and-salad period, and the one that outlasted all the others, the adoration for strawberry ice cream and milk flavored with strawberry syrup. He never explained these desires, but whatever else was on the menu, he had to have the current favorite as well. He never spoke while eating, but in good Buddhist tradition concentrated totally on his meal, with only an occasional burst of laughter doubtless provoked by secret and hilarious inner visions.

I regularly visited my clients to bring them finished work or pick up new assignments. Bud, always curious about my work, accompanied me several times to advertising agencies. He would sit in the waiting room, watching the activity around him and smiling at the young secretaries. He liked to watch me draw, following all the stages until completion. One day he asked if he could give me a hand. Amused, I showed him some simple techniques, like painting the background colors in gouache. Felt-tip pens didn't exist then and rather than an airbrush I used miniature rollers that spread the paint very evenly. Bud adored it and would work non-stop. He would have painted all the walls of the apartment if I'd let him, and he was indignant if there was no job for him to do.

Gradually he discovered other gestures. It was as if everyone in the past had created an emptiness around him, preventing him from doing some of the very simplest activities, which made him feel helpless. He had always been told: "Just play the piano, Bud. We'll take care of the rest." By depriving him of all responsibility those around him had reduced him to an unbearable state of dependence and alienation. Decisions, initiatives, all the normal actions of daily life were denied him. I already knew that his legal status had been unusual to say the least.

American musicians would tell us how his business was nearly always controlled by a third party. Bud never saw a cent of the money he earned. From 1953 on, he had been declared legally incompetent and a guardian had been appointed to handle all of his affairs. Oscar

Goodstein occupied this function for a year and half and collected his fees and royalties. Bud had his rights restored in 1956 but in people's minds Goodstein was still his "keeper" and remained his de facto guardian for years. The record companies never questioned this arrangement. It had simply become a habit with them.

Slowly, I suggested to Bud that he could begin to take care of certain things in his life for himself. He seemed embarrassed at first, then curious, and then finally pleased with himself when he carried out a task on his own. For example, I designed and printed some greeting cards for him, and he would send them out himself in reply to letters he received from devoted fans the world over.

When I made lunch he watched me closely, amused that a man could cook. I offered to teach him some basics, and his first efforts were very funny. The first dish he tried was scrambled eggs, but he misjudged his own strength and instead of scrambling the eggs, he pulverized them! He learned how to make a real French vinaigrette, with just the right proportions of all the ingredients. On the other hand, making mayonnaise was for him nothing short of a miracle.

Doing these things gave him pleasure and as he gained assurance, his ability to communicate grew as well. Perhaps we had found one of the keys to unlock the ivory tower into which he had retreated.

Once on the way home from a visit to Buttercup, we found ourselves driving through the rush-hour crowds. We had put the top down on the convertible, and I was scanning the sky, hung with dark clouds. Near the Gare Saint Lazare we were immobilized by a traffic jam. The streets resounded with the din of honking horns, as people rushed to and fro, their faces grim, running up the steps of the railroad station, or vanishing into the mouth of the Métro. The whole scene had the appearance of a gigantic anthill. Bud moved closer to me in the car and put his hand on my arm. I looked over at him and saw anxiety in his eyes. "Say, Francis," he whispered, "we're not like that, we're not like them, are we?"

TUNE FOR DUKE

(Recorded in Paris, February 1963 [Mythic Sound])

At the beginning of February I received a phone call from Duke Ellington. During his last trip to Paris, Duke had witnessed the change in Bud and had undoubtedly talked about it to other musicians. Among those who were happy to hear of Bud's improvement was Frank Sinatra, a longtime admirer. Frank offered to finance a recording with him and asked Duke to supervise the session.

Bud was overjoyed. Sinatra had often come to hear him at Birdland and one memorable night when his playing was transcendent, he had invited Bud for a drink at his table. No one knew which of the two was more enthusiastic, but when they clinked glasses in a toast, both glasses shattered!

Duke was delighted that Bud had agreed, and he asked me to encourage him to write some new compositions for the occasion. For me, Duke was one of the great masters of his time, and I was surprised at the interest he took in musicians of Bud's generation. I was naive. Like all the true greats, Duke was timeless and deeply involved in the evolution of music. In 1953 he had even thought of asking Charlie Parker to join his band as first altoist. It would have been a glorious venture, but Bird declined with the wisecrack, "Forget it, man. You can't afford me!"

Anyway, the record was going to happen and Bud set to work.

The minute Buttercup got wind of the project she phoned to speak to Bud. The conversation was heated. Her high-pitched voice could be heard from the receiver as Bud held it further and further away from his ear, looked at it in horror and finally hung up. I called her back and determined that all she wanted was assurance that the session would take place. Bud had intimated that if she was present (and he knew quite well why she would be present!) he wouldn't play. I managed to convince him that the music was more important than anything else and he finally gave me his word.

For this occasion, Bud wrote a number of new tunes. He would sit at the piano, staring at the keyboard, one hand on the lid, the other soundlessly caressing the keys. Suddenly, he would play a melodic phrase, repeat it at regular intervals, and note it succinctly on the paper at a stupefying speed, marking the notes, alterations, and punctuation all at once. Then there was a long silence until the birth, just as rapid, of the next phrase.

Sometimes he would keep the sustaining pedal down until the complete extinction of the sound. In the silence I could hear the harmonics fade one by one. The next instant came a rippling phrase, with astounding spaces, in which you could hear the same harmonics of the note that had just died away. These moments made me hold my breath. He didn't seem to make any effort, yet large drops of sweat had formed on his forehead, which he quickly wiped off with the back of his hand. When the moment of grace was over, he would break his concentration, stand up as if he didn't know what had just taken place, and walk away, leaving the music paper on the stand. This writing seemed not to mean anything to him and I never saw him look at it again.

One of the new compositions was dedicated to the Duke, with the title "Tune for Duke." He wrote a medium tempo piece, "Let's Go Away," a fast tempo one, "Free," and a ballad that I took to be for us, "For My Friends."

For the session, Buttercup insisted on Kansas Field as the drummer. I suggested Gilbert Rovère on bass. Duke liked him enough to hire him for his own orchestra. The session promised to be tense. Bud was against the choice of Kansas Field and refused to see Buttercup, who stayed wisely in the booth. To try and calm things down, Duke suggested I stay next to Bud in the studio.

From the beginning the atmosphere was heavy, in the literal sense of the word, for Kansas Field was not exactly the light and subtle drummer Bud would have wanted, but he managed, as always, to find the pulse he needed. Duke was delighted and while Bud played he went behind the piano, did a little dance step and whispered in his ear, "Play, genius, play! Do you know you're a *genius*?"

Duke asked Bud to play "Satin Doll" and, as Bud didn't know the tune, Duke whistled it for him. "Could you whistle the last part of the refrain again?" asked Bud. Duke obliged, but Bud stopped him after three measures. "That's okay, I got it." And indeed, the tune was recorded without a hitch, in only two takes, the first one having been thought a little too slow.

Then he did "Dear Old Stockholm," which was very popular with musicians at that time. These standards were used by the company in place of some of Bud's originals, most likely for commercial reasons.

The sessions ended well. Everyone was satisfied, though not for the same reasons. Bud had once again worked for the honor—and Buttercup got the check. The record came out as *Bud Powell in Paris*. He was glad it was over and pulled me outside, refusing to stay a minute longer. That evening we went out for a candlelit dinner at a friend's restaurant in Montmartre.

This recording session was the only one Bud was offered during that whole period. But he played a lot at home and I even persuaded him to put some of his old pieces back into his repertoire, including some studio tunes he had never played again, like "Cleopatra's Dream," "Crossin' the Channel," and "Blue Pearl." Sometimes he'd be lying on the bed and would leap up, rush to the piano, and play an explosion of phrases and progressions that were unbelievably lyrical and moving. This inspiration seemed to come all at once. I could feel he was suddenly tormented, feverish, unconscious of his surroundings.

When Bud asked me to play, I was so embarrassed at first that I was nearly paralyzed. But I couldn't go on refusing forever (any pianist will understand how I felt). Finally, with his kind encouragement, I began to get back to my music. He showed me harmonies and progressions of his tunes that I had had trouble with. His patience was extraordinary as he tirelessly repeated his explanations. What great piano lessons they were, and what a lesson in modesty from a musician of his stature!

I had composed a tune called "The Squirrel" and one day he asked me to teach it to him. I found the situation too funny for words, but he insisted, so I gave in. It took no patience whatever on my part, for he instantly memorized every detail and made it sound better than I could ever have imagined. Later, he played the piece for our friends Johnny Griffin, Art Taylor, and Dexter Gordon, never omitting to mention that I was the author. Another masterful lesson in thoughtfulness and humility.

Our studio was the scene of many memorable evenings with Johnny Griffin, Babs Gonzales, Dexter Gordon, Sonny Rollins, Hank Mobley, Art Taylor, and the regulars. Bud loved these parties and enjoyed playing host. He seemed to feel more at home and more and more sure of himself. Our American friends were at first amused, then astonished, and finally they came to accept that Bud was really a changed man.

HOT HOUSE
(Recorded in Toronto, May 15, 1953 [Debut])

W e went to see Dizzy Gillespie in a concert at the Palais des Sports. Lalo Schiffrin was on piano and Leo Wright soloed on alto sax and flute, with good taste and plenty of feeling. I had imagined that after the concert Bud and Dizzy would have a lot to say to each other but it wasn't so. They kissed each other, exchanged a few perfectly ordinary words and that was it. The real dialogue was in their eyes. We had gone backstage to say hello, and I was surprised to see how many of the musicians seemed afraid to talk to Bud. Some openly avoided him. One, a more expansive type, teased him as one would a child, then vanished. These reactions made Bud very nervous. He rolled his eyes and finally withdrew into a corner by himself. I never saw him really talk with anyone. It gave me a glimpse of one of the reasons for his timidity and mistrust of people.

Many people played dumb with him, using a condescending tone that I'm sure he noticed. Of course he was simple and even naive but this kind of provocation, which hurt him every time, made him withdraw even more into himself.

The day after Dizzy's concert I was practicing the piano when Bud came up and sat beside me. I stopped playing at once.

"Go on, go on," he said. "When you finish the piece I want to show you something."

I was playing "All the Things You Are," and I finished it off quickly, curious to know the reason for this unusual intervention.

"Look at this introduction," he said, and played the intro made famous by his and Bird's interpretations of that tune. "You see those chords and changes?"

"Sure Bud. Of course I know them. It's you who . . ."

"Well, you see, it was Birks first showed that to me. Go ahead, try it. . . ."

Bud always called Dizzy by his real middle name, Birks, just as Dizzy always called him by his given name, Earl. He patiently went over the harmonic progressions several times, articulating slowly so that I could visualize what he was doing. Then he said again, "You see, a long time ago, Birks did that with me, and now I'm doing it with you. He showed me that."

Then he segued into "'Round Midnight," playing the coda as well, and added, "Birks wrote that too, and he taught it to me. He showed me lots of things like that, you know. . . ."

Bud spoke Dizzy's name with the respect that he generally reserved for Tatum and Thelonious. I was astonished to learn that Dizzy had written the intro and the last part of "'Round Midnight." Bud went on to tell me the whole story of the piece, which was even more surprising: "When I was playing with Cootie Williams in 1944, I did most of the arrangements for the band 'cause I was the only one who could write music. I was working a lot with Thelonious then and I wanted Cootie to put 'Midnight' in the repertoire. He didn't want to, but he finally agreed to, on the condition that he himself would write a second part for the piece. At the time, you see, it had only the main theme. After that, Dizzy wrote the beginning and the end when we played the piece with his orchestra."

Later, Cootie told me that Bud had threatened to leave if he refused to put the piece in the program. He was not yet twenty years old, but his musical authority was already respected by everyone in the group. It was later on that things changed and life took charge of curbing his fiery temperament.

Bud was reserved and profound. His secretive nature led him to shun company. He opened up only to a certain category of people, often far removed from his artistic circles. He bloomed within our group of friends because they saw him as their ideal. Their behavior, like his own, was natural, straightforward, and unequivocal. They were tolerant and understanding. Nothing about him surprised them. This was, of course, the best attitude to take toward him.

During the long days we spent together, Bud only spoke when he absolutely had to. Otherwise, his communication consisted of smiling and making faces. I too learned to keep silent, to speak only when it was really necessary. We communicated through music and our looks told us we were on the same wavelength. At first, Bud's questions were brief and focused on my musical tastes.

"Do you like Fats Navarro? What do think of Sonny Rollins? Do you like the way Sonny Stitt plays?" "Oh, you've got Erroll Garner's records," he remarked one day with a frown. The great fame of Erroll Garner seemed to upset Bud, to the point, according to some people, of not wanting to be called Earl. At the beginning of his career, Bud had adopted the stage name of Earl Palmer, but he soon dropped it because it sounded too much like Erroll Garner.

We would talk about our favorites, sometimes making a game of it. I'd cite, for example, Fats Navarro, and he would counter with Freddie Webster. I knew Webster only from having heard him with Fletcher Henderson's orchestra and I couldn't see how he could be compared to Fats. "How can you prefer Fats?" he'd say. "If you never heard Freddie with us, then you can't know."

At times, too, he'd come up with an unfamiliar name. "Do you know Elmo Hope?" Elmo was a childhood friend whom he adored, and I, for shame, had never heard of him. Bud raved about him. "You gotta hear Elmo. He's fabulous. His stuff is very hard. He does some things that even I have trouble playing."

I was intrigued, knowing that Bud never said things like that lightly. As for Charlie Parker, he never said a word. He wouldn't talk about him, any more than he would about himself. One would have thought they had nothing to do with each other. Could this silence conceal some secret friendship? One day, however, in a moment of extreme openness, he confided, "We once went on tour together, and after the concerts we'd get invited to parties. There were lots of women . . ." His eyes took on a mischievous sparkle.

"Yeah? And what happened with Bird?"

"Oh, we had fun, and the others, well, they had fun watching us."

"What did you talk about, the two of you?"

"About nothing. We didn't talk, that's all."

And I couldn't get another word out of him about Bird.

Then came the big question. "Do you like Thelonious Monk?"

"What a question! I love him. He's a genius!"

His eyes shone with happiness.

Our main topic of conversation was still Tatum. I myself had been completely shaped by his music, which had brought me directly to Bud's. I tried, as did all my friends, to get down all the wild figures and flourishes of Tatum. Bernard Peiffer, Georges Arvanitas, Martial Solal, and René Urtréger had all worked like mad on Tatum's fantastic runs. René had even taken some of Bud's intros that Bud had gotten from Tatum.

One day, while we were having lunch, Bud suddenly stopped eating and closed his eyes with a blissful smile on his lips. We were listening to a Tatum solo from the famous Toronto concert. All at once, he placed his hands on the edge of the table and, to my amazement, began to move his fingers at breathtaking speed. He was reproducing note for note, move for move, every last detail of Tatum's racing interpretation. He went on till the end of the tune, absolutely faithful to the model. Then with a burst of laughter, apparently pleased with himself, he went back to his meal.

There was one other subject that always got a reaction out of Bud. I contended that Billie Holiday was the greatest vocalist. He disagreed, softening his reproof with a little smile. "No, Francis, the greatest is Sarah Vaughan. Don't you like Sarah, Francis?"

"Of course I like her. I have all her records. I like her because she's completely a part of your music. But Billie is more moving. And besides, I think Sarah got a lot from her."

We never agreed on this point. I have always suspected Bud of preferring Sarah for reasons that were not purely musical. If certain confidences are to be believed, his feelings for the young sweetheart of bop were more than simple affection.

When we had exhausted these subjects of conversation, Bud would ask for a little money to go for his customary walk. I always dreaded the moment, knowing I had to show firmness along with friendship. I couldn't refuse him a few francs and couldn't preach just before he went out, as that would only add to his frustration. I had already spent long hours explaining how bad alcohol was for him and why I, as a friend, wanted to protect him from its effects.

He always promised but he never kept his word. He'd walk as far as the corner bistro, spread out his fortune on the counter and negotiate with the waiter the amount of *vin rouge* it would buy him. Two glasses were enough to make him feel strange and more than two were disastrous. Alcohol had a devastating effect on him: his walk became unsteady, his speech slurred and he could no longer synchronize his movements or control his behavior. His was a painful paradox: the man was obsessed with drinking and yet he couldn't hold his liquor!

Without the Largactyl, Bud became more sociable. He began to initiate conversations. His main interest centered on my parents and relatives. A thousand times, he asked if I still had my mother and father, if they were legally married, if my sister was my real sister. I had to describe our family relationships in detail, but it never seemed to satisfy him. His interest in the subject was so obsessive I began to think that a clue to his own unhappiness lay in his relationship to his own family.

Despite his reserve, he gave me to understand that his childhood had not been a happy one. His parents didn't get along, largely because of another woman, and eventually they separated. For someone as sensitive as Bud and so in need of affection, this must have been a great emotional blow.

I had told Bud about my relations with my family, how my taste for jazz had caused huge family quarrels, my mother lamenting my musical orientation, my father fuming about the money they had wasted on my music lessons. "All the sacrifices we made, so that you can play this 'music of savages'!"

On top of that, I never stopped talking about some American jazz musician, a certain Bud Powell, who was an absolute genius. It was nothing unusual. Thousands of teenagers have lived through the same sort of family drama.

In short, after I left home at nineteen, my relations with my parents became sporadic, then stopped altogether. It was from the press that they learned Bud was living with me. A neighbor of theirs, my childhood friend and a devoted reader of *Jazz Hot*, had shown them an article about it. Curious about the situation, they let me know through my friend that they wished to meet this man I had talked about during all my teenage years, and they would be pleased to invite both of us for Sunday lunch. It was hard to refuse, even though I feared that Bud's behavior might confirm the validity of some of their criticisms. I was also afraid Bud might be put off, or hurt by their inquisitorial attitude toward me. But in the end, my desire to show Bud off and to prove my friendship won out, and I accepted the invitation.

My mother phoned to ask what sort of food Bud liked to eat. Since he was then going through a passionate *pâté* phase, I suggested a *pâté* for starters and anything else to follow.

The following Sunday we arrived at noon. Bud was as excited as I had ever seen him, and I was more than a little nervous. When I introduced him to my parents, Bud acted the man of the world, smiling yet reserved. I had bought a bouquet of flowers, which he presented to my mother. He didn't speak, but devoured both of them with his eyes. I held my breath. It seemed to me that in a flash, in a matter of seconds, his angelic smile had seduced my diehard family.

My mother led us into the dining room where the table was beautifully laid with a large vase of flowers and napkins folded fanlike in the glasses. She had gone to great pains to make a really elegant French Sunday lunch. She pointed to the *pâté* in the center of the table, saying she had made it specially for Bud. Not understanding what she said, he asked me to translate. When I did, his expression went from surprise to wonder then to unadorned greed. He made me repeat what she had said to be sure he'd understood correctly, then gave her a big wink to express his gratitude and sat down slowly and majestically on the chair nearest the *pâté*. One more time he made me repeat that the dish had been made "specially for him." That was all he was waiting for! He reached out and put the entire *pâté* on his plate. We all looked on in awe, as he threw my mother one last radiant look, then tucked in and began eating "his" *pâté*. In the space of ten minutes the entire dish was consumed. I stared down at my shoes, not daring to meet my parents' eyes, cursing myself for having accepted the invitation. My aunt, who was also present, stared at Bud with what looked like adoration. The silence was unbearable.

Suddenly, my father put an end to my embarrassment by striding across the room exclaiming, "*Bon sang de bon sang*, my goodness gracious! I am forgetting my duties as a host. Just one moment, my dear Bud. You are going to suffocate! Please taste a little of this bordeaux. You must tell me what you think of it."

Bud smiled and swallowed the wine in one gulp. I thought I would pass out. This time my mother saved the situation. She pushed me toward the table, saying, "Dinner is served. Sit down, son. Can't you see that Bud is hungry?"

A glance round the table showed me admiration on all faces. "What a fine appetite," said my mother. "I like people who know how to eat."

"And I like people who know how to drink," added my father. "Here, my dear Bud. Have a taste of this wine."

"What'd he say?" asked Bud.

I was speechless. Now it was my turn to gulp down my wine. I needed to get over my emotions.

As tradition dictates, the guest of honor was placed on my mother's right. She took good care of him and he didn't need coaxing to take second helpings. Once all the serving was finished, happiness was visible on every face. At the end of the meal, Bud turned to my mother and whispered, in a confidential tone, "So, you're really Francis's mother?"

"Yes, Bud."

"Are you really his mother?"

"Yes, Bud."

"His real legal mother?"

"Yes, of course, Bud."

"You gave birth to him?"

"Why yes, Bud."

By this time no one else was speaking. He leaned closer and whispered, "He came out of your stomach?"

"Yes, Bud. That's right, Bud."

Utterly satisfied, he put his hand on the back of her neck, placed her head in the crook of his shoulder and gave her a resounding kiss on the cheek. I could feel the tears come to my eyes, and I looked determinedly down at my plate. Bud was a magician. His childlike candor had won over my whole family, and he hadn't even played a note!

Then, with a mischievous look, he held out his empty glass to my father and said, in perfect French, *"Papa, vin rouge, s'il vous plaît."*

As I think about it now, I realize that I had always thought of Bud as a spiritual entity and had had trouble associating this image with the physical reality that had now become part of my daily life. This kept me in an eerie, dreamlike state. Standing beside him as an enlightened amateur, I knew more surely as time went on that I would have to go on fighting to make those around me see things as I did.

In the early '60s the world of music had a very different face than the one we know today. The frantic race for stardom that can suddenly make or break the career of young artists didn't exist yet. Musicians were guided in their creation by a genuine search for originality. Their ethic was a greater honesty before their art, and in this respect Bud was a model of integrity. The pace of life was slower then, and so was the pace of artistic success. Bud's came early, thanks to his greatest qualities: a capacity (shown very early) for assiduous work and an infinite passion for the keyboard.

The week after the lunch at my parents', who made us promise to come again soon, the annual awards of the Django Reinhardt Prize took place at the Club Saint Germain, hosted by Maurice Cullaz. Bud and I were invited and we were accompanied by, of all people, my father, who wanted to attend the ceremony. Maurice presented the awards, introduced the celebrities in the audience without omitting Bud, of course, and then he invited the new prizewinner, Pierre Michelot, to play with any musicians of his choice. Just then, my father rose and called out, "Now, my dear Bud, you will certainly play something for us, *n'est-ce pas?*"

Bud asked me what he'd said, and I replied, "He said he'd like you to play for us."

Bud gave him a timid smile, but my father, with a broad wink that brooked no refusal, was already nudging him toward the piano. "Okay, papa, I'll play."

Had it been anyone else he might have refused. But he had never played for my father, and it was clear that he didn't want to disappoint him.

What followed was a fireworks display. The entire audience was enraptured but none more so than his newfound fan, his latest convert, my father.

This appearance at the Club Saint Germain created quite a stir in the jazz world and a lot of commentary on Bud's new life.

It was getting harder for me to persuade Bud to continue our visits with Buttercup. He always went in the end, but their meetings were increasingly bitter. She constantly berated him and still spoke to him as if he were feeble-minded. Bud would listen briefly, then turn to me and beg to leave. I imagine just being near that place in which he had been so unhappy and suffered such indignity was enough to arouse dreadful memories.

Our relations with my neighbors had not improved either, for Bud had no notion of community living and persisted in playing late at night. We still couldn't bear Bud's sadness each night when he had to go back to his hotel. For a long time, I had hoped to find larger quarters, where Bud could live with us all the time. Now it had become an obsession. I was beginning to earn a good living. I decided I would buy an apartment.

After visiting several, I chose four rooms on the fifth floor of 64, rue de Clichy. If we could get it, we could have a soundproof music room, Bud would have his own bedroom, and, best of all, we would no longer have the painful nightly separations. When I compared the price of the apartment with the amount of my savings, the affair seemed doomed, but I was so determined that I threw myself into my work with more vigor and enthusiasm than ever before.

I had spoken to Bud of the project and he—never one to worry about material problems—was already asking when we'd be moving. I couldn't disappoint him. I worked like a demon, and everything I did succeeded. Neither before nor since have I had such good luck in my profession. To this day it remains a mystery to me. Normally, any ad campaign requires at least three proposals, but this time my clients not only accepted my first proposal, they retained the other ideas for future operations. And more miraculous yet, they paid me in advance!

RUE DE CLICHY
(Recorded in Paris, 1963 [CD Team])

In a month and a half, we had scraped together enough money to sign the purchase papers. We collected the down payment even faster. My father contributed his savings and Nicole got a UNESCO loan. Our last remaining pennies went for a bottle of champagne that Bud opened, deliriously happy, in order to celebrate the possession of our new premises. It had all happened so quickly our heads were spinning.

The apartment still needed lots of work, but we had achieved our main aim, that of being together. Now nothing would disturb the sacrosanct peace of our musical evenings.

The rooms were laid out all in a row, with French windows giving onto a balcony over sixty feet long, looking out over the rooftops of Paris. Bud's bedroom was next to a bathroom, giving him full independence. Our bedroom, with its own washroom, was at the other end of the apartment, near the kitchen and overlooking the courtyard. The two rooms in between we intended to make into one large space that would serve as dining room and music room, and that would, of course, be soundproofed.

Our lifestyle at first was closer to camping than to bourgeois comfort, but we were happy. Bud was always smiling and our multiple household problems usually ended in giggles all around. Our first few pieces of rustic furniture were purchased at a little antique shop just around the corner on the Rue Vintimille. Bud went shopping with us and gave his opinion on all purchases. Slowly, we built our little paradise on the fifth floor, which would soon become a meeting place for all of Bud's friends. Honoring us with their visits were Max Roach, Percy Heath, Sonny Stitt, Art Taylor, Sonny Rollins, Dexter Gordon, Hank Mobley, Kenny Clarke, and Johnny Griffin, as well as our friends from Paris, Raymond Le Sénéchal, René Urtréger, Henri Renaud, Eddy Louiss, Raymond and Hubert Fol, and many, many more.

My professional career was booming. I must have found the philosopher's stone, for I was turning base metals (paint and paper in my case) into gold. Much of the inspiration came from Bud's presence and from knowing that he was finally happy. He seemed surprised at first by how we took care of him, but then he got used to it and came to accept that this was really his home. "This is home, Bud, once and for all. There's nothing more to be said." For him, as for us, it was a deep and lasting commitment. "Bud," we told him, "friends are like a family that you choose."

Yet the joy was still broken by moments of anxiety and despair. He sometimes looked as if he were doing penance for some unavowable sin. I cursed the society that had done this to him, that had exploited, tyrannized, humiliated, and finally abandoned him. Many thought that Bud was through as a musician and, more than ever, I was determined to prove them wrong. I hoped that as he recovered his health and strength, I would come to understand him better, to pierce the secret of his silence, his absence, his distress. I made little headway. Seven months had gone by since his release from Laënnec Hospital and I knew nothing more of his inner torment.

For the public, as for many musicians, Bud was always a subject of curiosity. Some made fun of him openly. He would take these tasteless jokes in stride and, although his eyes darkened with contained anger, I never saw him answer back. If someone had to be taught a lesson, I often took charge of it after Bud had left. Yet he never forgot an insult and was quite capable of bearing a grudge. Sometimes when the musicians teased him at the club, he didn't respond immediately, but when he sat down for the set, I could see that he was about to get even. Glaring at those who had just insulted him, he would start to play, creating music so relevant and so breathtakingly beautiful that it was better than any verbal retort. Then he would calmly leave the piano, a mysterious smile on his lips, and look them up and down as if to say, "Let's see who has the last laugh!"

One evening, after an incident of this kind, Bud had played with a fire and brilliance that were positively dazzling. When he finished, he did something very unusual. He grabbed the mike and, in a professional manner, introduced the musicians, ending with a line made famous by Pee Wee Marquet: "This evening, ladies and gentlemen, you have been listening to the amazing Bud Powell. Let's give him a big hand." Then, with a laugh, he turned to the jokers and stared at them until they lowered their eyes.

Sometimes after a set he would take advantage of the general excitement to sidle up to a table and, with a conjurer's skill, toss down the contents of a customer's glass. Then he'd walk casually over to our table and sit down next to me, all innocence.

I think a lot of musicians had a distorted view of Bud. Those who knew him longer than I had said that in his youth he had been "normal"—the word sounds so harsh in all its nakedness. I myself would have had no inkling of the way he was if I hadn't met some friends of his youth and childhood. All of them said he was always different and exceptional—different for his unusually quick mind and faculty of assimilation, in math, for example, and exceptional for his precocious musical ability and the distinctive musical choices he made. This combination of passion and intellect placed him outside the normal range from the start, and must have served to distance him from his schoolmates. On the rare occasions he alluded to his school days, it was with a certain bitterness. Had he already been excluded because of his "being so different"? Was he envied and taunted by those who wouldn't accept him for what he was? His old friends also agreed that Bud always possessed that childlike candor that some call naiveté.

The few times he ventured to talk of his childhood, he spoke of strained relationships between himself and his brothers. He was the one who ended up doing all the household chores, as Richie, "the spoiled baby," could always wriggle out of them, and William, the older brother, either forced or tricked Bud into doing his work as well.

Were Richie's feelings for Bud pure admiration? When Richie wanted to learn piano, he naturally turned to Bud, who was already an accomplished pianist, with classical training and a lot of experience in jazz. Bud started giving him lessons but gave up after a while because he felt that Richie's work was too haphazard and his attitude too insincere to warrant his older brother's attention.

The organist Jimmy Smith, who came from Norristown, Pennsylvania, near Willow Grove, where the Powell family lived, gave an interview to *Jazz Hot* (March 1958) confirming Bud's account: "I knew Bud and his brother pretty well. Richie and I used to play cowboys and Indians together. I'd go there every day and Bud would tease us, saying we'd never amount to anything. He said I had more spunk than Richie cause I at least wanted to learn and Richie was always putting things off for later. I used to watch Bud, the way he moved his hands. His attack was absolutely unique."

Richie eventually gave up the piano to try drums and asked Max Roach, who played regularly with Bud, for lessons. Max worked with him for over a year. "The results were nothing spectacular," recalls Jackie McLean, "and Max advised him to go back to the piano."

So Richie came back to Bud and promised to be studious this time. He must have been true to his word, for two years later he was a promising pianist, playing professionally, and would soon join the Clifford Brown–Max Roach quintet—another member of the Powell family who was not so ordinary.

Whenever Bud spoke of the terrible car accident that had taken the lives of Richie and Clifford, he would always repeat in a voice full of pain, "He was so young. He could've gone so far. You know, Francis, he was so young. . . ."

But despite his enormous musical authority and unusual intelligence, Bud was amazingly credulous in daily life, which often led to his childlike behavior. His repeated questions about my family made me realize how much he must have brooded about the most intimate reflections of his own childhood.

Being far from home and cut off from his loved ones was hard for him. His need for affection and lack of family ties after his parents' break-up must have halted his psychological development, something like a refusal to grow up. I felt he was always waiting for something to happen that would put him back on the road to adulthood. But it never did. With all those wounds Bud remained as vulnerable as a five-year-old child. Yet none of this ever seemed to affect his spiritual and musical integrity.

UN POCO LOCO

(Recorded in New York, May 1, 1951 [Blue Note])

Mental illness has often been evoked to explain Bud's case. Those who advance this theory have never understood that his music alone is the proof of his great lucidity, a rare equilibrium and clear-sightedness. Some musicians, too, have favored the simplistic explanation of mental illness to cover up their own deficiencies or lessen their own responsibility in his regard. By refusing to stand up for Bud they only confirm their own inability to follow or understand him intellectually.

Alcohol was a constant problem, so I invented a few stratagems to keep Bud dry and happy. I got hold of a bottle of "Quintonine," an old-fashioned remedy based on quinine tonic, and made up a cocktail by mixing it with some Bordeaux wine. One small glassful before lunch was enough to put him in great shape. It appealed to him and was a good stimulant too.

One morning I found him up at the crack of dawn, a suspicious sparkle in his eyes. Clearly, he hadn't been to bed. I ran to the kitchen and sure enough there was the bottle I had prepared the night before, empty! If I had any doubts as to the tonic effects of this potion, here was the proof of its effectiveness.

Bud had a great need for liquids and since he didn't like water, mineral or other, we had a serious problem on our hands. I got some alcohol-free beer and he was delighted when I told him he could drink as much as he liked. I neglected to mention, of course, that it contained no alcohol. I was amazed to note that, taking this for normal beer, he was able to get drunk on it, though without the usual drastic physical symptoms. He himself seemed puzzled by the minimal effect of the beer, no matter how much he drank. I realized then how much he sought this "second state" in which he found escape and relief of pain. In his desire to dull his feelings, Bud's organism, through its own chemistry, provoked an effect analogous to that of alcohol. More and more I understood how far from common his psychological make-up was.

The alcohol-free beer simplified our life and Bud's health improved daily. However, as long as his therapy was based on subterfuge, he would remain physically and psychologically vulnerable whenever confronted with realities.

I became certain that we should no longer regard Bud as a typical alcoholic, for the simple reason that he couldn't drink three glasses of wine without being sick or passing out. In the past, it seems, he had drunk to excess, evidently being able to hold it better. Now, with all the medication he had taken, his liver was in such a state he couldn't drink at all. He kept trying, though, always hoping, always seeking oblivion.

But as far as drugs are concerned, I wish to state that, despite all the legends to the contrary, Bud never took any drugs during the time he lived in Europe. His desire was for alcohol alone.

He seemed helpless to halt this race to self-destruction, despite the happy moments we had together. What looked like a wish to drink himself to death was in fact only a sign of how thoughtless he was, how unaware of the consequences.

Bud was devoted body and soul to his music, and miserable over the rise of rock 'n' roll. It was being played on all the radio stations and on the jukeboxes of cafés. The minute he heard a note, Bud would leap up and run like a bat out of hell. It was the best way to get him out of a bar. He'd be upset for a long time afterward, as if he'd undergone an emotional trauma, his eyes full of anger and reproof.

According to the old adage, "music soothes the savage beast." But the music manufactured for young people nowadays by the show business industry is, in its very inspiration, ugly and violent. Each generation has its period of revolt and young people have always thrown their energy into their music. But in general they have been inspired by beauty. Today's music gives rise to violence, if not to downright rage—they smash and burn and destroy. But aren't the young people of today merely unconscious victims of a frantic quest for profit? With its supermarket slogans, its trite and used-up themes, once proclaimed in nobler and more courageous battles, rock spells the death of music, in an unequal struggle between art and money. It offers no hope in this brutal society of ours. To express the passions of today's youth, there is more strength to be drawn from jazz than from all of the ersatz music that offers only greater degradation.

In my own life, jazz in general and Bud's work in particular have helped me to create and to overcome many difficulties. Bud's music made me happy. It is still the driving force of my life and a permanent source of regeneration. After years of listening, without ever growing weary, one question comes to my mind: could it be that, through the energy and emotional charge of his music, Bud held the key to some forgotten therapy, some sovereign remedy based on healing vibrations? The pure mathematics of his harmonic combinations, the balance of his melodies and perfect architecture of his rhythmic structures, resemble the admirable and mysterious works of the master builders of the Middle Ages.

If Bud was disturbed by the coming of rock, he was also unhappy about the anarchic experiments in free jazz that were starting to develop at that time, in Paris and elsewhere. We had gone to Salle Wagram to hear Charlie Mingus's band, with Eric Dolphy. Charlie had asked me to design a poster for the concert, and made me promise to come and to bring Bud. From Dolphy's first chorus, I saw Bud wasn't taking it well. He got increasingly nervous and started fidgeting frantically in his seat. Pulling his cap down on his head, he took my arm and tried to get me to leave. Our neighbors were giving us dirty looks. I was very embarrassed and had a lot of trouble convincing him that we should stay at least till intermission.

Over his protests, I dragged him backstage, telling him I'd promised Mingus. "No, Francis. I don't wanna go. Why is Mingus playing with Dolphy? That's not music, that's noise!"

I had never seen him so furious. He jumped at each squeeze in the harmonies and the rhythms, and the delirium of the rhythm section didn't help matters any. The novel formula advanced by Dolphy that "there are no wrong notes" never convinced Bud, particularly in this musical context, where the bop form was still quite apparent and where Dolphy's break-out attempts still sounded evasive, accidental, and uncalled for.

I understood better now why, during the Antibes concert in 1960, with Mingus, Booker Ervin, Ted Curson, and Dolphy, Bud had stopped playing completely as Booker and Eric traded fours, deliriously battling one another.

Going backstage was a delicate matter. Bud refused to talk to the musicians and just glared furiously at Mingus, who was obviously baffled by his attitude. I refrained from any comment and the tension between Bud and Mingus became unbearable. Fortunately, our friend Lili Rovère showed up and Bud's mood changed. She got him smiling again, but he still had only one idea in mind—to get away.

Taking Lili by the hand, he told Mingus we were in a hurry and dragged us off to the nearest bar. Once again, his reputation was to suffer from this behavior. People took him to be deranged, for no one could suspect the real reasons for his behavior. As for the concert that night, nearly everyone else found it brilliant!

I believe that Bud's attitude toward people was never unfounded. Those around him, in their casual way, were never aware of his extreme sensitivity. Bud, with his refined language, never accepted coarseness or vulgarity. At the first sign of rudeness, his behavior changed and he took his distance. Such people were immediately categorized as unacceptable, and he refused all contact with them again.

GLASS ENCLOSURE

(Recorded in New York, August 14, 1953 [Blue Note])

INSANITY: mental illness or derangement; unsoundness of mind; great folly; extreme senselessness.

Through all these revealing experiences, I felt I was getting to know him better and better, and beginning to understand his philosophy of life. Still, he could never be completely free or communicative. One day, when he looked sadder than usual, I decided I had to fight fire with fire. As he watched in astonishment, I took out a bottle of wine and sat down facing him, determined to storm the walls of his ivory tower. I launched into a long and passionate monologue that went something like this:

"Bud, listen to me. I love you more than anyone else in the world. I can't stand your suffering any more. It destroys me. I'm your friend, for god's sake, you can tell me anything. I want to understand. What troubles you so? Why so silent, alone in your pain? I'm not a doctor, I'm not a psychiatrist, but I think I can help you, protect you. I'm with you all the way. As long as I'm here, no one will hurt you. You must trust me. Talk to me, please . . ."

It came out all in one breath, with all the strength of desperation. When I stopped, I was breathless. Bud was stunned. His eyes, serious up to now, took on an expression more terrible than I had ever seen. He took a few deep breaths, like someone emerging from the water after a long dive. Getting hold of himself he seized my two hands in his and squeezed them with all his strength. Then, firmly, but also in a monotone, he said, "I hope your spirit will always be in accord with your being and comfortably installed in a strong and well-balanced body."

I was speechless. I wasn't sure I had caught the meaning of these seemingly harmless words, but his eyes were filled with the effort it had cost him and his voice was like that of a stranger.

In the form of a wish for me, he had tried to express his own torment. It showed his awareness of his struggle against the unknown, uncontrollable, and probably contradictory forces that tortured his mind, a struggle that had already inflicted its damage on his body. He let me glimpse the reality that he hid in shame, preferring alienation to inquisition. He had proven his lucidity. His was a combat between physical and psychological forces. Did this struggle really merit the name of schizophrenia? And did such a diagnosis, in a man of his creative genius, really entail hospitalization, electroshock, and high-dose narcoleptics?

I had sworn that as long as I lived it would never happen again. Bud's confession had sealed a pact between us. Now there were two of us who knew. He could count on me. Bud had given me the greatest proof of his affection and trust. From that day on, he rarely called me Francis any more, but generally "brother."

I don't remember whether we finished the bottle. The emotion was so intense it wiped out all else. But I had managed to force an entry into his world, to drive a wedge into his private space from which he would never exclude me again. I had stumbled on the best therapeutic tool—sincerity and total friendship.

A psychiatrist and jazz fan I had met at a club once gave me a talk on schizophrenia that was most discouraging. "Bud's case is a perfect example of classic schizophrenia. You won't get anywhere with him. At this stage, it's irreversible."

What could such words mean to me? He had never met Bud. All he knew was the poppycock reported by the press. When he told me I was powerless against the disease, all it did was to give me an imperative need to prove to the world that he was wrong.

From this event forward, Bud talked more openly with me. He no longer avoided my questions, but did his best to give straightforward answers. This was something new for all of us. Even Nicole was surprised at first. However, it didn't satisfy everyone, for when it came to other people's questions, he was as mute as before. In order to get an answer, I usually had to repeat the question myself. For the other American musicians in Paris, this was both irritating and frustrating, all the more so as Bud kept his innocent smile the whole time. I felt a lot of jealousy or resentment during that period from people whose main problem was that they couldn't hold a candle to his genius. Seeing him miserable and constantly in trouble lowered him in their eyes, and actually, comparing his existence to their own helped to bring him back to a set of human dimensions more acceptable to them.

Our new home was coming along nicely. Top priority was given to the soundproofing, so essential to our way of life. Workmen were around constantly but no one minded, as long as we were together. We lived in a state of enchantment that our dream was coming true so fast.

Bud took an interest in everything that was going on. We had built a huge fireplace and kept a fire going all the time. This became his favorite spot. From his armchair he could survey the whole room, watching as the various components of our life were installed one after the other: records, tapes, tape recorder, and record player were all in a wall unit behind the grand piano. We had our meals by candlelight at a large farmhouse-style dining table. Ever since the move, Bud seemed to be in good spirits.

Johnny Griffin had taken a room on the fifth floor of a hotel just next door and during his long stay in Paris he too became part of the family. To visit us, all he had to do was climb over the railing that separated his balcony from ours. I shudder to think of these acrobatic feats, especially when he'd had a few too many. Johnny's whiskey consumption would have put an Irishman to shame. I began to believe the expression made famous by Raymond Le Sénéchal, "plastered but lucid." Later on, Art Taylor and Dexter Gordon moved in, too, and the Hotel Rotary, Rue Vintimille, became the haunt of American musicians passing through Paris. Bud's presence was like a magnet and the quarter became a hotbed of jazz.

MOMENT'S NOTICE
(Recorded in Paris, 1960 [Mainstream])

O   ur friend, the guitarist René Thomas, an unconditional ad-
        mirer of Bud, was another of the regulars at our house. He
too lived nearby, at the Hotel Monnier. René was a tireless worker
who practiced scales all day long. So as not to disturb others he
stuffed Kleenex under the strings to deaden the sound. Bud often
asked him to play his own compositions, but he also played pieces by
Monk, Parker, and of course Bud, to whose melodies he was one of
the few who could do justice. One frequent request was a favorite of
René's, "Moment's Notice."

Bud liked it so much that one day René offered to teach it to him.
Bud sat down at the piano and watched closely as René showed him
the chords, as Bud had requested. Usually so quick, Bud made him
repeat the harmonic structures, as if to make the pleasure last. René
was in seventh heaven. At last, Bud played it through perfectly, looking René in the eye the entire time. The lesson had been long and I
had never seen René so happy. He kept whispering to us emotionally,
"I can't get over it. I've just taught Bud Powell a piece. What a gas!"
Professional difficulties had made René cautious with money and he
was not known for his prodigality. That day, however, in a burst of
generosity, he announced, "Okay everyone, tonight it's on me!"

"What did he say?" asked Bud.

"He says he's buying dinner tonight."

"Don't say a word, Bud," came one snide reaction. "It's a miracle!"

"Tell him to get some strawberry ice cream," said Bud, who was in
one of his ice cream phases.

Ignoring all the cracks about his sudden unaccustomed generosity,
René went out shopping and came back laden with food. We all ate
well and throughout the meal he remained attentive to Bud's every
whim. But as the evening went on, René's face grew longer. His good
humor vanished and his expression became positively glum. He stood
up and started pacing around the room. I began to get worried and
went to see what was wrong. He looked at me helplessly and, after a
long silence, confessed in a strained voice, "You know, Francis, that
tune, 'Moment's Notice,' that I showed Bud this afternoon? Well, I

just remembered. It was Bud who first taught it to me, just after he came to Paris, when we played together at the Caméléon."

From his seat, Bud was watching us, an innocent smile on his lips. No one spoke. The moment was full of pathos. In the following nights at the Blue Note René played "Moment's Notice" accompanied by Bud, who kept giving him mischievous looks.

Another guitarist, Elek Bacsik, came to play in alternation with Bud. Between sets, we usually sat at our table at the back, near the coat-check. But for this set, Bud led me to a table up front. He watched Elek carefully, saying, "Listen, Francis. Listen carefully. This guy's got some nice chord changes, good harmonies."

Simone Chevalier, who married our friend Jean-Louis Ginibre, the editor-in-chief of *Jazz Magazine*, was an excellent singer, by far the best at the Blue Note. One night, Bud seemed surprised to see her. "Simone, what a surprise! What brings you here tonight?"

"I'm singing, Bud. What else?"

"Oh, you're singing. Who with?"

Slightly embarrassed, she replied that she had been singing with him every night for the past few weeks.

In the traditional role of the sexy vocalist, Nancy Holloway also made a hit at the club. Bud accompanied her and, to keep the tempo, he followed her swinging hips more closely than Kenny's hi-hat cymbals.

After Nancy came another singer, Bobby Parker. She was a pretty girl who adored Billie Holiday and always began her show with a ballad in the style of Billie, full of heartrending intonations and in perfect control. But as she sang, she had an unfortunate tendency to speed up the tempo and the number usually ended in total chaos. Despite that, Samson François came faithfully to hear her. He found her charming and consoled her every night after the show, drying her tears.

Mae Mercer also sang at the Blue Note. Her style was closer to blues than to the music played in that temple of bop. Mae had an impressive physique, tall and muscular, with a masculine quality in her movements that shocked Bud each time. "Tell me, Francis, do you think she's really a girl?"

Her special charm found favor with a young, somewhat effeminate-looking bassist who didn't hide his fondness for her. One night, while Mae was singing, he stopped at our table to say hello. I wanted to tell him that Zoot Sims was in the audience and decided to make a joke of it, saying, "If you can guess what famous saxophonist is here tonight, you win a night with Mae Mercer."

"And if I lose?" he asked.

"Two nights with Mae Mercer," snapped Bud.

Naturally, Zoot sat in with Bud, Pierre, and Kenny, and when I closed my eyes I sometimes thought I was hearing Lester. I suppose it was his way of paying tribute in front of that legendary porkpie hat, in the famous photo by Herman Leonard that was nailed to the wall next to the bandstand.

THELONIOUS
(Recorded in Paris, December 17, 1961 [Columbia])

Kenny Clarke, one of the regulars of the Blue Note, was both the most charming and most secretive of men. I questioned him endlessly about the early days of bop. He had been one of its first creators and had a host of stories to tell, which he related during the breaks in his soft melodious voice. The heroes of these anecdotes were usually Thelonious and Bud. Kenny and Thelonious had been close friends since Minton's. At that time, they used to leave the club and walk to the subway together after the last set. To enjoy Klook's company till the last possible moment, Thelonious would wait with him on his side of the platform until the train pulled into the station. Then he would sprint across the track, jumping over the electrified third rail, right in front of the oncoming train. Each night he would cut it a little closer, like some daredevil stuntman, just to impress Kenny, his audience of one.

Of Bud's few real friends, Thelonious was the most loyal, the one who was always around when times were hard. To illustrate the mutual esteem of Bud and Thelonious, Kenny told me this story of their early days at Minton's:

Thelonious was the regular pianist at the club. One night he invited Bud to join the rhythm section consisting of Oscar Pettiford and Kenny. Monk introduced Bud and asked him to play. Some of the customers were displeased and the manager, Teddy Hill, demanded that Thelonious come back. Enraged, Monk thundered, "Are you deaf? Don't you hear what he's doing? If you don't listen to him, I won't play any more!" And they listened, to the point where he became one of the regulars, just like Charlie Christian, Charlie Parker, Fats Navarro, and Dizzy Gillespie.

Another great friend of Bud's, Sonny Stitt, dropped in when he came to Paris for several concerts. They hadn't seen each other in five years but their meeting was pure surrealism. Sonny came in and, without any preamble, announced that he had learned self-hypnosis and if he hypnotized himself his left leg would be heavier than his right one. Suiting action to words, he lay down on the floor and as Bud looked on with a fascinated frown, he closed his eyes and started to breathe slowly and deeply, having told Bud to check it out in about three minutes. When the allotted time had elapsed, Johnny Griffin, another witness to the experiment, told Bud to go check. Bud lifted Sonny's left leg, cautiously, as if handling a poisonous serpent. Then he lifted the right leg, once again the left leg, and finally admitted that he really couldn't feel any difference. They tried the experiment several times that day. In the end Sonny told Bud that if he didn't believe it, he could try it on himself. Bud later did and fell asleep for real!

When Sonny came back the following days, the main subject of interest was music. He wanted to hear Bud play and Bud struck his usual bargain, "Okay, but first let me have some *vin rouge*."

At that time Bud was playing Monk's repertory almost exclusively. He played majestically, letting the piano vibrate to the limits of its resonance. What a contrast with the frenzied rhythms he had recorded with Sonny, Curly Russell, and Max Roach in 1949! Bud seemed to want to transmit another message to his old friend, the calm and serene contemplations of an artist who has come to the point where he now wants to say only the essential—uncontrived beauty, art without artifice. The rapt faces of the listeners showed their deep emotion and immense respect.

Bud was playing regularly at the Blue Note and had become its star attraction. His name in giant letters out front attracted the who's who of the jazz world. With the first poignant notes, he could create an atmosphere. The public was mesmerized by his fingers. When he played a ballad, some people would try to dance, to the dirty looks of the fans and the waiters who stopped them immediately. "No, no, you don't dance to the music of Bud Powell."

The Blue Note waiters were not necessarily fans, but they all respected Bud and were all touched, at one time or another, by his music. All but one, that is, who was the cause of an unfortunate incident. Bud was always trying to scrounge a drink and one night (when I wasn't there, of course) the waiter in question, thinking he'd have a little fun, asked him to dance the twist in exchange for a beer. Bud would do anything for a drink and, awkwardly, he did a few movements of that vulgar dance that was all the rage that year, for the amusement of a few idiotic onlookers. When I learned what had happened I invited the waiter to step outside for some fresh air and strenuously advised him never to do it again. That was the last time Bud made a spectacle of himself. The customers were usually nice to Bud, too nice sometimes. They treated him like a child, not meaning to offend, but because they didn't know any better. His relations with the staff and technicians were generally excellent, though he was always more distant, even defensive, with the club owners. On several occasions I remember a waiter phoning me at home, without telling the boss, so that I could come and stave off some problem that was brewing.

I'd drive Bud to the Blue Note and usually listen to the first set. When my work permitted, I stayed until the end and we went home together. If I couldn't stay, one of the waiters would call a taxi, paying the driver in advance to take Bud home. To avoid losing his key, Bud wore it on a string attached to the inside pocket of his jacket. In fact, it was the only thing he had in his pockets, as Buttercup still kept all his papers.

I worried whenever I had to leave Bud alone, for there were always customers, unaware of his weakness, who would ply him with drink—some just for fun, others to get him to stay a while at their table. One drink was all it took. When he got up, his step was uncertain. The other musicians looked on concerned, knowing where it could lead if he went on drinking.

If we left together, we would go for long walks through the silent streets. Sometimes Dexter Gordon came with us and I can remember his warm and resonant voice echoing through the silent streets. He walked on one sidewalk and Bud on the other, while I took the middle of the street. Dexter didn't speak to Bud. He sang, in a perfect imitation of Billy Eckstine's languorous vibrato. Bud laughed till he cried. We wandered aimlessly. Time didn't matter. I remember those moments as something unreal. Dexter was blessed with eternal youth. Even close to death, nothing ever eroded his natural good humor. Bud's and Dexter's language, like their music, had a special sound, a kind of swing based on an inner tempo. They had recorded together very early. I owned the records of the Savoy sessions of January 1946, and I had listened to them until I wore out the grooves. It seemed inconceivable to see them there together, like two kids, strolling through the night.

During that period at the Blue Note, a tall elegant figure would come in two or three times each night, at precisely the same times. Smiling from ear to ear, he would watch Bud in fascination, never speaking a word while Bud played. It was Joe Turner, who was playing at another Champs-Elysées club, the Calavados, just a few minutes from the Blue Note. Between sets he would hurry over to catch Bud. This great stride pianist, who had known Jelly Roll Morton and

James P. Johnson, who had been friends with Fats Waller, Art Tatum, and Erroll Garner, was not to be classified among the fossils.

The great musicians who came through Paris never failed to stop in and see Bud. There were many of them, for in this period Paris was the jazz hub of Europe. Among those who came to the Blue Note were Stan Getz, Cannonball Adderly, Erroll Garner, Don Byas, Sonny Rollins, Count Basie, Carmen McRae, and Earl Hines. Oscar Peterson came too, which reminds me of a rather strange anecdote.

Bud was in good shape at the time, playing with a lot of verve, his inspiration sublime, giving full play to his emotions. He was just finishing the set with "All God's Chillun Got Rhythm" in a brilliant tempo, with a heady swing and mind-blowing ideas, when Oscar Peterson arrived. The friends who were with him (and who shall remain nameless, out of kindness) started urging him to go on right after Bud. No sooner had the piano stopped vibrating than Oscar was sitting down and, with all the delicacy you can imagine, he launched into "All God's Chillun" at twice the tempo. The audience was unmoved by this rendition, whose speed of execution was matched only by the banality of its ideas. Bud watched the cannonball whiz by, but I could see he didn't like it and was revving up his own engine once again. Oscar finished his number with a smile full of false modesty, to the applause of his cohorts. Bud sat motionless, gazing into space, consternation on his face. It took all of Ben's powers of persuasion to get him back to the piano. From the opening bars of his intro, I knew Bud was going to show the audience the difference between speed and haste. The bold, inspired phrasing, the sound of the instrument being played to its full technical potential, filled the room. Suddenly, Oscar was in a big hurry to pay the bill. Bud hadn't reached his second chorus before Oscar and his fans were out the door and gone.

I enjoyed doing blindfold tests on our friends, mainly on musicians who were very sure of themselves, making comments like, "That's a white man playing for sure," or "Anyone can tell he's black!" I liked playing, for example, a recording of Toshiko Akiyoshi with the trio of Ray Brown, Ed Thigpen, and Herb Ellis. Even though the rhythm section was not ideal for the Powell style, Toshiko showed in that record that she was without a doubt Bud's most faithful disciple at that time. It fooled a lot of listeners, including Dexter Gordon, Johnny Griffin, and Hank Mobley, who were astounded when told who it was.

Bud himself was surprised to learn that this crashing music, full of swing, came out of the nimble fingers of a fragile Japanese girl. It really became clear to him only when she came to visit with her husband Charlie Mariano.

Everyone was shy and we ate with hardly a word, staring at our plates. Toshiko was overcome with emotion. Bud, who was sitting beside her, suddenly broke the strained silence. He took her hand, looked straight into her eyes, and said, in a solemn voice, "You know, you're the greatest woman jazz pianist in the world." Toshiko lowered her eyes to his hand with a strange expression and two large tears rolled down her cheeks. Then as we all looked on, deeply moved, she began to sob. She withdrew her hand, left the table, and went to huddle against the piano, as we all sat there, silent and motionless.

Maurice Cullaz told the story that Bud had once asked Toshiko if it bothered her that her husband was American.

"No," said Toshiko, "what's wrong with that?"

"But what about Hiroshima?" said Bud.

Bud didn't beat about the bush when he wanted to know something. He didn't speak often, but his remarks could be surprisingly to the point.

Toshiko had cut her first record thanks to Oscar Peterson. During a tour of Japan, he and his musicians had gone out on the town after a concert. At the suggestion of local journalists, they went to hear a girl who they said played a wild piano in the style of Bud Powell. Later, Oscar got Norman Grantz to record her with his rhythm section. It was the beginning of her international career.

Since she was in Paris at the same time as Oscar, whom she hadn't seen for ages, she wanted to go to his hotel and suggested we go with her. She phoned from the lobby to ask if he could see her and mentioned that Bud was there too. Oscar answered that he didn't have the time, which elicited a bomb from Bud, another of his rare but pointed comments. "Let's go. Mr. Peterson has got a swelled head!"

It was not like Bud to criticize other musicians. When asked his opinion about anyone he invariably answered, "He's okay." That was his minimal response. If he really thought a musician was any good, he'd say, "Yeah, he can play." Only Tatum and Monk were entitled to superlatives.

To my mind, one of Bud's soundest trios was with Pierre Michelot and Kenny Clarke. Their playing came together into a perfect whole, flowing and powerful—we would have liked to hear it go on forever. There's no doubt about it, the drum style that best suited Bud and all the great players of the bop era was invented by the drummer who was among the closest to Bud, Kenny Clarke.

Just before they stopped playing together, a peculiar ambience had developed and Kenny seemed to get a kick out of maintaining it. The affair started one night during the break. Bud's drinks were doled out by the staff and he sat nursing his coke, convinced it had rum in it, as Jacques the bartender had positively assured him. In fact, Jacques would simply take the cork from the bottle of rum and run it around the rim of the glass. Kenny, who was watching from the bar, swooped down and tried to swipe Bud's drink. Taken by surprise, Bud pushed him away roughly. Kenny, still fooling around, got into a boxer's crouch, threw a left hook, then a right that caught Bud square on the chin. Naturally, he had pulled his punch, making it harmless, but Bud, startled by his speed, jumped back and stood there glaring at him in unspoken reproach. Kenny went back to join Pierre on the bandstand for the second set, but Bud absolutely refused to play. I had no choice but to take him home.

On the way back home, he poured out all his anger against Kenny, refusing to believe me when I said he was only kidding. Bud swore it was a hard right to the chin and he'd have been knocked out if he hadn't ducked so quickly. The next morning, far from forgetting the incident, he was more outraged than ever, describing the scene all over again, and waiting for my reaction.

"Well, brother? What are you going to do about Kenny?"

"There's nothing to do, Bud. It was just a joke."

"No, man. He tried to knock me out!"

"Bud, he was just making believe. I'm sure of it."

"You're not gonna do anything?"

"What do you want me to do?"

"I want you to go punch him back."

"Are you kidding, Bud? I can't do that!"

"Yes you can. You go beat him up!"

Nothing I said could make him change his mind and my amused expression made him even madder. He wouldn't go back to play unless I promised to teach Kenny a lesson that very day. The whole thing was getting out of hand.

That afternoon, from a client's office, I phoned Kenny to explain what had happened and to tell him my plan. He agreed to go along with it. When I got home and told Bud it was all taken care of, his face lit up. He made me repeat the story again and again, chuckling with pleasure. That evening when we walked into the Blue Note, Bud marched up to Kenny and looked him boldly in the eye. Kenny feigned a frightened expression, put his hand to his jaw, and exclaimed, "Oh, man, what a punch he gave me! What a punch!"

Bud looked instantly sympathetic, almost protective, as he asked him for all the details of the payoff once again.

Kenny kept our bargain and the trio played that night. Bud never forgot the incident and liked to tell the story, complete with gestures, to all who would listen. I was glad it had worked out that way. I admired Kenny's muscles on the drums, but I wouldn't have liked to measure myself against him in a fistfight.

People often found Bud's childlike behavior endearing, but once again it made me think how little he really knew of the adult world.

During his French pastry craze Bud made frequent incursions into the pastryshop across the street. With complete disregard for the amenities, he would stroll in, ignoring the customers on line, go up to the window where the cakes were on display and simply help himself to whatever he fancied. Then, with a charming *"Au revoir, Madame"* he would exit smiling, his mouth full of cake and his fingers full of whipped cream. When the shopkeeper presented me with the bill, she would say with an amused air, "Your friend was here again. He's very sweet. I'm so pleased he likes my cakes. You can tell him the chocolate éclair was on me."

His curious ways never shocked the neighbors. On the contrary, all the shopkeepers were fond of him, and the owner of the nearest bistro, Les Roses, nicknamed him *"l'homme heureux,"* the happy guy.

AUDREY

(Recorded in New York, August 14, 1953 [Blue Note])

T he next Christmas was the first in our new apartment and we decided to celebrate it in the company of our good friends. More than just a Christmas dinner, it was to be a real celebration that lasted three days and three nights. Bud followed the preparations with great interest. There were Roger, Vincent, Jackie, Mic, and their girl-friends, the old bunch of friends, united in common loyalty and generosity. What we bought for three days could have fed a starving village in China!

We bought fine wines, and, as we opened the bottles and put them aside, Bud looked on in amazement. This was incomprehensible and even a little barbaric to him. We tried to explain that the proper temperature brought out all the flavor of the wine just as the proper notes created a perfect harmony. His eyes sparkled as he listened and he watched as expert hands prepared the meats and salads, sauces and cakes.

The festive dinners we held regularly with friends were an opportunity for us to relax somewhat the stringent rules we had to observe for Bud. Yet wine, the essential ingredient to accompany the good food, had to be doled out sparingly. We couldn't let him overdo it. We all did our best to distract him from his obsession and he went along with good grace, knowing that eventually he'd get a drink. Aside from these special occasions, my warnings against drinking were repeated like a litany. He would seem aware of the dangers of drink but in the end would refuse to admit the obvious. Sometimes he'd become angry with himself, recognizing that I wasn't exaggerating and that everything I said was logical and in his best interests. Once I told him that my father, too, had trouble holding his liquor and it seemed in some way comforting to him to know that someone close to me was in the same position as himself. From then on, my words seemed to carry more weight.

This evening in particular we had to keep our eyes open, and with subtle humor and tact the friends managed to keep Bud in good shape the whole time. At a blissful moment after dinner, with a fire crackling in the fireplace, Bud suddenly stood up and walked over to the piano without a word. Sensing what was about to happen, I sat down near him to savor the moment. After a long pause, he sat down with slow and careful movements, looked gravely round the room, where everyone had grown silent, and announced ceremoniously, "On this Christmas of 1962, I would like to play a ballad called 'My Devotion,' dedicated to my wife, Audrey Hill."

He had never before mentioned her name or made any allusion to a wife. He repeated the title, then said the dedication over again in a voice filled with pathos, as if recalling heartbreaking memories. The first harmonies rose, heartbreaking and majestic, slow in the extreme, filling all the space and sweeping over us. I held my breath to keep from breaking the spell. Our eyes filled with tears. Bud watched us closely as he played, as if to assure himself that his message was reaching our hearts. The message seemed to say, "Beauty is so simple, don't you see? The secret is to tell the world your love is boundless, yet one must reserve the right not to be hurt too much." It was sheer bliss. Oh, Bud!

Bud was a magician. With him, everything had another dimension, graced with the simplicity of his spirit. He had changed our world, and our every gesture gained in quality, in purity. I felt I was becoming better for it.

If we got along so well with Bud it was because we were on the same wavelength. His need for friendship, warmth and affection was heartbreaking, almost painful in its desperation. When Bud loved someone, he was all tenderness, all pathos. He had no words to express his feelings. He would just take your hand and hold it tight in his for a long, long time, as if the physical contact reassured him. "Do you like me, Nicole? Do you like me, Mic? Do you like me, brother?" The eternal question, endlessly repeated with an inexpressible longing.

Never before had I felt for anyone such absolute love, to the point of making all other sentiments negligible. True friendship and love have this in common, that they make possible a total commitment to the other, to the friend, without a second thought. This feeling is the privilege of the absolute friendship that bound us to each other in an indifferent world.

If I have finally decided, after long hesitation and much reflection, to share these thoughts about my years with Bud, it is to show the stupendous power of such feelings. I think Bud knew what he was doing when he allowed himself to open up to me, just as he seemed to know, without ever questioning me, what would become of all his music I so relentlessly recorded. The fact that he encouraged me to do so made me even more certain of the importance of capturing the precious sounds on my tapes. It is the great privilege of friendship to act in such a way that outsiders, judging in haste, might deem wrong, but to know that it is justified by the profound motivation, unguessed and unfathomed by anyone else. Like the clairvoyant he often seemed to be, Bud knew from the outset what would be the fate of the treasures he gave to my recorder—another proof, if one is needed, of his lucidity.

Our evening ended in a state of ecstasy. Bud had held up all night, no more drunk than the rest of us. It hardly mattered, though, for our bedrooms were right there and, after a good night's sleep, the festivities continued the next morning.

A few days later I was listening to the tapes of that evening and heard again the name of Audrey Hill. I raised the question cautiously. "You know, Bud, you surprised us with that dedication. I vaguely knew you'd once been married . . . but . . ."

"Yeah, a long time ago. Audrey was white, you know."

"What happened? Didn't you stay together?"

"The marriage was symbolic. We never really lived together. We were separated right away."

"What do you mean?"

"We were separated right away. . . ."

He looked so miserable that I let the matter drop. The more I learned of Bud's past the more I understood the depths of his unhappiness.

During the days we spent together, as he watched me work, I would often turn the conversation to his past. I felt he wanted to talk about it, to try to explain it to himself. Sometimes, as he spoke, he would find some justification for his misfortune, and it seemed to relieve him. I was very pleased to be able to provoke these deep reflections by catching him at unexpected moments. I continued to draw him out, to try to free him from the protective shell that hampered him so.

Our friends had adopted Bud for better or worse. Nothing he did surprised or shocked them. A child could pull the wool over his eyes but, when pushed too far, he could come up with a pertinent crack, as in this incident with Ray Charles.

Bud had gone backstage to see Ray after a concert. He came up to him, gave him his hand, and said, "Hi Ray, it's Bud."

"Hey Bud! How ya doin'?"

"Okay, Ray. How are you?" And then, in his inimitable fashion, he blurted out, "Tell me, Ray, are you really blind?"

Ray was staggered, but after a minute he answered nonchalantly, "Nah, Bud. That's just for laughs!"

When his surprise wore off, Bud was first incredulous, then obviously stung, and shot back, "Well, you sure do look it!" And he turned on his heels and stalked off.

One night, Bud arrived at the Blue Note and immediately spotted an American soldier, a colossus with an army crew cut, standing stiffly at the bar, obviously dead drunk. The American Army was learning the lethal effects of French 90-proof brandy.

The bartender was serving him another shot as Bud watched with great interest. The soldier tried time and time again to pick up the glass but couldn't manage it. Finally, he managed to hold on to the glass, and with the stiff movement made famous by Erich Von Stroheim, he downed the drink in a single gulp and fell flat on his back.

Bud looked on admiringly, horrified as well. Like lightning, he stepped over the body, banged his fist on the bar, and ordered, "Same thing!" The customers all around burst out laughing, but Bud remained serious.

Bud's retorts could be disconcerting in their logic. One night Gil Evans came to congratulate him after a particularly brilliant concert. "Bud," he said, "you're the greatest pianist in the world."

"Oh yeah? Well then, find me a job!"

Another story, in a surrealist mode, shows how his mind worked. This one was told to me by Randi Hultin: "One night, Baron Timmy Rosenkrantz, a great jazz fan, ran into Bud in front of Birdland in New York. Probably hoping to strike up a conversation, the baron asked him for the time. Unimpressed by this opener, Bud looked him up and down, and walked away without answering. Four years later they met again. Remembering the embarrassing incident, the baron didn't say a word. Bud came up to him and said, 'Hey, Baron! It's four fifteen.'"

Another story, recounted to me by my friend Henrik Iversen, head of Danish TV, underlines once again Bud's surrealist spirit. Invited to Henrik's house, Bud calmly sipped a drink, whilst browsing through the books in the library. Suddenly he pulled out *Romeo and Juliet*, naturally in Danish, and, pretending to read, started to rattle off the text in English, not forgetting to turn the pages.

Shortly after this display, which had somewhat surprised his entourage, he begged for some manuscript paper from Henrik, and asked his permission to withdraw for a while to write two compositions, which, according to him were weighing on his mind. Bud retired for a while, to return joyously brandishing the score. Henrik, equally happy, rushed toward him and grabbed the sheets of music which Bud held out. Then, disconcerted, he said: "But . . . Bud . . . there is nothing on these pages—they're empty!"

Bud seemed surprised, then quickly took back the score and examined it carefully. Finally he assured him with great conviction, "But it's all there . . . between the lines."

There are also anecdotes concerning George Shearing, who liked to tease Bud. He would tell him, for example, that he wasn't really blind, he was just pretending so people would be nice to him. One night between sets, Bud took George out for a little stroll, then walked off and left him alone in the middle of Fifth Avenue traffic. He watched, from the sidewalk, heedless of his cries for help, as George flailed his arms and didn't dare make a move. Was Bud really trying to get at the truth or did he just want to play a trick on George?

Many of these stories have a grain of cruelty. Musicians can be cruel, particularly when they feel they have scores to settle. For one thing, Bud didn't like the fact that Shearing was his "permanent replacement" at Birdland each time he couldn't make it and, for another, he didn't appreciate what he took to be pure imitation of his programs and his style. Johnny Griffin reports that one night, fed up watching George play *"à la Bud,"* Bud waited until George was leaving the stage behind his wife, then stuck out his foot. George fell flat on his face. On a similar occasion, Bud went up to him while he was playing and knocked on his head like he was at the door, asking, "Anybody home?"

Nasty? Yes, but no more so than Shearing himself, who was once scheduled to follow Thelonious Monk on a TV show. Monk was finishing his number and when the technicians told him he could enter the studio, he said, "No, I'll wait till they've finished tuning the piano."

As I got to know Bud, I felt that his character was not always in tune with the level of his genius and that he was often troubled by the demands his creative powers made on him. His surprising behavior and curious actions masked his personality. He often shocked or at least disconcerted those closest to him, who were hurt at having their genuine friendship rejected. How can this attitude of his be interpreted? Wasn't it a behavior cultivated as a natural defense, an ultimate reflex to protect his perpetual toil? In his silence and his apparent idleness, it always struck me that Bud's mind was mobilized by private and tyrannical occupations. His private life was thus dissociated from his music, the former given less importance than the latter, to which all else was sacrificed.

Speaking of the search for solitude reminds me of a story about Charlie Parker. An acquaintance of Parker's was constantly hanging around, trying to be with him. One day Bird told him that he no longer wanted to have close friends, for he was bitter about friendship. Pressed for an explanation, he said a friend had once played a dirty trick on him, something really unforgivable: he had the nerve to up and die on him!

Bud, too, needed this solitude. At the same time it weighed on him. I can still hear his plaintive voice saying, "Francis, I'm nothing but a nomad. I have nothing, no home, no family."

Each time, I replied in all sincerity, "Bud, this is your home. Nicole and I are your family—the real one, the family of the heart."

He would smile then, take my hands in his, and look deep into my eyes. A few seconds later, he would be back in his own private world.

I respected his silences and his meditations. I understood them and even learned some lessons from them. His behavior seemed an expression of the wisdom he had attained in order to survive. The structural equilibrium of his music and the mastery with which he expressed it could only spring from a deep philosophy. Bud had managed to remain himself and save his soul. What mattered for him was to use his exceptional gifts to the fullest. The rest was of little importance. His moral elegance matched his work. By isolating himself from a society increasingly cut off from true values, he managed to accomplish his own miracle. All his life, he developed the faculty of cutting himself off, until the retreat into himself had become natural. In his inner world he could discover the truths of the future.

However, inspiration, knowledge, and hard work are insufficient to explain the absolute mastery of Bud's improvisations. The most striking characteristic of his playing lay in daring to take all risks. His total abandon at the paroxysm of pianistic possibilities leads one to think that he had utterly mastered the art of the trance and could, in that state, reach the heights. This extraordinary energy in support of the most beautiful ideas ever executed on piano was already evident as early as 1946, in "I Want To Be Happy," with Sonny Stitt (on the record *The Bebop Boys*); or the original "Tempus Fugue-it" in 1949 (*The Genius of Bud Powell*); or "All God's Chillun Got Rhythm" and "Move," with Miles Davis and Sonny Stitt, from the 1949 Carnegie

Hall Christmas concert; or, much later, in 1960, "Shawnuff," "Get Happy," and "John's Abbey," with Pierre Michelot and Kenny Clarke. Each is a tour de force concealed by the apparent ease that can only arise from a state of grace. Without resorting to daily practice, Bud was able to summon up his incomparable sound and tremendous energy at the piano when the circumstances required it. In the necessity and exaltation of the moment, he reached the summit of his art.

Here, for example, is an anecdote told to me by Max Roach about Bud's comeback to Birdland in 1949 (after an absence of two years following a psychiatric hospitalization). Oscar Goodstein set up the evening and invited Curly Russell and Max Roach to participate. The club was packed and Bud got an impressive standing ovation, in response to which he launched into "I Want To Be Happy" in a tempo defying the most extreme laws of piano mechanics. By the end of the tune, the audience was on their feet. Every pianist knows what it means to be away from the keyboard for any length of time—much less for two whole years. Yet Bud had an uncanny ability to recover all his means when he needed them. And there was also his amazing memory, only present by fits and starts after the electroshock treatments at Creedmoor.

For once a film about jazz was playing in Paris. It was *The Connection*, a film directed by Shirley Clarke, which dealt with the subject of drug addiction. It featured Jackie McLean's band, which included Freddie Redd, Michael Mattos, and Larry Ritchie. Because of the touchy subject and the miseries it brought to mind, which I feared might arouse bad memories, I thought it best to see it without Bud.

The film was tough, the talk of drugs was crude, and the shadow of Bird floated over the whole production. Bud would surely have been upset by these broken people, each in his own hell waiting for his fix of heroin. I was glad I hadn't taken him along.

When I got home, though, I wanted to talk with him about Jackie McLean, who had impressed me a great deal in the film. I kept trying to find a way to bring up his name without giving myself away. "Bud," I said, "I've been thinking. . . . Do you know, oh, what's his name again?"

"Jackie McLean?" he asked, with his innocent air.

He had come up with the name spontaneously. I hadn't given the slightest clue. For the first time, I realized he had the ability to read my mind and to answer questions before I even asked them. As time went on, such occasions became an everyday occurrence. Bud had the gifts of a medium, with so-called paranormal abilities. His musical inspiration alone was the most significant sign of his extraordinary talents. He was never fooled by false appearances. He could tell real friendship from its counterfeit and had no trouble spotting the phonies who constantly hang around musicians. There were certain arrangements he accepted out of sheer necessity—I'm sure he had no illusions as to their real nature.

Our relationship was founded on trust, sincerity, and the certainty of mutual affection. Bud was quick to feel my every concern, which, more often than not, had to do with the ups-and-downs of his health. His morale was fragile, and periods of euphoria were quickly followed by ones of deep depression with a disturbing regularity. After reading a book on the influence of the planets I became convinced that his mood swings most often corresponded to the phases of the moon.

One evening after dinner, I had put on one of Bud's recordings and, as we listened in the growing darkness, the notes rang out with eerie clarity, sounding almost unreal. All at once, in a voice both worried and admiring, he asked, "Francis, tell me, who's playing?"

I smiled and didn't answer right away, but seeing his anxiety, I finally replied, "Why Bud, it's you. Who else could play like that?"

He stared at me for long minutes as if to make sure I was telling the truth, then stood up, walked to the piano, took hold of the corner of the lid and didn't let go. His back was to us and Nicole looked questioningly at me. When I came up behind him I saw his face reflected in a mirror. His eyes were brimming with tears.

He was holding on to the piano for dear life with all the strength of desperation. Embarrassed to intrude into his privacy, I averted my eyes. I put my hand gently on his shoulder but he didn't budge. That's all I can remember of the incident. But the next day, upset by having glimpsed once again the depth of his disturbance, I checked the calendar and confirmed that it was indeed a full moon. Similar happenings recurred periodically with cyclical constancy. At such times he was overcome with doubt and in constant and feverish need of consolation. We had to protect and reassure him, to remind him he was our dearest friend, our closest kin, for whom we would spare no effort. All his life he had suffered from a lack of love. Yes, he had been admired as an artist, but never loved for himself, as he understood it. He had gradually taken refuge in solitude, refusing all contact, expressing his pain only through his music.

After playing a song at a breathtaking tempo, Bud could go into a gorgeous ballad of heartrending beauty. As he evolved, his music went from the complex to the essential. No musician was ever more absolute or more sincere. One day I hope the whole world will hear "Dusky 'n' Sandy," "I'll Keep Loving You," and "Time Waits." The future of music will be all the better for it.

At the outset of this book I explained that if I waited so long before writing it, it was because I was afraid of being too subjective. I was fifteen when I discovered Bud and his music had given rise to a veritable passion. It was like love at first hearing. I had recognized sounds that were in some way part of my own personal chemistry.

Nothing since then has modified that first emotion or altered the certainty of my feelings. My technical progress has only reinforced my understanding of his conception. Many years have gone by but my innermost conviction is unchanged. Besides, a further study of classical music, a deeper knowledge of Thelonious Monk's music, a discovery of the works of McCoy Tyner, Herbie Hancock, Chick Corea, and Keith Jarrett, and a total commitment to the stupendous production of Bill Evans have only served to bring me closer to Bud, to throw more light on his genius, and to convince me even more of his importance. All these giants borrowed elements, consciously or unconsciously, from his revolutionary material. No pianist today can claim not to be indebted to him, even though some feign ignorance and others use the keyboard like a washboard. Without the slightest doubt, the real leaders, like McCoy Tyner and Herbie Hancock, are the direct heirs of Bud and Bill.

The charges made against Bud are in fact charges against a man who all his life refused corruption, mediocrity, and complacency. His alienation was deliberate. For Bud, music was a matter of life and death—no concessions, no compromise, honesty before all. It is in terms of such high ethics that we must see his personality. He never talked about his work, never explained it; he left us the task of discovering its philosophic message. Only careful listening can reveal its code.

When Bud was scheduled to play the first set, we would arrive at the Blue Note well in advance so he'd have time to relax. The club was empty except for Itla's brother, Jacques, behind the bar. One night we watched as he painstakingly filled bottles marked Bordeaux with cheap red wine we had baptized "the gut-killer." I thought of all the lucky tourists who had come to France to taste all that vintage Bordeaux! Bud was following his every move.

"Watch out," I said, "if you don't behave, they'll give you some."

"Why," he asked, puzzled. "It's wine, isn't it?"

"It's wine all right. But don't pee on your shoes after drinking it. It'll eat a hole right through the leather!"

After the set, we'd go over to the Little Bar on the Rue de Berri where Bud could have a pastry as a reward for his efforts. His favorite was *baba au rhum*, but he would have liked it even better if it was all rum, without the pastry.

At one point, Chet Baker came to play in alternation with Bud. From the first time he played, Chet cast a spell over us all. He was accompanied by Georges Arvanitas, Luigi Trussardi, Daniel Solano, and Luis Fuentes. He placed a chair at stage center and played sitting down. The music was poignantly beautiful and he was totally concentrated.

One night while we were under his charm, Itla, Ben's wife (whom Bud called Hitler), came in, bundled up in her fur coat. She stared at Chet, hunched over on his chair, and, without even pausing to take off her coat, strode to the front of the room, glared at him, then called out to Ben, "What's the meaning of this? Get this guy to stand up! Real professionals play standing up!"

Itla was the real boss and Ben reluctantly carried out her command. Chet came brutally back to reality, the sound stopped and our dreams along with it. He stood up very slowly, signaled the musicians to stop and, without a glance at Itla, walked calmly out of the club, his trumpet on his shoulder, followed by the rest of the group and by the angry customers.

Lester Young got a big kick out of Itla and Jacques, whom he nicknamed "half a motherfucker" in part because of his size but also because, he said, knowing his sister, he was entitled to extenuating circumstances.

THE SCENE CHANGES
(Recorded in New York, December 29, 1958 [Blue Note])

Once again the fortunes of Bud and Buttercup seemed to be taking opposite paths. Bud's health and morale were improving all the time and his last date at the Blue Note had been a big hit. The good news only made Buttercup nastier than ever. Her needling reached new heights, though it no longer seemed to work on Bud. The money she picked up every night, as punctual and as gracious as a tax collector, was not enough to calm her down. She saw Bud escaping from her clutches and feared that his latest successes wouldn't rub off on her. To make matters worse, she could feel that Bud, Nicole, and I had become a close family. Never before had Bud looked her in the eye so confidently. His hangdog look was gone and in its place was a tranquil and philosophic smile.

Over Bud's protests, we kept up our visits with Buttercup in order to avoid a complete break. On our way to the Louisiane we would drive past the palace of the Louvre and Bud never failed to ask, "Hey, how's King Louis doing?" One day, as I was telling him about Louis XIV, we arrived at the Place de la Concorde. It was six o'clock and I was maneuvering through the rush hour traffic when Bud noticed an ice cream vendor at the foot of the Obelisk in the middle of the vast square. He was in his ice cream phase and let out a shout, "Hey brother, look! Let's get some strawberry ice cream."

I was beside myself. I tried to explain how impossible it was with this kind of traffic, but when he had a craving for ice cream, there was no reasoning with him. There was nothing to do but get out of the car and make my way to the ice cream stand, amid the horns of the blocked cars and the insults of the Paris drivers, never known for their kindness or patience. Bud sat calmly eating his double scoop of strawberry, indifferent to the murderous looks all around.

To avoid putting temptation in Bud's path, we continued not to drink in his presence. We hid the liquor bottles among our cleaning products, and sometimes at night we would hear him rummaging through the kitchen cabinets or under the sink. We took the further precaution of marking the bottles with false labels saying poison

161

(complete with skull and crossbones), vinegar, sulphuric acid, kerosene, and the like. Thus, their levels remained intact and so did Bud.

He seemed oblivious to his own self-destruction. He treated his body as if it didn't concern him, as if he saw no relationship between cause and effect. He had horrible memories of his hospitalization, but seemed unaware of what had brought it on.

His teeth were in terrible shape and we planned to have some dental work done, but were waiting for his health to improve before we began. We had also realized that he was not eligible for French medical benefits and had no medical insurance whatsoever.

One evening I took him to the Blue Note, stayed for the first set, then went home to work. At 2 A.M. the phone rang. It was Toshiko, who was at the club with her husband Charlie Mariano. Bud had disappeared during the break. After much searching, he had been located at a bistro on the Rue Colisée. He was in an awful state. Before leaving the club, he had been seen with some young Americans, and he had undoubtedly talked them into giving him some money. The bartender at the bistro confirmed that he had served him two hundred francs worth of scotch. This was far beyond his tolerable dose of two glasses of red wine.

Nicole and I jumped in the car and headed for the Rue Colisée. The sight that met our eyes was worse than we feared. Bud was unrecognizable. His face was puffy and his lips and cheeks were swollen. His eyes looked glassy and dead. His movements were slow and uncoordinated and he could only utter incoherent sounds. He had fallen down in the street and his clothes were spattered with mud. Collapsed on a chair, he couldn't even hold up his head. Toshiko and her husband were helping him to sit up as a small crowd looked on with disdain. He was indeed a grotesque and pitiful spectacle.

I felt broken. I could no longer hide my anguish and my eyes filled with tears. Nicole was sobbing quietly. With one last effort, Bud tried to say something, but all that came out was an incomprehensible gurgle and he fell back against Toshiko, who tumbled down along with him. We had to get him home at once.

Putting him to bed was no easy task for he weighed 190 pounds and was not being cooperative. But as soon as he hit the bed he fell into an exhausted sleep. Nicole and I, despite our weariness, had trouble falling asleep that night.

SO SORRY PLEASE

(Recorded in New York, January 1950 [Verve])

T he next morning Bud was the first one up. He knocked timidly at our bedroom door and then came in—cleaned up and
fully dressed. His face looked tense and his eyes were anxious. I didn't
recognize this look—it contained something grave and highly irregu-
lar. He looked at us without saying a word. And then with immense
sorrow in his eyes, he said in a flat voice, "I never want you to cry because of me. Never ever again."

We were pretty astounded that he should be the one to bring up
last night's drama. "Don't you realize, Bud, how much pain you
caused us? How much we worry when you let yourself go like that?"

"I don't want you to cry any more."

"But Bud, when you hurt yourself, you hurt us too."

"Well then, I promise you I won't take another drink. I swear it,
never again." And there he stood, erect and solemn, waiting. What
could we say? After so many broken promises, we no longer dared to
believe his word.

The day went by normally, though we were still in a state of shock.
I was quite nervous taking him to the Blue Note. Ben was furious
about the night before and everyone maintained a careful silence. I
had some urgent work to do so I went home. I would see Bud when
he came back from the club. That night, he came home right after the
last set. He looked at me as if waiting for approval of his punctuality.
Then he said he wasn't hungry and was going to sleep.

The next day was ordinary as well. After lunch he took his walk
around the neighborhood. He enjoyed sitting on café terraces watching the crowds go by. I was still nervous about these outings. As
usual, he said he was going out and asked me for a little money.
"Okay, Bud, see you later."

When I could, I accompanied him to make sure nothing went
wrong. This time, however, I let him go alone. Determined to see
what would happen, I followed him a few seconds later. As always,
Bud walked slowly, with long strides, his fists clenched, his right arm
swinging. With his cap pulled down on his head, he had the relaxed
look of any other passerby. When he reached Place Clichy, he turned

right and sat down, as if exhausted, in a chair on the terrace of the café La Havane. I stopped at a shop window across the street, keeping an eye on him all the time.

A waiter came out to take his order and I waited, my heart beating. He came back bearing on his tray a large glass full of a glowing pink liquid—miracles never cease!—a strawberry milk. I knew the contents of the shop window by heart by the time Bud called the waiter, paid his bill and sauntered out into the street. I continued to shadow him at a safe distance. He crossed the square and sat down at Le Wepler, another large café. Again I watched in secret and again the waiter appeared with a strawberry milk. By the time the same scenario had been acted out in a third café, I was jubilant, though still keeping my fingers crossed that the miracle would last.

Bud had made a full circle and I realized his walk was over. I rushed home by another route and quickly sat down at my work table. He came in, glanced at my drawing over my shoulder then sat down quietly next to me, looking pleased. I asked no questions and he never spoke of where he'd been. For the next four days I continued to follow him, living through the same fears and the same jubilation.

The courage of his decision was never taken seriously by his entourage. Perhaps they had reasons to be skeptical, but I thought they could at least have shown some outward signs of respect to Bud. Instead they persisted in teasing him, even going as far as initiating tasteless provocations. It was obvious that no one ever believed him. He took it all philosophically, but I could see in his eyes that he was hurt once again.

Now that real dialogue was possible between us, I resolved to go even further. I was grateful that his effort had come out of an authentic consideration for us. Never had he been able to make such a resolution for himself. Now wine became the object of a running joke between us. We started putting a bottle of wine on the table at mealtimes.

"Bud," we would offer, "a little wine with the cheese?"

"No thanks, brother, I don't drink," he would say, with a look of mock indignation and a little half-smile, pleased with his own joke.

What he sought in wine was the effect more than the taste. His friendship for us and his desire not to hurt us were all that could possibly curb his self-destructive behavior. Bud had never accepted his physical limits or the catastrophic effect alcohol had on him. The endless sermons had grown monotonous. He needed to see for himself, which meant drinking again, and he never learned his lesson, as he never associated the result with its cause. Being denied any responsibility, he had been kept in an infantile state. He needed to be taught independence. He had to really *want* to take care of himself again.

A good way to begin was with his financial arrangements. Incredible as it may seem, Bud never saw the color of his money, either in the States or in Europe. Marcel Romano confirmed that since 1957, when he played at the Club Saint Germain, his earnings went to Buttercup. No one ever thought to question the arrangement.

Now, with the change in his behavior, we would attempt a new step forward. After the fifth day of trailing Bud around like a shadow, I decided to stop sneaking around and lay the cards on the table. After dinner, I said very simply, "Bud, I owe you an apology. I doubted your word."

He looked at me in surprise, curious as to what I was getting at.

"I'm ashamed to tell you, but for the past five days I've been following you on your walks. I was worried. I needed to know if you were drinking or not."

"What? You did that?" said Bud with a frown, hiding his evident inner satisfaction with a glower of disapproval.

"Yes, Bud. I was really afraid of what might happen. But now I'm ashamed of myself and I ask you to forgive me."

Bud looked liked a child who has just pulled off a good stunt. And what a stunt it was! Now he could live without constraints, without being watched all the time. We had overcome the last hurdle. I knew only too well the disastrous effects two little glasses of wine could have on him. But I could see that he had stuck to his promise and was stocking up on strawberry milks, and now I could really help him change his life.

Shortly thereafter, I said to Bud at lunch, "Well, if that's the way things are, we're going to settle a problem that's been bothering me for ages."

"What's that?" he asked, intrigued.

"You'll see. Just wait until tonight."

I didn't dare say too much, for fear that my plan might not work.

The salary a person earns is one of his basic human rights. I had in mind to settle the problem of Bud's money without further delay. That night at the Blue Note, I invited Ben Benjamin to our table.

"Ben," I said, "from this night on, and for reasons I will explain later, I would like Bud to be paid in person."

Ben looked at me as if I'd gone berserk and stammered, "But . . .
but . . . that's impossible. You're joking . . . ! You . . . you . . . you're
crazy!"

"No, Ben, I'm not joking. I'm very serious and I know what I'm
talking about."

By now his tone was categorical. "It's out of the question. Just forget about it."

"I thought you trusted me, Ben. Do you think I'd ask this lightly,
without a good reason?"

Poor Ben didn't know what to think. His sharp little eyes looked
into Bud's. Then he played his last card. "It'll be a disaster, Francis.
What will Buttercup say?"

"She has nothing to say. Bud works and he should be paid for it."

"Or else I won't work!" Bud cut in, looking as determined as Ben.

"That's right, or else Bud won't work."

This was the clincher. Ben rolled his eyeballs and gave a large
French shrug. "Okay, Francis. But you tell Buttercup and you take full
responsibility for the consequences."

"It's a deal. Trust me. I have no doubts about it. Bud's a new man."

Bud was overjoyed, though he tried to keep a straight face. Then
he jumped up, turned on his heel and walked off, leaving Ben deep in
thought.

A deal is a deal. The first night of the new arrangement was nerve-
racking. That very night I decided to give Bud more freedom by not
waiting for him. Before leaving, I asked a waiter to call a taxi as usual,
but to let Bud pay for it himself and to phone me when he'd left.
When the waiter called to say Bud was in the cab, I waited with a
pounding heart. At night, it would take no more than ten minutes to
get from the Blue Note to our apartment in Rue de Clichy. I was out
on the balcony precisely ten minutes later when I heard the distinctive sound of a diesel engine and a taxi pulled up out front. I hurried
back to bed, not wanting Bud to see how worried I'd been. I heard a
key in the lock, then silence for a long minute. My heart was pounding and the silence was endless. Finally, there was a little scratch at
my bedroom door.

"Francis, are you asleep, Francis?"

"Uhh . . . no, Bud, . . . uhh . . . not really. . . . Are you okay?"

"Can I come in, please?"

"Sure, baby."

Baby, that favorite word of Johnny Griffin and Babs Gonzales, had
become the term of address of all our close friends. I turned on the

bedside lamp and pretended I'd been asleep. But I couldn't hide my jubilation, for there in the doorway stood Bud wreathed in a triumphant smile, holding up a handful of bills, shaking them at me, all that was left of his meager pay. It was tremendously moving. I bit my lip, not wanting to succumb to the urge to cry. Good God, I kept telling myself, this is actually Bud Powell! I couldn't get over it.

The change in him was spectacular. Every day, he gained assurance and became more interested in everyday affairs. Until then, he hadn't even known how to buy a Métro ticket. Now I intentionally put him in situations where he would have to take some real initiative.

I gave him a wallet to hold the brand new identity papers we'd had made. In the past, Buttercup had always kept his papers, saying he'd only lose them. Without papers, it was inevitable that he'd be picked up by the police at any identity check. When I think of the problems he might have avoided if he'd carried even a photocopy of his passport! Every morning he would carefully slip his money into his new wallet. It was such an ordinary gesture, but it seemed so solemn when he did it. What a great change it meant to him. Buttercup and all those other birds of prey had cashed in on all his money unscrupulously for so long a time!

Now, every night, Bud took his taxi alone and came home without a hitch, as punctual as a banker. If we went to bed before he returned we left him a cold meal and a note saying how we'd spent the evening and what we had planned for the next day. When I got up in the morning and quietly checked his room, he'd be sleeping like a baby. On his night table was a growing pile of money, orderly piles of coins and banknotes that he took out of his wallet every day.

We had a little notebook in which we kept track of Bud's earnings. They were ridiculously low, considering that he was the main attraction for the customers. His fifty francs a night, the least of any of the musicians, had been set arbitrarily years before and was presented as a favor when the club took him back. From this measly sum they deducted the taxi fare (or two on days when I couldn't drive him to work), two packs of cigarettes, and even the matches, advertising giveaways! That didn't leave much, but he still tried to put aside some savings, besides assuring the support of Buttercup's son Johnny. Buttercup continued to send us all the bills concerning Johnny's expenses, as she had done in the past through Oscar Goodstein, Bud's lawyer Maxwell Cohen, and others. Now she sent the bills for Johnny as well as a multitude of others directly to Bud, some extremely farfetched, all hastily scrawled on bits of paper. Bud would look them over angrily and then he would turn them over to me. It wasn't hard to detect when she was cheating. A phone call to the alleged creditor sufficed to confirm our doubts and we would simply ignore these items, limiting the expenses to those that really were for Johnny.

Bud was relearning adult life. This is hard to explain to those who didn't know him, to those who never saw how this man lived. His musical genius and his infantile behavior created an ambiguity that seemed strange even to me, and I of course knew him intimately for a number of years. His childlike naiveté always remained, but his dependent state had been deliberately reinforced by the constant refrain of, "You play the piano. We'll look after the rest."

When he first started playing with Cootie Williams's band in 1939, he was only fifteen and his father officially entrusted him to Cootie's care. Many years later his father told me that it was at that time Bud first came into contact with alcohol and marijuana. The consequences were catastrophic from the first and were ignored by all those around him. This was the start of a process that would lead to his repeated hospitalizations and ultimately to the loss of his rights. Through it all his genius remained, and they kept on saying, "Just play the piano. We'll look after the rest." They even started saying, "You'd better not even try to look after the rest." If Bud made an unexpected move there were always new reprisals, even commitment in state hospitals. What could he do, the "presumed incompetent," but to submit?

Here at last was a possibility for Bud to begin rebuilding his life. Though inadequate from a financial viewpoint, it was more honorable than it had been before. Through force of circumstance, I now became involved in matters far removed from those that had made me take an interest in him. I tried to be discreet, but my position was not an easy one. In the realm of music, Bud was my model, my master. This rescue process with a person of his stature posed questions of conscience. How far to go? What ambiguity existed for the critical eyes of outsiders! I was sure that Bud had to learn to be a responsible adult again. I never thought of myself as correcting a deficiency, but rather as righting a wrong, giving him the means to undo all the harm that had been done to him: the alienation of an artist in a most perfidious world.

While the basics of daily life were of little interest to him, he could be completely demoralized by something as inconsequential as losing his cap or his beret. It didn't matter if we were in a hurry to leave, the cap had to be found right then. During our outings in my little convertible, losing the cap in a gust of wind was nothing less than a catastrophe, particularly if the car behind us had the misfortune to run over the precious object. In the car, therefore, he got in the habit of pulling the cap well down on his head. We once suggested jokingly that it would be safer to turn it backwards in the manner of bicycle racers. He flatly refused, giving us a dirty look that made it clear that this was no joking matter. Whenever I took a turn a bit sharply, like a racing driver, he would grab hold of his cap as he glared over at me, half angry, half amused.

"Not bad, eh? Are you having fun, Bud?"

He would turn the question to Nicole in the back seat. "You okay, Nicole?" Her carefree laughter reassured him.

Sometimes our expeditions took us out of the city. On sunny days, the whole gang would get together for a picnic in the Chevreuse Valley. Loaded down with provisions, we would take off in a roar of engines like a racing car event. Roger had a Triumph TR3 like us, Vincent a Panhard, Jacky a big Chevrolet convertible nicknamed "the calf," and another painter friend an MG. Bud was exultant as the whole armada snaked its way through traffic. If other drivers were upset by our antics, Roger had only to get out of the car with a monkey wrench in his hand to cut short any aggressive behavior. Bud looked on in admiration. These adventures were a change from his usual routine and opened up a new world for him to take an interest in.

The country was a constant source of discoveries. He became curious, attentive, asking lots of questions on inconsequential matters. Sometimes I would take him for a sort of pilgrimage to the surrounding rural villages where I had grown up. He adored these excursions. At the time, this area was still largely agricultural. People who had settled there from all parts of France had kept their folk traditions as well as their archaic tools. It was not unusual to see a horse-drawn wagon or a farmer dressed like a medieval peasant, with a pitchfork on his shoulder. Or to see young kids raking up horse droppings from the streets. Bud's eyes would pop out of his head. For him it was like visiting a zoo.

We would sometimes pay a visit to old friends of my parents who welcomed us around their fireplace with the traditional homebrew. Bud would observe this simple, timeless country life in incredulous silence, saying only after we had left, "What are they, Francis? Are they peasants, or what?" Or, "How can they live like that?" Or if the decor of the cottage looked more like a medieval hovel than an English country pub, he would laugh and say, "It looks like something out of an old movie."

Bud loved our apartment with its wooden beams and rustic furnishings, the old table and benches. From his armchair by the fireplace he could tend the fire that we kept burning in summer as in winter. He could be counted on to keep it going. We didn't live in the country but it certainly looked like it. We used electricity mainly for the record player and the electric shaver. Most of the lighting was from candles in our wrought iron candleholders.

We often did our cooking in the fireplace and Bud learned to like the skewered and spit-broiled chickens that our friends from Les Halles brought us to fill out our meals. Bud was really a perfect dinner guest, with a taste for all kinds of things that most Americans wouldn't touch with a ten-foot pole, like snails, frogs' legs and the famous *andouillette*, a tasty sausage stuffed with tripe.

More and more, Bud began to experience music as we did. For us amateurs, music meant passion, joy, and beauty, without the uncertainties of the professional musician, who is always worried about the future.

One morning I looked up from my work to find Bud standing in the doorway looking fresh and rested. I had spent days searching feverishly for new poster ideas for a brand of apéritif. He came over, looking strangely excited, and I could see that he had a question to ask. I had a large array of bottles on my work table, along with documents about the product. For a split second I thought they had awakened his old longing and that he was about to ask for a drink. "Francis," he said, a sense of urgency in his voice, "do you think I could get a job?"

"A job? What do you mean, Bud?"

"I don't know, something I could do?"

Bud had surprised me before, but this knocked me out! I wasn't sure what he meant. "But you're a musician, Bud. A great one. That's your job."

"I mean another kind of job. Do you think there's anything else I'd be able to do?"

When my amazement wore off and I started thinking about his question, I realized what a sensitive question he had just brought up. I recalled being told that Bud often said he wished people would treat him less like a musical phenomenon and more like a human being.

Now that he was enjoying music for itself and without the troubles of a professional musician, he had begun thinking about this question once again. In this relaxed atmosphere, he began playing more often and his music became more spontaneous, stronger, and more concise. There was more conviction and a sureness in his work that no accompaniment could weaken. Even if the tempo faltered, the pulse kept all its consistency, so forceful was the inner inspiration. His means of expression gradually became more sober. He had already extracted the best from Tatum's language by stripping it of all artifice. Now he could continue the process, paring down his own style. With more concise phrasing came a more convincing vocabulary and a fresh harmonic code. Both emotion and esthetics were now expressed only by the barest essentials and deepest sentiments.

Bud was asserting himself more each day. One evening, coming back from a walk, we met Nicole in the staircase. "Where are you going?" asked Bud.

"Shopping for dinner."

"What are we eating tonight?"

"I don't know," she said. "I'll see in the shop."

A good bit of our budget in those days went for fixing up the apartment, and we sometimes had to scrimp on food. But we always made sure there was a nice piece of meat for Bud. It had not escaped his notice that the menu wasn't the same for all of us. "How about steak for everyone?" he suggested.

"Oh, not for me," said Nicole. "What about you, Francis?" she asked with a wink to show the state of our finances.

"Get a steak for Bud. I'm not planning to eat much tonight. I have some work to do."

"No," said Bud. "Tonight we'll all have steak. I'm paying!"

"Oh no, we couldn't do that." My reply had been instantaneous, and Nicole echoed my refusal. To touch Bud's money seemed a sacrilege to us.

"Why not?" asked Bud, saddened by our reaction, when he had made his offer so happily. "I've got money," he added, showing us his wallet.

I suddenly realized how sharp my answer had been. I was embarrassed at the thought of using Bud's money, but I forced myself to answer in a light tone, "Okay then, it's your treat, Bud. Thanks, that's really nice of you."

Very excited, he reached hurriedly for the money in his wallet, then stopped, momentarily puzzled, not really knowing the value of the wad of bills he held out.

"Twenty francs is plenty," I said, "too much, even."

"You'll bring me back the change?" he asked Nicole.

As long as I live, I will never forget that meal. Bud supervised the cooking of the meat and watched every bite we took with pleasure. "How do you like the meat? Is it tender? Is it tasty? Did you have enough to eat?" He was the host and we were his guests. His face was wreathed in smiles and the meal was joyful. After dinner he left the table and went to sit in his chair by the fire. As he sat, his face clouded over and his expression filled with disapproval. Nicole and I noticed the change but didn't say a word. All at once, he leaped to his feet and started firing protests at us. "Don't think I never noticed that I was the only one who had meat at every meal. If you have problems, you have to tell me, 'cause I have money now. You mustn't deprive yourselves for me. I love you. Don't you two know that I love you?"

At that instant, I could've died. It was too much. I tried to hide the tears that rose to my eyes. Nicole, who was facing Bud, was crying openly. We couldn't speak. My throat was knotted. How could I explain that we couldn't bear to spend a cent of Bud's money for ourselves? Yet how selfish it had been to deprive him of the pleasure of giving us something in return. We would simply have to take care that such a situation didn't occur too often.

Everything I ever did for Bud, like my various activities in the world of jazz, was purely voluntary. I wrote for magazines, took part in radio, TV programs, concerts, and festivals, and designed innumerable posters and record jackets. I always saw it as my personal and spiritual luxury. To the casual observer, such an attitude may have been incomprehensible. Now, 25 years after the fact, I don't seek to convince or to justify what I did, nor to convert anyone to these principles. I have remained unconditional. For me, this policy seems the only one compatible with the integrity of those who created this quality music, music too often exploited after the demise of its creators. It's even painful for me to have to enter into such explanations. Once again, such principles seemed natural and simple to me, given the examples I had had in my childhood. None of this ever seemed exceptional or extraordinary to me. Today, alas, the ethics of such behavior are beyond the comprehension of certain "rational" minds who have gone so far as to impute other, more treacherous, motives. I can only pity those who have never known the profound joy of sentiments like these.

Those who so carefully looked after Bud in the past always had a personal interest in his business. They saw to it that he was in good health because he provided them with a lucrative activity, a service. Often, they got more out of it than he did. Generally speaking, his earnings were split down the middle—fifty percent of his pay went to Bud and fifty percent went to his "watchdog"—and there were even some who went so far as to submit expense accounts for their "services"! In short, the more Bud worked, the more these fine people earned. If he wouldn't or couldn't work, for whatever reason, enormous pressure was brought to bear on him.

To illustrate this point, here is a letter from Bud's mother, Mrs. Pearl Powell, to Bud's attorney, Maxwell T. Cohen:

Jan 21/57

Mr. Cohen
Dear Sir,

I rec'd your letter telling me about my son Bud Powell. I am so sorry he is drinking so hard. It seems to me he is very upset over money matters. He says he works and never have [*sic*] money like other men. I know it is hard to work all the time and never have anything. Has he ever seen his bank book? You see Mr. Cohen I am not considered as a mother.

Yours truly,
Mrs. P. Powell

Naturally, the American musicians passing through Paris had not failed to notice the change in Bud. They were flabbergasted by his new way of life and his considerably altered state of mind. Bud played a great deal and soon regained all his means. He was once again a figure of authority among his fellow Americans who, when they got back to the States, brought with them a wealth of enthusiastic stories about Bud's restoration.

Buttercup had been relieved to see him go, but now that he was the talk of the town it was starting to bother her. Everyone was talking about his "rebirth" and his success at the Blue Note. She acted nastier at each visit. Bud was more and more reluctant to go, and now he categorically refused to enter the hotel itself. I could imagine how he must have dreaded this place where he had really hit bottom. Buttercup never knew how much it took to persuade him to go see her, and when we got there all she had for him was anger and scorn.

In another letter to Maxwell Cohen, Bud's mother expresses concern about the ongoing relationship between Bud and Buttercup (Mrs. Edwards):

Mr. Cohen
Dear Sir,

Bud went to Europe and never told me anything. I rec'd a phone call since he has been home. Mrs. Edwards called and he talks about one minute to me. Mrs. Edwards tell [sic] him everything to do and he is like a child with her. I don't know his address.

Yours truly,
Mrs. P. Powell

At just about this time I received a letter asking me to report to Police Headquarters at my earliest convenience. It was from the Brigade des Moeurs, the famed Paris Vice Squad. I wondered what it was about, but figuring it must have something to do with Bud, I thought it best to take along some articles about Bud and me that had appeared in the press. It did indeed have to do with Bud, but I hadn't suspected exactly what had prompted their call. To my great surprise, the policeman handed me an anonymous letter. It was brief in the extreme, saying simply that Bud Powell, living at 64, rue de Clichy, was taking drugs. The poison-filled bomb had been thrown! Who could have wanted to send such a letter? What could be the point? The feeble nature of the accusation was obvious to the police. My response was to show them the clippings, all of which dealt with my efforts to get him away from his destructive surroundings, and to let them judge for themselves.

This was in fact the last attempt to hinder my actions. But I knew now I could expect the dirtiest kind of maneuvers. I never mentioned this incident to Bud, thinking of how shocking it would be to him. It convinced me more than ever that I was on the right track and that the longterm goal, for which I would fight to the end, was Bud's rehabilitation—to restore his dignity as a man and his reputation as a musician, and to help him to initiate his own responsibilities in his own business affairs. He knew why I was doing this, and this new disposition in our lives took priority in the rebuilding of his morale and his aim in life.

IN THE MOOD FOR A CLASSIC
(Recorded in Paris, July 31, 1964 [Fontana])

The great classical pianist Samson François was a frequent visitor to the Blue Note and he rarely missed a night when Bud was playing. Most of the time he would show up after the first set and stand quietly in the back, just soaking up the atmosphere, and then he'd head for the first empty spot he saw near the bandstand. I enjoyed watching this great musician as he sat listening to Bud, his head in his hands. After the set he would look on in obvious admiration, but he never tried to speak to Bud. He would retreat into ecstatic silence like any ordinary listener. He'd be talking to Nancy Holloway or Bobby Parker and despite their obvious charms his eyes would often be on Bud. Several times he said to me in a confidential tone, "You know, this man's a genius. What a pianist! What a virtuoso! He's got it all."

I had spoken to Bud about Samson, saying that, to my taste, I felt that he was the finest interpreter of Chopin and Ravel. From then on, Bud, too, was impressed and would often stare at him intensely without saying a word. One night I couldn't stand it any longer and decided to introduce them to each other. For once, Samson was sitting alone in the back of the club, so I went up to him and invited him to our table. "Samson," I said, "I'd like you to meet Bud, who is eager to make your acquaintance."

Though he didn't understand my words, Bud was already on his feet, looking very dignified and not a little intimidated. The introductions were made (for form's sake) and they stood there clasping hands and staring into each other's eyes for a long, long time. It was another instance, I thought, of the eloquence of silence. They didn't exchange a word that day, nor many more in the days to come, but their mutual feelings spoke louder than words. That night, Bud seemed to be playing just for Samson, and I thought I heard in the ballads a certain intimation of a Polonaise.

At home, life was more harmonious than ever. Bud was cheerful and went to the door himself to greet the friends that came to call each day while I went happily along with my work. He was more and more reluctant to leave for the Blue Note. After our candlelit dinners, he would have preferred to sit around and chat by the fireside. If we couldn't go with him to the club, we'd phone for a taxi. It was always just at that moment that he would think of an extraordinary story he wanted to tell us. Or else he'd lock himself in the bathroom, and it took all our pleading to get him to come out.

One evening, after we'd phoned for the cab, Bud launched into a hilarious story about life in jail. In one of the New York State prisons, he said, the inmates were required to keep fit and the guards forced them to do gymnastics. We could already hear our taxi's diesel engine as Bud was saying, "They had to do push-ups, you know. Do you know what push-ups are? Do you do them?"

After seeing that I didn't know the word, he got down on the floor and did a few push-ups, then collapsed with a long grunt, completely exhausted. I helped him to his feet and all would have been well but for one detail. We were in the midst of soundproofing the apartment, and the floor was covered with a sticky plaster-like substance in preparation for the laying of the carpet. His black suit was now covered with a pattern of fine white lines. He tried to look contrite (as I did, too, calling down my apologies to the cabdriver) while Nicole cleaned him up as best she could.

Bud was particularly fond of René Urtréger, whom he regarded as one of his spiritual sons. By the time he was 22, René already had a number of Bud's tunes in his repertoire. He was one of the first European bop musicians. After the 1956 Birdland tour with Lester Young and Miles Davis, he went on to the Blue Note, where he alternated with Bud. Quite often, Bud would stay to watch him play. His friendly smile encouraged René despite his awe in the master's presence. Surprising as it may seem, Bud had the gift of stimulating people, not paralyzing them.

At that time, René had a motor scooter and when the weather was good he would take Bud home. Bud gripped him from behind, scared to death, but loving every minute of it. But when René Thomas borrowed the scooter, it was Urtréger's turn to be scared. Thomas had never managed to find second gear. He drove exclusively in first, with roars of indignation from the tortured motor. Urtréger was worried sick about his scooter, but Thomas drove gaily around the block with Bud looking on in admiration.

When I didn't have too much work, I stayed for the second set and waited for the club to close. After long goodbyes and a lot of kidding around with the other musicians, we would leave at dawn, or more exactly at that magical moment we called "the blue hour," that time just before daybreak when the sun has started to come up behind the shadowy, still sleeping buildings. Before getting into the car we would stroll through the deserted streets, the silence broken only by the first clangings of the garbage collectors. After a night of great music, we always savored the stillness. It felt strange to be going home to bed just when the rest of the world was waking up and getting ready to storm the cafés in search of their morning croissants or café au lait. When "the blue hour" was over, we quietly climbed our five flights without breaking the romantic spell of our wanderings.

One morning while I was working and Bud was alone in his room, I heard him speaking some incomprehensible words. Without leaving my desk, I called out, "What is it, Bud? Did you speak to me?" There was no answer, so I went to his room.

He looked at me intensely and repeated, gravely enunciating each syllable, "*Ghai-ril-magh-doo-be-Alayheem.*" Then in a plaintive voice, he chanted in a minor key, "*La-i-la-ha-il-Allah!*"

"What's that all about?" I asked, amused.

He gave no explanation, just repeated the incantations like a haunting litany. Only later did he tell me about an Arab prophet who had come to the States bringing a new philosophy. He translated the phrases, insisting on the seriousness of the message, "Not like those who have taken the wrong road and who are cursed by Allah," and "There is no god but Allah."

"Do you believe in God, brother?" he asked me one day.

"Not in a religious sense. I only believe in beauty, Bud."

"So you don't believe in God?" he repeated, worried.

"Do you?" I asked.

He hesitated a long time. Then, making a great effort to articulate his thoughts, he finally said, "There's something."

"Really? And what is it, do you think?"

"I don't know. Something you can't explain. But that prophet who crossed the ocean to talk to us, he knew, you see."

We often spoke of this prophet and each time Bud repeated the phrases with the grave and pensive air of someone seeking a revelation. Certain appearances notwithstanding, Bud didn't really follow the doctrine of "turn the other cheek." Rather than the Christian philosophy that governs our society, he seemed to have a different outlook, in which Islamic ideas had taken a certain hold.

A number of bop musicians eventually converted to Islam. Dizzy Gillespie told us this story about a recording session with the arranger Gil Fuller. When a number of the new converts interrupted the session to kneel toward Mecca and pray, Gil was flabbergasted, but Dizzy was moved to tears by the sight and tried to explain to him, "You've got to understand them. They've been hurt bad and they're looking for escape."

"It's the last refuge of those who don't know which way to turn?"

"Oh, they know which way to turn, all right!" answered Dizzy, "They turn east!"

Indeed, many converts changed their names, Walter Bishop becoming Ibrahim Ibn Ismail; Kenny Clarke, Liaquat Ali Salaam; Art Blakey, Abdullah Ibn Buhaina; Edmund Gregory, Sahib Shihab, to mention only a few, and, of course, Cassius Clay, the most famous of all, who became Muhammad Ali.

Speaking of religion, I knew that the pianist Mary Lou Williams, whom I had met several times in Paris, had made some sporadic incursions into Catholicism. She was doubtless searching for an inner peace that her social life had never brought her. During her mystical periods she tried to convert some of her cronies. Bud, who was very fond of her, was one of them. It's true he was badly in need of help of one kind or another. During one of these periods, some time before 1947, Bud had replied to Mary Lou with the following poem:

THE GREAT AWAKENING

I was sitting in the garden one late afternoon
And out of the sky a feather fell
And not a moment too soon.
I didn't stop to regard from what source it came
I only know it lifted me out of the depth of shame.
You see, I never really lived, all I've done was exist. . . .
For all the joy I've ever known, was from a knife, a gun or a fist.
I came up the hard way, that is, the boys, a drink and a broad
But from this moment hence, I'm drawing my sword.
And I'm going to cut the weed of temptation, before it entangles me,
And live the way GOD intended, this short and sweet life to be.
Oh, but there's one thing I've not cleared up, and that's
    the missing link,
From whence that feather came, has started me to think.
And as I look up at GOD's operation, a school of pigeons flew by,
It was then that I knew where it came from, GOD had used a spy.

Apparently, Bud used to write poems for all his compositions. What a terrible shame that none of them survive today! They were never written down or copyrighted, and in the course of his chaotic life almost all of them have been lost.

When Bud was alone, he would sometimes laugh out loud and then he would grow sad and moan till the tears ran down his cheeks. Even after he began talking more openly to me, he could never give an explanation of these states.

Though he stopped drinking alcohol, Bud remained a great drinker. He consumed vast quantities of milk or fruit juice. He drank everything in one gulp and would hold the empty glass in his hand when he'd finished. Sometimes he would raise his glass as if to propose a toast, then lower it after a few minutes and go back to his private meditations. We never knew what prompted such gestures, but I often thought of what he had told the psychiatrist at Laënnec Hospital about his dreams and the internal voices he heard.

I might have regarded these symptoms as signs of some sort of mental disorder were it not for the fact that I had noticed other, even more surprising, phenomena. For example, he would ask for news of some friend or other and, quite often, in the minutes that followed, the friend in question would phone. Or else he'd be humming a tune in the car, which would make me think of turning on the radio, and when I did, what should be playing but that very tune? One day, he was whistling "If I Had a Hammer." I was vaguely familiar with this little ditty and was surprised that he would sing it. Wanting to cut it short, I switched on the radio and there was the pop star Claude François, belting out his French version of "If I Had a Hammer."

Bud would often stare down at his right hand, examining it with disturbing intensity, stretching out each finger, then he would slowly bring them together to make a fist. He would keep the fist clenched tightly, exerting great pressure all the while. He would turn his fist in all directions, looking at it in astonishment, then quickly slip it into his pants pocket and leave it there for a long while.

His way of walking was sometimes odd as well, especially when he lifted his knee nearly waist-high as if to avoid an invisible obstacle. It was all most unusual, but I was never really shocked by it and I thought it best not to react.

During his long meditations, he would often bend his head backward as if looking at some elusive image over his head. His eyes would roll back in his head and he'd remain motionless for a while, then come back to reality without the slightest transition or discomfort. Some observers felt that this was only a trick of his to cut himself off whenever he didn't feel like talking to someone.

I never asked him about these acts, not out of any embarrassment but rather because I felt I'd glimpsed something very private. Dr. Harris, of Seattle, Washington, a physician, pianist, and friend who did extensive research into Bud's case, told me the conclusions he had reached:

> In regard to Max Roach's views . . . that the beating Bud received at the hands of the police might have been a cause of some of his later problems . . . the idea that Bud might have been made epileptic by a beating over the head is at this point only an hypothesis. . . .
>
> For me there is no stigma attached to being epileptic, for as I mentioned in our telephone conversation I am epileptic myself (it is this very fact, along with my own research pertaining to the mechanisms of epilepsy, which has led me to see a certain possibility where others had not seen it). Thus, it is difficult for me to understand the fact that some people will not want to consider the possibility that Bud was an epileptic because for them this disease carries such terrible associations. Some, including yourself at present, will not readily accept the idea that Bud might have been epileptic simply because they are not familiar enough with the manifestations of this disease. For example, while you mention that you have never heard of any usual manifestations of epilepsy in Bud's life, in almost the next sentence you mention that he heard voices. Apart from the usual psychiatric interpretations of that phenomenon, it is a fact that auditory hallucinations—including hearing voices—are one form of epileptic manifestation. What I am talking about is a far more subtle form of epilepsy, rather than the stereotype of the *grand mal* seizure or whole-body convulsions which I'm sure most people call to mind when they hear this word. Actually, the French term—"absence"—expresses the idea of the *petit mal* variety of epilepsy, which is what I have and what I think Bud had. The precise symptoms depend on exactly what part of the brain has been injured. This injury would in no way be visible to the naked eye, even if it could view the brain directly. Yet, the injured area has acquired the property of spontaneous activity (that is, activity without an external stimulus or willed internal stimulus). If it is the area concerned with normal hearing, for example, the individual may at times "hear things" which aren't there. These may be "records" of the past—as in the case of hearing symphonies—or voices speaking for the first time. After experiencing such sensations, the individual may or may not lose consciousness for a brief period of time. If he loses consciousness, he may nevertheless carry out movements of parts of his body (including turning the head, facial grimaces, staring with the eyes or blinking rapidly) which appear to the observer as if they were deliberate. . . .

In order to better understand the significance of certain behaviors that various observers had described to him, Dr. Harris delved into Bud's music by accurately retranscribing the compositions and also some of the improvisations. This step, an unusual one for a doctor, taught him a little more about Bud's reactions. He went on to explain:

> I think that the content is so strong (that is, the chords are so richly voiced, and there are so many notes with such a strong pulsation in the line) that the brain is literally driven into "overload" and if the person doing the playing has any tendency toward seizures the music will thus trigger their occurrence. The onset of the seizure has a terrible subjective sensation (I feel as if I am going to become paralyzed, or lose consciousness and die); since I know what is happening to me I can deal with it, but if Bud didn't know what was happening to him it would have been very frightening to him to have such experiences, I'm sure. All I have to do to stop the sensations is to stop playing for a short time. This may have been what Bud was doing when he paused in the middle of playing, as several critics have described, or simply sat at the keyboard without even beginning to play. In those instances, he may have begun to experience odd sensations as soon as he got near the piano, and was afraid to play because that might worsen the way he was feeling. I doubt that he would have told anybody about this, even you, because it is very difficult to explain. Words cannot begin to express how I feel when a seizure is starting, and what it feels like to "fight this off" and return to a normal state of mind. . . .

There is much to be said for this theory, as in some countries epileptics are regarded as the psychologically privileged, endowed with paranormal faculties. This is true of shamans in Soviet Asia, or in Java where, at the first sign of the malady, they are isolated from the rest of the population and kept apart from community life. They remain in isolation until such time that they can be initiated as healers, then begin to carry out their role, something between witch doctor and psychiatrist.

These strange signs that appeared periodically never failed to shock Bud's entourage. It gave him all the more reason to want to hide, to avoid confronting the society of the "healthy." Dr. Harris is still pursuing this line of research. He had noticed similar phenomena in Thelonious Monk toward the end of his life and advised him to see a doctor at that time.

Besides his interest in my parents, Bud often questioned me on the events of World War II. During his European tours he had seen traces of the bombings and felt concerned by this conflict. Thelonious Monk had felt the same way. As early as 1940 (perhaps informed by Nica de

Koenigswarter, who was herself a cipher agent during the war) Monk had put on a beret with the Free French insignia and went around calling out, in perfect French *"France libre, France libre!"*

Such reactions are significant in people who possess this kind of sensitivity. By echoing the events taking place halfway across the world, they too were resisting in their own way. Bud asked me repeatedly about my father's activities in the *Résistance* and he drank in my every word. Each time he came back from a tour, he questioned me about the events of the war and seemed moved by my answers. For a while his music would reflect this obsession, with ballads of tragic power and heart-rending emotion, like long laments. Then suddenly the music would explode in a shower of liberating ideas. Bud didn't need to talk much. Music was his best form of expression. The titles themselves were often closely related to the latest events in his life.

While he was in the hospital he wrote "Glass Enclosure" (the controversial title refers to being a prisoner of a glass of alcohol). "Hallucinations" was written when he was getting electroshock treatment and "Oblivion" and "Wail" expressed his feelings about these events. "It Could Happen to You" is a clear warning while "Everything Happens to Me" shows his helplessness in the face of uncontrollable outer forces. These responses in musical form were quite frequent. Unfortunately, they were probably never understood by those for whom they were intended.

All these events led me to meditate more and more on his inner universe. Bud made me realize to what extent emotion and sensitivity are the true content of a work of art. In this respect, the critics were often far from understanding Bud's real motivations in the evolution of his work. He expressed only the essential, without the slightest complacency. As a result, his endless labor combined perfect lucidity with an urgent need to search, to question, and, endlessly, to begin again.

For all of these reasons he remains for me a genius at all times, whatever his performances may have been like. Where others find fault, I see the sublime. When Bud began to pare down his style, many saw it as a loss of creativity. I found in it both a lesson and a source of reflection. Musical ideas, melodies and phrases that could easily have escaped me in the past now appeared with brilliant clarity. By this new approach, I realized that Bud was expressing an affirmation. In the clear, remarkably logical and structured phrases, there was nothing left to chance. Also significant, and a sign that he was feeling good, was the constant subtle humor that permeated his improvisations. These fleeting references, perfectly integrated with the ideas, were like so many winks to the initiates. Withdrawn as he was, and seeming to refuse all communication, there was still a brotherly feeling in this approach. Brotherly because he had humbly opted for simplicity, for more detachment of voices and sounds, in order to allow a better understanding of his intentions and a greater perception of fundamental beauty. It illustrated once again the generosity of the man and his music and his will to express a message of whose importance he was fully aware. As time went on, I would say to myself more and more, "Bud is really up there in the higher spheres. There can't be many others with him there."

Bud was still pulling them in every night at the Blue Note. At various times the bill was shared by Lou Bennett, René Thomas, Dexter Gordon, and Charles Bellonzi. Bellonzi, who was Kenny Clarke's best pupil, played with Bud on a number of occasions, very well indeed, and to his great enjoyment.

A new record date was set up with Blue Note for May 23 at the CBS studios. It brought together the whole gang—Dexter Gordon, Pierre Michelot, and Kenny Clarke. It was quite a session! Bud also took part in a session with Dizzy Gillespie, to accompany Mimi Perrin's Double-Six, and in another with Pierre Michelot and Kenny Clarke. Bud was transcendent and so was Dizzy who, to my mind, had rarely played so well.

Each time, the contract was negotiated by Buttercup, something Bud favored less and less, for even if business was booming for her (Bud had cut three records in six months), he himself got very little out of it. I found the situation revolting, even though I could see some secondary benefits—that is, the peace and quiet it brought us. In an effort to console Bud, I would say casually, "Oh, just forget about Buttercup. When things are like this, at least she leaves us alone. All she cares about is the money."

Meanwhile, though, I was footing the bill for Bud's board and replenishing his wardrobe. I could understand that Bud felt hurt for me and for himself being used and exploited once again. But I was surprised by the indifference of the other musicians. They were close enough to us to be aware of the situation, yet they all maintained good relations with Buttercup and turned a blind eye to her scheming ways. Of course, she still had the pseudo-status of manager and, as such, exercised a lot of influence. All contract negotiations were done through her at the Louisiane and any number of times she would recommend musicians. They all seemed to accept this. Once Johnny Griffin got mad and let her have a piece of his mind, but her screeches of protest cut all further discussion short. The attitude of the others was extremely ambiguous. Only Babs Gonzales, who disliked Buttercup, had the courage to tell her what he thought of her without mincing his words.

As spring approached, visiting groups of Scandinavian musicians began to descend on Paris. They were tall and blond, and you could spot them a mile off by their large stature and blond hair. One day on the terrace of the Café de Seine, Babs caught the eye of a group of other foreigners, eleven Dutchmen, all jazz fans who recognized him, who had come to make the rounds of the Paris clubs. He sat down in their midst and settled in for a couple of drinks. Since each of them wanted to pay for a round, it was not long before they were all completely potted. In a burst of generosity and a tender thought for Buttercup, Babs invited them all to the hotel for dinner. He left them and rushed off to tell Buttercup that some VIPs were on their way with contract plans for a big tour. He gave her some money and told her to hurry up and get a big dinner ready. All excited by the project, she ran to do the shopping and set about preparing the meal. At eight o'clock sharp, the first Dutchman showed up, a blond giant with a build like a rugbyman. He asked for Babs and was told to come in and wait, that he wouldn't be gone long. Babs watched through the crack of his bedroom door, which happened to be across the hall. The second one followed, then the third, fourth, etc., all paraded in before Buttercup's astounded stare. By the time all eleven of them had pushed their way into the little room, there was not an inch of space and not an available surface to sit on. What an evening that must have been, with no room to eat in and a bunch of guests who couldn't speak any English! Of course, Babs himself never did come. He stayed in his room and gloated, sipping his glass of scotch.

I received a phone call from Henri Renaud who was producing a jazz program for Radio Monte Carlo. He had also been pleased to see the change in Bud since he had come to live with me. Henri was known as a journalist, but he had also played piano in the Paris clubs, most notably with Clifford Brown in 1953 and with Lester Young in 1958. An early lover of bebop, he was an unconditional fan of Bud's music. He wanted to devote an entire program to his music and to interview him, if at all possible. The second part of the plan sounded dubious as Bud rarely talked much to journalists. We went to the studio and, as usual, in order to get an answer, I had to reformulate all the questions Henri asked. The conversation went something like this:

"Who are your favorite pianists, Bud?"

"Al Haig. He's my idea of the perfect pianist." (Bud was aware of Henri's passion for Al Haig, and I suspect he said this just to please him, for in all our conversations, he had never expressed the slightest interest in Al Haig.)

"Can you mention some other pianists you admire?"

"Well, I said Al Haig . . . Let's see now, there's Billy Kyle, Hank Jones . . ."

"You say at first you were strongly influenced by Billy Kyle. Bud, who was your master on the piano?"

"Art Tatum."

"Did you spend a lot of time with Tatum?"

"Well, you see, Tatum used to come pick me up to go for rides in his big Lincoln. He had this sky blue Lincoln. I'd go riding in his car."

"Who's your favorite composer?"

"Thelonious Monk. He's been one of my favorites for a long time. We used to hang out together all day and all night in the after-hours clubs."

"Aside from pianists, Bud, who are your favorites on trumpet and saxophone?"

"On sax, Johnny Griffin. On trumpet, Miles Davis."

"And what bass players do you like?"

"Oscar Pettiford when he was alive. Now I like Tommy Potter. He's a good bassist."

"Who are your favorite accompanists?"

"Max Roach. Ray Brown."

Bud was working pretty steadily during this period. We were trying to give him a lot of support and affection. I was spending all my nights at the Blue Note, where I had my reserved seat near him at the piano. Watching his hands while he played was a fascinating spectacle, just for the sheer beauty of the motion. Comparing him to other musicians, I noticed that the beauty of the music matched the perfection of the movements.

For a pianist, there is real enjoyment in the simple mechanical execution. The movements of the fingers reveal all the magic of the esthetic, even before the sound is heard. I can remember, for example, when my neighbors gave me too much trouble, I would go on playing with my hands above the keyboard. Without touching the keys or producing the slightest sound, I already felt half the pleasure I was seeking.

PERDIDO

(Recorded in Toronto, May 15, 1953 [Debut])

And so our routine might have comfortably continued if not for the fact that Bud was showing some disturbing signs of fatigue. He had always been slow in his movements, and I rarely saw him rush, whatever the circumstances. But recently we had begun to notice that his pace had slowed down even more. Climbing our five flights of stairs seemed to use up all of his energy.

Though he ate well and got plenty of rest, weekends in the country and frequent time off from his work had no effect. He slept later than usual. One morning I looked in while he was sleeping and saw that he was perspiring heavily even though it wasn't very warm. Then he started losing weight. Any effort was exhausting. His movements were painfully labored and he seemed to be carrying a heavy load all the time. Even if nothing spectacular was evident, all these signs revealed that something was wrong. I decided he had to see our friend Dr. Teboul for a complete check-up.

Bud dreaded any contact with the medical profession. I managed to persuade him that we were just going to see a friend for a routine visit. At the first glance the doctor looked worried. He examined Bud, then signaled to me to follow him into the waiting room.

"Francis, your friend has tuberculosis, and it's in a very advanced stage. It's awful. He must have had it for years."

"But that's impossible," I blurted out. The news hit me like a ton of bricks.

"I'm certain of the diagnosis. Of course, we'll do the usual tests. But I have no doubt whatsoever."

My world caved in. Just as everything was going well for Bud, here he was betrayed by his body. I felt crushed and helpless, and without the support and friendship of Dr. Teboul, I don't know how I would have survived this period.

I went home with Bud, feeling miserable but trying not to show it. Bud acted unconcerned, asking no questions. In private, I told Nicole the bad news, and we got through the evening trying to hide our anxiety, clinging to the vain hope of a possible error.

The next day we took Bud for his tests, saying once again it was just a check-up. The results were even worse than we feared. Tests revealed that Bud's condition was contagious by direct contact. His lungs were perforated in many places and there was one enormous cavity of nearly three inches just over the left pectoral lobe which the doctors were very worried about.

The news of Bud's tuberculosis sent the Paris music world into a tailspin. All those who'd been around him were scared out of their wits, particularly those who used to tease him by drinking out of his glass. Kenny Clarke ran to have a test, then Hazel Scott, who often kissed him on the mouth, then Ben Benjamin and all the Blue Note staff. A sudden panic hit our little world—there was something comical about these musicians, usually so carefree, suddenly finding they had all kinds of symptoms. If it hadn't been so serious it would have really been laughable.

Fortunately, no one had caught the disease. Nicole had the beginnings of an infection and had to go and rest in the country. But Bud's case seemed desperate. Only surgery could save him, and even then the doctors were afraid it might be too late. No one understood how it could have gotten this bad without more obvious symptoms. For one thing, Bud had exceptional resistance. But he was also inured to suffering. True, tuberculosis can be dormant for years before the onset of symptoms. Only regular check-ups can reveal its presence and Bud hadn't had a check-up for years.

The hardest thing was to conceal our anxiety. Now we were facing a new and desperate battle, which would entail a new break in our lives. Just as Bud was responding to the security of family life, the doctors were saying he had to be hospitalized within 48 hours. Dr. Teboul recommended us to Dr. Gilbert at the Hospital Foch in Suresnes, who immediately reserved a private room.

Fearing Bud's panic, we decided not to tell him until the last minute. We tried to appear cheerful and talked about plans for the coming days. On the eve of his hospitalization, we took him to the movies to see *The Great Escape*, a title that turned out to be strangely prophetic. Bud insisted on sitting in the first row and after the show we went straight home. We left him alone for a few minutes, just long enough for Nicole to do some shopping and for me to park the car. By the time we got upstairs Bud was gone. He had his own key that hung on a hook in the hallway and he took it each time he went out. With a sinking heart I ran to the hallway. The key was in its place. Bud would never have forgotten to take it with him. I knew why he had run away, and yet no one had mentioned hospitalization and we had done our best to act normal. I might have known that Bud, with his paranormal abilities, would sense something wrong and make a run for it.

Now we were more frightened than ever. The doctors had agreed that time was of the essence. We tried everything to find Bud. I phoned Buttercup, without much hope, as well as all the other friends or acquaintances Bud might conceivably have gone to. He was nowhere to be found. That night and the whole next day we continued to comb Paris, but without any luck. I had the idea of contacting the radio stations and asking them to broadcast bulletins—among others, our friend Philippe Adler made several announcements of Bud's disappearance, complete with his full description. By the third day we were beside ourselves with worry and exhausted from lack of sleep. We had no desire to eat and spent most of our time roaming the streets and calling hospitals and police stations, all in vain. One person was always posted by the telephone, just in case.

That afternoon I went to get a haircut. The barber was halfway through when the phone rang. It was my sister. She had just had a call from a woman who thought she recognized someone resembling the description on the radio. He was in a café on the Rue de Paradis. Nicole and a girlfriend of Johnny Griffin's were already on their way. With my hair half cut, I left the barber standing there with his scissors in his hand and leapt into my car, which was parked out in front, and drove off.

It was Bud all right. Nicole and her friend got there first. They spotted him at once, pale and thinner than ever, with a three-day beard. As soon as he saw them, he scampered away quickly. They caught up with him and convinced him to sit down with them and have a drink, but when he saw them talking to the bartender, he got scared and ran away again. In a panic, they asked the bartender to call the emergency number for the police.

When I reached the street I saw our friend Mic on his motor scooter. I left the car, jumped on the back, and off we went at full speed, jumping sidewalks and taking one-way streets the wrong way. At last, we saw Bud, pursued by a police car. He saw us coming and stopped. Falling into my arms, he said in a dying voice, "Francis, I can't take any more. I'm tired."

"Come on, Bud, please. We're going back home."

Where had he spent the last three days and nights? Had he eaten? Slept? We never knew. When we got home, the only words he spoke were the desperate plea, "Francis, I don't want to go to the hospital. I don't want to have an operation."

How could he have known about our arrangements? No one had breathed the word hospital, much less operation. He would never cease to amaze me. He took a bath and got into bed, exhausted. We brought him his meal and he fell asleep instantly.

For me it was a sleepless night. We had only a few hours together before I would have to take him to the hospital. It was too late to break it to him gently. I had to tell him what was happening and why we had hidden the truth from him. I had to explain that this was the only way for him to recover his health. He reacted like a frightened child, saying he would be okay if only he could have his treatment at home. Going to the hospital was like being abandoned. I told him he had to have faith in us, that we would do everything to make him get well, that he would be surrounded by kind and devoted people. I must have come up with the right words, for all at once he seemed resigned to his fate and started asking specific questions about the hospital and the doctors. I could reassure him on that score as I knew we had retained the best specialists.

His treatment was indeed accomplished in a wonderful atmosphere of friendship and concern. The entire staff gave him special care and did all they could to make his stay more pleasant. He was hospitalized on September 17, 1963, and it was none too soon. Dr. Gilbert, the head of the section, told us that in another 48 hours it would have been too late. So luck did smile on us a little amid all the misfortune.

Bud was put on "attack treatment" as soon as he arrived and with all the sedation and heavy medication, I assume he was unconscious a good part of the time. For us, waiting to hear the first results was unbearable. The reports were encouraging. His body was reacting well and the doctors said he was already stronger. After about two weeks, I was authorized to visit. I had waited impatiently for this day and was feeling very emotional by the time I arrived at the hospital. I opened his door and tiptoed into the room. Bud was propped up against two large pillows, an IV drip attached to his right arm. He seemed to be asleep. Then he opened his eyes and turned his head slowly toward me. After a moment of hesitation, his expression went from doubt to stupefaction. Making an enormous effort, he whispered,

"Francis, why didn't you come before?"

"You weren't allowed to have visitors, Bud. You needed a lot of rest. Now the doctors are satisfied. You've made good progress and they say you'll soon be cured."

A gleam of hope flickered in his eyes.

"When can I get out, Francis? Soon?"

I knew he would need at least two more months in the hospital and that afterwards he would have to go to a sanatorium.

"It's hard to say for sure but you have to stay confident. You're on the road to recovery. We'll get you well as soon as possible."

"I don't want to have an operation," he begged again.

He was still terrified of this possibility and I worried about it myself.

"I'll speak to the doctor. Don't worry. For the time being, everything's okay."

The doctors were still sure they would have to operate. There was no point in discussing it with Bud. It would only upset him unnecessarily. I was now allowed to visit him regularly as long as he didn't talk. He was short of breath and got tired quickly. I would sit by his bedside and hold his extended hands, and tell him in full detail everything that went on at home. When I talked about the messages of sympathy that were pouring in from everywhere, a pale smile lit up his thin, drawn face.

The press, eager as always for juicy stories, had once again latched on to the Bud Powell case. But one good effect it had was to make fans write to him. Most of the mail came from the States. Some letters were really touching: "Bud, I have been desperate since I learned the terrible news. Please, grab a hold of yourself, you must cure yourself and come back to us. Do that for me and for all those who love you."

Sometimes the tone was deliberately provocative: "Bud, you must cure yourself quickly. We all need you, the world of music has broken down without you."

Or this rather blunt letter from a pianist named Marcello: "I've heard you haven't been quite well lately. . . . Dig me man, and get well, or I'll come and shit on your grave!"

A ten-year-old fan named Linda sent him a photo of herself, on the back of which she wrote in her childish handwriting: "Dear Bud, I am one of your most loyal fans and I wish I could meet you and hear you in person. My father is teaching me to play 'Monopoly' & 'Sub City.' Linda."

There were postcards that said simply: "Here, you have real true friends. Get well quick, we're waiting for you. . . ."

Many women, too, sent him poignant letters, offering to write regularly to cheer him up and make his hospitalization more pleasant.

All these signs of friendship and sympathy were full of tenderness and passion. I read them aloud to him as he didn't have the strength to read them himself. He would ask questions, then make me repeat certain phrases that were particularly touching. I held his hand and looked at the dripping IV and my heart ached for him. Poor Bud! He'd been fighting an uphill battle for so long.

I dreaded the moment when the nurse would ask me to leave. His eyes would beg me to stay and I knew I'd be miserable for the rest of the day. He would start new conversations, using any pretext to prolong the visit, like a child refusing the inevitable. Knowing how much he needed rest, I would have to spend our last minutes together pleading with him to accept the discipline recommended for him.

On one occasion, I said goodbye firmly and left the room. I was nearing the staircase when a sound behind me made me turn. There was Bud running after me. He hadn't been out of bed since his admission and was very weak and staggering. He was barefoot, and I saw with horror that he had pulled out his IV. I helped him back to his room and made him promise never to do this again, or he would be jeopardizing the good results everyone was so happy about. He got back into bed, suddenly docile again, and before my horrified eyes, calmly stuck the needle back into his arm.

Nothing about Bud should have surprised me any more, but I still had occasion to be amazed. One day, Dr. Gilbert announced, his own voice filled with disbelief, "You may not believe this, but the latest tests show that the three-inch hole has practically healed. In my opinion, an operation will not be necessary. In my entire career as a specialist, I have never seen such progress. It is unbelievable, absolutely amazing!"

I felt like saying, "You don't know the half of it!" as I thought to myself of Bud's other astounding abilities.

I was able to tell Bud the good news myself. In an effort to raise his spirits, I explained that he himself was responsible for these encouraging results. By keeping up his morale and following the advice of the hospital staff, he was going to make spectacular progress. For us, this was another sign of his inner strength, despite his appearance of a man worn out and prematurely aged. At the time, Bud was only 39 years old, but he looked over 50.

Soon I was called into the hospital's administrative office and informed that, as I suspected, Bud had no medical insurance, not even the minimum coverage that any French worker has. I guaranteed that I would take responsibility for paying all of his hospital bills. It would cost a lot, but I had no hesitation. My work was going well and now I had another reason to work hard. Money for me has never been an end in itself, but rather a means of solving certain problems. The objective now was to get Bud well, whatever the cost, and bring him home with us. The hospital bills were sent every two weeks and I tried to pay them promptly.

When the news of Bud's illness reached New York, Henri Renaud phoned me to say he had received a letter from Oscar Goodstein, who had just learned of the situation. They had met while Henri was on an American tour in 1953, and Goodstein was the manager of Birdland and Bud's legal guardian.

Goodstein said in his letter of September 8, 1963, that he heard from Buttercup's mother, Mrs. Harris, that Bud had "a touch of tuberculosis" and that Bud would need $200 before X-rays could be taken by the hospital. Goodstein didn't trust Buttercup or her mother, so he wrote to Henri and his wife Ny to "do [him] a favor." He enclosed two checks to Bud's order—one for $200 and another for $100—and asked them to find out if Bud was really sick or if it was "another trick of Buttercup to get more of Bud's money." Goodstein was happy to help Bud if he was really sick, but he wanted to make sure Buttercup didn't "get her hands on this money" if he wasn't actually sick. He asked Henri and Ny to give both checks to Bud and let him do what he wanted with them. He also urged them to write of Bud's actual condition, "whether he is working and where, who he's living with, how he looks, and if he is happy."

A few days later, Ny received a phone call from Goodstein, who had taken things firmly in hand. At my suggestion, Ny turned over the checks to the American Embassy, to the consul, Mr. Lamprecht. This was intended to avoid any ambiguity. But the social service at the embassy, unaware of any change of address, sent their notification to the Hotel Louisiane, where it was received by Buttercup. Once she got wind of the checks, her reaction was not long in coming.

On one of my visits, I was very upset to find Bud terribly agitated, and I knew how much he needed rest and absolute calm. There was panic in his eyes and his first words were, "Francis, please, don't let them send me to a psychiatric hospital. I don't want to go. . . ."

"What are you talking about, Bud? Where'd you get that from? What does that mean?"

"Buttercup came to see me. She said if she wants, she can have me committed."

"Don't worry about that, Bud. You know perfectly well she has no rights over you. And anyway, who said anything about a psychiatric hospital? I don't know what she's talking about."

Bud stared at me, not yet calm but somewhat relieved by my own assurance. But he still looked worried and I had the feeling he hadn't told me the whole story. There had to be something more to frighten him so. At last he admitted, shamefaced, "Buttercup made me sign a paper. I didn't want to, but she threatened me, if I didn't . . . so . . ."

"A paper? What kind of paper?"

"I don't know. She said I had to sign it or else she would have me locked up. . . ."

"So you signed?"

Bud nodded slowly like someone in deep thought. I was beginning to understand. Buttercup's visit could only have a connection with money.

"Bud, I beg you. Never sign anything without talking to me first. You know Buttercup has no rights over you."

But the following week another letter came from Goodstein. He was worried about the two checks, as it appeared that neither of them had ever been paid to the hospital. He had received a telegram from the State Department in Washington, DC notifying him of Bud's condition and asking him to send money to the American Embassy in Paris, so he called Ny to see to whom she had given the checks.

In his letter of September 15, 1963, to Henri and Ny, Goodstein made it clear that Buttercup was not Bud's wife. He already had a wife—"a white woman by the name of Audrey Hill Powell"—who lived in California. Bud and Audrey had been separated for years but they remained man and wife. He asserted that Buttercup had no legal or moral right to touch Bud's money or to take anything else that belonged to Bud. He suggested that until Bud recovered, all money would be sent to him care of the American Embassy, and that afterward, Henri, Ny, or I should get his checks for him. He advised that they call the police and have Buttercup put in jail if she tried to take away Bud's money.

Goodstein mentioned in his letter his plans to contact the musicians' union to get permission to run a benefit to raise "a large sum of money for Bud" in mid-October. He also said he would try to get Bud's four music publishers to pay an advance against future royalties and to send checks directly to the American Embassy in Paris.

And finally, he kindly thanked me "from the bottom of [his] heart" for all I had done for Bud, and hoped that we would be able to meet in person one day.

I must make it clear that at this time no one really knew what Buttercup's actual rights were or what authority she had over Bud. Her absolute gall in front of police and hospital authorities had made people wonder. When Henri and Ny told Goodstein of our problems with Buttercup, he immediately answered in a letter dated September 25, 1963, that he had sent a check to the American Embassy in Paris for Bud's account, and that no one in the Embassy would give the money to Buttercup; it was to be used strictly to pay Bud's hospital bill. He also told Henri and Ny that he sent a letter to the Special Consular Services of the State Department notifying them that Buttercup had no legal claim on Bud and that they should advise the Embassy in Paris.

In the meantime, he had sent another check, for $411, through the same channels. The hospital never saw a cent of that, either. Buttercup had made Bud sign a power of attorney and she picked up the checks as quickly as they arrived. Mr. Lambrecht, the consul, was furious. He had tried several times to make her return the money, but to no avail. Buttercup took the position that, as a mother, she had certain priorities. Everything had happened so quickly that no one had had time to sort out the legal situation.

On October 24, I wrote to Goodstein for the first time, thanking him for his letter, bringing him up to date on all of the events, and also reassuring him that Bud's health was improving remarkably.

> I have received your very kind letter and was touched by your enthusiasm and sincerity. I want you to know that reading your letter gave Bud much pleasure and renewed his confidence.
>
> This evening I went to the Hospital Foch in Suresnes where Bud is now, and per your authorization turned over to the Office of the Cashier your two checks totalling $300. The head Cashier told me he summoned Buttercup several times to have her pay the bill with the money she had received for this purpose. No word was heard from her. She contacted me by telephone. She said openly that she didn't want to give this money to the hospital, that they could wait, and that she had in mind sending Bud to a free state hospital for the rest of his treatment. . . .
>
> The major menace seems to be that she claimed that once Bud was in a mental institution no one would have any more contact with him and she could do what she wanted with him. Buttercup has signed an agreement with the American Embassy making her responsible for Bud's hos-

pital bills. This was, of course, to keep the Consul from getting suspicious, though he hadn't objected when she asked him for the money. Now she claims to be using this money for other things. . . .

Oscar replied at once. He did all he could to reassure us in his letter of October 26, 1963. Unfortunately, it was too late to stop payment on the check he had sent to the American Embassy. He had just received cancelled checks for it and for the two checks he had sent to Henri and Ny. He assured me that it would be the last time Buttercup would "be able to rob Bud of his money" and encouraged me not to worry. He planned to demand from the Embassy proof that the money sent to them was used to pay some of Bud's hospital bills and "when they contact Buttercup and learn that she did not use the money for the specific purpose it was sent, you can be sure that the Embassy will cause her more trouble than she can stand."

Goodstein said that the authorization that Bud had signed under duress would do Buttercup no good since he wasn't going to send any money to the Embassy in the future. As for her threats to send Bud to a mental institution or to take him back to the United States, he wrote to me: "you and Bud can tell her to go jump in the ocean or go and lose herself because she has no authority or legal claim on Bud Powell and is in no position to carry out any of her threats."

He reminded me that our efforts were not in vain; that "Bud Powell's name will be remembered and people will speak about the great contributions he has made to our modern music." He was quite emphatic about Buttercup's interventions. He wrote: "If I was in Paris now, I would take that fat miserable woman by the seat of her pants and throw her in a garbage can where she belongs, for all the wrongs she has done him."

But there was no stopping Buttercup. To everyone's despair, she continued to proffer her threats. To be on the safe side, I informed Goodstein that she had just told me: "because of the bad influence, according to her, of the people who are now concerning themselves with Bud's affairs, she intends to pay the hospital tonight and get in touch with 'her doctor' in order to get Bud transferred to another hospital tomorrow morning. . . ."

I made one last try to make Buttercup listen to reason. I sent her a special-delivery letter saying:

Buttercup,

I am hoping for some good sense and understanding on your part. I ask you to try to put aside any personal feelings. Don't let your pride come before Bud's health.

Try to understand with me that the main thing we all want is to let Bud continue his excellent recovery. Stopping his treatment now could kill Bud.

Personally, my only wish is that Bud doesn't take any risks and that he starts up his treatment again as soon as possible. He has made spectacular progress, but stopping his treatment is all the more serious because his illness should have required an operation. The doctors were trying to avoid an operation by giving him especially powerful treatments. Thus his body is used to these high-powered treatments. Stopping them now could be fatal and the person who keeps him from a doctor's care is taking Bud's life in their hands. He still has holes in his lungs measuring two inches in diameter. He is still contagious and therefore dangerous for all the people around him, especially your son Johnny.

I am completely agreeable to drive Bud back to the Sanatorium as soon as possible. This is the last friendly approach that I am able to make to you and I am doing it for Bud's sake. I will be at home all day and you can telephone me to give me your decision. I hope you will think it over very carefully and realize its seriousness and how important it is for Bud.

There was no reply. But Goodstein answered immediately, mentioning for the first time the name of Bud's lawyer, Maxwell T. Cohen, who was about to take things in hand himself. Oscar wrote in his letter that he knew how worried I was about Buttercup's threats since he was over 3,000 miles from Paris. He reassured me that Maxwell Cohen, Bud's attorney, would be granting me authorization to represent Bud in France. He also told me that Cohen promised to go to Paris to get the courts and the police to "punish Buttercup if she does a single thing to hurt Bud," and that he would have her prosecuted for misappropriation of Bud's funds if she did anything wrong. A few days later, I received the following letter from Maxwell Cohen:

November 4th, 1963

Dear Mr. Paudras:

Our mutual friend, Mr. Oscar Goodstein, afforded me the privilege of reading your correspondence to him with regard to Bud Powell.

I think that you are handling a difficult situation in a most sensitive and commendable manner. All of us in the United States who feel the way you do about Bud are most grateful to you.

A publishing company has contributed $500 towards Bud's welfare. A concert conducted at Birdland resulted in approximately $800 in income. The check was given to me to be forwarded to you for transfer to the Foch Hospital.

As Bud's attorney may I be very specific in designating you with authority to act on my behalf. As Bud's attorney I shall be acting on his behalf. Very specifically I would request that the check be transmitted to the hospital and that the hospital be instructed that no part of this check is to be given to or credited to Buttercup.

With very good wishes, I am

Most sincerely yours,
Maxwell T. Cohen

At last, it seemed that the proper actions had been taken to stop Buttercup's intrigues and manipulations. Mr. Lamprecht had made this case his own personal business, and after a final warning from him, Buttercup ceased her interference.

If I drag out all these sordid events, it is, for one thing, to clarify a few points that seem very confused in many people's minds, and also because they are inseparable from this painful episode in Bud Powell's life. I want to show how even in the most desperate moments, nothing was spared him. I hope I will be forgiven for going into such lurid detail, but it seemed necessary for me to show why Bud behaved as he did. So often, his strange behavior was misinterpreted by those who really didn't know all the facts.

The usual bunch of friends all visited Bud at the hospital. They showered him with pastries, which he put away with stupefying consistency. I have never seen anyone who could eat as much pastry as he did. We watched him eat with fascination and delight, taking his appetite as another sign of his eventual recovery.

Johnny Griffin sometimes came to see him too, but of the musician friends, he was, alas, the only one. Bud asked again and again why no one else came to see him. Perhaps it was the tuberculosis that frightened them away. I could find no good excuse to offer for their absence.

BLUES FOR BOUFFÉMONT

(Recorded in Paris, July 31, 1964 [Fontana])

Bud's recovery was spectacular. The doctors announced that the "attack phase" of treatment was over and he would soon be transferred to a sanatorium. I could just imagine his reaction to that news! He was already asking when he could go home. Most sanatoriums are in the mountains far from Paris, which would mean I wouldn't be able to visit very often. But once again, thanks to the kindness and understanding of the doctors, Bud was admitted to Bouffémont, a sanatorium situated in the outer suburbs of Paris. It was normally reserved exclusively for students and his admission there was indeed a special favor.

It took all the arguments I could muster to convince Bud that this was not a hospital but a rest home where he would be on a kind of long vacation. He said it didn't sound like a vacation to him, but I prevailed upon him to accept it with good grace.

Bud was so relieved at not having to undergo surgery that he went off to Bouffémont without protest. As soon as we met Dr. Joussaume, the director of the establishment, I saw that he had taken to heart all the special recommendations the doctors had made for this exceptional patient. To provide the freedom and tranquility he needed, Bud was given a private room. It had tall French windows opening onto the spacious grounds, with a view of ancient oak trees bordering a lush green lawn.

The room had a bed with a movable meal tray, a table, two chairs in front of the large window, and a wardrobe unit. By the bed stood a small table with a bedside lamp and a radio with preset stations. It was functional and somewhat spartan in appearance, but really quite comfortable. He could walk down the hall to the nearby lounge and had easy access to the grounds.

The warm welcome made me feel better. I could relax now, feeling that Bud would be in good hands. He even seemed to like the place himself. I can never express enough gratitude to the doctors, the staff, and even the other patients for all the consideration they showed Bud during his stay. Once again he had won over his entourage. It was a comfort, for I knew he'd be there for quite a while.

The problem of payment came up again. I explained Bud's situation to Dr. Joussaume and signed an agreement to pay all the expenses of board and medical care.

As in the past, whenever there was serious trouble, Monk gave a hand. He and Bud remained lifelong friends despite their silences and long separations. As soon as he heard of Bud's plight, he suggested a benefit concert in his honor. Oscar Goodstein made all the arrangements for this exceptional concert and sent the proceeds to the sanatorium. The proceeds were slim, however, once deductions had been made for taxes, royalties, and other charges. But whatever the sum, the most important thing for us all was the affectionate gesture that Monk had made.

On November 22, 1963, the radio announced the shocking news that President Kennedy had been assassinated. Johnny Griffin climbed over his railing and onto our terrace to tell us the news. When I got to Bouffémont I found Bud in a terrible state. He kept repeating over and over gravely, like a litany, "They shot the president of the United States."

He said it over and over again, slowly and clearly as if trying to fathom its meaning. The words didn't really seem to touch him, but the obsessive way he repeated the phrase heightened for me the total insanity of the event.

The main building of the sanatorium had a large day room where all the patients met. On one side of this lounge was a counter where they sold a variety of items the patients might have missed: food, soft drinks, candy, and cigarettes. Not wanting Bud to feel hampered in his choice, I had told him everything was free. He needed no further coaxing. In an effort to accelerate his recovery, he took it upon himself to frantically consume as many different kinds of well-chosen delicacies as he possibly could. He went from sweets to sardines to canned ham and *pâté*, and washed it all down with alcohol-free beer. The lists of his purchases leave me bewildered to this day. Here, for example, is the list I was given for the date of January 4, 1964:

1 canned ham
2 cans of tuna
1 pack Gauloise cigarettes
1 can of sardines
1 box of chocolate (36 pieces)
1 beer
1 box of matches
4 cans grape juice

1 canned mackerel
2 beers
2 Nuts candy bars
1 *pâté*
1 *pâté*
1 pack Cheese Puffs
2 beers
2 beers
2 beers (!)
1 can chicken liver
2 beers
1 can anchovies
1 pastry
1 pack Gauloise cigarettes
1 box of matches
1 can of sardines
2 beers
2 beers

In short, a day well-spent! Eating became his favorite occupation. The minute the bell rang for meals, he would rush back to his room to await delivery of his tray. This lavish diet, added to the fresh air and enforced rest, yielded results. He gained back his normal weight and soon exceeded it.

I had bought him two pairs of pajamas and a pair of fleece-lined felt bedroom slippers of the "Docteur Jéva" brand, well known in France at the time. "You'll see," I told him, "it's like walking on clouds. They may be ugly, but they're the convalescent's equivalent of a Rolls-Royce!"

He seemed dubious at first, but when he tried them on, his beatific smile left me no doubt as to their comfort. After having adopted the French beret, he had now been converted to Dr. Jéva's bedroom slippers.

As it was a students' sanatorium, the patients were mainly young people and some of them knew who Bud was. There were even some jazz fans among them, who invited him to join their games and pastimes, but unfortunately to no avail. He preferred to be alone. He watched everything that went on around him and told me how fond he was of some of the young people. He was touched by their discretion and impressed by their knowledge of music. There was a large hall with a stage and, I was surprised to discover one day, a grand piano. During one of my visits, I was told that at the urging of some patients (who must have had great powers of persuasion) Bud had given a private concert. I was overjoyed to hear it. If he agreed to play, it was an incontrovertible sign of recovery.

Dr. Joussaume kept me informed on his progress. One Monday morning he phoned to report the following anecdote: Bud had agreed to give another recital for the patients and this time for the medical staff as well. After the concert Dr. Joussaume had gone up to the stage to thank him and give him the traditional embrace, to the enthusiastic applause of the audience. Several days later, the doctor gave a lecture in the same room on the evolution of tuberculosis and the course of treatment. Bud was in the audience with the other patients. He had noticed Bud smiling and listening attentively though he didn't understand a word of French. When the talk was over, Bud strolled up to the stage to congratulate the doctor, embracing him just as the doctor had done the day of the concert. The audience broke into gales of laughter.

Bud was becoming himself again. His humor was coming back and that too was a good sign.

Dr. Joussaume never failed to keep me posted on Bud's doings and some time later offered another amusing story. He was having lunch with fellow doctors in the staff dining room when Bud came in and stopped behind his chair. Placing his hands on the doctor's shoulders, he leaned gently over his head, picked up his wine glass and drank it down in one gulp before the amazed stares of all the others. Then he calmly wished them *"Bon appétit,"* and walked out smiling from ear to ear. "What could I say?" said the doctor. "He had done it all so sweetly!"

When I mentioned the story to Bud, he replied in all innocence that since this was a sanatorium he assumed it must have been alcohol-free wine!

I also heard that Bud had found his way to the kitchens. He would drop in several times a day and even though he knew no French he got on so well with the cooks and serving women that they adored him and pampered him with all kinds of little between-meal treats.

All these anecdotes reflect the atmosphere that Bud had the good fortune to find at Bouffémont. The doctor still remembers his rather exceptional patient in the following terms:

Powell was unlike the other patients because of his greater maturity but mainly because of his gentleness. He was very withdrawn when he arrived but gradually he integrated himself into the community, especially when he began to play. When he found we had an excellent piano, he played all the time, just for himself. Sometimes patients would listen and they were enthralled. His music brought calm and serenity. I asked him if he would give a little concert and he kindly agreed. He was to give several for the whole sanatorium community.

He was nice to everyone and the staff were all fond of him. With the nurses his relationship was like mother and son.

You were of great help to him, as psychologically he was like an infant. He was passive, taking no interest in his own health and I think he was unaware of the problems he caused. He never understood the seriousness of his illness but always had confidence.

The hardship of his life, his family problems, etc., may all have contributed to his illness. Tuberculosis is often linked with psychological factors in its evolution and its cure. Antibiotic drugs were used at the time but there is no denying the importance of the psychological aspect. In his case, his psychological state undoubtedly played a decisive role in his treatment. He flourished at Bouffémont and by the time he left his condition was greatly improved.

We did have some administrative problems with him as his papers were in the hands of a certain Altevia Edwards. When our letters to her went unanswered, I informed the state prosecutor's office and a police investigation was ordered.

The police had called on Buttercup to question her about the matter. The police report reads as follows:

Subject has great difficulty speaking French. When informed of the purpose of our visit, she told us through the hotel manager that she was not the mistress but the legitimate wife of Mr. Bud Powell. She states they were married on March 29, 1957, in Montclair, New Jersey, and that that state does not issue marriage certificates.

Buttercup had an answer for everything! There was one small detail, however: Bud had married Audrey Hill on March 9, 1953 and his divorce was still pending on the date she gave for their supposed wedding. So either she was lying or the marriage was bigamous.

The police report went on:

Mrs. Edwards declares that her husband, a musician of talent and fame, is the victim of a plot to isolate him and exploit him for recordings. Consequently, to protect him from dishonest affairs, she has initiated legal action with a view to his transfer to a sanatorium in Switzerland. Her husband's identity papers are presently in the hands of her attorney in Geneva. Mrs. Edwards is therefore unable to submit these papers as requested by the head doctor at Bouffémont.

I had written down my phone number for Bud and he could call me whenever he liked from a phone in the lounge. Sometimes he would call and say hello, then remain silent. The mere fact of having me on the line seemed to comfort him, and I made conversation alone as best I could. I was always moved by his need to stay in touch.

The solitude in which he lived most of the time was sensitively described by the journalist Jean Wagner in *Cahiers du Jazz* no. 9:

> To this day, I am always astonished when I come face to face with a man whose works have been and still are vital to my life. The frequency of such encounters, I am not ashamed to admit, has in no way dulled the surprise or the wonder.
>
> These were my thoughts the other day as I sat beside Francis Paudras driving towards Bouffémont, on the way to see Bud Powell in his sanatorium. It's sad, a sanatorium in winter. At close of day it all takes on an indefinable hue of dirty gray.
>
> Silhouetted against the darkness, the patients walked slowly, as only those walk who unconsciously seem, for the moment, to have no hold on time. The overall effect was eerie and unspeakably sad.
>
> And there in the middle of it all was the sweet round face of Bud.
>
> I was alone with him for about an hour while Francis talked with the head doctor. We didn't exchange three words.
>
> He was there, immobile in front of me. He looked out the window at the trees and the lawn. He looked at me. He touched my hands but said not a word except "How do you feel?"
>
> But during that hour of mutual silence, his presence alone sufficed to maintain a strange atmosphere, to give another color to the anonymous little room.
>
> The tragedy of this man before me was the tragedy of a solitary artist who has but one language to communicate in—music. And if everyday life is so painful, if not impossible for him, it's because so few perceive the language of music. When Francis came back, he was transformed. Francis Paudras, through unfailing friendship, a friendship based on an acute perception of Bud's musical universe, has been able to penetrate Bud's world, a world that is more and more opaque. Francis Paudras is for Bud a sort of bridge between the everyday reality he flees, and which flees from him every day more intensely, and his own reality, the only one which, in his eyes (and rightly so, even though he's not conscious of it), is worth being lived.

When we left the sanatorium night was falling. Bud kept looking at Francis. Like a child, he tried to delay his departure. It was moving to see this man trying to hang on to one last bit of warmth before finding himself alone in the night, amid the strange surroundings of a lonely chateau.

The Christmas season was approaching, with its traditional festivities, presents, good wishes and visits of friends. How could we be merry with Bud locked away in the sanatorium, huddled in his loneliness? Once again the doctor was extremely understanding. He knew the importance of good morale on a patient's recovery. During the war, he had done remarkable feats both as a doctor and as a member of the Resistance. He knew the psychosomatic nature of this type of illness and this viewpoint was beneficial to us. When I spoke of our sadness at spending the holidays without Bud, he first spoke of his medical condition—Bud was still contagious, very weak and a strict sanatorium regimen was indispensable. Then, thinking it over, he added, "Still, there may be a solution."

I had already asked him if it was possible to put us on medication as a protective measure. Now he thought that could indeed be the solution. We would be put on Rimifon and Bud would be allowed to come home with us for the holidays. And so it was decided, then and there, to release him, as simple as that! Thank you, doctor, once again, for the marvelous Christmas gift. When I told Bud, he was beside himself. As the days went by he grew more and more impatient, flooding me with phone calls to ask again and again what day he was leaving, what date, what time . . . then forgetting and calling to ask again. The apparently childlike behavior had a deeper sense. It was simply that he dared do in utter simplicity what most pseudo-adults refrain from doing out of pride, for fear of looking silly.

UNA NOCHE CON FRANCIS

(Recorded in Paris, July 31, 1964 [Fontana])

As Christmas approached we got busy getting everything ready for the big day. I had to do some finishing touches on the decorations, mainly in Bud's room. I worked on them until the last minute and was a little late in leaving for Bouffémont. I had told Bud I'd pick him up at six o'clock but by the time I arrived it was eight. Night had fallen and I found the little world of the sanatorium effervescent. A big party was just getting under way for those patients who had to stay. Bud wasn't one of these so I went to find him in his room. I gently opened the door and he barely turned his head as I entered. He was sitting on the edge of the bed, sunk in his thoughts, looking in the depths of despair. When he realized I was there, his face lit up and he exclaimed almost incredulously, "You're finally here! I thought you weren't coming." Then he added, softly, "It's nice of you to come." And finally, in a worried tone, "You did come to get me, didn't you?"

I was angry with myself for having been late, suddenly aware of how worried he must have been as the time dragged by. "Of course I'm coming to pick you up. Forgive me, Bud. I'm sorry I was late, I had some work to finish. I hope you didn't think it was all off. All the friends are waiting for you—Roger, Mic, Vincent, Ranci, Yvette, Mireille. The whole gang is at home."

He didn't seem to believe me. Without wasting a minute, I helped him into his overcoat, and when he had pulled the cap down securely on his head with an expert gesture, we headed for the exit. A few patients greeted him in the hall and wished us a merry Christmas. I felt like a parent taking a child home from boarding school. Bud was grinning like a schoolboy at the top of the class who has just been rewarded with permission to leave.

In the soft light of the car, his face had that "Mona Lisa smile." All through the ride he made me repeat the details. "Who's there? What will we eat? How long will I stay? Will there be cake?" He delighted in my answers, and for me, Christmas had already begun.

We reached Paris and climbed up the five flights as slowly as possible. When we got to the door, I was pleased to notice he didn't seem out of breath. I remembered how badly he had struggled before his diagnosis. We rang the bell several times and the door opened to a great gust of laughter. It was a triumphal entrance. Nicole and all of our friends were very moved, Bud no less than the others.

When the kisses and greetings were over, Bud looked around the room. We had fixed up a traditional Christmas tree, a fire was crackling in the fireplace, and the whole apartment shone in the candlelight. The party began. Roger, in a white apron and chef's hat, was busy tending the spit on which a beautiful turkey was roasting. Great platters of seafood were brought out onto the long table. We had done our shopping at the best vendors in Les Halles. It looked like it was going to be a great evening. Bud didn't stop laughing and our friends, as always, were full of good cheer. The record player poured forth our favorite music—Bud's, of course—and our fifth-floor walkup had an air of paradise.

Bud was an excellent dinner guest. He enjoyed eating and particularly loved the traditional order of dishes. As soon as he came to live with us, he always observed, at first with open curiosity, and then with great interest, how we organized our meals. From then on, he never mixed all the courses on one plate, as many Americans do, but savored the progression of the dishes: hors-d'oeuvres, meat, vegetables, cheeses, dessert.

With his "special" diet at the sanatorium, full meals plus the snacks the staff slipped him, the rest of us had trouble keeping up. Dr. Joussaume had recommended we be reasonable and see that Bud didn't get to sleep too late. Bud had agreed, but in the general euphoria, I hardly dared look at the time. When the last pastries were consumed, the signal was given to open the presents under the tree. We told Bud to go have a look, too. There were presents for all of us but by far the most were for Bud, as everyone had wanted to give him something. There were a number of nice ties and the stiff-collared shirts he liked so much. I had bought him a watch. He acted like a kid, opening the packages with exaggerated slowness and exclaiming at each gift.

Now it was his turn to give us his Christmas present, the best present of all. He walked to the piano. The moment was sublime. Fortunately, my tape recorder was in good working order and that memorable evening is recorded in all its intensity and magic. His music expressed a *joie de vivre* probably never captured before and undoubtedly represents a unique document among his works.

It was a moment of grace, and the audience thrilled to each modulation. But at last we had to admit it was bedtime. As our Christmas parties always lasted three days, with friends camping at the house, it wasn't hard for me to persuade Bud to go to bed.

It was still early for Christmas Eve and the party went on. Bud's playing had made me feel like playing, too, and I sat down at the piano, stimulated by the aura of music in the air. All at once the door opened and there stood Bud in his smart dark blue pajamas, looking as dapper as if he wore a tux, and smiling from ear to ear. "If Francis is playing, I'm coming back!"

The festivities started up again. We had to bring out the turkey, then cheese, then cake before we could get him to go back to bed. I guess we weren't very convincing because he came out three more times that night, giggling like a naughty child and each time with a new excuse.

The three days spent together showed that Bud's recovery was progressing nicely. His "home leave" had quickened the train of events. Dr. Joussaume was always open to new ideas, and now his patient's great progress had given him an idea. After checking the latest tests, he authorized me to come and get Bud every weekend, with the condition that Nicole and I stay on our preventative medication. The one cardinal rule was: no excess, and no unusual strain. Bud was delighted and promised to follow the rules to the letter.

Every Saturday I came to get him after lunch, at one o'clock. He was always ready by nine in the morning and refused to have his lunch at the sanatorium. I could never make him remember that he was not allowed to leave until one o'clock. He'd be waiting outside on the front steps in his raincoat, his cap on his head and an impatient look on his face. As soon as he saw me, he ran toward me with uncommon vitality and literally pushed me to the gate. One day, I found him on the steps as usual, but this time surrounded by a group of young people. When Bud stood up to leave, one of the boys hurried toward us. I stopped Bud, thinking the young man had something to say to him.

But it was to me he spoke.

"Hello," he said. "I don't want to bother you, but could you . . . That is, if you could convince Bud to . . ."

"Convince him to what? I don't understand."

"Bud's been trying to get out of it, but we'd really like it if he'd give our friend a return match."

"Return match. What do you mean?"

Another boy walked up.

"Well, you see, we noticed Bud alone a lot of the time, so we asked him to join us for a game of chess."

"Oh yeah? What happened?"

"At first he said no, but we insisted. He said he didn't play very well, but..."

"It's probably true. I never saw him play chess. Or any other game either, for that matter."

"Well, he finally agreed. He had a faraway look, kind of absent-minded during the whole game. He didn't even seem to be paying attention. And then, when no one was expecting it, he suddenly called out, 'checkmate!' And then he got up and left. Ever since, he's refused to play a return match, and that's not fair."

I said I thought it was true that he didn't play very well and he had probably won by luck.

"That's impossible," said the boy, "our friend just happens to be the French national chess champion!"

Bud didn't say a word about it. In the car, he was very quiet. He just stared at the road with a little smile. After a while, I asked, in a neutral voice, "Bud, do you play chess?"

"Oh, a little. My father taught me when I was a kid."

He gave no further explanation and continued his contemplation of the road. On our way home Bud liked to stop off, always in the same little bistro, for some sweets and a glass of his favorite, strawberry milk. I had learned to like it too. And he'd smoke his eternal Chesterfields. He never stopped smoking. At first, the doctors at the hospital had forbidden him to smoke, but then they decided that it was worse to deprive him of it, as long as it was in moderation.

Every Sunday there was the heartache of returning to the sanatorium. As he put on his raincoat to leave, he seemed to be getting back into all his pain. It reminded me of when I was at boarding school, unhappy each time I had to go back. I'd promise to phone the next morning to have a little chat. But sometimes he'd phone before I even had a chance to get back home. The telephone was his lifeline and he used it to the hilt. The conversation was always the same.

"When are you coming to get me?"

"Saturday, Bud, not until Saturday. Be patient, it's only Tuesday."

"Not till Saturday?"

"No, you know very well it's a special privilege."

"You really can't make it before Saturday? Okay, what you been doing? Do you think you can come before Saturday?"

It was impossible to talk about anything else. Sometimes, we would hang up and he'd call back immediately to start all over again.

One Saturday, as soon as I'd arrived, he announced, "Francis, I've written a tune for you. It's called 'Una Noche Con Francis.'"

To prove he wasn't joking, he sang it to me in the car. My knowledge of Spanish was very limited. But I understood the meaning of the title. Our Christmas party had left a happy memory for us all, and he wanted to commemorate it musically.

"Why's the title in Spanish?" I asked.

He just laughed and said nothing. But the tune was sufficient explanation. Its Afro-Cuban beat and lively rhythm evoked the festive mood of the evening. I was proud of the marvelous present Bud had given me.

His creative impulse didn't stop there. The next weekend Bud announced he had written some more tunes. There was every sign of a rebirth. Our trips home from the sanatorium were enlivened by his songs. He couldn't wait for me to hear his new compositions: "Blues for Bouffémont," a real blues if ever there was one, expressing the sorrow and resignation of one haunted by fate, "Heyadididee" and "For My Friends," both still unreleased, and "In the Mood for a Classic," a tune full of bounce.

The tunes he wrote during this period are particularly classical. Except for "Blues for Bouffémont," they express the newfound joy that went along with the improvement in his health. His progress continued. The last exams showed that the worst was over. He was no longer contagious. We could now stop taking our medication.

Henri Renaud was following his progress and now phoned me to suggest a visit to Bouffémont and if possible an interview about his new compositions. This interview was recorded on my portable tape machine:

> Henri: Bud, you told me that you just wrote a new composition while you were in Bouffémont. What is it called, and can you give me some idea of it?
> Bud: I wrote "In the Mood for a Classic" (Bud begins to hum the tune).
> Henri: Bud, whom did you write that tune for?
> Bud: To my dear friend, Randi Hultin.

The interview wasn't easy. As I expected, he remained deaf to Henri's questions and as always I had to rephrase each question to get an answer out of him. Besides, Bud was still on medication and was somewhat drowsy at that time of day. But we did manage to get a few responses.

Henri: How are you feeling?
Bud: I feel fine, thank you. The doctors say I'll be well soon and I'll go home. They said it's improving fast.
Henri: Bud, what have you heard recently that you like?
Bud: Well, Charlie Mingus is nice, and Toshiko is nice. I think she's a very technical pianist.
Henri: Do you often listen to the recordings of Art Tatum?
Bud: I'm crazy about Tatum. He's still my best friend, one of my good friends.
Henri: What are your latest compositions?
Bud: Three new tunes: "In the Mood for a Classic" is one, "Heya-dididee" is another. "Una Noche Con Francis" is the other.
Henri: Bud, do you know Bill Evans?
Bud: I heard him on records only. He's nice. He can play. I heard he's sick.
Henri: Me too, but I can tell you he's doing okay. Bud, thanks so much for welcoming us, and so long.
Bud: *Bon soir, je vais revenir bientôt.*

That day he played his new tunes on the music room piano and I shot a little 16-mm. film. A photo essay was also made of the event by Dolly Schmidt, the wife of French filmmaker Jean Schmidt, whom I had just gotten to know. Jean Schmidt had made a moving and sensitive film about the life of gypsies whose caravans were systematically expelled from one village after another. The film, called *Kriss Romani*, had made people more aware of the plight of these people and the denial of their rights.

Schmidt was interested in Bud's story and suggested we write a scenario together relating the episode of our first meeting and tracing all the events that led up to his present resurrection. It was in a way an anticipation of the movie *'Round Midnight*, but with one significant difference—we would have Bud play his own role and, of course, compose and direct the music for the film. An item about the project appeared in *Jazz Hot* (January 1964) entitled "Concerning Bud Powell—will the cinema finally pay homage to jazz?" Alas, the film was never made, for the simple reason that it never found a producer. One could cry today to think how powerful such a document could have been. Bud's screen presence was incomparable. His feelings passed with an unbelievable emotional charge, mainly because he had no artifice. He was simply and sincerely himself.

One project that did come off was through the help of Philippe Koechlin, the editor-in-chief of *Jazz Hot*, who closely followed all of the events concerning Bud. His friendship and consideration were valuable at a time when I was trying to cope with a difficult situation in the face of general indifference. He tried to find ways to help me pay the debts I had incurred in relation to Bud and introduced me to Jean Tronchot, another editor at *Jazz Hot*, who was also artistic director of the jazz department at Fontana records. Philippe knew I regularly recorded Bud at home and he suggested that Tronchot put out a record based on my tapes, if Bud agreed, of course. The private nature of these recordings, the confidential and intimate climate of the music, made them unique. Bud was excited about the project and we spent part of the weekend picking out the tunes and timing them. Among the works we chose were some solo ballads and some fast pieces he had played with me, as a duet. When Bud played, I would sometimes pick up a pair of brushes and accompany him on a newspaper. When he did the same for me, I discovered he was a very exciting drummer.

Jef Gilson, who was then sound engineer at Vogue, was very helpful. He offered to do the necessary corrections and editing, and he made the master free of charge. The album came out on the Fontana label, entitled *Bud at Home*. On the cover was a nice shot of Bud seated comfortably in his armchair.

We carefully followed coming concerts, in the hope of a visit by Thelonious Monk, Dizzy Gillespie, Art Blakey, or another of the old-timers. We were delighted to read that Monk's quartet was coming on February 23, 1964. We found out when and where they were arriving, and since it was on a weekend when Bud was in town, I proposed that we go out and meet his old friend at the airport. He was all excited at the thought of seeing Monk again. Musicians don't often go and meet other musicians. A friend of mine took along his 16-mm. camera to film the great encounter.

It turned out to be a brilliant idea, for the scene was moving indeed. Thelonious and Nellie were absorbed in the usual formalities and at first didn't notice Bud. But as they came through the last control, Monk looked up and spotted Bud in the crowd. He stopped for a split second, in disbelief, as if an apparition was there before him. But Bud was already walking toward him, his arms outstretched, a broad smile on his face. Thelonious put down his bags and put his arms around Bud. It was a long silent embrace, then Thelonious stepped back to look Bud over. Obviously, he couldn't believe his eyes, Bud had changed so much. Bud looked over at us and, taking Monk by the waist, dragged him insistently over to introduce us to him, in terms that I'll never forget. "Thelonious, this is Nicole and Francis. They're my friends, my best friends. They take good care of me, you know."

I was moved and somewhat intimidated. Thelonious didn't let go of my hand and looked into my eyes with his grave and penetrating look. While Bud wasn't looking, he whispered very softly, not hiding his surprise, "Bud's in great shape, man, great shape!"

It was wonderful to see them like that, looking at each other with obvious love and admiration. Thelonious, the colossus, with his fur hat, and Bud, a little pudgy, looking very Parisian in his canvas cap. I never again saw Thelonious looking so relaxed and happy.

A number of friends were there—André Francis, Jean-Louis Gini-bre, Lucien Malson—and a great many journalists. They all tried to talk to Thelonious but after a few words he'd turn away and look at Bud. No one managed to get an interview: he had eyes only for Bud!

That night we were all at the Olympia. We went backstage before the concert to see the musicians and friends, including Kenny Clarke. Everyone was talking about a tour the quartet had just made in Japan. Bud was fascinated by the anecdotes about the trip. He never took his eyes off Thelonious, hanging on his every word. All of a sudden he came up to him and, in a confidential voice, said, "Is it true that Japanese women . . ."

Then he stopped, embarrassed. Thelonious waited. Bud glanced around to make sure no one else was listening and went on, ". . . that they got . . . you know, that their thing goes sideways?"

There was a roar of laughter. Bud's face wore the expression of a child playing a prank. Thelonious made believe he was deeply meditating then, in a very serious tone, replied, "Now that depends which way you look, man!"

The answer left Bud puzzled. He wasn't satisfied. Everybody put his two cents in, and the "clarification" grew hazier by the minute. Then someone came to call the musicians, cutting short the fascinating discussion. That night, the music was electrifying. Thelonious was in fine form. Bud insisted on seeing him afterwards. Monk was delighted with the concert and its reception. He couldn't stand still and kept dancing around his dressing room as Bud watched in admiration. Thelonious and Nellie wanted to go out to eat and invited us to join them. Nicole was tired and went home, but the rest of us went to Gaby and Haynes. All the American musicians who passed through Paris knew this place where you could get real American "soul food" until the early morning hours. Thelonious chose a table on a platform in an alcove. He sat opposite Bud and took care of him all night, mobilizing all the waiters to make sure Bud had everything he wanted. That night he could see for himself Bud's astounding appetite. The only conversation was about the quality of the food, as dish after dish paraded across the table to Bud's plate.

When we got back home, Bud asked me to put on a record by Thelonious and started dancing to it the way Monk had done while the musicians took their choruses. Bud was very excited and we went to bed late that night. Before heading for his room, he said good night, then added in a conspiratorial whisper, "Tell me, Francis, do Japanese women . . . ?"

Oscar Goodstein had never ceased to take an interest in Bud's health. However, his financial aid stopped, as Bud's resources in the States had apparently run out. In a letter to me dated January 20, 1964, he explained that it would be difficult to raise more money for Bud in the United States and, therefore, it might be a good time for me and the musicians in Europe to arrange a benefit for Bud in Paris, to pay for the balance due to the Hospital Foch and for the remainder of Bud's stay in the sanatorium.

Philippe Koechlin had written several times about Bud in *Jazz Hot*. He was in a good position to know the financial difficulties we were having and he suggested holding a benefit concert. The news of this project spread fast among musicians. Seldom before had there been such solidarity. Some musicians, like Donald Byrd, even offered to pay their own expenses in order to participate. I stayed up a whole night making the poster for it. I was exhausted, but looking forward to the great event.

The concert took place at Salle Wagram on March 13, 1964, and it lasted a full six hours. It might have turned into a real jazz festival except that the organizers had limited each group to two tunes. After the concert and the goodbye kisses we set out for home, where we had planned a small party with only the closest of our musician friends. The gang from Les Halles had volunteered to look after the catering.

Bud was on home leave again but there was no question of his staying up so late. He hadn't gone to the concert. It was 3 A.M. when the first guests arrived and they were surprised to find him up. With a bright smile, he stood guard at the buffet table, waiting impatiently for the company. On the large table and several small ones was the most fantastic array of seafood imaginable. People were arriving by waves, so many that we were worried where to put them. By the time the doorbell had rung its last, we were fifty people strong, mostly musicians, all wanting to see Bud and congratulate him on his recovery.

That night he was the center of attraction. I told him that he was the host and he threw himself into his role, greeting his guests with perfect manners. All that remained was to attack the mountains of clams and oysters and sea urchins—a feast for a millionaire. Bud was all ears, wanting to hear all about the concert, exclaiming over each detail. Suddenly, he said he wished we could do it all over again at the house, with everyone who was there.

The large room had of course been fully soundproofed and there was no problem as long as all the doors and windows were kept closed. But with all the people there that evening we had to open them in order to breathe. Hazel Scott began the festivities, followed by René Urtréger, accompanied by Donald Byrd, then Johnny Griffin, and so on, all night long.

At 5 A.M. the party was still going strong when the fun was rudely interrupted by a series of insistent rings of the doorbell. The guest nearest the door went to open it and when he saw who it was he told Bud to get me, quick! Bud's smile vanished as he ran over and whispered in my ear, "Francis, it's the police."

With so many people making so much noise at that hour of the morning, I knew there'd be no use arguing. I went to the door like a lamb to the slaughter. The sweet aroma of an exotic herb floated in the air. I took a deep breath before opening the door. Two ominous silhouettes, with their distinctive hats and dark capes, stood motionless in the doorway. I was already calculating the odds against me. I opened my mouth, then froze, thunderstruck. "Lucien! . . . Lulu!"

"Francis!"

"Lulu! . . . you old son-of-a-bitch! What are you doing here?"

The police officer standing before me was none other than my childhood friend Lulu. What a shock to see him in a cop's uniform! Lulu and I had climbed trees together, broken windows with our slingshots, set off firecrackers at school and tossed stinkballs in the sacristy when we were choir boys. We had also listened to Fats Waller, Art Tatum, and Bud Powell. He was the friend who had shown my parents the article in *Jazz Hot* that had told about Bud living in my house, "Lulu! Well, I'll be . . . Well, come on, don't stand there on the doorstep. Come in."

And we fell into each other's arms. His colleague didn't know what to make of it all but was soon grabbed by outstretched arms and pulled into the festivities. "Come on," said Lulu. "He's a friend from way back. We were kids together. Our parents played cards together."

There wasn't a clean glass left in the house but someone found two cereal bowls, filled them with champagne and handed them to the newcomers. Lulu explained he had fallen on hard times (he was an upholsterer by trade) and had joined the police force as a temporary expedient in order to support his wife and family. By the time we'd introduced them to the friends, refilled their bowls with champagne and reminisced a little about the old days, an hour had gone by. Bud was looking at me again as if I were some kind of magician. I had saved him before from police and doctors, but this was beyond belief! Our uniformed friends took their leave, eyes twinkling, saying they'd come back and see us sometime.

"So long, Lulu. Regards to the family."

In the hallway, grim-faced neighbors were pacing up and down in their bathrobes. We had a few more run-ins later on, but they never again tried calling the police to stop our musical soirées. Maybe the gods were with us after all!

Bud continued to get better rapidly. The understanding attitude of the doctors certainly helped, as did his superb diet, rounded out by his purchases at the canteen. He had now accepted the sanatorium routine and although the weekly separations remained difficult, he seemed resigned and serene.

Each weekend was planned down to the smallest detail, the one aim being to pamper Bud. The contingent from Les Halles arrived laden with the usual seafood, a large roast beef or leg of lamb and, of course, the indispensable pastries. It was like Christmas every weekend.

Bud's smile never left his face. Despite the hardships of this period, it left me with wonderful memories. I felt this trial had brought us closer. Now it wasn't just a great musician I saw in Bud, but a fragile human being, full of hope, slowly regaining his taste for life with his home, with his family. He was bright and optimistic, and more communicative than ever before.

Then came an event that would profoundly affect our lives. Nicole and I had long wanted a child—now we learned that she was pregnant. In keeping with our Bohemian lifestyle, it was logical that the pregnancy came first and the marriage second. As soon as we had some free time, we set the date at the local town hall, with Bud as my best man. Our family ties became even firmer. Bud was overjoyed and became extremely solicitous of Nicole. He took an interest in her pregnancy, asking her many times how she was feeling, when the baby was due, or if she felt it moving.

When I suggested he should be the baby's godfather, he agreed instantly. My explanations about the role of the godfather in case the father died prematurely left him bemused. We were glad this would forge yet another tie with our family, and Bud was extremely proud and happy of what was in store. Being godfather to our baby became an obsession of his and he kept reminding us that, whatever happened, no one but he should fill this role. During this period, his attitude underwent a further evolution. His view of life seemed more realistic and he took a greater interest in everyday pursuits. It was a real turning point and proved that our efforts had been worthwhile. Bud was getting well and became happier than he had ever been.

One day, out of the blue, he looked at me curiously and said, "Tell me, Francis . . . are you black or white?"

I was taken by surprise. "What do you think?"

"I don't know." He stared at me harder than ever.

"What do you think, Bud?" I asked again, amused.

"I think you got soul!" he replied in a grave voice.

It was obvious that until then he had never thought about the color of my skin. In a way, it was the greatest of compliments. If he hadn't noticed this detail, it showed he was no more obsessed by it than I was and nothing had ever come between us to bring the matter up. For my part, I had long ago given up the idea that jazz is the exclusive property of one people. Was classical music reserved for whites? Bud played Bach and Chopin as well as anyone, maybe better. Jazz has become a universal language. Those who play it and love it recognize one another, and they are of all cultural and racial origins. Of course, no one should be unaware of the original creators, but the particular genius and the triumph of jazz is to have become the music of the intelligent world. Bird once told a bunch of musicians, "Jazz should be written down so that it can be transmitted. That's the only way it can become important and universal."

Yet jazz is a selective discipline. It has its chosen few. You don't just learn jazz. You come to it as you come to religion. If certain predispositions are there, and especially a strong love for this music, at that point a lot of hard work and perseverance will do the rest. A music that is miraculous by its improvisation, a music of creators devoted to constant and spontaneous writing, it has attracted people who resemble one another, who share something strong. This common denominator, which no one should ever try to identify, is one of the most significant possibilities for peace among men. A music of love for one great church, a universal religion of which Bud was one of the high priests. Bill Evans once said, with complete lucidity, and with his usual sharp focus, "I hope my music will contribute to the building of a better world."

We knew that soon Bud would be fully recovered and allowed to come home. The long-awaited day came sooner than expected. The last test results and Bud's excellent morale had led Dr. Joussaume to make an exceptional suggestion. (For that matter, everything about this doctor was exceptional, and I will be forever grateful to him.) Now, besides the special favors and weekend passes, he had considered the amount of money the hospitalization was costing us and, knowing how carefully we carried out his instructions, he thought the last phase of treatment could be taken care of at home. This plan was accepted in general euphoria.

Bud had to go for regular check-ups. As for the quiet pace of life and the limits to be respected, we were already used to that. So Bud came back to Rue de Clichy and our life resumed its normal course, with just a few restrictions that Bud accepted with great docility. For his cure to be completed without any setbacks, he had to get enough rest and eat a well-balanced diet. As a bonus, he was surrounded with our unbounded affection. Summer had arrived and we started visiting friends in the country. Again, the rhythms of Art Tatum resounded in our lives and Bud grew stronger. I threw myself into my work with renewed vigor since my good friend was back. His music had enhanced my life and his presence made my every act seem sublime.

Happiness is an abstract notion, but now I felt it was almost palpable. Through the most uncanny events, I had the feeling that everything was calculated, preordained, that the trials I was going through were necessary and inevitable. These eerie impressions were incommunicable in their very nature and also in the utter simplicity of our feelings. We understood each other with a glance, a word. Language, with its jumble of useless words, had given way to another, more perfect, communication.

Bud's last check-up went well. He was completely cured, though still fragile, and we had to be vigilant.

He worked at the piano assiduously and with obvious pleasure. I suggested he might want to go back to some of his compositions that he hadn't played lately—"Un Poco Loco," "Tempus Fugue-it," "Dusky 'n' Sandy," "Bouncing With Bud," "Oblivion," "Dance of the Infidels," "Hallucination," and "Glass Enclosure"—and he started working on them again. He also played some classical pieces by Bach, Chopin, and Rachmaninoff. These were for his own pleasure, and not because he had any intention of including them in his programs. I was fascinated to see how these pieces came back to him, for he played without a score. He had some trouble at first, but wound up playing them brilliantly in the end. He enjoyed these exercises and liked listening immediately to the recordings I made. His ability to remember music from so long ago was impressive. I realized he was recomposing everything by analysis. Some harmonies, excellent though they were, differed from the original ones in their subtlety and didn't sound quite as assured, but on the next few tries, he would always end up getting them right.

The news of Bud's return traveled quickly around Paris and the phone rang all day long. Everyone wanted to speak to him or to know how he was. During the seven months at the sanatorium there hadn't been many visits. Bibi Rovère and his wife Lili, Johnny Griffin, and the great organist Eddy Louiss and his wife Martine were the only ones who made it aside from the intimate friends. But Bud's life had often been like that. Maybe that was how he learned to live with his solitude.

This solitude created a distance between not only the public at large, but also musicians close to him—close in appearance, that is. I think Bud avoided certain relationships to escape from a milieu he never felt was really his. Even in his youth he had shown some reticence to enter the professional world of jazz. What he liked best was to play as an amateur, for music's sake alone, accompanied by his childhood friends Andy Browne and Ray Perry on violins and Jessie Drake on trumpet.

After a few weeks Bud started asking if we could go back to the Blue Note. I had a hunch he felt like playing. I called Dr. Joussaume to ask his opinion. His tests were excellent and in the best interests of his morale the doctor agreed that Bud could play as long as he didn't stay up too late.

During his entire hospitalization, the Blue Note had never taken down the sign outside presenting the house trio, The Three Bosses— Bud Powell, Pierre Michelot, and Kenny Clarke. When I pointed this out to Ben Benjamin, he apologized, making up a lot of lame excuses. The three famous names had continued to attract customers from far and wide and the waiters had orders not to mention Bud's absence. They would show the customers in, saying simply that the musicians would be there soon. I was worried about Bud's reaction if he saw his name being used like that, but fortunately that first night he didn't notice. The Blue Note gave him a warm welcome, with a standing ovation from musicians and audience alike. By way of thanks he played a set that was positively mind-blowing. Ben instantly offered him an engagement for the coming weeks. The contract was signed with the one condition the doctor had stipulated: Bud would play only the first set, to enable him to get to bed early.

With its great pianist back, the Blue Note recaptured the atmosphere of the good old days. Bud played with Michel Gaudry and Larry Ritchie. Larry was the fine drummer I had seen for the first time with Jackie McLean in the film *The Connection*. He positively worshipped Bud. Thanks to the complicity of the three musicians, this trio had found a new sound and an original pulse. Bud had great authority over his partners, but that didn't stop him from listening attentively to them. True, he imposed his music, but he did it using their particular strengths with great intelligence. How often have I heard musicians say, "Tonight, I'm playing against so and so." This comment reflects a sad reality. But for Bud, music had to come out the winner in any kind of confrontation. He made use of everything, even the imperfections or weaknesses of others. He involved the personality of each musician, matching their intentions and drawing even the least able into the final whirlwind. Through Bud, they gave the best of themselves, discovered unsuspected capacities and unparalleled joys.

His comeback on the jazz scene was greeted with lukewarm attention by blasé critics, comfortably settled in their preconceived notions. Through indifference, they perpetuated the usual errors that had so damaged Bud in the past. Nevertheless, he continued to play with enthusiasm and to evolve revolutionary ideas, unsuspected by the so-called experts. His ideas prefigured the great lines that a new generation of pianists would soon develop. Today we are fortunate to have a young generation of writers who closely follow living jazz.

Just at that time, Oscar Goodstein, in response to the latest news I had given him, unexpectedly made me the following offer. He suggested that if it was possible for me to take a leave of absence for ten to twelve weeks to bring Bud to New York with me, he would forward airplane passage for both of us from Paris to New York, as an advance against Bud's earnings. Oscar would schedule Bud to perform at Birdland and pay him $500 each week. (He would pay the bass player and drummer separately.) He figured that it would cost me and Bud less than $150 a week to maintain ourselves in New York and the remaining $350 could be saved, resulting in approximately $3,500 after ten to twelve weeks of consecutive work.

Oscar realized that this might be an imposition on me, but he felt I was "one of the few persons that [he could] absolutely trust to take care of Bud." He reassured me that the smoke-free air in Birdland, due to their ventilating system, would not affect Bud's health and that they would have a doctor check Bud's health every week.

This suggestion, intended to help pay off the sanatorium expenses, sounded interesting, but I was hesitant. Nicole, though she was feeling fine, would soon enter a difficult period of pregnancy. Bud was also surprised by the offer. At first he expressed no particular opinion, but in the following days, he seemed more and more excited by the idea and began asking me a host of questions about the conditions of our stay, questions that I was in no position to answer.

Our friends—Johnny Griffin, Dexter Gordon, Art Taylor, Kenny Clarke, etc.—all seemed enthusiastic about the proposal and the idea began to take hold in our minds. Oscar inundated us with letters, each more inviting than the last, all emphasizing the exalting prospect for Bud Powell of a triumphal comeback to New York. Alan Bates, an English producer, also loved the idea. As for me, fairly ignorant of certain aspects of American life, I was not unduly worried about the project. I found myself dreaming of Bud's glorious comeback. Bird was gone. So were Billie and Lester. After six years away, it was time for Bud to return. The American fans would be overjoyed and I was sure they'd give him a warm welcome. In any case, unless there was some obvious danger, I would do nothing to hinder any project that might help Bud, that would put him back on the pedestal he so rightly deserved. All things considered, it seemed like a marvelous adventure. Nicole, always ready to do anything for Bud, encouraged me to go, and so it was decided, to unanimous glee.

Bud had a visit from the Norwegian journalist Randi Hultin, a woman he had met in Oslo during his 1962 tour. In an interview she later gave me, she relates her second meeting with Bud:

When I arrived in Paris in July 1964, Buttercup took me to the Blue Note, and when Bud saw me, he burst into laughter. Strangely, he couldn't stop laughing, and Buttercup didn't let me talk to him then, so I returned to the Hotel Louisiane, where I was staying. The next day at noon I asked Buttercup if it was possible for me to see Bud. "Wait a minute. He's coming," she said. [In reality, Buttercup had called me right away to ask me very urgently to come and bring Bud, with no other explanation.] So we were sitting outside the Café de Seine when you and Bud arrived. Bud looked at me, took my hand, and immediately Buttercup started to talk about the Chicken Shack, her club and grill in Paris, which she managed. "Everybody thinks that I stole the money to start my club, but that's not true," she said.

I asked Bud, "Do you feel good now?"

"Randi, did you know I was sick?" he asked.

"Sure. Everybody all over the world knew you were sick." And he was smiling.

During that time Buttercup kept on talking about the money she hadn't taken and suddenly Bud said, "Francis, let's leave. You see now, Buttercup, Francis is taking care of my business."

And I was shocked because I had never heard him talking like that before. So I asked Bud, "Please, Bud, can you give me your new address?"

Buttercup broke in, "No, no. I can give it to you," still always trying to control the situation.

But Bud interrupted her sharply. "No, Randi. If you have a paper and a pencil, I'll write it down. Are you going to come listen to me?" he added. . . .

When I came by the Blue Note Ted Curson was playing opposite Bud, and Bud asked me if I came to listen to "this other guy."

"Yes, sure. But first of all I came to listen to you."

"Are you sure, Randi? But you know I think he plays much too modern for me."

So when he went up to play, he took my hand again and said, "Will you please come up with me on the stage?" Then he asked me what I wanted him to play for me. Ron Jefferson, the drummer, had been telling me about "In the Mood for a Classic," so I asked for that. It was so beautiful, it broke my heart. He had changed so much since the last time I had seen him in Scandinavia. He was talking so fluidly and normally with the musicians and all. . . .

One evening, Francis, you were sitting in the club with Alan Bates, who was the producer for that new record Bud was going to do. Bud told you then, "Remember, Francis, 'In the Mood for a Classic' will be dedicated to Randi on the record."

And you asked him, "But Bud, why didn't you dedicate 'Una Noche Con Francis' to me?" and Bud said, "Oh no, 'cause 'Una Noche Con Francis' sounds Spanish . . . !"

I asked him some other questions about the new tunes for the record.

He mentioned the song "Heyadididee" and said, "Let me have your pencil. I have to write the name down for you, it's too difficult."

Then he said, "Let's get out of here, Randi. I want to go to the bar."

So, we went across the street, not too far away, and he ordered two drinks and paid for them immediately. What a shock to see that for the first time! And he explained, "You see, now I take care of all my own money."

At that moment Art Taylor showed up with two English women. Bud asked, "Are you French?"

"No, we're from England."

"How do you like Paris?" Bud asked.

It was amazing to see Bud talking like that, and Art Taylor began to tease him, asking him, "Hey Bud. Can I borrow ten francs from you?"

"No!" said Bud, and he covered all his change with both hands. "I can't afford it, Art, because I'm going to go to America soon, and you know that I have to be very, very economical. Randi, do you want another glass of red wine?"

"Sure, Bud. But this time I want to pay for it."

"No, no, Randi, I'll pay for it. I can pay for it."

Then Bud continued his conversation with the two English ladies, suddenly turning to Art Taylor and asking, "Art, do you remember who gave you your first gig?"

"Of course, Bud. It was you. But since then you've worked with great drummers like Max Roach." And Bud laughed deeply.

And I told him, "It's so fantastic to see you feeling like this."

"But you know why, don't you—Francis," he said, still laughing. "But you know, Randi, we have to go now. To rest. Doctor's orders. Did you know, Randi, that Buttercup stole my passport? Randi . . . do you like Buttercup? How do you like Buttercup? . . . "

I answered, "I know what you mean. She's terrible."

Bud said, "Randi you have to understand that Francis lets me have all my money now, and tells me that I can keep it all and do what I want with it."

We kept talking and he tried to figure out what had happened during his time in Scandinavia, and I reminded him about that terrible story with the famous sandwich, the one Buttercup had spit on. He asked me, very anxiously, "Randi. Did I eat that sandwich?"

I laughed because I couldn't recall, but after all it was not really so funny. . . .

Randi stayed in Paris for several days and visited the house often. We would go to the Blue Note together and then go home and have our mini-Christmas parties. There was a deep bond between them.

Ever since Johnny Griffin had moved into the Hotel Rotary, his agent Alan Bates had become one of the regulars at our house. Bud's new compositions and the fact that he was in good shape prompted Alan to suggest a recording session featuring mainly originals.

For this session, Bud chose two musicians he knew well, Michel Gaudry and Art Taylor, his old friend from New York. They hadn't played together since the tour with Jacques Hess in Italy in 1961. Larry Ritchie had been chosen first, but he had suddenly been called back to New York to see his mother. We never saw him again. The sessions were carefully prepared. Michel, intent on supplying Bud with the accompaniment he needed, came to the house to rehearse in the afternoons. I remember that for "Heyadididee," which in the end wasn't on the record, Bud had asked him to produce a kind of clock sound on the bass, a kind of tick-tock effect. I recorded these rehearsals, all of which sounded new and fresh, and I think I prefer them to the recorded versions.

Bud and Art didn't communicate with words. Art's attitude was always cautious and when they met it was always in silence. He adored Bud and was one of those who always said he was the greatest. He told me that in the old days of Birdland, Bud never spoke to him, even on stage. On one of the last days, they met at the door of the club. Bud seemed surprised to see him and exclaimed, as if they hadn't seen each other in ages, "Hi Art, how ya doing? What are you up to these days?"

Art looked at him in amazement, "Bud, I've been playing with you for the past four months!"

Was it a put-on or had he really lost the notion of time? I think Bud lived, intermittently, in a parallel world that distanced him from certain realities. Sometimes he himself was puzzled by it. But I'm sure he kept it up on purpose, because it gave him the protection and isolation he sought. At first it may have been deliberate, almost a provocation, designed to shock or disconcert. When he knew he was being watched, Bud could play his eccentricity to the hilt—for example, standing for hours in front of a mirror, grinning broadly and admiring the effect from every angle. How could anyone not be put off by such behavior, as were many young musicians who admired him in the fifties?

The recording session for Alan Bates took place on July 31, 1964 in a little studio in Saint Germain des Prés. Bud, remembering the session with Duke, was worried that Buttercup might get wind of it and show up. We hadn't heard from her since her visit to the Hospital Foch had shown her true motivation. Alan agreed to negotiate finances with her, but she was forbidden to set foot in the studio. Bud had sworn that if she were there, he would stop playing at once. His wishes were respected and the session went off without a hitch. Buttercup waited in the booth and left once again with a check. The music and our peace of mind had priority.

Randi Hultin came back from Antibes that day after spending a few days at the festival. She phoned and Bud invited her to join us. She told me:

> I remember that evening at your place. Bud was so happy when he heard I was coming.
>
> I was anxious that he would ask me about the festival. In fact, before I left, Bud wanted to know who was playing over there: Count Basie, Lionel Hampton, Ella Fitzgerald, etc. He said, "Randi, will you tell everybody Bud Powell says hello?"
>
> Over there I ran into Buttercup, who was speaking to everyone like they were still together. She didn't tell anyone that they were now separated. So I said hello to everybody for him. They asked how Bud was, and I told them the truth. Ella was with Beryl Briden. When I asked her if I could take a photo of her, she answered, "Oh, you're always walking around with that camera," in an irritated tone. So I thought it was probably not the right time to tell her that Bud said to say hello.
>
> Bud had seen a television show about the festival and he wanted to know what Hamp and Roy Eldridge had said . . .
>
> So I said that everybody was so happy to know that he was in good health. He asked me suddenly, "Randi, did Ella brush you off?" That was so typical of Bud. He could always read my thoughts.

The record came out under the title *Blues for Bouffémont* and was reissued as *The Invisible Cage*, with the mention "Editing and remastering by Jef Gilson and Francis Paudras." To be more precise, Alan Bates could have added that our contribution had been on a friendly and purely voluntary basis.

The album included three new compositions by Bud—"Blues for Bouffémont," inspired by his stay at the sanatorium; "Una Noche Con Francis," referring to our Christmas celebration; and "In the

Mood for a Classic," dedicated to Randi Hultin. They are fine examples of the immense mobility of Bud's style. He sounds calm, thoughtful, and serene. His inspiration and swing show him to be back in good health. But the climate differs greatly from that of his earlier sessions and was seen as a weakening of his abilities, an appalling error of judgment with respect to a new stage in his creation. What would one think of a painter who eternally reproduced the same canvas? Of a writer who continually repeated the same story? One of the facets of Bud's genius was to express new feelings through a familiar repertory. One had only to listen to him every evening at the club to realize that no tune was ever cast definitively in one particular treatment. This priority given to creation seems to me to be one of the major elements that make jazz such a living music. For an artist of Bud's caliber, music was inseparable from daily life. A musician who does not understand this fundamental law is not a visceral creator. He is subject to any passing trend or fancy. His work, interesting though it may be, is all too often the rehash of a common and impersonal musical discourse—in short, music worthy of being lumped with parlor games and other frivolous and trendy pursuits of society. For some, this may be enough. I myself prefer the surprises offered by Bud. I fully agree with the remarks that Berlioz wrote at the top of his score for *Romeo and Juliet:* "As the public has no imagination, pieces that appeal only to the imagination have no public." The whole problem is there. When I see the great mass of people flock to music that is banal, lacking in substance and vital necessity, I always feel I am living in a world of the deaf.

In short, whenever Bud played differently, people thought he wasn't playing well. Many forgot the good fortune they had been given to see and hear a living genius. Some nights, when he was feeling melancholy, he would completely alter the program and play a series of ballads, one more heart-rending than the next. On such occasions, some loudmouth who had come just to have a good time would be annoyed and come out with a nasty comment. When these comments were translated for Bud by some ostensibly well-meaning soul, he was always deeply hurt by them. Though he always knew his own talent, disobliging remarks depressed him. He would begin to doubt his own work and find greater value in that of Tatum and Monk. Incensed, I would try to show him that no pianist was free from his syntax or the originality of his creative ideas. I would illustrate my words with significant extracts from records of a number of pianists and compare them to his own early works, tunes he had created back in the forties. Despite my efforts, he would look sad and continue to deny his importance in the world of music.

I was witnessing the drama of pure creation and artistic uncertainty in a scrupulous human being assailed by anxiety and doubt. In his quest for the essence, his language was often trimmed down to a rare purity and perfection. This search for simplicity was always misunderstood by those who wanted to hear nothing more from him than the fleeting sound captured on their old records, the music they had digested in their youth. They had grown old, whereas Bud escaped from time. To seek the greatest simplicity is the sign of someone who is genuinely superior to others.

As for the world of classical music, shouldn't they, too, have listened to these towering works? Bud knew and loved the classics and felt them as part of his own musical family. But classical musicians never listened to him. Certain that they possess the truth, the musicians in the classical world look down on jazz but most have no inkling of what jazz really is. How many conflicts are there between the conservatory professors and their young students who are interested in jazz as well as in classical music?

A friend, the bassist Luigi Trussardi, tells a joke that nicely illustrates this mentality. "Why are there more classical musicians than jazzmen who can read music?"

"Because with classical musicians, more of them are deaf than blind."

This sad conclusion is inescapable when you think of all the jazzmen who are self-taught, compared with the multitude of classical musicians who are plodding, unmotivated and mediocre, with the blasé mentality of civil servants.

Nicole sometimes took my place now to accompany Bud on his infrequent visits to Buttercup. Once in a fit of rage Buttercup grabbed Bud in the hotel corridor and tried to retain him physically. Nicole fought like a fury and just missed getting a kick in the stomach, not a great idea in her advanced state of pregnancy. She managed to get Bud away from this screaming harpy and bring him home. But this put an end to our visits. Bud was beside himself with worry about Nicole and he broke off all relations with Buttercup.

Bud was now on the wagon with a vengeance. I would have liked him to be able to take an occasional drink and I sometimes offered him a drop of vintage bordeaux or a taste of a fine bottle of burgundy, for some special occasion. His reply was always the same: "Come on,

Francis, you know I don't drink!" His will grew stronger as his health improved. We had never been happier.

The summer had arrived and the warm weather made our trips to the country even more enjoyable. In the open convertible, we would drive down to see our friends in the Chevreuse Valley, admiring the countryside and the animals on the way. One day, when we passed a horse and wagon, Bud said to me, "Francis, I don't want to die without riding a horse." He would often reiterate this wish. It sounded like a plea. One day as he watched me working I asked if he wanted to draw something himself. He produced a splendid drawing of a horse, with a vision as fresh and candid as that of a child. I told him I liked it but he was unconvinced and, when I went to take the drawing, he quickly crumpled it up and threw it in the wastebasket.

My mother often came to visit and I relived the joys of my childhood. Bud was very fond of her. She always brought cakes that they ate together. I would watch them surreptitiously as I worked, not wanting to intrude on the touching twosome. Bud acted more than ever like a child, timid and tender, always thoughtful and delicate. I was always struck at such times by his enormous need for affection. In situations like this he could reveal himself completely, whereas in encounters of importance he would retreat within himself and remain untouched by demonstrations of great friendship.

In mid-afternoon, my mother would make some hot chocolate. Bud never left her side. Sometimes he would take her hand and lead her to the piano and the loveliest music in the world would fill the room. I wanted time to stop. He looked deep into her eyes and played "April in Paris" or "I'll Remember Paris" or some romantic piece by Chopin, then break the emotion with a joyful laugh. My mother would stand and kiss him, then come over and whisper in my ear, "Bud is such a dear. What kindness! What an artist!"

My happiness was complete. It was like a second chance, compared to the loneliness and indifference in which I had lived during my youth. Their duets were a pleasure to hear. The intensity of his message to my mother reached new depths. His creation took on a new dimension. I had noticed that in all of Bud's melodic lines, he rarely exceeded the register of the human voice. Perhaps that is one of the keys to the mysterious fascination he held for his audiences. What is more moving than a voice? What instrument is better capable of transmitting the message of the soul? Bud played with urgency whenever there was an imperative message to express. Maybe that was why he was so reluctant to play on command.

In the interim, Buttercup had opened her "Chicken Shack," an American-style restaurant where she cooked soul food. She also did some singing, accompanied by Bud Saviano on guitar and Roland Haynes on bass. She had a pleasant voice and a real feel for music. What a shame she never developed her talents. It would have been far more profitable for her and certainly more peaceful for Bud.

LUSH LIFE

(Recorded in New York, October 5, 1956 [RCA Victor])

Our friend Roger phoned one day to tell me he had just taken a summer job as manager of a seaside restaurant near Granville, in Normandy. He had fixed up one of the rooms as a little night club, complete with piano and bass, and was expecting us for the holidays with the whole gang. This heavenly little spot, l'Escale, was in a town on the coast of Normandy called Edenville, a name full of promise.

It sounded like a fine idea. Sea, sun, music, and friends—what better way to complete Bud's convalescence? Paris was sweltering in a July heat wave so we decided to leave at once. I told Bud there'd be all the seafood he could eat and he was already licking his lips.

Firmly settled in the Triumph, along with Vincent, we set off for Edenville. The top was down on the car and Bud's cap couldn't resist the acceleration, and kept flying off his head, and we had to stop a few times to pick it up. There were a number of sandwich stops as well, as the fresh air was already having an effect on Bud's appetite. He seemed to get hungry every fifteen miles and it took us all day to cover the two hundred or so miles between Paris and Edenville.

Roger had found some young musicians passing through and hired them to play at the club. By the time we got there the place was already humming with music and the musicians were dying to meet the great Bud Powell in the flesh. Roger, his sister, and brother-in-law had prepared a dinner to Bud's taste. The evening we arrived Bud played with great gusto and the young people welcomed him with an ovation.

HAPPY BLUES IN EDENVILLE

(Recorded in Edenville, August, 1964 [Duke])

The holiday goers at the little beach resort soon became assiduous fans. Admission was free, drinks were cheap, and the club was jam-packed every night. It was wonderful to see the young people listening in fascination, sitting on the floor when all the seats were taken, grooving to a music that most of them had only just discovered.

On the beach, Bud was the center of attraction. Most of the young people just watched him from a distance, but some overcame their shyness and went up to say hello and to try and start a conversation. Generally, there was no answer. Bud, reserved as always, would merely look at them and smile. One exception was a young Welsh girl called Rini who had come to France to study French. She caught Bud's eye right away and since she spoke English, they could converse easily. It looked to us like a little flirtation was underway.

Bud was not a bathing buff. In fact, I never saw him swim. Each time I asked him to join me in the water, we would go through the same scenario. After much coaxing he would reluctantly step into the water, only to freeze in horror as the next wave rolled in. When I teased him he followed me with a pinched little smile, at a safe distance. As the wave went out his smile would return, only to vanish again with the next incoming wave. The expression on his face followed the ebb and flow of the sea.

On the coast of Normandy the beaches are long and broad, and at low tide become even more impressive. During the afternoon, some of the gang went for excursions, others napped or fooled around. Bud and I often found ourselves alone for a few hours in the middle of a quiet, empty beach, far from all agitation. Bud enjoyed these quiet moments. Sometimes he seemed so deep in meditation that I wondered if he was still on this earth.

One day as we were leaving the hotel, I noticed on a table a telephone receiver with its wire cut. I picked it up and put it in my bag, thinking of a possible trick I might play. On the beach we were alone, as usual, lost in the midst of a sandy expanse. The tide was way out and all that was visible on the horizon were a few people out looking for shrimp. We sat without speaking or moving, in the infinite stillness, staring out to sea. During one of these moments, I slipped the receiver out of the bag and in the voice of a busy man disturbed by an intrusion, I simulated a conversation in English. Bud looked out to sea. He didn't bat an eyelash. I went on with my imaginary conversation, "Bud? Yes, he's here, right next to me. . . . They want to speak to you, Bud." He looked a bit surprised but accepted the receiver I handed him and, taking a deep breath, said a hearty "Hello?" Then he frowned, shook the phone, and said, "Too late. They hung up."

I laughed alone, but I was laughing at myself, for Bud had shown no surprise and instantly went back to his dream world. I never knew if he was putting me on or not.

He watched me swim, with a worried and sometimes downright disapproving air. I never dared stay in too long and we walked back faster than we had come down. Back at the hotel Bud sat down at a table where an assortment of pastries was always mysteriously waiting for him.

Nicole's pregnancy was beginning to show and Bud worried about her a lot. "Can you feel it moving?" he asked for the thousandth time, with mingled concern and admiration.

There were still three months to go and if we went to New York the child would be born in my absence. This upset Bud, but in spite of that he spoke with growing interest of our impending departure.

Every evening he delighted us all by playing solo or in a trio with two young amateurs, Jacques Gervais on bass and Guy Hayat on drums. I alternated with Bud, although it was no easy thing for me to follow the master himself.

Johnny Griffin kept in touch regularly and at one point, when he was between jobs, Roger invited him and his wife Marilyn to come out and join us. That was all we needed to round out our tumultuous evenings. Our little club was white-hot! Every evening there were turnaway crowds. Jazz had turned this quiet little beach town on its head.

Every day another of the gang showed up from Paris and soon our whole "family" was together again at Edenville. I think we were the only guests of the hotel, which had suddenly found itself a great jazz center. Our friend Jean Tronchot was there and so was Mike Hennessey, an English journalist who wrote for *Melody Maker.* We lived in perfect harmony, in a world of jazz.

Every evening after some stupendous music, we all ritually gathered in the hotel kitchen where Roger, with his usual generosity, emptied fridges and pantries and served up mountains of food. Bud always looked forward to this bedtime snack, his appetite never lacking. After Bud's performance, the others took a chorus and the show went on. The gang exchanged wisecracks in their Les Halles slang. Bud made me translate, rocking with laughter at the jokes and stuffing himself on the huge sandwiches. When we said good night our sides ached from laughter and overeating.

Amid the constant merriment, our departure date was drawing near. Goodstein kept pressing us to set a definite date. He was impatient to start promoting Bud's much heralded return to Birdland. I had to make some final arrangements and tactfully inform my clients I'd be away for a while, but all were most understanding. At last our departure was set for August 16, 1964. We returned to Paris drunk with sun and music. The holiday had been wonderful from every point of view, including the constant revelations of new aspects of Bud's personality. Who would have suspected two years ago that he was capable of having so much fun?

We had kept in touch with Dr. Teboul and had gone to see him a few times for tests. Now we had a chance to meet his wife, who was a psychiatrist of the Jungian school and had done some serious studies on schizophrenia. Bud had been diagnosed as schizophrenic in the United States, and I told Mrs. Teboul about his history and the harsh treatments to which he had been subjected. She had been interested in meeting Bud. Their meeting was brief and I never knew what transpired between them, but when it was over, she had been clear and to the point: "Francis, your friend has one of the most acute and characteristic cases of schizophrenia that I have ever had occasion to see. Be careful. These people are unpredictable. As long as he's calm, there's no risk. He needs attention and affection. But believe me, at this stage, you will never be able to communicate with him. You will achieve no satisfactory results."

I had listened without surprise. I was used to this type of comment. But my stubborn efforts with Bud made it impossible for me to admit that his case was hopeless. True, he hardly spoke at first and seemed to be elsewhere. But things were different now.

Before leaving for New York I wanted to spend an evening with the Tebouls to show off Bud in top form. I wanted Mrs. Teboul to hear him speak and maybe even play and to see how our relationship had progressed. I wanted her to see that no diagnosis is ever definitive, that patience and friendship can work wonders.

The Tebouls came to dinner with their seventeen-year-old daughter. I placed Bud between father and daughter and facing Mrs. Teboul, so they could all talk to him as they liked. I had reminded Bud how helpful the doctor had been during his hospitalization. The table talk was lighthearted, starting with our upcoming New York trip. Bud was smiling and took an active part in the conversation. Mrs. Teboul, surprise written all over her face, listened with growing interest. When dinner was over, Bud turned to the daughter, took her hand, and said in a gentle voice, "Francis tells me you're studying piano, mademoiselle. Would you play something for me?"

She was very nervous. We had listened to some of Bud's records during dinner and everyone was moved, which made it even harder for her. But the most upset of all was the mother, who couldn't believe her eyes or ears. I still remember her words as they were leaving. "Francis, I prefer to forget everything I saw and heard tonight. It's enough to cast doubt on everything I said."

Thank you, doctor, for those words. They continued to guide my conduct.

Her husband still remembers these pleasant moments we spent together. He was kind enough to share some of his memories and this warmed my heart:

> I was very struck by that evening. Bud was really cured. One can see the importance of psychological factors—he wanted to get out of the hospital, so he got well.
>
> The evening at your house was extraordinary. My daughter has never forgotten it. His kindness was unbelievable. She tinkled away at the piano, proud to show him what she could do. Then Bud went to the piano to show her something. He was perfectly charming—to make her happy, he played for hours. I hope you have the tapes! We were really very pleased.
>
> I think getting Bud off the Largactyl did him a lot of good. As for electroshock therapy, no analysts believe in it today.
>
> If Bud had schizophrenic tendencies, I believe they were slight. In any case, there was never any question of treating him with psychotherapy. When you possess such genius, you have to let it explode. It's amazing to see how someone can let all his spontaneity come out if he feels protected. He was protected and was therefore free to blossom.
>
> He found in you someone with whom he could express himself and he came to life again. With your affection you were able to "repair" the parental image. Your friendship and admiration for him (to which I can bear witness) completely changed his behavior. He was unrecognizable. You played a fundamental role in his life. Basically, in cases like that, the only things that work are love and friendship.

Alan Bates, conscious of the financial problems I was coping with as best I could, had mentioned the tapes I had at home. The record *Bud at Home*, produced by Jean Tronchot, was encouraging as it had been well-received, both by the public and by the critics. Alan suggested that we do another. Using the tapes seemed a good idea as there was no way we could set up a record session with Bud before our departure. Once again Jef Gilson kindly stepped in—always ready to help out where Bud was concerned. With Bud's help, we selected a number of tunes. For the best way to pay him, I had an idea I thought might work. In order for Bud to be covered by national health insurance he had to have some sort of regular salary. We decided to put him on a monthly salary basis, which would give him at least partial coverage. Everyone thought it was a good idea and Bud signed a contract for the production of two records a year from my tapes or recording sessions. Alan also became Bud's agent and was to find engagements for him. Alas, the events that followed made it impossible to ever put these new arrangements into practice.

I finished up my illustrations, took care of some last-minute red tape and then helped get Bud outfitted from head to toe. We made the rounds of the department stores and Bud used his own savings to treat himself to whatever he liked. We ordered two tailor-made suits, one in beautiful gray flannel and the other a dark blue serge, some dress shirts, bow ties, and a few of the black string ties and black socks Bud was so partial to. We got some casual clothes for daytime wear, a blue blazer, some lightweight pants and a windbreaker. For his New York comeback, Bud would look his best. I was eager with anticipation, for I was bringing home a happy man.

THE LAST TIME I SAW PARIS

(Recorded in New York, 1951 [Verve])

Thinking back today, I must say that despite his enthusiasm about returning to the States, Bud had always shown some signs of unspoken apprehension. It seemed normal to me after such a long absence. As for me, the unanimous encouragement of all our friends set any fears to rest. Bud was going to be back on top, buoyed by the certainty that he had recovered all of his powers, ready to plunge into a new life, freed from the spectres of the past. He would no longer be dependent, but liberated in his actions and movements, responsible for his own money and free to dispose of it as he wished. I dreamed of the moment he would be back among his own, his human dignity restored, a man conscious at last of our need for him and his art. With each passing day he was more cheerful, more sure of himself. This was the man with whom I was about to board a plane, with no heavy baggage other than a stubborn determination and a heart full of hope.

Our departure was greeted by many a tear. Though the prospects seemed excellent to us all, the separation was painful. Goodstein had sent us two one-way tickets. Our American adventure was about to begin, even sooner than anticipated. At home, Bud was in constant preparation. His every gesture was so slow that I wonder today if he wasn't trying to call it all off. Was it a revealing sign of last-minute hesitation? We got to the airport without a second to spare, and had to run to catch the plane. Bud ran slower than me, and we nearly missed our take-off.

We caught our breath and were barely strapped into our seats when Bud was already asking when we would eat. His good humor had returned. He didn't have to wait long, and though the meal was copious, that didn't stop him from asking for a few extras, which were graciously provided. The flight attendant was amused by his impressive appetite. The flight seemed to me very short. Bud asked the same questions over and over again. Who would be at the airport to meet us? Would there be any friends, musicians? I had no answers to give, but it helped to pass the time. Night had fallen. A voice was announcing that we would soon be landing at Kennedy Airport. Bud had stopped speaking and his expression was grave once again. As for me, I was very nervous.

Coming off the plane, we were met by a photographer from *The New York Times*. Then came the long wait for customs and immigration clearance. Bud went through without a problem, then it was my turn. The police officer who stood in front of me was a colossus of a man, over six feet tall, with long hairy arms that gave him a distinctly simian air. His face, with its naive, candid expression, seemed to be there by accident. "If man descends from the apes," I thought, "this one didn't descend very far!" Cautiously I handed him my passport. He looked it over, then stopped and stared at my visa.

"You here on business?" he asked.

"No, as a tourist."

"Huh? not for business?"

"No, I'm just here with a friend."

He looked again at my visa and a glint of what might have been taken for intelligence crossed his face. "But you've come for business reasons?"

"No, I'm simply here to accompany Mr. Powell."

Bud was waiting on the other side of the cubicle, looking worried.

"Well, you *are* Mr. Powell's manager, aren't you?" He was beginning to sound irritated.

"No," I said, firmly, horrified by such a suggestion. "I am a friend and I am accompanying him during his visit to New York."

He was beginning to see the light. If there were a tax on brains, he would have been exempt. He flipped through my passport again and read a paper attached to the visa that explained the purpose of my trip. Apparently, something was wrong with the visa. The colossus called over one of his colleagues and talked with him for a while. Then he came back and barked, "Your visa's not in order. We're putting you on the first plane out!"

The earth reeled beneath my feet. I didn't know what hit me. Everything seemed unreal, like in a nightmare. Meanwhile, Bud was being jostled by the passengers clearing the checkpoint. I made one last effort to get the cop to listen to my explanations. Completely ignoring Bud, he dragged me into an office, motioned me to a chair and took another for himself. He turned it around and sat down on it backwards, facing me with his arms folded on the chair back. The other officer joined him and the two of them took turns grilling me. I felt like a character in a bad detective story. I tried to be as clear as possible, choosing my words carefully. All at once, the cop stood up and sent his chair across the floor in exasperation. I understood the case was finished. "That's enough of that," he said. "You'll be on the next plane out."

Just at that moment, Bud, whom everyone had forgotten, strode into the room and in a voice full of authority that I had never heard before began shouting at the two cops, "What is this? I've been away from home for six years. Now I'm back with a friend of mine. For three years he housed and fed me and nursed me when I was sick, and now I can't even invite him to my own country? What's the meaning of this? I want to know what's going on here. My name is Bud Powell, I'm a musician, and I want him to come home with me!"

The tirade poured out like an icy torrent. I was terrified of the reaction it would provoke. I thought of all the stories I'd heard about the police and black people in America and I feared the worst.

The two cops were even more bewildered than me. After a silence, the giant suddenly turned calm and affable. "Well now, in that case . . . Hold on a minute, let's see what we can do . . . Do you have any money?"

In all innocence, I told the truth. "No, but we're expected by Mr. Powell's employer, who will take care of our entire stay."

At that very moment, who should turn up in the doorway but Oscar Goodstein. When we were late, he had gotten worried, verified that we were on the flight, and realized that some sort of problem must be preventing our clearance. With a big smile, he introduced himself as Bud's employer, said he would take responsibility for everything, and got them to let me stay, on condition that I get my visa modified.

Now Oscar greeted us with open arms. He was of average height, with gray hair, slightly balding, and a pleasant, open face, like a provincial businessman. From the first moments, the pace at which he told us what he had in mind for us made it quite clear that he was a model of efficiency.

He had seen Bud for the first time in February 1950, and it was a revelation that had changed his life:

> I had sold my oil holdings and planned to go down to Florida with my family to take it easy for a while. But in February 1950 I paid a visit to a friend of mine who was the owner of Birdland. It was there that I heard Bud for the first time. I was a lover of classical music then and had a big collection of classical records. I had studied piano as a kid and my sister was an accomplished musician. The first thing I remember feeling about Bud was anger at the way he totally upset all my musical values. I put off

my departure for Florida and went to hear him play every night that week. I felt I just had to work with him, that this was the kind of work I wanted to do. So I broke the news to my family: Florida's out. New York is where our future is! Within a month I had become Bud's personal manager.

I was still amazed by what Bud had said to the police and the tone in which he had said it. The hangdog Bud, cringing before cops and doctors, or resigned in front of a bullying Buttercup, was now a thing of the past. With a gesture of authority, he took me by the arm as soon as my passport was returned and dragged me energetically outside. We quickly headed for the airport snack bar, where Don Schlitten and Dan Morgenstern were waiting. Don took a few pictures and we sat down to have coffee.

After my momentous entry into New York, I began to have the feeling that things weren't going to be as easy or as exalting as I had imagined. Bud was looking at Oscar, strangely solemn, without saying a word. All the compliments on how well he looked didn't seem to change his somber mood. Something new had just happened. By an inevitable process that I didn't really understand until much later, Bud was experiencing a series of flashbacks of his past, a past that was to reappear before him and that I would now have to learn to live with.

At the start of his career, Bud was the typical example of the artist coveted by crafty businessmen. Caught between cops, doctors, lawyers, and journalists, he had never understood what was happening to him. His only business was music. Furthermore, at the time his employers were part of that nightlife underworld in which gangsters, drug dealers, and pimps could get rich without being bothered. Jazz musicians had no choice if they wanted to work. Bud had a visceral hostility for club owners, middlemen, and other denizens of this world. When he was in their presence he became nervous and distant. Those days in which he (like so many other young talents) had been exploited by his employers under the guise of a false paternalism had marked him for life. It was a strange period, when managers could impose their will on musicians, could blithely decide, without consulting them, everything concerning their contracts and their pay. Such contempt could not fail to disturb sensitive minds, and could even warp their personalities forever. A musician's life on the road is tough enough, but in those conditions it was often unbearable. As in the boxing world, the club and dance hall owners were dependent for their livelihood on the crooks and thugs who ruled as masters over the universe of jazz.

Bud had never forgotten that life and remained deeply traumatized by it. Like so many artists, he was credulous and extremely vulnerable.

MEDIOCRE

(Recorded in New York, January 13, 1955 [Verve])

Oscar suggested we go straight to our hotel. He had booked us into the Hotel Woodward, on the corner of Broadway and 55th Street, right near Birdland. We had a large room with twin beds, a full bathroom, and a small kitchen. Feeling that my presence was indispensable, Oscar had gone so far as to put us in one room. Personally, it didn't bother me, but out of respect for Bud, I thought he should have had his own room. Bud made no comment. In any case, there was nothing to be said: Oscar had made all the arrangements. He explained that the hotel would be paid directly by him as would the Italian restaurant across the street where we could have our meals. So we didn't have to worry about transportation, as long as we didn't leave the neighborhood. We had kitchen facilities, so we could always prepare a snack after the show. There was an ancient refrigerator that sputtered like a dying motorcycle, a gas hotplate that looked like a prewar model and that I distrusted at first glance, and a wall cupboard that seemed to be central headquarters for all the cockroaches in the building. The walls were papered in faded gray with an old-fashioned pattern.

We arrived without much money, the last of my cash having gone to replenish Bud's wardrobe and to buy a stock of tapes to record at the club. I had taken along a small portable E.M.I. tape recorder and a Sennheiser microphone that picked up a really good sound. Informed of our financial situation, Oscar gave me a $20 advance for expenses and handed Bud $10 for pocket money, telling us not to spend too much. Then, assuring us we had nothing whatsoever to worry about, he left us to settle in, saying he'd see us later at Birdland.

It was very hot in New York in that month of August 1964 and unfortunately the room was not air-conditioned. We did have space, however, and we would have to make the best of it. I took a shower, changed to light clothes and left for the club. Bud said he preferred to lie down and rest a while. I was tired too, but I couldn't wait to see the famous Birdland. My head was full of images of the mythical place I had dreamed of so often, the club that had seen the likes of such celebrities as Tatum, Bird, Bud, Fats, Dizzy, Garner, Sarah, and so many others.

THE FRUIT

(Recorded in New York, February 1951 [Verve])

Those first steps through the streets of New York remain an extraordinary memory. I was excited by the discovery and crushed by its scale. The splash of brightly lit buildings far exceeded all the photos and movies I had seen. The din of the city was deafening, the street sounds magnified by the canyon walls, like some giant echo chamber. The ghastly screams of ambulances and police cars made my hair stand up. Waves of cars flooded the avenue in a mighty stream, in a din of honking horns and the throbbing of powerful engines. In France in 1964 there was nothing to compare with it. I covered the distance between the hotel and Birdland in a semi-conscious state and found myself at the front door of the club. When I spotted the sign above the canopy with those magic words, "Birdland, Jazz Corner of the World," I was dumbstruck. Feverish with excitement, I walked down the few steps and pushed open the door. I was hit in the face by a tempest of sound, a sensation I will never forget. On the bandstand, which looked ridiculously small, Slide Hampton's big band was playing a raging up-tempo piece. As always, Slide led the band like a locomotive engineer. Then Lloyd Price, the singer, came on strutting like a wrestler and the band played even louder. Irma Franklin (the sister of Aretha) came on next to perform a duo with him in a hilarious show that ended to thunderous applause. The whole thing was pretty raunchy but the music and the swing were first-rate.

I stood motionless at the door between the two bouncers, Johnny Gary and his cohort, a giant with a bald head and a build like George Foreman. I was completely subjugated by what was going on when a hand tapped me on the shoulder, "Hey Francis! There you are, man! Shit, man, you finally got here! God-*damn*! Shit, man, we been waitin' for you!" It was Lee Morgan, whom I'd met in Paris with Bud in 1959 at the Théâtre des Champs-Elysées. "Come on, I'll introduce you to some friends."

We made our way through the room to the bar on the left, where Lee introduced me to George Tucker (a bassist who died soon after) and some other friends. "So Bud is finally here. Son of a bitch! Come on, man! Tell us all about it."

"Yeah, he's here all right. You can take my word for it."

"Where is he, Francis? Shit, man, everybody's waiting for him. Goddamn, since he left . . . you know, man, he's been gone one helluva long time!"

"Oh, he's resting at the hotel. He's tired, it's a long trip."

The band had just finished playing and the audience applauded like mad as they left the stage. I heard a familiar voice, a high-pitched nasal voice I knew from records, and turned to see Pee Wee Marquet, Birdland's midget emcee, former mascot of Sugar Ray Robinson, who was announcing the program for the next set.

By now a circle of newcomers had formed around us. The news of Bud's return had spread like wildfire and everyone had something to ask. Obviously, Bud had been awaited like the Messiah and I was assailed with questions. All at once, Lee announced he had to leave.

"Shit, I got a gig in half an hour, I gotta split! Hey man, I got a problem. I got no money to take a taxi. Oh shee-it, I'm gonna be late."

Everyone suddenly put on an indifferent air. I felt as if I were the only one who'd heard him. I had known Lee well in Paris. He had seemed nice, always kind to Bud, one of the few who treated him with esteem and didn't tease him unbearably. "Listen, Lee," I said. "I've got $20 on me, but no change. If you can break it, I can give you some money."

"No problem," he said, and with the dexterity of a magician he grasped the bill as soon as it was out of my wallet. Without a second's delay, he was up the stairs and running out of the club. And if the poor guy hadn't died a few years later, I would say he's running still! I never saw him again my whole time in New York and my $20, my entire fortune, had just flown off to a destination I did not yet suspect. I stood there, bemused, as everyone else did, determinedly studying the ceiling. "Okay," I thought to myself, "I dig. I get the picture."

Well, I certainly hadn't wasted any time. Ten minutes in the place and I already had a real good taste of American reality. I found Oscar backstage and he introduced me to a man named Max, a big bruiser who looked like a heavyweight and who helped run the club. He seemed engrossed in counting out a huge pile of bills into the drawers of a cash register. He glanced up at me so quickly I felt I had become invisible. Then he turned back to his dollar bills, mumbling a weary, "Hi ya Frank."

Oscar told me to come back with Bud first thing in the morning. "There's work for you guys to do. You'll have to get his cabaret card as soon as possible. But don't worry. I'll explain everything . . ."

After this friendly reception, I decided to go back to the hotel. Bud wasn't sleeping, he was sitting on the edge of the bed, staring into the swirling smoke from his cigarette. I didn't mention the incident with Lee Morgan, but went straight to the sink and gulped down a large glass of water. My first night at Birdland I was $20 poorer, and I hadn't even been offered a drink!

It was late at night before I fell asleep. The next morning, I awoke with a start from an eventful dream in which trucks were transporting vast numbers of big bands, and realized that our room was just over a garage of tourist buses, coming and going non-stop. Bud was still sleeping soundly. Oscar had asked us to show up at ten o'clock and there wasn't much time to get ready so I resigned myself to waking him up.

The club looked bigger than the night before. The cleaning women were busily vacuuming around the tables. A sickening odor of stale smoke hung in the air. Oscar was waiting in his tiny office, a mountain of papers on his desk.

"Hey Oscar, how ya doin'?" said Bud, trying hard to sound cheerful. I was surprised to see him like that, as he was usually so quiet and indifferent with people. He seemed more like a child than usual, a scared child making a big effort to be pleasant and cooperative.

These reflections were interrupted by Oscar saying we had to leave at once for an appointment at the musicians' union. He explained that to work again in New York, Bud had to pay his back dues for all the years of absence. Without trying to understand any more than that, I said okay, figuring that Oscar certainly knew what had to be done better than anyone. On the way, he told us Bud would also have to get a new cabaret card, since he had lost his old one before he left for Paris. He didn't think it necessary, I suppose, to tell me why.

A lot of musicians had been in trouble with the Narcotics Bureau or the Liquor Authority and had lost their cards through court decisions. Since the card was absolutely compulsory, they were thus effectively barred from working in New York. Billie Holiday and Charlie Parker, just to mention two, were among the artists who found themselves in this position.

Much later, Kenny Dorham said to me, "Can you imagine, Bird would stand there in front of Birdland and not be allowed to go in?" And he'd say to us, "Ain't that something? I gave that place its name, its fame—and here I am on the sidewalk like a black sheep."

Oscar said that to get his card back, Bud would have to have some medical exams and go through a little red tape.

At the union office, he explained the situation quickly and started counting out wads of dollars to the man behind the counter. If I remember correctly, the back dues came to something like $900. I was horrified to see Bud's money disappearing before he had even begun to earn it. "No problem," said Oscar. "I'll advance Bud the money. We'll work out the accounts later."

As we left the office, he explained that he would keep careful accounts. He then added another detail I hadn't thought of—the air fare would be deducted from Bud's earnings as would the expenses for food and lodging. I had hoped this might be at the expense of Birdland, as it was they who chose the hotel and the restaurant, not even leaving us the choice of staying with friends. Everything was moving too quickly for me. At this stage I let myself be dragged along into the whirlwind.

The next day several magazines, newspapers, and radio stations asked for interviews. The journalists gave us a warm welcome, all apparently surprised by the change in Bud. *Down Beat* (September 24, 1964) related our arrival as follows:

> Pianist Bud Powell, one of the pioneers of modern jazz, returned to the United States August 16 after an absence of more than six years . . .
>
> Powell, who was stricken with tuberculosis in 1962, only recently emerged from a long period of convalescence. Accompanied by his close friend and companion, the young French commercial artist Francis Paudras, the pianist appeared to be in excellent health and good spirits upon arrival at New York's Kennedy International Airport.
>
> . . . Paudras, who is credited by Powell's friends with nursing the pianist back to health and shielding him from undesirable influences, was highly praised by Oscar Goodstein, Powell's American personal manager.
>
> "Without this man, Bud might not be with us today," he said, and Powell nodded agreement. "Bud is coming to Birdland to show his appreciation for the benefit we ran for him last year and other things we did to help. It's a blessing that Francis agreed to come along—even though his wife, back home in Paris, is expecting a baby next month."
>
> Powell was asked what he was looking forward to the most during his stay in New York. "Handling my own dough," the pianist, whose financial affairs in the past have frequently been in the hands of various guardians and trustees, said with a big grin.

The New York Courier of August 29 headlined: "BUD POWELL, JAZZ GIANT COMES 'HOME' FROM PARIS." The article went on to say:

Bud's father, William Powell
(Courtesy of Celia Powell)

Bud's mother, Pearl Powell
(Courtesy of Celia Powell)

(Photo by Francis Paudras)

Bud and Francis
(Photo by Mary)

Francis improvising on the piano
(Photo by Mic)

Bud and Buttercup
(Photo by Alain Chevrier)

Bud and Art Blakey
(Photo by Jan Persson)

Francis, his sister Noëlle, and Bud
(Photo by Mary)

Jacques Hess and Bud
(Courtesy of Jacques Hess)

(Photo by Francis Paudras)

Duke Ellington
(Photo by Alain Chevrier)

(Photo by Nils Edström)

Oscar Pettiford
(Photo by Alain Chevrier)

(Photo by J. M. Ploton)

Charlie Mingus
(Photo by Francis Paudras)

Francis, Bud, and Randi Hultin
(Courtesy of Randi Hultin)

Skip and Kirsten Malone
(Photo by Francis Paudras)

(Photo by Mary)

Buttercup, Johnny, and Bud
(Photo by Kirsten Malone)

Wailing on the piano
(Photo by Kirsten Malone)

Holding hands as he so liked to do
(Photo by Nils Edström)

Randi Hultin
(Courtesy of Randi Hultin)

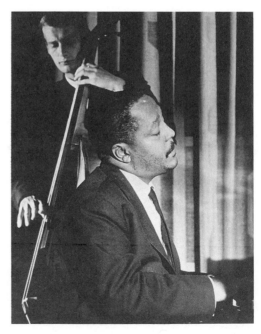

(Photo by Nils Edström)

Bud in performance
(Photo by Jan Persson)

Buttercup, Francis, and Bud
(Photo by Randi Hultin)

Bud and Nicole
(Photo by Francis Paudras)

(Photo by Francis Paudras)

Thelonious Monk and Bud
(Photo by Francis Paudras)

Toshiko Akiyoshi and Bud
(Courtesy of Toshiko Akiyoshi)

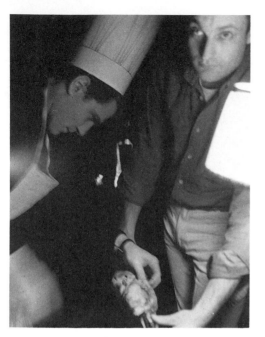

Roger and Francis
(Photo by Mic)

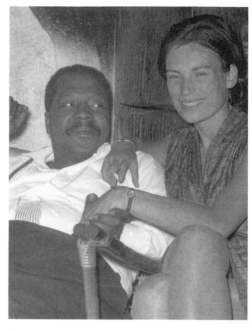

Bud and Noëlle
(Photo by Francis Paudras)

Bud, Anita Evans, Franck Nizery, and Francis
(Photo by Mic)

(Photo by Francis Paudras)

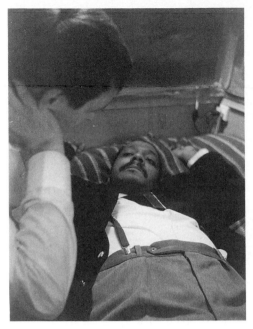

Francis and Bud
(Photo by Mic)

Francis and Bud
(Photo by Mic)

(Photo by Francis Paudras)

Dr. Joussaume, director of the sanatorium
Bouffémont *(Photo by Francis Paudras)*

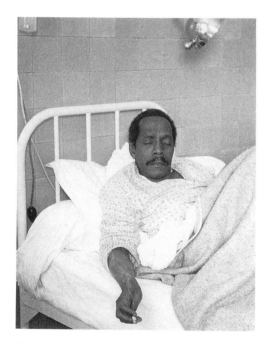

Recovering from tuberculosis
(Photo by Francis Paudras)

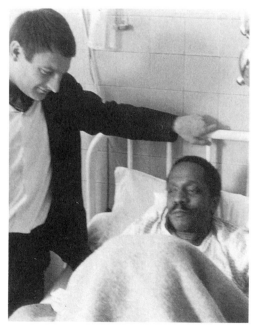

Francis and Bud
(Photo by Mic)

(Photo by Francis Paudras)

Bud and Francis
(Photo by Dolly Schmidt)

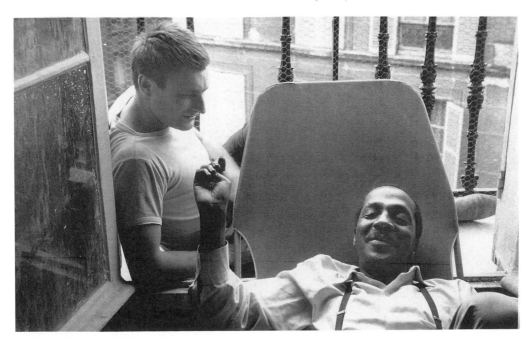

Francis and Bud
(Photo by Mic)

Francis and Bud
(Photo by Mic)

Francis and Bud
(Photo by Mic)

Bud on holiday in Edenville, 1964
(Photo by Jean Tronchot)

Francis and Bud
(Photo by Jean Tronchot)

Bud and Rini
(Photo by Francis Paudras)

Johnny Griffin and Bud
(Photo by Francis Paudras)

(Photo by Francis Paudras)

Francis and Bud
(Photo by Mic)

(Photo by Francis Paudras)

Arriving at Kennedy Airport,
New York, 1964
(Photo by Don Schlitten)

Francis and Bud
(Photo by Don Schlitten)

Maxwell T. Cohen, Bud's attorney
(Photo by Francis Paudras)

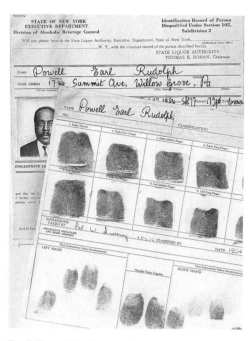

Bud Powell's fingerprints
(Francis Paudras Collection)

Birdland poster
(Francis Paudras Collection)

Façade of Birdland in New York City
(Francis Paudras Collection)

(Photo by Nils Edström)

Bud and Francis
(Photo by Dolly Schmidt)

(Photo by Nils Edström)

Thelonious Monk and Bud
(Photo by Francis Paudras)

Nica de Kœnigswarter
(Courtesy of Baroness Nica de Kœnigswarter)

Max Roach
(Photo by Francis Paudras)

Bud and Margareta Johnson
(Photo by Francis Paudras)

Margareta and Bud on Fire Island
(Photo by Francis Paudras)

(Photo by Francis Paudras)

Marshall and Roz Allen, Margareta, and Bud
(Photo by Francis Paudras)

Receiving the Schaeffer award
(Courtesy of the Schomburg Library)

(Francis Paudras Collection)

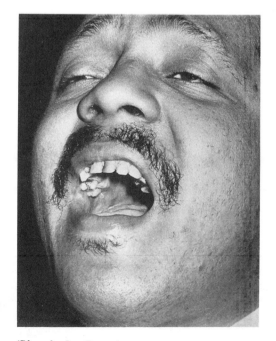

(Photo by Jan Persson)

Paul Chambers
(Photo by Francis Paudras)

Bud's father, William Powell
(Courtesy of Celia Powell)

(Francis Paudras Collection)

Bud and his group
(Courtesy of Celia Powell)

Andy Browne
(Photo by Francis Paudras)

(Courtesy of Celia Powell)

(Francis Paudras Collection)

Freddie Jones
(Photo by Francis Paudras)

Francis and Thelonious Monk
(Photo by Mic)

Courtesy of Charles Delaunay)

Bud Powell and his brothers Richie and William
(Courtesy of Celia Powell)

Cecilia Powell, Bud's daughter
(Courtesy of Celia Powell)

Frances Barnes, Celia's mother
(Courtesy of Celia Powell)

(Photo by Francis Paudras)

(Photo by Francis Paudras)

Babs Gonzales
(Francis Paudras Collection)

Prophet
(Photo by Francis Paudras)

(Photo by Francis Paudras)

(Photo by Francis Paudras)

Francis and Ornette Coleman
(Francis Paudras Collection)

Barry Harris
(Photo by Francis Paudras)

Nica de Kœnigswarter
(Photo by Francis Paudras)

Francis with his son Gilles
(Photo by Mic)

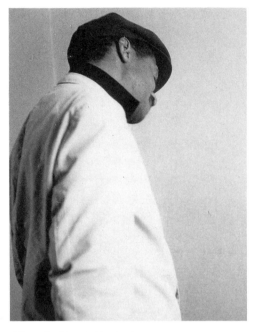

(Photo by Francis Paudras)

Francis
(Photo by Mic)

(Photo by Jorgen Leth)

Bernard Stollman, chairman of ESP Records   *(Photo by Jan Persson)*
(Photo by Francis Paudras)

(Photo by Jan Persson)

April 17, 1979

I, FRANCIS PAUDRAS, hereby transfer, assign and convey to CECELIA J. POWELL, daughter of EARL RUDOLPH ("BUD") POWELL, all of those certain tape recordings which have heretofore been in my possession embodying performances of Bud Powell, alone or with others. Such assignment is made without any conditions and with the express intention that CECELIA J. POWELL shall have all rights of title and ownership with respect to such tape recordings and shall be fully free to use such tapes as she, in her sole and absolute discretion, may determine.

Witness

MAX ROACH

x _____
FRANCIS. PAUDRAS

On the 17th day of April, 1979, before me personally came and appeared FRANCIS PAUDRAS, to me known and known to me to be the person described in and who executed the foregoing instrument and he duly acknowledged to me that he executed the same.

x _____
(Notary Public)

Letter given to Celia Powell from Francis Paudras
(Francis Paudras Collection)

Max Roach and Francis
(Photo by Anita)

(Photo by Francis Paudras)

Bud Powell's tombstone
(Photo by Francis Paudras)

(Photo by Jorgen Leth)

(Photo by Jorgen Leth)

(Photo by Jorgen Leth)

(Photo by Jorgen Leth)

The man who inaugurated and introduced a new mode (and mood) of jazz expression to the world more than 20 years ago returned "home" last Sunday after an absence of more than six years.

It was a "new" Bud Powell who stepped off Air France flight 025 at Kennedy Airport last Sunday, accompanied by Parisian press agent Francis Paudras (who befriended the pianist when he became ill in Paris), to be met by Powell's close friend and American personal manager, Oscar Goodstein.

Bud was heftier by about 30 pounds, more personable and communicative then he had ever been, and he was sober—stone sober.

And talent he STILL has in abundance as evidenced by the success of the recent sides he cut in Paris.

It is expected that Powell's long-awaited date at Birdland will again establish his place in jazzdom's Hall of Fame.

But the warmest welcome of all the press was that of Allan Morison for *Ebony* and *Jet* Magazines. Allan had always been a loyal fan of Bud's and one of the few journalists to follow closely the tragic episodes of his life, from the time of his first confinements in psychiatric hospitals.

I took advantage of these interviews, particularly those on the radio, to transmit an appeal to Bud's childhood girlfriend, Frances Barnes and her daughter, Celia, who was also Bud's daughter, in the hope of meeting them as soon as possible.

Celia's name had acquired for me an almost mythical significance. It was the title of a tune Bud had composed in 1948 and it was the first piece of modern jazz I had learned as a teenager. Later I was to hear that the same tune had served to open new pianistic conceptions for a great number of my friends. René Urtréger and Georges Arvanitas in France and Walter Davis Jr. and Barry Harris in the U.S. are all very attached to the piece to this day.

In my efforts to help Bud get on his feet again, I thought it was important for him, now that his health was better, to find something concrete to hold onto, like his daughter. Bud seemed to regard Nicole and me as family, but perhaps his paternal feeling would be a stronger bond yet. I hoped that such a meeting would reinforce the responsible adult behavior he was slowly recapturing.

Among the things we had to do was pay a visit to Maxwell T. Cohen, Bud's lawyer since 1953, and also Charlie Parker's. Actually, Max was the prime attorney for most of the musicians in New York, and some years later he was responsible for getting the famous cabaret card regulations repealed, after a memorable battle with the authorities concerned.

Oscar had given me a check for $700 for Max Cohen. According to him, that was the amount of back fees owed for various actions taken on Bud's behalf before he left for Europe. The future revenues of Bud were dwindling dangerously before he had even set foot in Birdland!

In Max's waiting room we saw several other musicians sitting around, and Ahmad Jamal came out of the office as we went in.

I was surprised to discover that this pleasant and friendly little man was the one who coped so well for so many years with all the sticky problems of jazz musicians. I had expected a rugged, driving brute like the kind we used to see in American movies, but here was the opposite of the stereotype. He was chubby, nearly bald, with a graying beard, and a sparkling smile, the image of a small-town judge. He greeted us with great kindness and seemed sincerely happy to see Bud. Bud, too, looked pleased to see him again and was once more very outgoing, more willing than usual to answer all Max's questions. I felt his nervousness again, but this time mingled with a sense of friendship for someone who had obviously played an important role in his life. Max gave us a letter of introduction to the Liquor Authority, where we were to ask for a certain Mr. Gillespie, who had Bud's whole file. Max was requesting the necessary clearance to get the cabaret card at once. We left the office to rush off for this next appointment.

After a long wait, Mr. Gillespie called us into his office, which was about as warm and cozy as a prison cell. He leafed through Bud's file as if it were a pile of dirty laundry. As his face went from surprise to astonishment to positive distaste, Bud sank lower and lower in his chair. Bud was sweating buckets and the time seemed interminable. He took some notes, then told me we would have to come back with the following documents: narcotics test, medical certificate after a complete check-up, and a police attestation with official ID and fingerprints. In short, just what an artist needs to feel in perfect shape.

I was beginning to wonder what we had gotten ourselves into. Here I had brought back home the uncontested master of the keyboard, the idol of pianists, at the top of his form, full of love, generosity and enthusiasm, ready to release the treasures of his genius, and he was greeted like a delinquent or a criminal.

Already, Bud wasn't looking at me with the same eyes. He seemed embarrassed for me and I felt in a confused way that his old distress had begun to take hold of him again. The smile that lit his face a few days ago was gone and all my attempts to reassure him didn't cheer him up. Still, I felt, I was here beside him and together we could face all obstacles. He had nothing to be sorry for and once these hassles were over, we would find once again the excitement and joy that had brought us so far.

HALLUCINATIONS

(Recorded in New York, March 7, 1953 [Base])

We made an appointment for the very next day to take a narcotics test. I had no idea what the test consisted of and as I calmly took Bud to the doctor's office, I was convinced it was nothing but a formality. The waiting room was packed and unbearably hot. Against the dark walls of the dreary room were pallid faces, looking as if they'd been dropped by accident on top of disarticulated bodies, like puppets in grotesque positions. Their haggard eyes stared at us, and the odor of fear they gave off made me feel a sudden wave of nausea. The bodies were in constant movement, with jerky, nervous gestures. Each oblivious of his neighbors, they frantically scratched their legs, their trouser legs rolled up. Others were doubled over, their heads on their laps, arms clutched round their waists. Their bulging eyes examined skinny hands with stiff and outspread fingers. They picked their noses, torturing dilated nostrils. I watched in horror the pale faces covered with convulsive tics, frozen in derisive grins, open mouths writhing in soundless screams. It was a descent into hell. I didn't dare look at Bud and forced myself to stare at a crack in the planks of the filthy floor, trying desperately to empty my mind in the hope of finding my inner music. The sound of fingernails endlessly scratching dried skin and the convulsive movements of their wretched limbs kept up an obscene background noise, punctuated with furtive groanings.

I was trying to contain my anxiety when a sudden gesture of Bud's made my blood turn cold. He had pulled up his pants legs and sunk his nails deep into the flesh, scratching his shins incessantly back and forth. When I turned to look at him, I saw his eyes rolled back in his head.

I firmly grabbed his arm to stop the horrible scratching. He froze, looked at me with eyes both questioning and troubled, in which I could find nothing familiar, nothing comprehensible. He pulled his arm away and went back to his frantic scratching. "Bud, what's the matter?" I whispered helplessly.

The whisper felt like a scream amid the furtive rustling movements. Just then, a door opened and a tall man in a white coat appeared, pushing before him a sort of automaton. With a glance around the room he noticed us and came over slowly. I stood to greet him and handed him the paper that Mr. Gillespie had given us. He looked Bud over with an expert eye, put a hand on his shoulder and, with a soft and knowing voice, whispered in his ear, "Okay man, when did you have your last fix?"

"I didn't take anything," answered Bud, like a child who's lying, just waiting for the slap. I was stunned, voiceless, terrified by the unbelievable scene.

"Come on, you can tell me. Don't be afraid."

"I didn't take anything," said Bud in the same voice, stammering, unconvincing.

Still stunned, I followed Bud as the doctor led him away, speaking in a calm and reassuring voice, "Okay look, we'll do the test, right? Come with me."

My brain began to function once again and I quickly recapitulated all the events since our arrival in New York, trying to find at what point a significant event could have escaped my attention. I tried desperately to recall something suspicious that hadn't caught my attention, but try as I might, nothing came to mind. I hadn't left Bud for a minute. The first night, of course, I had left him alone in the hotel room when he said he wanted to rest. I had been gone at most an hour. It all seemed impossible and grotesque.

Bud removed his jacket, rolled up his shirtsleeve and tentatively held out his arm. The doctor carefully examined the inside of the arm and took a blood sample. He transferred the contents of the syringe into a test tube filled with a colorless liquid. He shook the tube, put in a stopper and told us to wait outside. "It won't be long," he said.

The wait was a veritable Calvary. Without a word, Bud again started scratching his calves, his head turned upward and his eyes rolling. The doctor returned with a paper in his hand. He held it behind his back, leaned close to Bud, and asked, "Okay, now will you tell me when you had your last fix?"

I felt I was going mad. The nightmare wouldn't end. Bud, like a hunted animal, replied, still with no conviction, "I didn't take anything, doctor. I swear I didn't . . ."

My mind was racing. I was more and more convinced that this whole thing was a horrible mistake. Everything became clear. Over the years I had observed Bud closely. I now remembered all the signs I had seen before of his paranormal faculties. All at once, I lost my temper. Without even thinking about what I was saying, I stood up, and said brusquely, "Please doctor, that's enough. Mr. Powell hasn't taken anything. I'm sure of it. I haven't left him since we arrived. So do me a favor, just cut it out!"

The doctor was taken aback. He looked incredulous, as if he couldn't believe his ears, and didn't say a word. He averted his eyes, glanced down at Bud, who was looking at me in desperation, then literally flung the paper in his face, turned on his heels and walked off. I grabbed the certificate, took Bud by the arm, pulled him up from the bench and we took off, fleeing from that antechamber of hell.

Meanwhile, a storm had broken out in the sweltering city, a New York summer storm sending sheets of warm rain down on our heads. I walked without thinking, holding tight to Bud's arm. He stared straight in front of him. Water dripped from our clothing. My feet made squishing noises in my soaking shoes. We walked for a long time without looking for shelter. I felt broken, overcome by the nausea that had not yet dissipated. At last, we stopped under the awning of a shop and I carefully took the certificate out of my pocket. The result of Bud's test was, of course, negative.

This horrifying episode made me think further about Bud's strange psychological make-up. I knew that he was hypersensitive and suggestible, but this was positively uncanny. I had noticed in the past that a child mistreated by its mother or a dog beaten by its master was enough to make him miserable for the rest of the day. I remembered the look on his face, invaded by such despair, when he played "I'll Remember Clifford" and Buttercup would tell him to "think real hard" of his brother Richie. I can only imagine the suffering it must have caused him.

Bud had just lived through the suffering of the people around us. He had felt their withdrawal symptoms and made them his own, much as a medium takes into himself the tormented spirit he's trying to reach. Without wanting to, he absorbed the emotion and the suffering of others. Each time a situation was recalled for him, he lived through it all over again in a sort of flashback. I began to understand the depth of his fear of the outside world and his need to shut himself off, to seek refuge in his inner world. I thought of Bud's words, the first he had spoken seriously to me, and their meaning became clear to me now.

TOPSY TURVY

(Recorded in New York, October 5, 1956 [RCA Victor])

The next day couldn't possibly be as bad as what we'd just lived through. There were standard medical exams to go through and a traditional blood test. I didn't expect any problems, as our weekly check-ups in Paris with our friend, Dr. Teboul, had always been quite encouraging. Except that they took up a whole day, with endless waiting in a variety of waiting rooms, the tests confirmed that Bud was indeed in good shape. The blood tests found no alcohol in his blood. It looked like we were well on our way to obtaining the cabaret card. The only thing left was a final police check and then we could return to Mr. Gillespie.

Day by day I saw a change in Bud's behavior and felt his morale going downhill. From the day we arrived, he had lost his good humor and enthusiasm, and began to resemble his old self, one that I had known only too well. Throughout all the recent hardship, I felt him clinging to me again as he had in the days of his worst insecurity. I could no longer reassure him as I had done in Paris. Did he realize that in this hostile universe that was so new to me, I had no control over the situation?

I made a superhuman effort to distract him from our problems, but ultra-sensitive as he was, I know he felt all my own anxiety. Perhaps I was naive at the time, but still, what could I make of such a reception, one that had wounded his pride and shattered all of his hopes? He had arrived "clean," healthy, and stronger than he had ever been, and now his illusions were gone. He had been disappointed, too, that none of his friends had met him at the airport, and he referred to it again and again. I thought of his radiant smile when he went to meet Monk at Orly Airport and how happy Monk had been. I remembered how surprised Charlie Rouse and Ben Riley were to see Bud, as in the States the word was out that he was dying. Now in his own hometown, no familiar face was there to greet him. Bud was once again alone.

I hadn't been back to Birdland since the first night, since Bud always preferred to stay in our hotel room. I had managed to get a TV set installed and we killed time by watching all the programs till the

251

Late Late Show. Every evening I wrote to Nicole or our other friends, never mentioning all the problems we were going through. Bud spoke less and less. Only the mention of Paris and our friends back there got any reaction out of him. He would smile sadly and say something insignificant. At my insistence, he would scribble a few words at the bottom of my letters, then relapse into the abyss of his inner world.

Ever since our arrival, New York had been in the grip of a heat wave. The pocket money Goodstein sparingly doled out to us quickly vanished with the vast quantities of cigarettes and strawberry milkshakes Bud consumed. We took to going places on foot to save money, but in the summer heat these walks were exhausting.

Of all the red tape we had to take care of, the worst were the visits to the police. Bud dreaded each one despite my reassurances that he had nothing to fear. Our last one hadn't gone very well. Bud was nervous and the police didn't fail to notice it. I tried to appear casual despite my anxiety. After a series of nasty and ambiguous questions, they motioned Bud into an adjoining room for the customary fingerprinting. I had never witnessed the process. Each joint of each finger was inked separately, as well as the palms and the sides of the hands. Bud was perspiring profusely. At one point he wrenched his hand away from the cop who held it and tried to wipe his dripping face. The ink on his hands mingled with the sweat to form big dirty blotches. Between his anxious expression and the black rivulets dripping down, his face became a weird-looking mask. The cop looked on in contempt and my presence did nothing to improve the situation. I had made the mistake of letting my nervousness show and the look he threw me was both quizzical and threatening. Once more, I had to explain who I was and what I was doing there, and once more they didn't seem to understand a word I said. It was just like the scene at the airport, only this time Bud no longer dared to intervene.

Impulses of rebellion flashed through my head, seeing him so helpless once again. How could they subject an exceptional human being to such revolting treatment? He had come only to bring happiness to others. Why did he have to suffer these indignities? I felt guilty for not having realized beforehand what he would have to go through. I might have known that this would be the price to pay before he would be allowed to share his gift of love and beauty with a hard and ruthless world. We returned that night to our stifling hotel room like hunted animals returning to their den. We didn't speak—Bud resigned to his shame and I finding nothing I could say. It had been rough on us both. I knew he felt awful, both for causing so much trouble and for being unable to explain his strange behavior.

At last, when the silence had become too heavy to bear, I suggested we have an early dinner and set about preparing the meal in our kitchenette. He followed my movements as always, but without a single question. I could tell his mind was elsewhere. All at once, as if on a sudden inspiration, he asked, "Can I go out for a walk, Francis? Is there enough time?"

"Sure, Bud. Dinner isn't ready yet. Anyway, I won't start without you."

I was just setting the table when he came back. I could see at a glance that he'd been drinking. There was not the slightest doubt. I had seen it too many times before. He couldn't have had much, but in those few minutes he had undone all the work we had painfully accomplished together. I felt overcome by an immense fatigue. Avoiding his eyes and trying to hide my distress, I announced that dinner was ready. He answered with studied kindness and, in a drink-thickened voice, tried to make meaningless small talk. He was testing to see if I'd noticed anything. He never knew just how obvious it was and I, with great effort, hid my feelings and made believe I followed his incoherent talk.

The next day things were back to normal, but I knew that Bud was vulnerable again. I couldn't bring myself to blame him for what had happened, after the horrendous days we had spent, so I said nothing but resolved to be more vigilant than ever. I cursed the circumstances that endangered all our hard-won progress. I saw the destructive process that Bud had known all his life, because he was "different."

Once again, the ruthless system of a closed-minded society was wiping out the supportive surroundings Bud had built up for himself. It was just what had happened in the past, with one difference. This time, I was there, looking on in disgust but with the knowledge that I would one day bear witness. It is because of these obstacles that I will not accept the slightest criticism of Bud.

The worst of our ordeal was over. Now we had to go back to Mr. Gillespie with the various certificates and authorizations, to complete the investigation and get the famous cabaret card. We made an appointment and were received by Mr. Gillespie, who looked over the documents, seemed satisfied with their contents, and said Mr. Goodstein would hear from him promptly. Early the next morning I received a telegram asking me to come to his office at once. I lied to

Bud, saying I was going to the corner drugstore, and with great anxiety, headed over to Mr. Gillespie's office.

Mr. Gillespie greeted me in a peremptory manner and, in a tone devoid of any courtesy, accused me of concealing important information when filling out the forms. According to him, we had lied about events that were not only serious but also prohibited by law. I was totally bewildered but my innocent air and my flood of protests did nothing to calm his wrath. He continued his accusations, finally blurting out, "Don't act so innocent. You know very well that Earl Powell made a serious suicide attempt and you are certainly aware that that is a criminal offense in this country."

I was speechless.

"It is my duty to tell you that your concealment of this fact will seriously jeopardize the cabaret card."

I tried to explain that I had met Bud in 1956 when he arrived in Europe and knew nothing of his past before that time. I also said I had no authority to discuss this kind of subject. That stumped him. Just like the police at the airport and the police station, he assumed I was Bud's manager, doubtless appointed to look after the man and his business. It seemed hopeless to make him understand that my role was of mere friendship. Such things as friendship and loyalty seemed to be unknown in his vocabulary so I gave up and suggested he get in touch with Bud's lawyer, Max Cohen, to clarify this delicate point.

Max searched through his records and did find a trace of this horrible episode. Some years before, Bud had taken a razor and slit open his left armpit. He was taken to the emergency ward nearly dead from loss of blood.

Later on, I thought a lot about this terrifying suicide attempt. Assuming that he had done it in a moment of desperation, why had he cut the armpit and not, as is far more widespread, the wrist? Even in deepest despair, had he had misgivings about destroying that marvelous machine that was his left hand? We never talked about this episode and all I've just said is pure speculation. However, thanks to the astute eyes of Jackie Deghelt, a physiotherapist, it offers a plausible explanation of Bud's odd way of walking that only his close friends had noticed. I have already mentioned how Bud walked swinging his right arm, his left held rigid at his side. Jackie further observed (through watching my films) that Bud's left hand moved little at the piano and that he always held his left arm stiffly extended. When he played, the impulse came directly from the shoulder. This relative immobility is a type of compensation often seen in patients with arm injuries. To avoid discomfort, they truncate the gesture or try to assist with another part of the body. The way Bud used his left hand was fully concordant with an arm and shoulder injury. Still, Bud's left hand was firm and solid, and his movement on the keyboard was positively amazing when you think that he may never have recovered full use of all the ligaments of his arm.

I was glad I had left Bud at the hotel, thinking of the shock it would have been to bring up this horrible memory. Max Cohen gave me a letter for Mr. Gillespie, explaining the incident and also clarifying my relationship with Bud. Within 48 hours, the matter was settled. Goodstein phoned to tell me the card had finally been issued and Bud's grand premiere had just been officially announced to the press. He had even sent an invitation to Mr. Gillespie so that he could judge the quality of his client for himself.

By now my morale was at an all-time low. We had been in New York for a week and not once had there been any mention of music.

Oscar called us down to Birdland one afternoon to show us the piano they had rented especially for Bud. It was a Steinway and Bud obstinately refused to try it, simply repeating, "It'll be okay, Oscar. It'll be okay."

Not wanting to leave it at that, I sat down at the piano and ran my fingers over the keyboard. The touch felt good. Though nothing exceptional, it seemed sufficient and I figured Bud would get the most out of it. At last we were entering a positive phase, and about time, too, as Bud's strength was declining slowly but surely. With the unremitting heat and discomfort of the hotel, where the garage made it impossible to get a good night's sleep, we were physically undermined day after day. I tried to appear cheerful and keep Bud's spirits up.

All the papers announced his return to Birdland and evoked as always the spectre of his past troubles. Despite all the publicity, we still hadn't seen a single friend and I didn't dare broach the subject with him. To distract him I often took him to the movies, choosing those with air conditioning. After dinner at our usual restaurant, we would end our evenings quietly in the hotel room in front of the TV.

With all the red tape I was beginning to have a better idea of what musicians had to go through in the United States, particularly if they were marginal in any way. The musicians' union, the American Federation of Musicians, had demanded all Bud's back dues, to be deducted from his future earnings. Later I wondered why they couldn't simply have taken them out of his royalties. All these years, the union hadn't taken the slightest interest in the problems of one of its most il-

lustrious members. I had always naively assumed that the union regulations must in some way have been dictated by its members. In fact,
jazz musicians had little say in this structure that controlled so much
of show business. Besides, the strongarm tactics of its leader, James C.
Petrillo (who had learned his trade in Chicago), made it clear that the
existing structure would not easily be changed.

The methods of the musicians' union were undoubtedly more
beneficial for performers of light music and varieties than for the jazzmen, who were in the minority and most of whom were poorly informed. What the jazzmen did feel was the union's iron fist. The
cardinal rule was obedience, and the regulations were applied to the
totality of the profession, irrespective of working conditions or esthetic considerations. The rules made sense perhaps for show business
in general, but were not particularly compatible with the creative spirits of the jazz world. And so a kind of "protected zone" was created,
whereby some could get work, while those others of a more rebellious
nature were effectively boycotted. This kind of set-up appreciably altered the future of pure jazz. Petrillo's actions, notably in prohibiting
all new recording between 1942 and 1944, had had the effect of ob-
scuring the bop current at a time when it was in full flower, preventing its diffusion and thereby its assimilation. The fruit of the musical
investigations of the period has been lost to us today. By stifling this
tremendous musical revolution, the Union seriously compromised the
future of its creators. Audiences missed out on the phenomenon and
went on to throw themselves into lesser types of music that, unlike
jazz, never lacked for clever promoters, ready to exploit the ignorance
of the general public. Jazz, truly a music of the people, a means of
peace and communication, was to enter a sort of clandestinity.

Now we were nearing opening night and a telegram arrived from
Frances Barnes and Celia. Our messages had finally reached them.
Bud was extremely moved. They were living in North Carolina and
said they couldn't come to New York right away. Still, I was glad
we'd reached them and hoped we'd see them sooner or later. I thought
it would be good for Bud.

The great day finally dawned. Bud Powell would be back at Birdland. In the excitement of opening night, all the hassles of the cabaret
card faded into a bad dream.

On the afternoon of the opening, Oscar asked us to come to the
club to meet the two musicians he had hired to accompany Bud. I
had hoped for some old hands that Bud had played with before, but
Oscar said he couldn't afford such seasoned musicians. We met the

young drummer Horace Arnold and the bassist John Ore, whom we'd seen in Paris with Thelonious. When the introductions were over and the musicians had made their preparations, Bud went back to the hotel to rest. Like a true pro, he knew how to save his energy, but I felt his inner excitement, which had been missing for a long time.

As the hour approached, I grew more impatient myself. I thought of the importance of the event, imagining the curiosity of those who had said Bud was washed up and of the others who would be seeing him for the first time. For young musicians in America, Bud was a myth. He had left in March of 1959 and was coming back five years later, while in his absence a whole new generation of artists had been born, most of whom looked to Bird and Bud for their inspiration.

I was also nervous about the critical reaction. Bud was silent but tense, a perfect lesson in concentration. Time seemed to be moving very slowly. At last it grew dark and I was relieved when he started getting ready. The suspense was growing unbearable.

For the occasion, he put on his grey flannel suit, a spanking white shirt and a nice new black bow tie. He was always a classy dresser, but tonight he looked stupendous.

Night had fallen and New York, with the tall, brightly lit buildings, seemed to have a particularly festive air. The avenue took on a new magnificence and the noise of the city was more exciting than ever. I felt reconciled with America and ready to forget all the pain of recent days.

We went to eat at our old familiar restaurant and I appreciated the surroundings for the first time. Our meal felt like a gala feast and I savored every delectable minute of it. Each dish tasted delicious and for dessert I ordered Bud's favorite, strawberry tarts.

It was always a pleasure for me to watch Bud eat. He was like a child when he liked something, and the tarts were his passion of the moment.

Comfortably seated at the table, he picked up the tart brimming with strawberries and with deep concentration raised it slowly to his mouth. He sat far back in his chair and, with his ample and exaggerated gestures, the tart was traveling a very dangerous path indeed. I suddenly had a vision of gooey strawberries running down his white shirtfront and the beautiful flannel suit. There wasn't much time to spare and any slip would be a catastrophe.

I held my breath so as not to interrupt the delicate maneuver and didn't move until the last bit of tart was safely consumed and Bud licked his lips with an ecstatic smile.

The evening was off to a good start. In my nervousness, I had completely forgotten about my own tart but when it came to food, Bud didn't miss a thing. Knowing I didn't care much for sweets, he politely asked if I was still hungry, and before I could answer, he had taken it off my plate and was prepared to consume it, too. With bated breath, I went through the long, slow process all over again, but our lucky stars must have been with us, for the suit remained spotless.

THE BEST THING FOR YOU

(Recorded in New York, September 1964 [Roulette])

T
he fateful hour was approaching. A glance at my watch confirmed that it was already a quarter to ten. Bud was asking no
questions; he trusted me. He had only to look at me and he knew
how things stood. He was radiant and extremely calm. All his senses
were awake and his energy was growing by the minute. I had lived
beside him for so long and had observed him so closely that I could
feel the slightest variations in his behavior.

I asked if he wanted anything else and told him it was finally time
to head for Birdland. We had only about two hundred yards to go. We
walked slowly, without speaking. The city streets were full of life, the
bright lights seemed garish and the traffic exceptionally heavy. I
caught a glimpse of the front of Birdland from a distance and it
seemed to me there was a line out front under the canopy. I was beginning to worry about how to get through the crowd of customers
but as we got nearer I could see what was going on. Two rows of men
stood facing each other in front of the entrance and before we could
realize that they were in fact an honor guard for Bud, we were in
their midst and I began to recognize some familiar faces. Up front on
the right was Bobby Timmons, his eyes sparkling with happiness, and
alongside him we saw Wynton Kelly, Barry Harris, Kenny Dorham,
Walter Davis, Walter Bishop, McCoy Tyner, Charles McPherson, Erroll Garner, Babs Gonzales, George Tucker, Sam Jones, John Hicks,
Billy Higgins, Lonnie Hillyer . . . There were others, but memory
fails me.

Bud had taken my hand, as he always did to cross the street, and
he paused for a second when he heard some scattered applause. He
walked on toward the staircase and just as he drew near, Bobby Timmons reached out to take his hand and give it a fleeting kiss. Instantly
the others did the same, with a devotion and fervor that was absolutely heart-rending. I heard some brief comments and recognized
some young musicians, their faces contorted with emotion. Bud was
squeezing my hand with uncommon force, his face illuminated with
joy as we walked down the stairs amid our guard of honor.

The doors were wide open and the club was packed to the rafters. Bud had not yet reached the last step when a thunder of applause exploded in our faces. "There he is . . . That's him. It's Bud, it's really him . . ." It was breathtaking. Bud vanished into a sea of outstretched hands reaching frantically to touch him, hold him. Everyone wanted to see him, talk to him, exchange a friendly wink. "Bud. Hey. It's me, Bud. Over here. How ya doin'? You look great, man! . . ."

What waves of love, of passion flowed from the assembled crowd! Pushed toward the bandstand, it took a while before he reappeared in the limelight, and then the applause broke out again, twice as powerful. I had instantly found myself alone, trapped by the teeming, excited crowd, and I stood there savoring my solitude. I let myself go, caught up in the intense emotion that had electrified the room.

The applause grew louder, reaching a crescendo. It was deafening. Bud stood stiffly on the stage and looked out with an almost embarrassed smile at the faces straining toward him. When Pee Wee Marquet came out, I thought the club would explode. The audience, on their feet, was clapping wildly without a stop. Bud looked admiringly at the delirious crowd. I had never heard such an ovation. Pee Wee tried for the second time to take the mike and failed.

Amid the shouts and whistles, Bud took a tentative step toward the piano, then stopped as the applause doubled in intensity. The audience had not yet had their fill. The standing ovation lasted seventeen minutes! Afterward, Pee Wee told me, "Francis, I've been emceeing at Birdland for over fifteen years and I never saw anything like that."

All at once, as if by some magic signal, the room grew quiet, with a stillness so deep it was almost painful, the only background noise the faint whir of the air conditioner. All the customers were in their places, seated or standing, pressed against one another, all eyes turned to the piano. The bassist and drummer waited solemnly, their eyes also trained on Bud. He arched his back, threw back his head and the music flowed in all its awesome beauty. I knew so well that movement that announced quick-tempo tunes. In any case, Bud never made introductions. With a simple "One, two . . . one, two, three, four," he would tap his foot sharply as if to get the machine moving, and the locomotive was off, powerful, majestic, unstoppable. The audience recognized "The Best Thing for You Would Be Me" and clapped once more in homage to the humor of the title.

Will you believe me if I say again that this was the finest moment of my life? Lost amid the packed crowd, I fought to hold back the tears. I was overcome with euphoria. I was deliriously happy for Bud and proud to have come so far with so many difficulties. We had over-come indifference, adversity, provocations, suffering, illness, financial problems, and now, all at once, our victory over the impossible took on all its meaning.

When the first set was over, Pee Wee could finally talk into his mike, though the silence was only relative. Frank Foster was sharing the bill with Bud and the other musicians were setting up their equipment. I inched my way backstage and found Bud surrounded by a group of friends. He greeted me with a big laugh and the traditional, "Hey brother, how do you feel?"

Oscar Goodstein was in seventh heaven. I could read surprise on the radiant faces and the comments I overheard also revealed their amazement. "Did you see Bud's face? It's amazing how happy he looks. No kidding, he's in great shape. Unrecognizable. Look at that smile . . ."

It was sheer bliss. I hadn't failed. I was beginning to repay my debt to the man who had enhanced my life, this man broken by a lifetime of hardship. I had won my battle to bring him a little comfort. Bud knew he had a true friend. He never doubted the love I had for him. That certainty remains today the finest jewel among my treasured memories.

That night left me reeling with joy. From all around came words and signs of friendship and I abandoned myself to the flow of good feeling. In my dreams that night, the buses in our underground garage carried screaming crowds clapping with all their might. I awoke not knowing for sure if it was all a dream and despite a troubled sleep I felt fit as a fiddle.

This time the press gave Bud's comeback an enthusiastic reception. *Time* wrote on September 4:

> When Bud Powell left Manhattan for Paris in 1958 [*sic*], his friends prayed that the change of locale might somehow exorcise the demons that had plagued him for much of his life. Instead, Powell sank even deeper into his private inferno. After five years abroad he was a shattered, empty-eyed hulk, a stranger to himself and his music.
>
> Yet, amazingly, last week Bud Powell, now 39, was back on the U.S. jazz scene, cured of T.B. and fat as a Burgermeister. The metamorphosis was complete when Powell forcefully struck the first chords of "The Best Thing for You Would Be Me." His attack was robust and sure, erupting in a series of crashing, dissonant chords, then retreated in flights of delicate, melodic figures. His audience vociferously agreed that he was still a master, his performance a giant step up from limbo.

The architect of Powell's recovery has been Francis Paudras, a 29-year-old commercial artist from Paris, who is Bud's most devoted fan and full-time guardian angel. Paudras lives with Powell, doles out his food and money, protectively escorts him everywhere to keep him on the straight and narrow. "People say Bud is crazy or lost or silent," says Paudras, "but he is really in a state of grace."

For the first time in years, his message is hopeful: "Please tell everybody that Bud's O.K. and he's feeling fine and he's ready to play."

On September 7, *Newsweek* ran the following:

Bud Powell came home last week. On opening night a jam-packed Birdland was rich in musicians, including Thelonious Monk, Max Roach, Charlie Mingus, John Coltrane, Quincy Jones, and Kai Winding. There is no modern jazzman anywhere who doesn't owe Bud Powell. The pianists owe most and say so. Bud pioneered the techniques of the modern jazz piano in those postwar days when be-bop liberated jazz from the prison of stereotyped swing. Few musicians needed the new freedom of musical language more than Earl Bud Powell, who, drummer Kenny Clarke said, "used to do all the things that Monk wanted to do but couldn't." Powell was a man driven to find new expression for his intense musical vision. . . . It was a great stroke of luck when young Francis Paudras, a fervent admirer of Powell's music, appointed himself Bud's unofficial caretaker. These days Paudras watches over Powell like a Gallic Saint Bernard—without the brandy . . .

In Robert Sheldon's column in *New York* Magazine:

One of the most influential figures in modern jazz, Bud Powell, the pianist, has come home to roost at Birdland for a month. . . . Typical of the reverence that he inspires was the comment of Horace Silver, pianist, who is also appearing at Birdland. Said Mr. Silver, "Bud is one of the great sources. He says more in five measures than most piano players say in five minutes."

Dan Morgenstern expressed his joy at Bud's return in an article in *Down Beat* on October 2:

When Bud Powell mounted the bandstand at Birdland for his first appearance in his homeland in more than six years, the packed house gave him a standing ovation. It was a spontaneous and moving vote of confidence in a musician who has had more than his share of trouble and whose eagerly awaited return had been accompanied by persistent rumors that this once-great player was now just a shadow of his former self . . . Nevertheless, from the opening "The Best Thing for You Would Be Me," to a delightful "John's Abbey" through a rhapsodic "Like Someone In Love," . . . there were moments of inspired music making. . . . Not the least moments were

Powell's readings of two selections from the Thelonious Monk canon: Monk's own "Epistrophy," and Denzil Best's and Monk's "Bemsha Swing".... Powell played Monk's "I Mean You" in absolutely masterful fashion, his inventions bolstered by Moses' expert phrasing and time. Powell's sense of humor (like all great players, he has one) was evident here . . .

Bud's triumphal comeback to New York also inspired some pertinent remarks by Harvey Pekar, in *Down Beat* (October 22). To my great satisfaction, he reversed in one fell swoop the mixed critical reaction that had previously prevailed. All at once I felt reconciled with American journalism. Pekar seemed to see that Bud had reached a new phase in his music:

> Though few knowledgeable observers would deny that Bud Powell ranks as one of the greatest and most influential jazz pianists, only a fraction of his career and recorded output has been discussed intensively.
>
> Powell's style has evolved in a manner unlike that of any other jazzman. Two giants contemporary with Powell, Charlie Parker and Dizzy Gillespie (who almost could be said to belong to the musical generation immediately preceding Powell), didn't alter their approaches significantly after about 1946. But a person comparing a Powell solo from that period with one recorded about a decade later would find it hard to believe that both were played by the same person. . . . Many of these [later] records have been dismissed by critics, but as a body of work, they constitute a fascinating and high-quality output. But to see them in proper light, one must consider what came before them. . . . Perhaps Powell's playing here heralds the beginning of a great new period in his career. If he can get himself together again, we may not have heard anything yet.

From our first days at the hotel, we had become friendly with George, the doorman. George worshipped Bud and gave him special treatment. With our peculiar working hours, the rules didn't apply to us. At any time of day or night we could have a cup of coffee or hot chocolate and if by chance we had forgotten to shop, he would bring us sandwiches for our midnight snack. I was beginning to get used to this life that was so new to me.

Still feeling a little out of place and not sure how to proceed, I had not yet brought my recording equipment down to Birdland. My tape recorder, compact for its time, was nonetheless cumbersome and very heavy. I had to think of a way to set it up in a way that would be permanent. Our reserved table was to the right of the stage near the kitchen doors. I decided to attach my only mike to one of the pillars up front to get the global sound. Then I could keep the recorder near me and thus monitor the quality. We went to the club one afternoon to check it out. There was no problem, except for one detail—according to Oscar, recording was absolutely prohibited. "Personally, I have nothing against it," he said, "but we'll be in for trouble if the union finds out." Even with Bud's permission, the rule was very strict. I couldn't see the logic in it. Bud was all for it and he had no contractual obligations with any label. When I told him I wanted to try anyway, he said to go ahead.

The second night at Birdland was a repeat of the first. A sell-out crowd applauded Bud with the same fervor. The staff looked astounded as I went tranquilly about my recording. My mike wire that trailed across the path leading to the kitchen was about as discreet as a high-tension power line. The reaction wasn't long in coming. By the second set, I started to get some flak, first from some busybodies prying into matters that were no concern of theirs, then from Pee Wee Marquet, who took it upon himself to be the spokesman for the musicians' union. But since his explanation of why recording was banned was no more convincing than the others I had heard, I decided to keep on with it, but a little more discreetly from now on. I knew it would be useless to discuss the matter and hopeless to make them understand that I simply couldn't bear to let this music vanish forever. With Bud in complete agreement, I was convinced that these exceptional moments had to be preserved.

To perfect my installation and put an end to unwanted comments, I went back to the club with Bud the next afternoon. Birdland's sound system worked on three mikes: one in the piano, another on the bass and the third for general background. There were other standing mikes that could be used for the horns. I decided not to use any movable equipment but opted for attaching my microphone to the piano mike, turning it slightly toward the bass. The drums would always be audible enough. I ran the wire behind the stand and let it out near our table. All I had to do was hook it up and that was that. I had my recorder within reach under the bench. Bud watched my preparations with a conspiratorial air. He offered to give it a try and since it worked perfectly we left for a walk around the neighborhood.

That evening, everything went smoothly. Bud, who had a sense of humor, looked me right in the eye and spoke into the mike, loud enough for me to hear, "Are you ready, Francis?" That way I could start recording right at the beginning, without wasting any tape or missing the openings.

One evening, at the end of a rousing chorus I'd been listening to in a state of rapture, Bud suddenly panicked. He stopped phrasing and just played a few chords. The bassist stood expectantly. Bud's eyes searched for mine and in an anguished voice he called out, "Francis, what am I playing? What's the piece?"

Fortunately I was able to give him the name of the song, and Bud, with a look of relief, went on without a hitch. Bud would get so involved in a chorus that at the end of a daring exploration he could completely lose touch with something as basic as that.

Once the equipment was set up correctly, I had no further trouble. I could discreetly handle the apparatus hidden under my seat and back at the hotel at night we would listen to see how the trio sounded. While the recorder was running, I would move over to the other side of the room, to the space they called the bleachers, reserved for fans too broke to afford a regular table. It was an enclosed area near the bar and close to the stage where they could listen to the music without eating or drinking. The admission was $4. It was the favorite spot of all the musicians, who came nearly every night. The most regular of them all was Barry Harris. I would sit next to him and together we would revel in the same emotions. Bud knew where we were and would often look over in our direction. In the center was the dinner club, the biggest part of the room. The bar was on the left near the band, and on the right was a row of booths.

Between sets Bud and I went regularly to hear Mary Lou Williams who was playing at the Hickory House, a minute away from Birdland. Barry wasn't working much in New York at the time and by a curious coincidence, Mary Lou would get sick two days a week, every single week, to be replaced, of course, by Barry. She was a close friend of Bud's but strangely enough she never came down to Birdland so we had to go to the Hickory House to see her. The piano was on a high platform in the middle of a circular bar, and there we could observe the musicians all around without embarrassment. Each night when we arrived, Mary Lou's face would light up as if filled with sudden inspiration. She seemed completely changed, the sound grew louder and her articulation more vigorous. Sometimes, with a knowing smile, she would play a long phrase that evoked one of Bud's tunes. Holding on to the edge of the bar, his fingers would twitch with a sudden agitation as he devoured her with his eyes.

I knew his reactions well enough to spot the sure signs of real interest. I was sure he was reproducing, right there, some of the figures she played. After all, Mary Lou was one of the family.

STAR EYES
(Recorded in Stockholm, April 23, 1963 [Steeple Chase])

O ne Monday morning the telephone rang and a woman's voice at the other end spoke in French, with a charming little English accent. "My name is Nica de Koenigswarter. I'm an old friend of Bud's and I'd like to invite you both to my home." Of course I had heard of Nica, the Baroness de Koenigswarter, whose reputation as a patron of the arts and friend of musicians was legendary. "I understand Bud's off this evening. If you like, I can come pick you up. We'll spend the day at my house, then go out to dinner." We had no particular plans, so we accepted with great pleasure.

Nica arrived right on time. It was my first meeting with a very great lady. I know I use a lot of superlatives. This is not because I like to gush, it's simply that I feel very fortunate to have met so many wonderful people in my life. I also have a handy faculty for forgetting what is negative, dull, or mediocre (with the sole exception of Buttercup, who deserves to be remembered!). But my entire vocabulary pales in Nica's presence, and I need to run for my thesaurus to find enough superlatives to describe her.

Our friend George, the doorman, let us know she was waiting downstairs. We went down to find a gorgeous Bentley convertible purring softly in front of our door. Nica greeted us with a dazzling smile. In a few seconds, she had asked about everything and when she was satisfied that all was in order she invited us into the car. "We'd better leave the city right away. The traffic is going to be terrible."

Nica maneuvered her Bentley with the skill of a racing driver. A cigarette holder between her teeth, she took the turns at breakneck speed without batting an eyelash. Bud sat in the back with his cap pulled down tight on his head. He was used to convertibles from our little TR3. As she drove, Nica gave Bud news of all his musician friends. She was fascinating. Listening to her, I lost all track of time and, as if by magic, before I knew it we had crossed the Hudson River to New Jersey and were pulling into Nica's driveway.

As we got out of the car, a cat came up to greet us, brushing against Bud's leg. Still as sensitive as ever to cats, he jumped aside with surprising agility. I still remembered the episode with Bill Coleman's tomcat. Nica put the car in the garage and opened the front door. The spectacle we saw made Bud freeze in his tracks. In the doorway, a dozen or more cats were looking us over with cool curiosity. Nica couldn't have imagined the extent of Bud's fear of these creatures. When I explained the situation, she quickly locked up her overly friendly pets, then invited us into the house.

We went directly to the upper floor. A wooden staircase led to a vast room in the middle of which stood a black Steinway baby grand. Three of the walls were covered with extraordinary photos over shelf upon shelf of thousands of tapes and records. The fourth side was an immense window overlooking the Hudson River, with the New York skyline framed as if on a giant movie screen. Down below, some boats were lying at anchor and seagulls glided in the limpid air. The minute I saw the room I was overcome with emotion. It had the serenity of a chapel and the open piano was like a living presence. On that piano Monk had composed his greatest songs, along with Bud and Sonny Clarke.

Nica knows hundreds of musician stories and has a unique gift for telling them. Even when it's not the greatest story, her voice alone is enough to keep the listeners enthralled. Bud was on cloud nine as Nica recounted a flood of good news. (Where bad news is concerned she becomes amnesiac.) Later, Barry Harris arrived and his face lit up when he saw Bud. His passion for Bud was equal to my own (and René Urtréger's back in Paris) and to see him react just as I did to Bud's music made me surer than ever of my convictions, if such a thing was possible.

Soon Nica said it was time for dinner. She suggested we go to a restaurant in Greenwich Village near the Five Spot, where Charlie Mingus was playing with his group. So after dinner we headed for the club, where Teddy Wilson was already waiting at a table that had been reserved. Jaki Byard nearly had a heart attack when he saw Bud walk in. There was a flutter in the band and after exchanging a few looks, everyone was informed of his presence. The set ended and the embracing began. Bud happily drank in the compliments on how good he looked. The club slowly emptied and a cheerful and animated conversation was struck up at our table. As the musicians went to put away their instruments, Teddy Wilson, at Nica's request, launched into " 'Round Midnight" with some harmonies of his own. I was surprised to hear this tune, not usually in the repertoire of musicians of his generation. Mingus came out plucking notes on his bass as he carried it in front of him and the evening took off again. Teddy gave Bud some significant looks, motioning toward the keyboard, but Bud simply smiled his beatific smile. Barry went to the piano and, with a knowing look at Bud, started to play a series of pure Tatum clichés. Bud was jubilant, when suddenly his attention was attracted by a strange-looking bearded black man who had come timidly up to our table. He looked like one of those winos who hang around night-clubs panhandling and calling you "Sir" as they open your taxi door for you. He couldn't have been over 25. His hesitant steps toward the piano intrigued Barry, who stopped right in the middle of a cascading arpeggio.

"Play, man. That's nice Tatum. Go on, play. . . ."

We all raised our eyes to stare at the intruder. Barry resumed play-ing but kept a worried eye on the man, who placed a dirty hand on his shoulder. "Hey man," said Barry with a jerk of the shoulder, "get away, will ya?"

"Play man, play," said the drunk. "Hey, do 'I Know That You Know'. . . ."

Bud looked on amused. He seemed accustomed to that kind of character and he was the only one still smiling. Barry was mechani-cally playing the tune and had already slowed down to look for some harmonic combinations in the language of Tatum.

"No, no, A-flat and D," said the drunk, swaying dangerously on unsteady legs.

Barry looked annoyed, than patiently went on with his hesitant in-terpretation.

"Nah, put an A-natural there," said the guy, pointing an authorita-tive finger at the keyboard.

Barry stopped dead and, in a flippant tone with a heavy dose of irony, said, "Hey listen, maybe you want to play it yourself?"

Not fazed in the slightest, he shrugged and answered between two hiccups, "Okay, man, if you want, I can try."

He sat down awkwardly as we all watched in amazement. His dirty sweater of indeterminate color had a hole in the sleeve and his elbow was sticking out. He placed his skinny hands on the keyboard and attacked the tune in a dizzying tempo. I suddenly had a feeling that some practical joker had put on a record by Tatum (the Toronto concert) with the famous solo rendition of "I Know That You Know." The evening ended with all of us listening to this phenomenal pianist and urging him on. As we left I told Barry how surprised I was, and he said in a blasé voice, "Oh, you know, in New York, you can expect anything. There's some incredible talent out there." He was right. I had already realized it, but this particular time was exceptional. Nica took us back to the hotel. It had been a marvelous day.

In the days that followed, each time we saw Nica was a veritable delight. Nothing was too good for us. Every thoughtful gesture was made with utter discretion, as if it was perfectly natural. Once and for all, I was certain that she was the great lady of jazz.

Pretty soon Bud began to show signs of dissatisfaction with his drummer. Horace Arnold was young and lacked experience. I passed on his comments to Goodstein, who said he couldn't afford the better-known musicians. Knowing how sensitive and demanding Bud was about his rhythm section, I tried to argue with him, but it was to no avail.

Then providence intervened in the person of Max Roach, who dropped in to see us one morning at the hotel. Bud was very happy to see Max. They had last met in Paris back in 1959 when he had come to give a concert at the Théâtre des Champs-Elysées. He invited us to his house for dinner the following Monday, which was the musicians' night off at Birdland. The club was open only for jam sessions, the occasion for young musicians to play in public and mix with the professionals who came to scout out new talent. There was one pianist, I remember, by the name of Kirk Lightsey, unknown at the time, who made a tremendous hit each time he played. A lot of pianists were always there for these fabulous contests.

When Max heard we wanted a new drummer he spoke to Goodstein and recommended a very promising student of his, J. C. Moses. That evening Max and Abbey Lincoln came to the club with J. C. Moses, who did a tryout on the second set. Horace took it well. Playing with Bud was a memorable experience for him in any case.

For his famous dinner, Max put on a mysterious look and promised us a surprise. Bud was dying to know what it was, but no matter how many times he asked, Max wouldn't say a word.

During that week, I met a lot of people and got to know some of Bud's old friends. The press continued to give him excellent notices and Birdland was packed every night. But I couldn't help thinking it was pretty strange that none of the old-timers ever showed up at the club.

Kenny Dorham, who had been there to meet Bud on opening night, didn't come into the club but did join us for lunch nearly every day. Kenny was a wonderful guy and his friendship and respect for Bud were touching. I remember him well and have never accepted his sudden death. I think he was underestimated. Perhaps he was overshadowed by the "greats," Dizzy, Fats, and Miles. This fine musician, who was also, incidentally, an excellent boxer, earned his living teaching at a music school. He deserves to be listened to more closely, for in my opinion he was one of the subtlest trumpeters of his time. I urged Kenny to come down to the club, but he said he never set foot in Birdland any more and I was too embarrassed to ask why. He declined all my invitations and I didn't insist.

Every night on our way to Birdland we ran into Erroll Garner. This towering figure of the music world was surprisingly short. Erroll's eternal problem on the road was that there was never a piano stool high enough for him, especially since he liked to sit very high. This seemingly minor detail became a major preoccupation until he hit upon the idea of taking along a phone book, the Manhattan phone book, to be exact, which he said was just the thickness he needed to be at a perfect height. He traveled with it under his arm and if people expressed surprise at the strange hand baggage, he would answer, "Well, it's a good book, even though it's got too many characters for my taste!"

Each time Erroll saw us, he would feign surprise, although we met at the same place every day. Bud would smile knowingly and Erroll, with his unfailing good humor, would tell me over and over again, "Bud's a genius, you know, man, a real genius."

He'd walk us to the club, give Bud a friendly hug and then disappear into the crowd. Each time I asked him to come in, he gave the same reply as Kenny Dorham. It was all very puzzling.

During the same week, Babs Gonzales showed up at the hotel too. We would have a bite together every night after the show. Babs was a friend from way back. He had been coming to Paris regularly since 1948 and remained a loyal friend until the end of his life, till the last days he spent at my house. We were fond of him and he of us. He was the quintessence of the bop era, and in my opinion, the only real singer (except for Dizzy) in the bop style. He had a very distinctive sound and his own special language. The direct heir of Cab Calloway or Lester Young in the practice of musicians' slang, he would comment on the most ordinary events like a true poet of the street. His corrosive humor hid a deep melancholy as well as a touching naivete. He said to me one day, "You see, Francis, I've had two great lessons in my life. The first one came from Fernandel, who said 'Babs, make people laugh. That's the only thing that's real.' The second lesson was from Josephine Baker. I was telling her about my money problems, and she advised me, 'You know, Babs, banks get robbed, lawyers are crooks. Once my hotel burned down with all my savings. And you gotta look out for pickpockets. So my advice is: walk on your money!'"

I wasn't sure what he meant, so to illustrate, he pulled off his shoes and socks and, to my amazement, there were stacks of dollar bills inside his socks and under the soles of his feet.

"Voilà, la la," he said. "No problem. C'est la vie, la la . . ."

Babs was the eternal showman. He took life philosophically. Nothing was too serious to make fun of. He was the only person who could make Bud laugh till he cried, and he did it every night at our late night suppers. He'd be waiting for us outside the club, then we'd do some shopping and go back to the hotel to eat and listen to the tapes of the evening. We would go to bed, our sides aching from laughing so hard. Sometimes, when Bud finished early, Babs would invite us to a restaurant. Some of those dinners ended badly, for the general hilarity caused by Babs's antics was a bit too noisy for the management's taste and we'd have to beat it out in a hurry.

He too refused to enter Birdland. I couldn't stand the mystery any more and asked him point blank the question that had been bothering me so long.

"You know Bird was banned from the club. It wasn't only that he lost his cabaret card. He also had a fight with Goodstein."

I had never heard the story, so Babs told it to me. It seems Bird showed up to play one evening in shorts. Goodstein was furious. They got into a shouting match and finally came to blows. From that day on, none of the oldtimers would set foot in the club. The next day I mentioned this to Goodstein with a disapproving air and, right away, he got angry. To justify himself, he went to a shelf in his office and took down a big envelope, from which he carefully extracted some photos. "Look at these. You'll see!" There in the photo was Charlie Parker, looking like a Boy Scout, his bare legs sticking out of what seemed to be Bermuda shorts.

Years later, Bird's girlfriend Chan told me her version of the incident. Just before leaving for Birdland one night, Bird noticed that his only suit pants were not ironed. Chan immediately started to iron them but, interrupted by the doorbell (the arrival of a delivery man), she went away leaving the iron on the pants. By the time she got back, the room was filled with smoke and one leg was burned through at calf level. Bird's immediate reaction was extremely logical. He picked up a pair of scissors and cut the legs off just below the knees. Then he put on the hastily shortened pants, jumped in a taxi and headed for Birdland. That was all there was to it, a story that had been blown out of all proportion.

Whether Babs's story was the real reason or not, none of Bud's old friends ever went near the club. The only one who ever broke the rule was Max Roach. After Max had left, Oscar was in such a state that it simply proved it was probably better for the old crowd to stay away. Max had apparently insulted Oscar at the very "scene of the crime" and brought up all the old grudges. Oscar was fuming all night, so Bud and I thought it best to slip out quietly and unnoticed.

Apart from that minor incident, the Birdland engagement was going well and the audiences were as enthusiastic as ever. J. C. Moses got more and more into the spirit of the trio as he grew more familiar with Bud's repertoire.

One morning we were about to go out for breakfast when the doorbell rang. I opened it to find a young man standing there. His face looked familiar but I couldn't place him at that moment. "Is Mr. Powell in, please?"

"Yes, of course. Your name . . . ?"

"Ornette Coleman."

Of course I had heard of Ornette Coleman. He had begun to make a name for himself in Europe. I had his records with Charlie Haden, Scott Lafaro, and Paul Motian, and I liked a number of his compositions like "Ramblin' " and "Invisible." I called Bud and Ornette introduced himself. "Good morning, Mr. Powell. My name is Ornette Coleman. I'm a saxophonist and all my music is based on the intervals and changes of the sevenths in your left hand."

Bud couldn't find a word to say. Later on, Ornette became a close friend, one who was always there in times of trouble. When people mention the existence of a generation gap among musicians, Ornette, with his exceptional sense of friendship, proves it wasn't necessarily so.

With all this pleasant company, the days went happily by and the night of Max's invitation finally arrived. Max and Abbey Lincoln gave Bud a welcome fit for a king. I have always been struck by the extreme courtesy of musicians of their generation, compared to the offhand attitude too frequent in the younger set. However friendly they may have been, the relationships of the oldtimers were always based on respect.

Max introduced us to another guest, his painter friend Prophet. I knew of him through one of his paintings that had been used as a jacket illustration on a record by Monk and Coltrane.

Bud's muteness still posed a problem. Ever since I had broken through his silence, he would answer my questions spontaneously, as natural as could be, to the great surprise of all observers. With other people, however, he remained incommunicative, to the point where, in order to get an answer from him, I always had to repeat the question. I had seen this behavior before and thought it was reserved for strangers, in order to protect his "splendid isolation." Now I saw that he did the same thing with old friends, even with someone as close to him as Max Roach. So I got in the habit of providing a kind of simultaneous translation, an odd situation, but one that everyone eventually accepted. Dr. Teboul had explained the phenomenon as follows: "Ever since he consented to communicate with you, or through you, you are for him like the airlock of a submarine. You represent the only gateway of communication between his world and ours. It shows the absolute confidence he has in you." After hearing that, how could I help but feel a great burden of responsibility?

The doorbell rang. Max hesitated a second, and announced, "I think that's the surprise I told you about."

He went to the door and there in the doorway stood the surprise, a gigantic figure with a very unexpected hairdo.

Bud asked me, with a false air of wonder, "Who's that, Francis?" Of course I had recognized Sonny Rollins. This was the big surprise promised by Max, but he looked all the more surprising for the weird Mohican haircut he wore at the time.

A little embarrassed, I replied, "Why it's Sonny, Bud." With a sweet smile and mocking disapproval, Bud's first words were, "Hey Sonny, where'd you get the funny haircut?"

Clasping Bud warmly in his arms, Sonny explained that he had merely adopted the hairdo of his ancestors. He had brought Max a present, two small Indian drums from the tribe he belonged to. Abbey bustled about the kitchen and the dinner was succulent. It was our first real American meal since our arrival. Prophet, the painter, had brought along an eight-mm. movie camera and he filmed part of the evening. He'd gotten in the habit of filming musicians in the privacy of their homes and later I had the chance to see some extraordinary footage, of Thelonious in particular.

Max mentioned his latest recording session a few days before and right away, Bud asked if we could hear some of it. Sonny too wanted to hear and urged him to put the tape on. I was genuinely touched by the warm, close feeling that they had for each other. Max put the tape on and as soon as the music started, Sonny knelt down and remained there, motionless, during the whole tape, back straight, shaking his head occasionally to punctuate a few modulations. I was deeply moved and so was Max. It was the only time we saw Sonny. We talked by phone many times but of course he too never went to Birdland.

I was also happy to meet Prophet, who became a good friend. He had painted the musicians of that generation and the walls of his apartment were covered with their portraits.

Bud couldn't bear waiting to see Thelonious any longer, so the next day, I decided it was time to call on him. According to Babs, he wasn't likely to show up at Birdland. I didn't have his phone number, so the best thing seemed to be to go to his house and leave a message, as he was often away on tour. We got there in the early afternoon. I was pretty well convinced that he would not be at home. I rang the bell, we waited a while and were about to leave when the door opened and there stood Thelonious himself, a towering, silent figure. I had stepped behind Bud and now they were face to face, their faces nearly touching.

They stood there as if hypnotized for what seemed an eternity without a word or a movement. Nothing in their faces betrayed the slightest sentiment. Just as I was beginning to think no one would ever move, Thelonious took Bud by the shoulders and pushed him into the apartment, uttering the enigmatic words, "Come on in, I'll do the airplane!"

At his Paris concerts, we had gotten used to his strange wanderings around the stage while the musicians improvised their choruses. With his stumbling gait, he would venture very close to the edge, just over the orchestra pit, keeping time to the music with jerky movements of his whole body, while holding his arms straight out like a child imitating an airplane. Sometimes he would pretend to fall off the stage, giving the front row spectators a bit of a scare. "I'll do the airplane!" At that moment, the words seemed so out of place I wasn't sure I'd heard him right.

Thelonious led the way, with Bud behind him. We entered a small room taken up by an immense grand piano, which looked even larger for the lack of space and more peculiar for the pile of dishes lying on its lid. The back of the piano was in the kitchen and the keyboard in the living room. Thelonious sat right down to play, lifted his hands high over the keys, looked down at his feet and pressed down both pedals. With a slow, extremely calculated movement, he pressed down hard on the keys and remained like that, head down, back bent over, body pressed against the keyboard until the sound faded away.

First the piano let out a low rumble and the dishes began to shake until they started vibrating with the resonance of the strings. The density of the sound imitated to perfection the roar of a formation of bombers. Suddenly, it brought to mind a very precise memory. During the war, when there were air raids, we would listen for the American Superfortresses coming in to bomb the German positions. Flying very high to get above the anti-aircraft fire, they produced a low, dull, very distinctive sound that no one who lived through that period ever forgot. It was this sound that Thelonious had just reproduced. The roar died away like the planes moving off as Thelonious sat there, still bent over, and turned his head slightly to give Bud a questioning look. Repressing a smile at first, Bud finally burst into guffaws of laughter that brought tears to his eyes. Thelonious offered us a drink, but had to drop the idea after a thorough search of his liquor cabinet under the kitchen sink turned up nothing at all.

I sat there watching them for a long time. They seemed content to look at each other, without a word, mischievous smiles on their lips. They said a lot with their eyes.

We saw a lot of Thelonious in the days that followed and each time Bud was elated. Their relationship was *extra-ordinary* in the fullest sense of the word. Nothing about it was ordinary—it was always charged with emotion, full of the unexpected. I think I have never felt so strong an emotional current between two people. Their silences were quite untenable and the intensity of feeling that passed between them made me feel like an intruder.

By now our first horrendous week in New York was for me no more than a disagreeable memory. Bud, however, still seemed upset by it, and I noticed signs of a growing weariness. At the time, I didn't know exactly what kind of treatments he had been subjected to in the past, nor was I aware of the constant pressure he had lived under. The past now pursued him and he lived in anguish of finding himself in the same situations all over again. It wasn't just his illness or his misconduct that led him into the hospitals and courtrooms. Other causes had contributed, more arbitrary and more dangerous. From the moment he had had a guardian, he had lost his individual prerogatives and had fallen into a life of submission to those who managed his personal as well as his professional life. Any lapse in conduct was immediately sanctioned. Max Cohen, who fought to help Bud recover his rights, has in his files documents galore proving this was so. Whatever he did, he was judged on the basis of his past history. His newfound assurance and good morale were eroded now and he was once again weak-willed and psychologically fragile.

We met lots of people at Birdland, most of them nice, some of them drunk, all of them enthusiastic. But few were aware of Bud's real problems. His reputation didn't help. Some fans would have done anything to spend a few minutes alone with him, and the easiest way to start a conversation was to offer to buy him a drink. Imagine my position. Bud never responded directly to this kind of invitation. Instead, he would give me an embarrassed, almost pleading look, as if putting his fate in my hands once again. I dreaded those moments. I tried to force him to take the responsibility of answering by himself. One good reason not to drink was the promise he had made to me, but a better one was the absolute necessity, imposed by his tuberculosis, to avoid alcohol. When I tried to explain to those unaware of his health problems why he couldn't touch a drop, I'd be letting myself in for some nasty cracks and sarcastic imbecilities like, "What's it to you? How much do they pay you to be his watchdog?"

I never tried to reason with customers of that ilk but sometimes, at the end of my rope, I would grab one by the collar, creating a bit of a stir in the house. The two bouncers assured me that they too would keep an eye open and intervene if necessary, and they warned me about the drunks and drug dealers who haunted the clubs in search of a possible client.

My major problem was to protect Bud's endangered health, the hard-won health that we had fought so long to regain. I was so happy when he'd stopped drinking and knew that he too was pleased to be in control again. Now I saw with consternation that he was once more putting himself totally in my hands. I tried to be more attentive than ever to his every need. I had completely stopped drinking in his presence. For someone like me who likes a drink and can hold his liquor, it wasn't very easy, particularly in the atmosphere of a nightclub, but in the end I was glad to share the burden with him.

In early September, Elvin Jones came to see us at the hotel. He too never came to Birdland but we'd met many times by chance during the course of our walks. Now that I think about it, we met too many people for it to have been by chance, so maybe it was intentional. Elvin was throwing himself a big birthday party on September 9 and wanted us both to come. He had made a name for himself with Coltrane, but I learned that he had often played with Bud in 1956 and

1957. Elvin's kindness is legendary and I was touched to see his deep feelings for Bud.

It was quite a party. Naturally, most of the guests were musicians. Though the occasion was Elvin's birthday, he saw to it that Bud was the evening's star attraction. I had wondered how the old friends would treat Bud and worried about how they would view my role in his life. The reality exceeded all my hopes. Max Roach, Thelonious, Art Blakey, Ornette Coleman, Kenny Dorham, John Coltrane, Babs Gonzales, Elvin, all of them were infinitely kind and tactful when it came to discussing Bud's health problems, gently offering advice or suggestions, which Bud accepted with good grace. For me, their elegant attitude and their gentlemanly qualities clearly showed the deep interest they took in Bud, and also the great affection they had for him.

As we explored New York in search of pleasant nightspots, I discovered the bars of Greenwich Village, haunts of the "drinking class," the "alcoholic cream of New York." Drinking to excess seemed to be an institution here. It surprised me to see women of all ages stewed to the gills, for in France I had never seen anything quite like it. In these smoky rooms we would sit until the wee hours, talking about everything under the sun, but we also met jazz fans and musicians and we could hear our favorite music while drinking abominable Californian rotgut. But nowadays, when I visit the States, I choose *good* wines, mostly from California!

Most of those whom I met in these clubs knew Bud well and had followed his troubled history over the years. *In vino veritas*, as the saying goes. When they'd had a few too many, I discovered they had a strange way of looking at the world. In their view, trying to protect someone from alcohol for his own good was seen as some sort of infringement on his free will. Their motto, in the name of freedom, seemed to be, "If he wants to drink, that's his business. If he wants to kill himself, let him."

Such remarks, coming from those who had heard about our relationship in the press, and often made to me directly, didn't work. I was never convinced by this philosophy, and some of the conversations ended in a pretty stormy fashion. In their muddled way of thinking, I saw the same kind of revolt I had known in Paris, in the St. Germain des Prés of the early fifties, when it was considered compulsory to hide one's feelings, to scorn real values, to shock at all costs by overthrowing traditions and institutions. It showed you were "hip." But these characters went even further. In the name of liberation, of throwing off all restraints, they merely sank deeper into an all-out egoism, an ailment already pervasive in American society.

In this little world, depravity was in. You had to be a smiling fatalist, with a pinch of sadism, as you looked at the ruins of the old values that certain poor innocents like me still tried to hold onto. The only things worth living for were sex, drugs, and alcohol. Only then could you qualify as hip, which was how they saw themselves. Otherwise, you were square, as I must have looked to their eyes with my outmoded principles. While these encounters might have had a negative effect on Bud, in fact they did the opposite. Without a word, he would burst out laughing, to the great discomfiture of the speaker mouthing his empty phrases. Or he would gaze in disgust at the pitiful women hanging on to the bar. Deep down I found his reaction comforting, for even in his own pain he never espoused this third-rate philosophy. At the start of such conversations he would listen to both sides, then finally he would agree with me. I felt very strongly that he appreciated my firmness. Taking my side was the best proof that he was still aware that what was at stake was his health.

Our days became busier, more active. We would often run into Kenny Dorham, Erroll Garner, Babs or others, always "by accident," of course. Lots of others hovered around Bud, people who seemed at loose ends and whose attitude toward Bud was one of pure adoration. Bud, who sought solitude and shunned company, was always willing to spend some time with them. He had a knack of spotting those who were sincere.

However, when it came to interviews requested by newspapers and magazines it was very hard to mobilize his attention. The reporters always asked about his health and I feared they would bring up his history of mental problems. In these interviews, Bud became as I had known him at first, distant, apparently shut off in his own world, unconcerned by the questions asked. I always had to repeat whatever they said and then he would emerge from his reflections to utter a few syllables. That was his way of dealing with questions that were pointless or tasteless. I would try to steer the reporter into more productive areas, but few of them seemed interested in Bud's new musical expression. They remained obstinately attached to his music of the past and seemed to think any evolution impossible for him. My feeling that a sparer language was not necessarily a regression left them cold, as did my explanations of Bud's silence and his odd behavior. Sometimes they laughed openly when I suggested that it was his way of protecting himself from the world to remain in a "state of grace."

At the very least, they dismissed my ideas as romantic or merely naive. I would have liked to say, "Romantic? Naive? Perhaps, but I succeeded where the cops and doctors failed, so where does that leave us?"

In the liner notes for the reissue of *The Genius of Bud Powell* (Verve 2-2526), the journalist Neil Tesser wrote:

> Paudras' simple description of Powell's conflict dovetails precisely with an intriguing theory devised by the eminent psychotherapist Rollo May. In his book *Love and Will*, Dr. May wrote: "Both artist and neurotic speak and live from the subconscious and unconscious depths of their society. The artist does this positively, communicating what he experiences to his fellow men. The neurotic does this negatively. Experiencing the same underlying meanings and contradictions in his culture, he is unable to form his experiences into communicable meaning. . . . The relation between the artist and the neurotic, often considered mysterious, is entirely understandable from the viewpoint presented here . . ." The life and music of Bud Powell—the protean, promethean promise/threat of bebop—serve as concrete evidence that artist and neurotic can coexist.

MARGARETA

(Recorded in New York, September 1964 [CD Team])

Ornette often came to Birdland to hear Bud and one night he introduced a friend of his, Margareta Johnson. She was tall, fair and very feminine, her long blond hair showing her Nordic origin. She worked in the jazz department at Atlantic Records. It was as if their meeting had been preordained, for she and Bud hit it off at once. Margareta was a fine, sensitive woman who instantly understood Bud's personality. For the first time in a long time, here was someone for whom he was not an object of curiosity.

Meeting Margareta changed our lives and Bud's patterns of behavior. I thought of the solitude in which he had lived so long and of his pathetic answers at Laënnec Hospital when the doctor asked about his sex life. They met every night and naturally I tried to leave them alone. But each time I went away Bud would ask where I was going and insist that I stay. We had been so close for so long that it was never embarrassing. Margareta lavished attention on him. Now there was someone else who could be counted on to be vigilant in delicate situations, and I was able to relax a little. I learned much later that they had met in Stockholm in 1962, but fleetingly.

Bud had two childhood friends, both musicians, one a drummer and the other a violinist. They had been inseparable. One night during the break a waiter at Birdland came to tell me that some customers had invited us to their table. It was Andy Browne, the violinist, with his wife Barbara. Bud was overjoyed to see them after 25 years. Andy ordered drinks all around. When I said that Bud couldn't drink, his attitude toward me immediately hardened. Margareta backed me up and we ordered a Coke for Bud, but Andy slipped him some cognac under the table. When I spotted the maneuver I lost my temper and the situation rapidly deteriorated. "What do they pay you to do this dirty work?" he snarled.

Andy was built like a football player but in cases like that I lose all notion of caution. I grabbed him by the shirtfront, tipping the table and knocking over the glasses with a resounding crash. Luckily our bouncer friends stepped in and stopped the fight.

"Don't you worry," said Andy. "I'll see you outside."

At the end of the evening, Bud looked worried. He took my arm and steered me outside, where Andy, still violently aggravated, was waiting, with his wife and Margareta both trying to cool things down. Bud hung on to my arm and walked more quickly toward the hotel.

Behind us we could hear Margareta and Barbara trying to calm down Andy. When we reached the hotel, I saw that they were still behind us. We walked in and I was closing the door behind us when Andy blocked it with his foot. "Just a minute," he said, "I want to talk to you."

"It's no use. We've said everything there is to say."

"Let's shake hands," he said.

I was still angry. Nothing made me madder than when people doubted my intentions toward Bud.

"I apologize," he went on, "I didn't know who you were and what you were doing. Come on, forget it. Let's shake on it."

We made our peace and Andy became one of my best friends in New York. In the following days he even joined us to help protect Bud from the many pitfalls that crossed our path more and more frequently every day. We got to know each other better and thanks to him I learned a little about what Bud was like as a child:

> Bud wanted to be just like any other guy. What happened, when they found out that he could play the piano as a child, when we'd go to parties, they wanted him to play. But he didn't want to play. He wanted to be part of the party. Then he'd tell me, "I'd like to have a party once in a while when I wouldn't have to play." But he'd be afraid they wouldn't accept him without his talent. He wanted to play ball and do what all the other kids did.
>
> He was very smart in mathematics, just like Thelonious. He got ninety-five or a hundred and he only studied three, four weeks. He got the basics. So when you got the basics, why carry on with all that other stuff? He would study for a little while, then disappear and just come back to take the tests and be ready. That used to impress me more than the music...

Both Thelonious and Bud were very good in mathematics and physics, according to Monk's manager, Harry Colomby. It made us all think that music and numbers can really mix very well together. Andy went on:

> ...He would go to school to get all the basics, maybe for about a month. Then he didn't go back to school. He was fourteen or fifteen at the time. But he'd always come during the time for tests and he'd pass them high up. So he had no problem, then.

Bud wasn't concerned about much except playing. He wasn't concerned about working for a living, he was just concerned by [*sic*] playing the music . . .

Bud never spoke too much about what was going on in his family. He tried to keep it secret. To me, he did say. His father in fact just never came back home.

He loved to come over to my house. We were a large family, everybody was talking at once, the house was really alive and my mother never bothered him. When we got a piano, he'd come over all the time and he used to play a lot. My mother just adored him . . .

Another childhood friend was Freddie Jones. Recently, in his sixties and still as fervent an admirer as the rest of us, he filled in some more of the portrait:

I first met Bud . . . oh, it had to be around 1935 or '36. We were young boys together growing up in Harlem. I was a year ahead of him in school. . . . Bud was a piano player, while the rest of us just played out in the street. We enjoyed what he played but we did not recognize his genius. . . . At school, when he was using his hands for playing the piano, I was using mine for boxing. Bud was a small fellow, he wasn't too large. He was always protective of his hands, you know . . . at that time he knew what we didn't know.

We were kids together in the choir they had down at St. Charles church. They had a chapel downstairs. There was an organ there—one of those you had to pump—and Bud used to play and I'd have to pump the organ for him! Actually, pumping that thing for him was a real pleasure . . .

The first time I remember Bud playing in a group was in Alan Richard's band . . . kid's stuff, you know . . . 18, 19-year-old kids. They was all kids, and they used to rehearse in that corner store around 140th St. . . . and Bud was in that band. I remember that Bud's father used to be at those rehearsals. He was the superintendent of that building, or something. . . . Then he played in a lot of little dives around Harlem . . . not even clubs . . . just dives. I remember him playing at a club called Canada Lee's. I think this was at 136th St. and between 7th Avenue and Lenox. He played a solo stint there. Then, after he got out of school, I remember him going with Valaida Snow, I remember that stint. I saw him in Boston when he was in Cootie Williams' band. Lena Horne was the star of this particular show. I remember after one of those sets, we all went and hung out with this cat Ray Perry—Ray played violin and trumpet. I remember Bud running all these chords for Ray. It was something . . . I did not understand . . .

I remember at Minton's one time. I went there with Bud and Al Haig was the piano player. I remember Al asked him to sit in on a set for him, and Bud played the set and Bud blazed. Bud completely dominated, you know? Now, Erroll Garner was standing in the back of the house, looking on, and someone said, "Hey Erroll. You gonna play a set?" And Erroll said, "Not after that motherfucker, I ain't!" Now see, I remember that, you know . . .

Although the bop musicians boycotted Birdland, the great names of the previous generation were frequent visitors. Count Basie, for one, was a regular and was always enthusiastic about Bud. One evening, as I was listening to a particularly enthralling chorus, he came over to my table and said, "Come over here, Francis. I'd like you to meet a friend of Bud's."

I tore myself away from the music and followed him. He introduced me to a colossus who must have taken up two seats on the bench. Though the face was familiar I couldn't put a name to it. When we shook hands, my hand disappeared completely inside his. Count Basie understood from my expression that I couldn't recall his name, and added, "Of course, you know the great boxer, Joe Louis?"

I've always liked boxing and I had seen a number of his fights at the movies. But I was surprised to discover someone like him among Bud's acquaintances. I waited impatiently for the end of the set to see their meeting after so many years. Bud laughed out loud to see Joe, who had already enveloped him in his huge arms. Well, I thought, maybe we've found ourselves a new bodyguard!

I grew increasingly accustomed to our nocturnal lifestyle and liked watching the crazy mix of characters who haunted the club. There was pint-size Pee Wee Marquet, who couldn't haven't been over four feet even with his elevator heels, but what he lacked in size he made up in nastiness. Every night, he'd hang around me trying to wheedle a few dollars (that I didn't have) in exchange for a better introduction for Bud at the beginning of the set. Each day I refused and each day he was back at it, plugging away. Finally I lost my temper. From then on, his introduction of Bud was reduced to the barest minimum: "And now, ladies and gentlemen, here's Bud Powell."

Judging from the length of the intro he gave Herbie Mann, the poor guy must have turned over half his salary. In any case, at Birdland, money was king. Even the toilet attendant came looking for money, though to this day I don't know what he had to sell.

Every night, Margareta came to join us and was always with Bud. I was happy for him and I could relax a little and chat with the other musicians during the breaks without worrying that he'd get into trouble. Ornette dropped in one night after the first set to tell me that

Bill Evans was playing at the Café a Gogo in Greenwich Village. Bud and Margareta seemed happily occupied with each other, so I went off with Ornette.

I was really looking forward to seeing the only contemporary pianist who had caught Bud's attention over the past few years. I recalled the interview Bud had given to Henri Renaud, in which Bud asked about Bill's health even though he didn't know him personally. Very few of his records had reached France, but we'd heard "Waltz for Debby" and Bud had been impressed by it. Most other pianists, besides Tatum or Monk, usually left him cold, but each time we listened to Bill he seemed intrigued and made me repeat his name. He would ask to see the jacket, check the name of the composer of "Waltz for Debby" and sit deep in contemplation till the end of the record. Each time he seemed to be discovering it anew. When I told Bill in Paris in 1965 how much Bud had liked his music, Bill was deeply moved, adding, in a grave voice, "Please, don't say any more."

The Café a Gogo was a long narrow room and when we came in I was struck by the size of the piano, much longer than the standard concert grand. It was made of blond wood, nearly white, and extremely elongated. Ornette explained that the piano had been made specially for Bill by a devoted fan and presented to him as a gift. It had been designed with the bass strings much longer than usual. Bill loved that piano and later told me it had mysteriously disappeared during a ship crossing between America and Europe.

Walking through the doorway, I got a gust of perfumed air. Bill was accompanied by Chuck Israels and Paul Motian. I was impressed by his position at the piano. His forehead was down, practically touching his hands. His back, completely rounded, made it look as if he was an integral part of the piano. The hushed confidential sound of the trio was positively sumptuous. The audience sat in reverent silence. Toward the end, Kenny Burrell joined the group. At the end of the set, I was still in ecstasy when Ornette led me over to the bar to introduce me to Bill.

"Bill," he said, "I'd like you to meet a friend of Bud Powell's."

"Is he the one who brought Bud to New York?" he asked, and his eyes lit up with a fascinating smile.

"That's him," said Ornette.

All the papers had spoken of Bud's return in the company of a French friend and all the musicians knew about me. Bill's only reaction was to laugh out loud and give me a big hug and a kiss on the forehead. To this day, I cherish the memory of that gesture.

We became great friends, united until the end of his life in our mutual passion for Bud and in a certain conception of the piano. I only
regret that he and Bud never met. How cruel life can be! I imagine
they would have become inseparable. Bud was an exceptional human
being, and so was Bill. Neither of them was made to live in this society. Their freshness, commitment, and total honesty in their art had
made them both marginal and therefore perfect victims.

Ornette at the time was rooming in the Village with a woman who
worked as a sound technician. Their basement apartment was taste-
fully furnished, with fine modern paintings on the walls and round-
the-clock music that made up for the distinct lack of oxygen. We
started spending our afternoons there and the place soon became
headquarters for Thelonious and Charlie Rouse. I would bring along
the tapes of the previous night and we'd sit around listening in religious devotion.

I regret it never occurred to me to keep a regular diary in those
days, for there are many things I no longer recall. I did sometimes
take notes, though, and coming across one of these scribbled notes has
reminded me of the following anecdote:

> Monk has just walked into Ornette's and Mildred's with Charlie Rouse. I
> put on the tape of "Ruby, My Dear," recorded at Birdland last night. Bud
> plays brilliantly. He looks at Monk with a defiant air. Monk exchanges ad-
> miring glances with me on the sly, at every fabulous chord change, but he
> avoids Bud's eyes. The music swells, the tension mounts. Bud is very
> nervous, his fingers twitch as he relives each phrase and he looks at Thelo-
> nious in a stupor. The music reaches a climax of almost unbearable ten-
> sion, then it's over. There is applause, followed by silence. At last Bud
> speaks up firmly, a half smile on his lips, "Monk, go get some wine."
> Thelonious looks at me, ignores the order and bursts out laughing.

That's about how our afternoons went. There was never much conversation. Ornette listened respectfully to the sporadic remarks of his
eminent guests and well-chosen music filled the air. Sometimes we'd
have dinner with Ornette before going back to Birdland. On occasion,
I'd go out with Monk to do some shopping. Many people recognized
him in the street and would joke familiarly in passing. They'd pat
him on the back with, "Hey Monk, how ya doin', man?"

It shocked me every time. My own admiration for him was such
that a familiar gesture of that sort seemed somehow disrespectful.
Monk never answered, just grunted with his usual air of resignation.

Whenever we were alone, the conversation inevitably turned to Bud. Thelonious talked mainly of his youth, constantly bringing up his friend's brilliant qualities. "He could do anything, you know. He was extremely intelligent." And as if talking to himself, he'd repeat, "Yeah, he was very smart, very smart . . ." When I pressed for details, he merely added, "He was very receptive, you know. He could do anything. He could play the most difficult things. He'd grasp a new idea right away and develop it instantaneously with perfect ease." Then he'd get very tense and add with deep feeling, "Francis, nobody could play like Bud, nobody. It was too hard, too fast, unbelievable."

Thelonious remembered that Bud had studied classical piano. "Very young he acquired this great technique, you see. He could play 'fluid' without any trouble, really at ease." At this remark, he drifted off into his own thoughts.

Once I asked if he had shown Bud certain things. "Yeah, I'd play him my tunes and he could retain them right off. Bud was brilliant from very early on. I showed him a lot of chords, new combinations, reversed harmonies. Bud caught on right away, and with his way of playing the most complicated chords, he could use it in his own developments. Bud was a genius, but you know, he was so sick, and now he's fragile . . ."

There was something unreal about those walks of ours in the Village. I never would have thought that behind his imposing facade and distant manner, he could be so kind and so simple. True, he didn't talk much, but as soon as I brought up Bud, he opened up and spoke nostalgically of their early days. He seemed anxious about Bud's health. He didn't seem convinced that he was really cured. He still had in mind the brilliant young man with uncommon energy, the "phenomenon" with whom he'd shared the joys and certainties of creative genius. He probably also had other memories, less happy ones, when he referred to the awful treatments inflicted on Bud, though he never gave any details. He would quickly change the subject with a look of distaste and fall silent again.

Their feeling for each other was rare, unique. Of all the artists and musicians I've known in my life, I never felt the same unspoken communion. Each time they met felt like it would be the last.

MARSHALL'S TOWER

(Recorded in New York, September 15, 1964 [unreleased])

In Saint-Tropez in 1963 I had made the acquaintance of Marshall Allen, an American jazz fan, through Bud's friend Anita. Marshall had two passions in life: Bud Powell and the ancient Cretan writing he was trying to decipher. His family fortune assured him a livelihood and he could indulge these hobbies to his heart's content. He came to Birdland where he met Bud for the first time, then invited us home after the last set. It gave me a glimpse into the extraordinary world of a fervent fan who had everything in life.

Oscar Goodstein offered Bud ten days vacation. We had mentioned that it might be nice for him to relax a little and breathe some fresh air. Marshall invited us to Fire Island, where he owned two houses, octagonal modern structures of wood and glass, designed by himself and built under his supervision. One was reserved for him and we were given the other. Two women friends were also around, one of whom, Rozlyn, later became his wife. Rozlyn was hip and fascinating, the brains of their household, fairylike, with a unique sense of hospitality. Margareta came too and this quiet stay, a far cry from our smoke-filled nights in the city, was a heavenly holiday. There was no piano, but when he was really happy, Bud would sing. He was suddenly inspired and spent the last few days composing new tunes. None of these has ever been released.

For Bud, creating music was as essential as breathing. Max Cohen related to me:

> Bud's ability and facility in creating was such that he could virtually compose at any time—and under any circumstances. At a recording session in the RCA Victor Studios, there was some uncertainty as to the number of originals and the standards to be recorded. Bud suggested casually, as a solution to the problem, that he would actually record two sides of a longplaying record with originals without repeating himself. An official in charge, unfortunately and unimaginatively adhering to the prescribed schedule, did not avail himself of the offer, thus depriving music devotees of forty-five minutes of spontaneously created music, which would have been composed as casually as anyone engaged in ordinary conversation.

Bud wrote a tune for our host called "Marshall's Tower," in reference to the famous octagonal house. He wrote one for Margareta, called simply "Margareta"; plus a song with a super-fast tempo and acrobatic harmonies, called "Oh Boy"; another dazzling piece named "Fantasia"; two more in a medium tempo in his traditional style, "Jumpin' With Me" and "Mama Nicole" (a fond allusion to the mother-to-be); and last of all, a heartbreaking tune, very meaningful at this particular time, entitled "No Dice."

On September 27, we celebrated Bud's birthday on Fire Island, just before our return to the club. I gave him a surrealistic sculpture I had put together with ocean-smoothed stones and driftwood picked up on the beach. I spent my days making these constructions while listening to Bud's records, selected exclusively by Marshall. Rozlyn made a birthday cake, complete with candles, and Bud blew them out to the traditional "Happy Birthday" sung by everyone. Each of us made a little speech expressing our affection and Bud responded in a timid voice, obviously moved.

Every day we took long walks on the beach with Margareta. It was a little paradise, a genuine haven of peace a stone's throw from the rat race of New York.

AUTUMN IN NEW YORK

(Recorded in New York, May 30, 1953 [Session Disc])

Back in New York, Bud went right to work at Birdland. Dakota Staton was doing the second half of the program, singing all the songs from her record *Late Late Show.* The next performer to share the bill was Horace Silver, so I was able to make the acquaintance of this wonderful musician. He knew of Bud's health problems and expressed his concern from the moment we met. He told me he too had undergone pulmonary problems in his childhood, which had ruined his career as a saxophonist. Horace was upset that Bud had never stopped smoking and, during the breaks, he did his best to turn him off tobacco. Bud hung on to his every word, smoking like a chimney all the while. In the end, Horace presented him with the handwritten music of his song "No Smoking" and Bud played it the very next day in the first set.

Horace's playing, which I listened to from the bleachers with Barry Harris, has left me unforgettable memories. Its tension and density were something extraordinary. I'd sit right up close to the keyboard, just at the foot of the bandstand, and watch in fascination as the sweat dripped off his face with the regularity of a clock ticking off the seconds. I had never seen anyone expend such energy. Horace gave himself completely, with total generosity, and I wonder today how such a slender, fragile-looking man could actually be able to stand up after such a performance.

Each Birdland program was simply awesome and I went from admiration to enchantment. Marshall came often and after the show we'd end the night at his place in the Village, along with Ornette. Together, we'd watch through the big picture window and wait for what we called the "blue hour," that magical time just before daybreak, which was our signal that it was time to go to bed. We had talked the night away on our favorite subject (musicians) and now that we were in a dreamlike state, drunk on music, we finally thought about going to sleep. Marshall put us up whenever he could and the brief hours we slept at his place were far more restful than our noisy nights at the Hotel Woodward.

At Ornette's, most often with Thelonious, we also met Cecil Taylor, whom Ornette introduced as *the* pianist of the future. When I wondered why Cecil wasn't in his group, Ornette said that no one was ready to play his music yet, but that Cecil would certainly be the one some day. At the time, Cecil worked in a factory for a living and only played when an opportunity came up. When I heard he didn't own a piano, I spoke to Marshall, who immediately invited him to practice at his home every day. Marshall had a Steinway baby grand and Cecil couldn't have dreamt of a better instrument. Cecil was still playing on bop structures then and he kept a worried eye on Bud's reactions.

After a late breakfast, Bud would settle himself in a cozy chair and sleep a good part of the afternoon. Cecil would take advantage of these moments to play some phrases and clusters that were pretty surprising to our ears at the time, conceptions that later became the distinctive features of his style. Bud would wake up with a start and flash furious looks around the room, shock written all over his face. Cecil would go back to a more traditional register with a contrite smile and Bud would drop off to sleep again. But he was only catnapping, because if ever Cecil dared to go off in this vein again, he'd be up in a flash with murder in his eyes. Bud never did accept this music, which nevertheless went on to make its way in the world. I must say, Thelonious too reacted this way sometimes, during our afternoons at Ornette's, when Mildred would put on a tape of that kind.

Nica de Koenigswarter once told me that Monk left the jazz scene because he wanted to distance himself from this current.

Nica phoned and set up a date to go hear Monk at the Village Vanguard. Max Gordon reserved a table for us as close as possible to the piano and when we arrived Monk greeted us with his composition "In Walked Bud." Bud was bubbling with joy and all through his choruses Monk was giving him little smiling looks. I had never seen Monk look so happy at the piano. He seemed to be playing for Bud alone—no one else existed around them. Nica whispered in my ear, "Look how he's sucking in his cheeks. He always does that in the great moments."

I'll bet Thelonious was sucking in his cheeks plenty during all the years when certain listeners with tin ears mistook his daring harmonies for wrong notes! Using fractions of seconds, inversions of chords on the relative and substitution chords, he was, in fact, imposing a perpetual interchange between his vast musical knowledge and his visceral need to break out of all molds.

One day, when he played a harmonic inversion that was just too obvious for his taste, he blurted out, with his typical dry humor, "Oh no, not that. That was a bad mistake!"

Rozlyn and Ornette came to join us and so did Margareta followed by Max Roach and Clifford Jordan. We were in fine company.

I told Oscar Goodstein that Bud had written some new compositions on Fire Island, enough to think about bringing out a new album of completely new and original material. He phoned Alfred Lyon, one of the heads of the Blue Note label, to talk about a recording session.

Bud played the new songs first at Birdland, then put a few finishing touches on them when he got back to the hotel. He would lie down, spread the pages of sheet music on the bed, and read them over. Then he would sing them slowly, punctuating certain passages. This was enough to enable him to imagine all the combinations he would build on the completely new structures. He didn't write down a single chord, just some numbering and punctuation. The rest was in his head.

In his new compositions, Bud was no longer seeking velocity at all costs. His tumultuous feelings came out as pure emotion, expressed through the sparest phrasing and stripped of all frills. In his music of 1964, Bud was taking every risk, changing and re-examining every former conception that the public already had, based on the stereotyped image of his style. He would glide into long, sinuous, nearly abstract phrases, hard to grasp at first hearing but which, on further listening, became perfectly clear and even inevitable. Finally, he took to playing with modes more than he had ever done before and with complete mastery. Later, when I became more familiar with the work of McCoy, Chick, and Herbie, I grew to appreciate this new exploration even more.

One afternoon, a date was set up at Birdland with Alfred Lyon and Francis Wolf. For the recording session, Bud had suggested Paul Chambers and Roy Haynes. Rehearsals were to begin the next afternoon at the club. Bud greeted Alfred and Francis with real pleasure, the first time he had ever shown any fondness for members of the recording industry. Everything was looking good for the project. Oscar talked to Alfred while Francis Wolf took some photos of Bud. When we had completed all that had to be done, Alfred suggested dinner at a Chinese restaurant. We looked around for Bud, but he had vanished! I made a quick search through the neighborhood, but he was nowhere to be found. It was then that Francis Wolf told us with some embarrassment that Bud had asked him for money, and he had given him

$20. Bud wasn't playing that night, as it was Monday, jamming night. There had been nothing to upset him all day long and we couldn't understand why he had gone off without a word. Before heading out for the restaurant, I left a message at the hotel telling him where we were. As the hours passed and grew late, and there was still no sign of him, I began to fear some probable new catastrophe.

At the restaurant, Alfred filled me in on Bud's life history. He had known Bud as a young man and he had also known Bud's entire family. He was on friendly terms with Bud's mother, Pearl, and he often went to see her at her home in Willow Grove, Pennsylvania. He thought she was overprotective of Bud and dominated him, and their relations were not always smooth. Alfred was fond of Bud and considered him the uncontested genius of his generation, dogged by tragedy all his life. He disagreed with those who saw Bud as mentally ill or looked down on him for what they considered his dissolute way of life. Bud had left the straight and narrow, of course, like many musicians of his generation, only it had hurt him more than it had the others. There was no contempt in his attitude toward Bud, just respect for a man who wanted desperately to live up to his own standards. Alfred recalled one night at Birdland when Bud had played with dazzling virtuosity. The audience was mesmerized by the energy he emitted. Transfigured, almost in a trance, Bud was pulverizing the keyboard. His speed of execution was so great that gradually he stopped pressing down on the keys and eventually was just moving his fingers above the notes without producing a sound. His face showed the ectasy of a music only he could hear. Naturally, the audience started getting restless and finally there were some jeers and whistles. The reaction wasn't long in coming. Two gorillas guarding the door strode up on stage, grabbed Bud under the arms and carried him out. His feet never touched the ground. Fearing the worst, Alfred had rushed after them and had gotten outside just as the bouncers were heaving him onto the sidewalk. Bud rolled over on the ground and immediately crawled under a car like a frightened cat looking for shelter. It took Alfred an hour to persuade him to come out so that he could take him home.

THE GONEST THING

(Recorded in New York, August 8, 1964 [unreleased])

Bud never showed up at the restaurant. I hurried anxiously back to the hotel, sure that I'd find him there, but his bed was empty. George the doorman hadn't seen him either. Just to make sure, I made one last tour of the neighborhood bars and then went to sleep, realizing there was nothing to do until I heard from him. I watched TV and finally fell into an agitated sleep. I had the feeling I'd slept only a few minutes when the phone rang. "Hello," a voice said. "Is this Francis, Bud's friend? This is William Powell speaking."

It was 5 A.M. I was numb with fatigue and it took a while before I realized it was Bud's father on the phone. I had heard a lot about him, of course, but since our arrival in New York, he hadn't given us a sign of life and Bud hadn't mentioned him at all. Strangely enough, Bud hadn't spoken of his mother, either.

"It's like this," he was saying, "Bud's been here at the house since last night. He's drunk and he can't stay here. So you'd better come and get him right away."

I was so groggy I thought I was having some kind of awful dream. As I hesitated, he added immediately, "I couldn't reach you any earlier. But you better come get him now. I don't want him here at the house. I don't want any trouble with him."

The cold, harsh tone of his voice brought me back to reality. I threw on my clothes, hurried out and took a taxi up to Harlem to the address he had given me. As we drove up I saw a little man standing in front of the building, attentively watching the passing cars.

"What's happening?" I asked, trying hard to sound cordial.

He pushed me ahead of him toward the house, looking around him all the while. He seemed nervous and angry, ill-disposed to talk. "Come upstairs. Bud's sleeping, but I'm going to wake him up and you can take him away with you. I just don't want any trouble, you know. There's no way he can stay here."

His mind was made up. There was no room for discussion. Before I had a chance to think, I was upstairs in the apartment. There, in a room with the door wide open and a bare lightbulb in the ceiling, lay Bud, sound asleep, fully dressed on the made-up bed. The room looked like a spare bedroom filled with boxes and suitcases. William shook Bud, who grunted a few times, then woke up and looked around in a daze.

"Okay, Bud. You gotta leave now. Francis is here. He's come to get you."

Bud stared at me without a word, looking so unhappy I could have cried. He remained seated on the edge of the bed and tried to speak a few words to his father. But William cut him off right away.

"No, Bud. You gotta go now. Come on, get up."

Bud gave me one last pain-filled look. Then he stood up slowly, arms dangling, head lowered like a punished child who had been beaten into submission. We made our way carefully down the stairs, Bud hanging on to my arm, then waited out front for the cab that William had called by phone. Bud could barely stand up straight and all because of a few miserable glasses of red wine. It was early morning and people were already leaving for work or coming out to do their shopping. Some of them said hello to Mr. Powell and looked with curiosity at Bud, who stood there swaying slightly, shifting his feet to try and keep his balance. Seeing their embarrassed and pitying looks, William said sadly, "That's my son, Bud. He's sick, you know."

In all my life I have never forgotten that morning. I felt as miserable as Bud, unwashed, unshaven, tired and disgusted. The taxi pulled up and the driver, surprised to see a white person in the neighborhood, talked it over with William. All the way back to the hotel, he kept looking at us in the rearview mirror, obviously intrigued by the whole situation.

"What happened, Bud?"

He wouldn't look at me but kept his eyes firmly on the floor and answered simply, "I wanted to see my father, that's all."

"But why didn't you say anything?"

"I don't know."

"But Bud, you should have told me. I was worried."

"I wanted to see my father."

"Of course you did, but why not tell me about it?"

"I don't know why. I didn't know if he'd want to see me."

"You've been drinking, Bud. I know you have. Why?"

"I wanted to see my father . . . I wanted to see my father . . ."

He repeated the words plaintively, speaking now to himself. He had seen his father, all right. I suppose the idea had been haunting him since we arrived. Did he need a drink to have the courage to face the home he'd left so long ago? I would never really know. At that point I couldn't speak, he looked so unhappy. The ride seemed interminable. The city was waking up. I felt thousands of curious eyes staring at us.

At the hotel, I suggested he have a bath and I ordered a hot chocolate from our friend George. In answer to all my questions Bud would only repeat, "I wanted to see my father." He looked more despondent by the minute, drained of all energy. He kept his head down and wouldn't look me in the eye.

I too was heartsick and numb. I remembered all the talks we'd had about his parents and there was no need for further comment. I felt closer to him than ever. It was 8 A.M. and the morning noises drifted up from the street. But I wished him good night all the same, put my arms around him and held him tight. "Don't be sad, Bud. I'm your friend. I'm with you. I understand."

His father called the next morning to ask if we got home all right, but he didn't suggest we meet again.

During their brief encounter that evening, what could have been said that led to another break in their relations, this time for good? Had he talked of his mother? Her recent death? William and Pearl had been separated for years but her death must have affected him. It was a wound I felt would never heal. Bud would live the rest of his life with this repressed love. Out of discretion, I never brought the subject up and in the end Bud never spoke of his parents again.

Perhaps Bud clung to his childlike soul in the hope of recapturing an interrupted childhood, of renewing relations with his parents and satisfying the terrible need for affection before entering the world of adults. This is not a subject I talk about lightly. Three years of close relations had shown me the desperate reality of his frustration.

That evening, before going to the club, Paul Chambers dropped in at the hotel. He hadn't seen Bud since Bud had left for Europe in 1959 and was very happy to meet him again. I found some comfort in his kindly presence. Paul talked about old times and managed to cheer Bud up a bit. He had no idea what Bud had just gone through and cheerily suggested he take some pictures. He had brought along an enormous camera that he seemed very proud of. I kept thinking, "If only he could have seen Bud two months earlier!" I felt incapable of explaining to friends why Bud had once again sunk into silence and misery. But after all, hadn't he come to represent the quintessence of sorrow? He was merely being true to his image.

Margareta was out of town for a few days and that depressed Bud even more. Paul came to pick us up every day for rehearsals at Birdland and shot vast numbers of pictures from all angles. The rehearsals were extremely brief. Bud was still very down after the incident with his father. He played his new tunes half-heartedly for Paul and Roy Haynes and refused categorically to rehearse with them. The next day Charlie Mingus came to join us, and the afternoon was happy and full of spirited conversation. Toward the end of the day, Bud suddenly decided to play "Autumn in New York." It was the most sublime and heart-rending version I have ever had the privilege to hear. In the following days Charlie joined us at the club regularly. Paul stuck around too, feeling that something was wrong. As for Roy, he came only in the evenings to keep an eye on what was happening. So our days were spent in the cool of Birdland while the city sweltered outside. I had a ball playing piano duets with Mingus. He enjoyed it too, for he loved the keyboard, and Tatum and Bud were his idols. (Needless to say, we had hit it off instantly.) But in the evening, by the time Roy arrived, Bud's enthusiasm was gone and he really had to drag himself to the piano.

When Alfred Lyon came to see how things were going, Bud suddenly announced he was dropping the whole project. This, despite the fact that he had just composed the last tune needed to complete the record, a piece he called "The Gonest Thing." Its title was certainly a reference to seeing his father for the last time.

So the sessions were cancelled and Bud's original manuscripts, left behind on the piano, were put away with the rest of my archives. He did play the tunes one evening at the club with John Ore and J. C. Moses, in honor of Margareta's return. It gave us just a taste of what the Blue Note label had missed. Paul Chambers was disappointed but when I filled him in on Bud's problems he became more solicitous than ever. It was a pretty idle period for him and he took to spending most of his afternoons with us. In his shabby black suit, he too looked like someone who had gotten a raw deal from life. It hurt me to see him, touchingly simple, extremely sensitive, looking a little bit lost in all the upheaval. For me he was the finest bassist of his generation. Paul and Bud didn't talk much. Their emotions passed without words. Paul understood right away that we weren't rolling in riches and every day we shared our meager pocket money to survive.

At the end of September a telegram came from Paris announcing I was the father of a baby boy. Our son Gilles had arrived at last. Bud greeted the news with joy, and I had a warm feeling to see him smile again. I had almost forgotten how happy he had been not so very long

ago. All at once, I felt a deep longing for all my loved ones and especially for the newborn son that I had never seen.

Our growing difficulties and Bud's low morale had me in a chronic
state of depression. Bud, excited by the prospect of being a godfather,
proposed on his own accord that we go out to celebrate the following
Monday in a little club in the Village. The mere mention of the baby
was enough to lift his spirits. For the first time, I brought up the idea
of returning to Paris and it seemed to me that was exactly what he
wanted. I felt our old intimacy coming back, the deep communion
that had been broken over the past few days.

That Monday, before our celebration, we went to see Gil Evans.
He lived in the Village in a building that was home to a number of
artists. The hallway was filled with a blue fog and an overpowering
smell of grass and by the time we reached his apartment on the top
floor, I was already high. Gil looked ten years younger than I remembered. His wife Anita had just had a baby, a little boy they'd named
Noah.

Bud's morale was now shot and his playing reflected it. As always
when he wasn't in good shape, he would expose a theme cautiously,
only to find his customary ease within the first few bars of the next
chorus. I had already noticed this in the past (particularly at the Blue
Note in the days when he was on Largactyl), and I understood that if
Bud had trouble with a certain theme, it was from a desire to respect
the way it was written. He had no problems at all in developing his
improvisations, which he could adapt perfectly to the possibilities of
the moment. This realization made me admire him all the more. After
all, who can claim to be perfect at all times? I dreaded the hasty judgments of those who knew him less than I did. As I observed the reactions around me, I thought to myself, "My God, what skill, what
lucidity! There's no one quite as hip as he. He can always manage to
come out on top. The elegance is still there. Even when he's down,
there's nothing to worry about. He's the prince of cool, with a chic all
his own—something pretty close to pure beauty." On occasion I'd
find him a little off for a couple of choruses and I'd feel frustrated by
what seemed to be a certain detachment in the treatment of the ideas.
But when I'd listen to the tape the next day and in the days to come,
I'd come around to the certainty that he was right again. With Bud,
everything was always perfectly suited to the needs of the moment. In
spite of his moods, or maybe because of them, his creation was a permanent and exciting adventure. The genius was always there.

A few days later, Goodstein called to say that Bud was going to receive a prize, the Schaeffer award, which would be presented at Birdland at a big ceremony with all the press and many jazz celebrities. It occurred to me that apart from coming in first in the *Jazz Hot* polls, Bud had never before been honored by any jury. He had never won a *Down Beat* or *Metronome* award or even a Grammy, for that matter. At last, I thought, some long overdue recognition! The name Schaeffer meant nothing to me and I imagined it must be some great artistic authority, so rare I'd never even heard of it. When I checked it out, I learned that Schaeffer was a brand of beer. What perfect irony! It's about time, I thought, that this great brewery was getting around to awarding its prize to one of its best customers! The award had already been given to Louis Armstrong, Duke Ellington, Thelonious Monk, and Ray Charles.

Bud and I were both surprised when the emcee called me up on stage in order to introduce me to the audience. A brief history of Bud's work and his enormous contribution to music nearly brought down the house. The award was ceremoniously presented by a pretty young actress named Roxanne Gilbert and Bud was asked to say a few words. "I appreciate very much that I got this award, and I'm glad that it was presented at Birdland, one of the finest nightclubs in New York." Then he timidly thanked the organizers and the audience, bowed with a tight little smile and disappeared backstage. Wynton Kelly and his trio played that night, with a very spiritual and moving tribute to Bud. The evening helped somewhat to improve Bud's morale and restore my own hopes, so I decided to put off for a little while longer our return to France.

We were contacted for an interview by a Philadelphia radio station. This interview turned out to be the smoothest, the most fluid, to my knowledge, that Bud had ever given. Unfortunately, I have no trace of it and have never been able to track down the journalist. Bud was teasing her throughout their talk and giving her the most incredible answers which she took perfectly seriously.

"Bud, who is your favorite pianist?"

"Dave Brubeck."

"Okay. And saxophonist?"

"Paul Desmond."

"What about a drummer?"

"Gene Krupa." And so on . . .

Bud was choking back laughter and his good humor renewed my confidence in the future. Things were looking up again. Art Blakey invited us to his farm in the country and when Bud heard there were horses, he positively glowed. "You've got horses? Oh, I'd love to ride a horse. I've always dreamed of going horseback riding."

I recalled how Bud often said, when we used to go to the country, that he didn't want to die without having tried to ride a horse. "No problem," said Art. "You can ride, it's easy, I've got all you'll need. I'll pick you up at the hotel tomorrow morning at ten. Be ready."

Early next morning, Bud was all dressed up in his new sports clothes and raring to go. We waited for hours in the hotel lobby but Blakey never showed up. It took Bud days to get over his disappointment. From then on, his morale remained fragile and his emotions went up and down like a roller-coaster. Luckily, Margareta came back to New York and Bud was happy again for a while.

I took advantage of her return to try to clear up something that had been bothering me for some time—the attitude of Bud's father. I called and asked if he would see me alone. He made it quite clear he didn't want to be mixed up in Bud's problems in any way, and only when I accepted that did he agree to see me. He showed no interest in his son except when he spoke of him as a child. Then his tone became gentle and his praise unstinting, and he talked with real admiration about what Bud was capable of at the age of ten or fifteen. To show me what he meant, he took out a recording machine he had made himself, which used spools of magnetic wire, obviously an ancestor of the Dictaphone. Then and there, I had the rare privilege of hearing Bud's earliest recordings. He played Bach, Chopin, Debussy, and also, almost in the same vein, "Body and Soul," "Tea for Two," "How High the Moon," "Honeysuckle Rose" . . . I was stunned to hear how the pulse and syncopation were already sketching in the structures that would one day be called bebop. The "pumping" left hand would frequently stop and do some strong off-beat chords that were later so characteristic of his style. The recordings were of excellent quality and Bud played with a virtuosity astonishing in someone of his age. William said he was incredibly gifted, could reproduce anything by ear, and already had a thorough understanding of harmonic systems. Where had he already drawn this knowledge at such an early age? As a pianist myself, I could compare Bud's precocious invention with my own efforts at the same age. I could hear in those recordings the essentials of Bud's language and syntax, enunciated clearly and with great authority. The music was almost abstract for its time and I could well imagine how much it must have shocked the young musicians of his generation, who could barely conceive of the sort of things that he was already performing with considerable brio. But alas, once William had finished talking about these childhood memories, he clammed up and that was the end of our conversation. I invited him to the club, but he never came to Birdland to hear Bud and we never heard from him again.

Having heard these early recordings (1934 to 1939), it always makes me smile when I read in the "highly specialized" journals that Bud Powell adapted the style of Charlie Parker to the piano. As I've said so many times, preconceived ideas don't die easily. There are plenty of Bud's contemporaries who reject this theory, like Kenny Clarke, whose integrity and authority in the matter seem to me unquestionable.

The music of that time was still based on the conceptions of Louis Armstrong and Earl Hines, whose trio work already showed a desire to break out of traditional structures. A quick rundown of the major bop artists, to see what style they were playing in during this period, is most instructive. In an interview with Maurice Cullaz in March 1962, Kenny Clarke said, speaking about Monk: "In 1936 he was mainly playing gospel and if he played jazz, it was with Bud Powell, at Bud's home. As a matter of fact, a lot of Monk's compositions were written in collaboration with Bud, on Bud's piano."

On the record *Trumpet Battle at Minton's* (Xanadu Records, 1941), Thelonious plays with Joe Guy, Hot Lips Page, and sometimes with Charlie Christian. This record set off a great debate, as some "experts" claimed it wasn't Monk playing at all, while others who had been present insisted that it really was him. What it shows, at the very least, is that Monk's style at the time was not so obvious as to be immediately recognizable.

As for Dizzy Gillespie, there is no doubt whatsoever that after he went to Teddy Hill's band in 1937, he was deep into progressive ideas. His encounter with the duo of Kenny Clarke and Bud Powell in 1938 must surely have set off some sparks. Kenny and Bud had been playing together for a year. Bear in mind that Kenny was the veteran of that group and that all those musicians had already put forth some pretty revolutionary ideas. Charlie Christian played some pretty advanced stuff with Bud and Sid Catlett (a major influence on Kenny). Dizzy went on to play with such accomplished musicans as Cab Calloway and Lionel Hampton, who would help forge his personality but certainly not enable him to crystallize his deepest aspirations. Then the members of this little avant-garde group who often met at Minton's welcomed Charlie Parker into the fold. He had just met Dizzy at the Booker T. Hotel in Kansas City and decided to come to New York. That was in 1939 and his stated aim was to meet Art Tatum. To pay his way, he didn't hesitate to wash dishes at the club where the great pianist was playing. He didn't stand a chance of playing there himself and was even met with a certain animosity, as testified by Don Byas. But he was content to soak up the music being played in New York at the time.

In Bob Reisner's book, *Bird: The Legend of Charlie Parker*, Parker himself recounts:

> I remember one night I was jamming in a chili house (Dan Wall's) on Seventh Avenue between 139th and 140th. It was December, 1939. Now, I'd been getting bored with the stereotyped changes that were being used all the time, at the time, and I kept thinking there's bound to be something else. I could hear it sometimes, but I couldn't play it. Well, that night, I was working over "Cherokee," and, as I did, I found that by using the higher intervals of a chord as a melody line and backing them with appropriately related changes, I could play the thing I'd been hearing. I came alive.

I can imagine Bud at this period, rubbing elbows with all the young lions in this hotbed of musical creation and just poised to explode. In a filmed interview with Kenny Clarke and Max Roach in Paris in 1984, Kenny told me:

> Bud and Charlie Parker were on the same level. Bud was just as heavy on his own instrument as Charlie Parker was on his. It became a battle of wits after a while because Bud really knew more about harmony than Charlie did. . . . Bird was jealous of Bud because of that. He used to want to beat Bud up all the time. We would have to say, "No, Bird—leave Bud alone." And Bud would ask, "Why does he want to beat me up, Klook?" We never really knew. But after, we began to understand why. Bud was superior musically to Charlie Parker, so it made Charlie angry. "How is it that you know more about music than I do?" But that's the way it happened . . .

Placing these events in chronological order helps put things in proper perspective and sheds light on an issue that few think about today. It's not a question of comparing the relative genius of these superb musicians. It's simply interesting to be aware of the possible influence each had on the others, at any given date, based on their personal development at that point. It seemed to me necessary to review, however briefly, some of the highlights of that crucial era so rich in musical discoveries. I regularly hear such comments from a lot of Bud's contemporaries, who'll say to me, confidentially, "You know, man, Bud was the master. He was the one who really found a lot of the things." These were whispered confidences no one seemed to want to shout from the rooftops. For me, they only confirmed my inner certainty. It's just that I found them a little *too* confidential. After a while, I decided to examine the idea by deliberately asking various people, in the course of interviews, what they thought, and pushing them to say more about it. Let us now give credit where it's due, even if it's a little late.

Here are some quotes collected over the years. Coming from such authorities as these, it's good enough for me.

Art Taylor: "Bud was the master. He was the greatest!"

Kenny Clarke: "Bud was the boss, no doubt about it."

Sonny Stitt: "Bud was the finest, the most subtle, he's always been at that level. He was the authority."

Sonny Rollins: "Of course Bud was the professor. He communicated his new ideas to all the musicians of this generation."

Paul Bley: "Francis, everybody knows that Bud was the master. This is evident."

Bill Evans: "He was the most comprehensive compositional talent of any jazz player I have ever heard presented on the jazz scene."

Max Cohen recalls a significant event that shows the respect they all had for Bud:

> Sometime in 1950, an unusual performance occurred in Birdland which is still discussed, with respect, by many of the principals. A combo consisting of Max Roach at the drums, the late Charlie Parker at the sax, Miles Davis at the trumpet, Freddie Russell at the bass and Bud Powell at the piano, were performing. There was a break and Bud began to play. The playing and the tone development were so extraordinary that the musicians, unknown to Bud, left the stand and Bud performed solo. When the other musicians complimented him on his performance, he appeared to be dazed and had no recollection of the fact that he had just completed, with incredible dexterity, 45 minutes of solo work of extraordinary content!

The basically new phenomenon of bop was the pulse, and no one but Bud had the drive that makes him unique, intellectually but also purely physically. Allen Eager, the faithful companion of Charlie Parker, told me one day: "Because of the level of his intellect, his musical choices and his exceptionally good taste, Bud impressed me even more than Bird."

Ira Gitler, a constant observer of the events of this period, declared in a filmed interview: "Bud had the New York style. Charlie Parker had the Kansas City style. Bud had the spirit of New York, with that special kind of urgency associated with New York, in his electricity. Growing up in the streets of New York had given him another way of looking at the world."

In a film I directed with Bud's cousin, Carolyn Dean, she commented as she showed me the piano Bud practiced on in the house in Willow Grove: "So many times I've seen Charlie Parker and Monk in contemplation, in front of the piano while Bud was working."

Max Cohen, who was Charlie Parker's lawyer as well as Bud's, wrote in his unpublished memoirs:

> I knew only one musical genius—defining this term as an extraordinary explosive but channelized creative force—Bud Powell . . .
>
> It is common knowledge, to the extent that names, places and dates are specifically mentioned, that many a musical composition attributed to a purported composer and profitably paying royalties was obtained by getting Bud drunk, placing him at the piano and inducing him to create while the performance was either recorded or rapidly transcribed.
>
> I was informed by the manager of Birdland, Oscar Goodstein, that he once returned to the club in the early hours of the morning to discover Bud playing the piano, completely drunk, and a noted band leader and his arranger copying Bud's music at great speed. Their exit from Birdland was at even greater speed . . .

Frances Barnes, childhood sweetheart and Bud's first wife, also has her word to say: "Duke Ellington was frequently coming over to the house. He used to make Bud play, and he would take a lot of notes. One day, I told Bud, 'Man, don't you know that he's stealing your ideas?' Later on, when Bud worked at the piano, we wouldn't answer the door anymore."

One of Bud's childhood friends, Andy Browne, told me that when Bud first played with a small group, he would sometimes leave the stage right in the middle of a number. Many people took it as a strange quirk or another sign of his anti-social behavior, but to his mind it was the exasperation of an innovator, impatient with the lack of understanding of his partners despite the many hours they'd spent rehearsing together.

Jackie McLean says the same thing: "We were rehearsing Bud's compositions, very difficult for us because we were novices compared to him and to his music. We were going over and over them until they were perfect. If by chance one of us happened to screw up during the set at the club, Bud would just split, furious."

So wasn't Bud in fact way ahead of everyone else, to such an extent that a conspiracy of silence was created around the importance of his role? Of course, a new musical conception was in the air. But this observation, while true, is a bit too simple. It was a movement that many took part in, but couldn't it be that one perceptive spirit, more precocious and musically cultivated than all the rest, had the good fortune to be incarnated in an inspired and prolific genius to create new structures that were solid and usable?

In the end, the egocentricity of some and the silence and legendary discretion of Bud made things cozy for a lot people.

Let me say one more time: the initiators were usually pianists and often they had their own big bands. The piano is an all-around instrument that permits the exploration of the entire world of music. To refresh the world's memory, I would mention such names as Fletcher Henderson, Jay McShann, Earl Hines, Duke Ellington, Stan Kenton, Fats Waller, Art Tatum, Nat King Cole, Count Basie, Thelonious Monk and, more recently, Bill Evans, McCoy Tyner, Herbie Hancock, and Keith Jarrett. From their concepts, even when they were not supported by their own bands, grew the new streams of music.

I never told Bud about my visit to his father. Anyway, he had other things on his mind, more interesting than that. I was delighted when I came home that day to find him smooching with Margareta.

CELIA

(Recorded in New York, May 1949 [Verve])

We got a telegram at Birdland announcing the arrival of Frances Barnes and her daughter, Celia Powell. The prospect of seeing them put Bud in a state of extreme excitement. We were to meet at the club just before the first set and all day long Bud was on pins and needles, asking me questions about this meeting that I obviously couldn't answer. His impatience was understandable. He had last seen his daughter when she was very young, before the hardships of his tortured life had torn them apart.

Birdland was still empty when we got there. The waiters were putting out ashtrays and setting up menus before the arrival of the customers. I immediately noticed two women sitting in the back. Frances and Celia had arrived before us. Frances stood and, a little embarrassed, gave Bud a kiss. Celia, a beautiful young lady of fifteen, sat rigidly staring at her shoes. Bud hardly dared to look at her. Frances asked her to stand and introduced her to her father. Bud gave her a timid kiss, smiling in wonder. There was a long silence as Bud looked from one to the other. You could have heard a pin drop. Then he took Celia's hands and they stood that way contemplating each other for a long long while. I lost all track of time, then came to with a start when I realized that, without my noticing it, the club had filled up.

The charm was broken by Pee Wee Marquet's shrill falsetto announcing Bud in his usual ill-tempered way. I didn't want to leave our guests alone so I decided not to turn on the recorder that night. How I regret it now! I think I never heard Bud play with such tenderness. For his first tune, Bud played "Celia," dedicated, of course, to his daughter. Listening to it then, the perfect logic and balance of the song, such a pivotal reference work for all future jazz pianists, made me more certain than ever that when Bud had composed it at Creedmoor four months before her birth, he'd had a strange premonition that the baby they were expecting would be a girl. There were tears in my eyes and I realized why it had been so important to find Celia.

Unfortunately, Celia and her mother had to leave the next morning to return to North Carolina. Despite the distance, we promised to keep in touch.

Alternating with Bud's trio, Blue Mitchell and his band had replaced Horace Silver. If I remember correctly, Lou Donaldson was in the band, as well as a promising young pianist named John Hicks.

BUD'S BUBBLE

(Recorded in New York, January 10, 1947 [Columbia])

O ne evening Bud and I chanced to see a fight in front of Birdland. Two black men were going at it, with a few others egging them on. Threats and insults flew. I could see fear in Bud's eyes and his hand gripped my arm. The circle of onlookers grew larger and their eyes shone with excitement. By the light of a nearby lamppost I saw the flash of a razor blade. Bud's grip tightened on my arm. The man with the razor blade was waving it in the air, grazing the other's face several times. All at once the other man, with a lightning reflex, grabbed a large hunk of wood that was sticking up out of a wastebasket near the lamppost and swung it with all his might straight at his enemy's forehead. The sound it made was like a watermelon splitting open. The man with the razor stopped in his tracks, then his eyes rolled upward and he collapsed in a heap on the ground. The other man took off, followed by the rest of his gang.

The body lay there with blood streaming from all the orifices. My first impulse was to go over but Barry Harris, who had witnessed the scene along with us, pulled me back roughly, and whispered, "Keep out of this." Someone gave the razor a kick and it disappeared out of sight. No one moved. Within minutes, two mounted policemen showed up, probably called by one of the Birdland waiters. They approached on their horses and questioned the remaining onlookers, but of course nobody had seen a thing. A few minutes later, a police van drove up. The cops loaded the body, more dead than alive, into the van, handling it like a sack of dirty laundry.

It had all happened so fast, I was in a state of shock. When I remembered Bud and turned to tell him we'd better go home, I saw he wasn't there. Barry and I looked for him both inside the club and around the neighborhood. There was no doubt about it. He had disappeared.

Pee Wee Marquet had already announced his name for the second set and the audience was becoming impatient. I could imagine how upset he was by the violence we had just witnessed, and it occurred to me that he might have gone back to the hotel. I hurried over to check, but no one had seen him. Oscar Goodstein was furious and there was nothing I could say. Even Margareta was puzzled by his disconcerting behavior.

Now the press would have a field day, painting Bud once again as an unstable individual with unpredictable reactions. That was how his reputation had been tarnished over the years, when in fact, where music was concerned, Bud was scrupulously serious.

Max Cohen cites a case in point:

> During one 10:30 performance in Birdland, it was observed that Bud's face was swollen and that he had developed a fever. He was rushed to Dr. Herman S. Harris and to Dr. Maurice J. Oringer, who subjected him to oral surgery. They removed an area of infection. Bud returned to Birdland after the operation and insisted on performing, notwithstanding the one-and-one-half hours of surgery. Actually, he had missed only one set. His great concern was that if he had failed to return to complete the evening's work, the rumors would spread that he had 'goofed-off' again. . . .

All things considered, I was forced to conclude that Bud's reputation in life had gradually cast its shadow on his work.

I spent the rest of the night searching the neighborhood and waiting anxiously for his return. The next day I called all of our friends, with no luck. I had the phone numbers of a few journalists, whom I asked to make an announcement in the papers and on the radio. As night approached, I grew more and more frightened at the thought of Bud roaming the streets. Just on the off-chance, I called his father and had to listen to his "I told you so" remarks, to the effect that this was exactly what he knew would happen and he had been right not to get involved. Then the thought struck me that Bud might have headed for one of the Harlem nightspots, and I decided to go up there to check them out for myself.

I had a hard time finding a taxi that would go to Harlem at that time of night. Finally a surly Italian gave me a fatalistic shrug and grudgingly agreed to take me. As we approached Central Park he locked his doors and asked me to roll up the back windows. Throughout the ride, he never stopped questioning me—why was I going to such a godforsaken place? And at night, no less! I was too worried about Bud to want to enter into long discussions with him, so I cut short the interrogation by pretending not to understand English. He just went on grumbling all by himself. "They oughta do something about it . . . Get rid of all these goddam niggers . . . Going around with knives . . . Slitting people's throats . . ."

The papers in France periodically reported incidents of reckless tourists getting in trouble, but tonight I couldn't care less. Bud was out there somewhere, maybe in trouble, and that was all I could think about. The cabdriver's vicious muttering went in one ear and out the other. This spate of abuse went on until I couldn't stand it any more and I told him to shut up, that I wasn't interested in his opinions. We were right in the middle of Central Park when he slammed on the brakes. I was looking out into the darkness, trying to figure out what had made him stop, when he got out of the cab, opened the back door and in a threatening tone, ordered me to get out. I stepped out without thinking and he took off like a shot, leaving me alone in the dark, blinded by the red lights of his car receding into the distance.

There was nothing to do but start walking. I walked quickly, all my senses alert for any possible danger. By the time I reached the first buildings I was a ball of nerves, every muscle in my body stiff with tension. The first passersby I met looked at me as if I was a Martian, but one of them gave me directions to the first place I wanted to check: Basie's.

My appearance at the club also created a stir, equivalent to the arrival of a flying saucer. I was the only white person present. I went straight to the bar and explained what I wanted, and within two minutes, Bud's name was on everyone's lips. The papers had talked a lot about Bud coming back to the States with a French friend and I understood this was what the customers were talking about. Some came up to chat amiably, others glared at me as if I had the plague. No one had seen Bud, but they suggested some other places I could look. One man offered to go with me and suggested we start with Small's. He looked nice enough but I was wary, secretly hoping he wasn't going to lead me down some dark alley and relieve me of my wallet.

We made a tour of the clubs but Bud hadn't been seen anywhere. Each time, my arrival in these all-black nightspots was a bombshell. In one club, Shirley Scott was playing with an alto player who sounded so much like Bird that for a few seconds he almost made me forget my troubles. Mostly, I stood at the bar, which usually had a mirror over it, so that I could see what was going on behind me. But I noticed that the mere mention of Bud's name was enough to quell any puzzlement my presence may have caused. The evening went by without a problem, except that I hadn't found the slightest trace of Bud. By early morning, I took the subway back downtown in despair.

I kept on phoning friends—Ornette, Thelonious, Max Roach—but no one knew a thing. I couldn't sleep despite my fatigue and spent the

day walking the streets like an automaton, poking into any place I
thought might have attracted Bud. At nightfall I went back to the hotel, beside myself with fatigue and worry. I had no appetite and
couldn't eat a bite. With each passing minute I was more certain of a
catastrophe. I couldn't figure out why the incident in front of Birdland could have disturbed Bud to the point of running away once
more without telling me. I went to the club and found Goodstein
more and more furious, with good reason, because the customers were
flocking in to see Bud and going away when they heard he wasn't
playing. By now he made no effort to be polite. He accused me directly of not having been vigilant enough. Disgusted by his attitude, I
went back to the hotel without even trying to defend myself. Just as I
collapsed on the bed, fully dressed, the phone rang. It was Bertha, the
wife of Bud's old friend, the pianist Elmo Hope. Elmo had just
walked in with Bud and had asked her to call me right away. All my
energy came back and I jumped in a taxi to go to their house in
Brooklyn. Both of them were waiting in the street when I arrived. It
was night and the neighborhood was none too reassuring. To allay my
fears, Elmo announced immediately that Bud was well and I needn't
worry. They had made him take a nice bath and he was now resting.
"He was really very tired, you know," Elmo said.

I looked at this sad little man, bundled into an overcoat, who also
seemed overwhelmed by the sorrows of life. In his plaintive voice he
was doing his best to reassure me and I felt a profound sympathy for
him. Bud had often talked about him and I felt as if I was talking to
an old friend. Bertha gave me the details of what had happened:

> Bud had been looking for Elmo. He had been asking a lot of people in
> the neighborhood in the lower Bronx where he could find Elmo. So, Bud
> was walking East and Elmo was walking West. They had to meet. This
> was the first time Elmo had seen Bud in years, and Bud told him that
> "I've been looking for you—I wanted to see you." So Elmo turned around
> and brought Bud back to the apartment. . . . By the time they had returned
> Bud was exhausted after walking up the two flights of stairs. He was
> breathing very hard.
>
> Elmo introduced him to me, and told how he had found him in the
> avenue. It was obvious that Bud was not a well man. He tried to talk to
> Bud, but it was difficult. Bud was really still panting to catch his breath.
> Elmo had to go to see his Mother's house and left Bud there with me
> alone. And I tried to make him comfortable, told him that everything was
> alright. Whenever I asked how he was feeling, he would just give this va-

cant stare. He was there for about four hours and he wouldn't eat any-thing. Elmo really wanted him to stay with us.

Upstairs, Bud was lying on a small iron bed in a tiny room painted dark blue. A single light bulb hanging from the ceiling shed its pale light on the whole sinister scene. Bud had a three-day beard, his hair was unkempt, his eyes expressionless, and he looked exhausted. His speech was thick and the few words he tried to say left me no doubt as to the cause of his sorry state.

I spent the night talking to Bertha and Elmo, telling them about all our tribulations, first in Paris, then in New York. After a while, Bud got up, painfully. He seemed a little stronger and asked if we could go back to the hotel. Our taxi felt like a phantom vessel. My nerves were taut and in my hypnotic torpor the lights of the city had a psyche-delic effect. Bud hadn't said a word about his latest escapade and I didn't have the heart to question him.

The next thing I remember, we were in the room and Bud was al-ready snug in bed. I had no recollection of arriving at the hotel and I almost felt I had dreamt the whole thing. I fell into bed and was asleep instantly. In the middle of the night I was awakened by a loud noise. A horrible odor filled the room. Terrified, I turned on the light, and saw Bud on the floor trying painfully to stand up. He had fallen out of bed and been sick. He looked dazed and helpless. I led him to the bathroom and ran a bath. He had thrown up all over the room, dirtying and staining everything in his path. I had to get it cleaned up and as I clearly couldn't do it all alone, I called Babs and Prophet. It was 4 A.M. but I knew I could count on them in a pinch. Sure enough, within half an hour they were there and the three of us worked together till morning on our unpleasant task. The last thing we had to do was change the mattress. Babs shelled out a couple of dollars and the problem was solved. I breathed a sigh of relief. If the management had learned of the damage, we would probably have been kicked out. By noon, everything was arranged properly once again and we were able to sit down to relax over a cup of coffee, as Babs regaled us with stories of his early years with Bud. Good old Babs, the heavenly vagabond who had never had the recognition his great talent deserved, who had borne so many disappointments with-out ever being crushed, a true brother to Bud, a true companion in misfortune. The next thing we learned was that Goodstein had can-celed Bud's appearance at Birdland. He had gone over his books and bluntly announced that as things stood, he didn't owe us a cent. Quite the contrary, we owed him! He had laid out for the plane tickets, the hotel, the restaurant, the back Union dues, Max Cohen's retainer and our pocket money. He advised us to think seriously about our future plans, and suggested that Bud could finish out the remainder of his contract later on, so we could go back with a little money to pay off the hospital debts, as had been the original idea. There was no way now we could go home early. We needed at least enough money for the air fares and our excess baggage. I felt the trap closing heavily around us and my melancholy thoughts went out to the baby who'd been born back in Paris.

I DIDN'T KNOW WHAT TIME IT WAS

(Recorded in New York, September 13, 1956 [Verve])

For a few days, Bud did nothing but rest, then finally he went back to Birdland. Margareta, and I did our best to cheer him up, but his spirits were alarmingly low. I still wonder about the real reasons for his total collapse. True, we had been through some painful moments trying to get the cabaret card. But after that, his success at Birdland, his meeting with Margareta, and his renewed contact with Celia had given him new energy and bolstered his morale. Ever since the visit to his father, everything seemed to be shattered. The old wounds inflicted by his family had never healed. His father's attitude, and whatever must have been said about his mother's death, had destroyed his last secret illusions. Time and again I have turned this question over in my mind, and I still believe today that this was the prime reason for Bud's tragedy.

There had once been talk of a Japanese tour, but now that was canceled too. The true friends—Max, Andy Browne, Ornette, Paul Chambers, Kenny Dorham, Prophet, Nica, Babs, Barry Harris—stood by Bud and came to see him regularly, at Birdland or at the hotel. On the other hand, the critics in search of sensational news, who had been noticeably absent, started in again with their eternal refrain on "the depressing Bud Powell case." Once more the hardships of his life provided the material to grind out their pointless and inconsistent stories.

The following days went by normally, though Bud never recovered his former dynamism. I talked with Goodstein again about the possibility of our returning earlier than planned but he couldn't come up with the plane fare. Margareta was planning to go to France, too. Meanwhile, Max Cohen was still trying to clear up Bud's marital situation. We knew that he had married Audrey Hill and that they had started divorce proceedings but no one knew quite how it had ended. Bud and Margareta were talking about getting married and this seemed encouraging for Bud's future. Margareta was a miracle of patience and sensitivity, essential for a tortured soul like Bud. With her kindness and constant availability, she was able to establish close contact with him, much as I had myself. His ability to trust her was a significant step, and I imagined that back in France, in a calmer society, Bud would find his equilibrium and settle down with Margareta in a quality relationship, finally putting himself in a position to establish a comfortable and stable existence.

J. C. Moses and Prophet cordially detested each other. I had never been close to J. C. and my friendship with Prophet seemed to bother him. In fact, J. C. knew that Bud didn't like him at all, neither the man nor his playing, and he took it out on me. Bud had told me this several times, but what could I do about it? When he learned Bud's contract was ending soon, J. C. took me aside one night backstage, looked me in the eye, and said softly, "You're not going back to Paris with those tapes you recorded. You know that, don't you?"

"No kidding," I said, "Is that so?"

"You sure are not," he said with an ironic smile. "I think you're going to give them to us."

During this exchange, some friends of his had quietly gathered round us, all of them wearing the same forced smile, just the way people wear the same hat. There in the club I had nothing to fear, so I said out loud for all to hear, "You're very brave on your own turf, but come see me in Paris if you want to play games. I have some friends who'd have a lot of fun with you!"

I kept my back carefully against the wall as we looked each other straight in the eye. No one moved, till at last, with a final sneer, J. C. called it quits. At the time he had joined the Black Muslims. In many ways, I was sympathetic to their position, my contact with the French *Résistance* having forged a certain idea of independence. I've had lots of animated discussions on the subject with Max Roach, during which I tried to make him see that all whites were not necessarily racists and slave-drivers, that some of us deeply loved the Black people. His answer was always the same: "Yeah, but you're different."

One day J. C. Moses and his strongarm boys came to the hotel and started up again. This time it was Bud himself who put him in his place. "What do you want my tapes for, J. C. ? How come? Are *you* the bandleader?"

He mumbled an unintelligible reply and left with his sneering henchmen, muttering threats that I'd hear from them again. Bud closed the door behind them without a word.

One evening at Birdland, Margareta left earlier than usual and when I found Bud after the last set, he was with a man I had never seen, who stopped talking instantly the moment I arrived. His eyes had a strange shine and a false air of cordiality. I was immediately on my guard. Bud introduced us and hesitantly asked if he could come back to the hotel with us. As I never liked to refuse Bud anything, I said okay. But instead of letting them go up together while I did the shopping as usual, I thought it best to stay with them. Bud wondered about this but I evaded his question. The atmosphere in the room was tense. Obviously, the man was waiting for me to leave before launching into his dealings with Bud. I moved about pretending to busy myself with various things but keeping an eye open all the time. As the minutes crawled by, the silence became heavier. Bud asked when I was going to do the shopping and I replied that I was not about to leave until our visitor was gone. Realizing that I was prepared to wait longer than he was, the dealer finally took me by the arm, drew me into the bathroom and unfolded a little envelope of white powder, saying, "Come on, man, don't fuck up the deal. You can have some if you want."

To tell the truth, I would have welcomed a little snort, but there was no way I could do it without Bud, and for him it was out of the question. For someone who's had tuberculosis, cocaine is a one-way ticket to the morgue. "Look," I said, "I don't care what you do, but there's no way Bud's going to use that shit."

"Go on, take it, man. It's on the house."

"The answer is no! As long as I live, no one's going to play around with Bud's health."

I was tired and this arrogant guy was getting on my nerves. Having failed with the soft sell, he now tried the tough guy approach. "I don't have to talk to you, only to Bud," he said. "Get out of my way!" With a determined look, he pushed me aside and started to walk back toward Bud's bed. At that instant I saw red. I grabbed hold of him with one hand and with the other, opened the door behind him and shoved him outside. He seemed to offer no resistance at first, but then he suddenly wheeled and shot out a right with his fist. All my years of judo had left me with some reflexes, so I ducked and at the same time, delivered a right to his face with all my strength. It struck its mark. He reeled backward, hitting his head on the wall with a sickening thud, and blood began spurting across the hallway, hitting the wall on the other side. A door opened and a haggard face peeped out, followed by another and another until all the people on the floor were standing in doorways in their pajamas to see what was going on. The night watchman came running up, took in the scene in a jiffy and announced that he was going to call the police. I grabbed hold of him just in time, explaining that considering the goodies this guy had on him, it might be wise, for the reputation of his hotel, not to bring the cops into it. Bud looked on without budging. Slowly, the dealer came to. Hearing the word police gave him back all his energy. In a split second, he was on his feet and running down the stairs without looking back. It took me an hour to clean up the last traces of blood. I gave no thought to the meal that night and Bud seemed too embarrassed to bring it up. We didn't talk about the incident but several times when our eyes met I thought I detected a look of friendship and gratitude in his eyes. I tossed and turned for a few hours, then finally fell into a restless sleep, disturbed by bad dreams.

I thought it best for Bud to have a medical check-up and suggested we go see Dr. Sheldon the very next day. At the doctor's office, he was seized with panic but I managed to reassure him. I could feel he still trusted me, but his old fear had taken hold again. The results of the check-up were excellent and we left feeling better. Bud never seemed to realize how close he had come to death. I kept reminding him that he owed his recovery to his own courage and tenacity and that he had to stay strong in order to put all those troubles behind him. But I felt like a struggling climber on a slippery uphill path.

The next morning I was still asleep when the phone rang. It was Ornette and from the sound of his voice I knew immediately something was wrong. "Francis, are you crazy or what?"

"Why? What's the matter?"

"Have you seen today's paper?"

"No, what paper?"

He read me the article that had put him in such a state. Some two-bit reporter, sparing none of the gory details, told how the great avenger Francis Paudras had beat up the wicked drug dealer. God bless freedom of the press! Always on the job! I had a fond thought for our friend George the doorman, who must have earned himself a few bucks for the information.

"You're out of your mind," Ornette went on. "Do you want to get yourself killed, or what? This is not Montmartre, this is New York!" I couldn't follow what he was saying. I was still half asleep and it was as hot as hell in our crummy hotel. "Listen to me," said Ornette. "Bud finishes at Birdland tonight, doesn't he? So just get the hell out of there. Pack your bags and get over here right this minute."

I couldn't believe my ears. "What are you talking about, Ornette?"

"I'm talking about that you're going to be in deep trouble if you don't get your ass out of that hotel pretty quick!"

"Okay, Ornette, okay, I'll call you back later."

I hung up. From my dumbfounded expression, Bud understood something was wrong. I explained what Ornette had said. He looked terrified and begged me to pack our bags at once. Ornette called back to say we should phone for a taxi and look both ways before going out in the street. I felt like we were in the middle of a Western!

Ornette turned out to be my best friend in New York and we did well to follow his advice. Despite the great distance that separates us now, our friendship has remained intact and I am deeply fond of him to this day. There's no doubt about it, when times are hard you learn who your true friends are. We showed up at Ornette's with all our paraphernalia. He had moved by this time and was living in a basement apartment, a real cellar complete with bare stone walls. It was pretty basic, but he had managed to make it livable with some very beautiful paintings on the walls, a big iron bed, a few benches, a music stand with a lot of sheet music and a vast number of books on architecture. He was studying architecture and had a consuming passion for geometry. On top of a pile of old books lay a violin in its case. He told me he had taken up the violin, though he never convinced me it was of much use, for the sounds he got out of that instrument were enough to make your teeth ache. A plastic sax, like the one Bird had used in Toronto in 1953, was on a stand next to two traditional brass saxophones, a tenor and an alto. The rest of the living space was taken up by orchestral scores spread out all over the room. The whole look was a bit disconcerting but it was cozy and I felt immediately at home. Ornette was the perfect host. He helped us settle in and invited us to share a delicious meal he had prepared. I knew our stay in New York was drawing to a close. Bud wasn't going back to Birdland and during our candlelight dinner I could breathe easily for the first time in a long time.

We were awakened every morning by Ornette's practice exercises on the alto. It was certainly better than an army bugle. He had found a simple method to loosen up his fingers. He would play a few of Bird's tunes at twice the normal speed, and he did it without a hitch. The effect was startling and put me in a good mood from the moment I opened my eyes. Bud loved it, and for the first time in ages I heard his legendary laugh. Ornette was pretty broke at the time and making ends meet became for us an "exercise in style." We shared our meager savings, as well as our friendship, and tried to forget our troubles.

I paid one last visit to Oscar Goodstein at Birdland. He agreed that the best thing for us to do was to go back to France as soon as possible. He showed me the accounts he had so meticulously kept, and the balance was still in the red. He made a long face as he said, "Poor Francis, you owe me $42," and then magnanimously added, "Forget it, it's on me!"

He was paying Bud about a third of what he paid Herbie Mann, but I learned that detail a little too late. He had taken it hard when Bud had disappeared and he preferred not to continue his engagement. We still didn't have our airline tickets and were effectively stranded in New York without any financial resources. Oscar suggested a way out. Bud was not under contract to any record company and could therefore record for any label he wanted. He called me back the very next day to say that a session had been scheduled with the Roulette label for October 12.

The situation in New York was depressing and I was in a hurry to set our return date. As soon as Bud signed the recording contract, Oscar took care of our tickets, making a reservation for us on Air France for October 14. I came to life at the thought that things would soon be set straight again. I would get Bud out of this hellhole, go back home to Nicole, and finally get to see my son.

Nica phoned to say that Thelonious would be playing a long date at the Village Gate. From then on, that's where we spent our nights. The club was very dark, with tables set up every which way and people walking about all the time. In the constant din, I had the feeling the show was more in the audience than on the stage. Thelonious was imperturbable—he just ignored the noise. We had a table reserved near the bandstand and we quickly felt without a doubt that the musicians were playing just for us. Margareta came for the first set and together we fell under Thelonious's magic spell.

One evening the spell was broken by a rather formal-looking character who came timidly to our table and introduced himself with a long and somewhat confused soliloquy. I was beginning to think I no longer understood English but was reassured to see that no one else had understood anything either. It's true, we had our minds on Thelonious. He handed us a business card that said "Bernard Stollman, Consultant Lawyer." He sat down uninvited and spent the rest of the evening declaiming his love for jazz and his passion for people like Bud. Margareta helped translate for me when his syntax went over my head. He spoke the hermetic language of the legal profession and certain expressions escaped me completely, as did the point of his endeavor. Between the long speeches I did manage to hear some soothing music. (I didn't have the same faculty as Bud for blocking out what he didn't like. I'm sure Bud only heard Thelonious.) With a loyalty that was positively touching, Stollman came back every night and when he learned of the troubles Bud and I were in, he offered to take charge. I told him Bud's lawyer was Max Cohen and he took his number and promised to get in touch with him. He added that he was an expert in royalties and everything would be worked out with no delay. When I told him Bud was only paid his royalties in dribs and drabs, and that I had to pay the hospital bill in installments, I thought he would have a heart attack. I listened with a skeptical ear, but was willing to give him a chance, after all that I'd been through. I gave him the information he needed to make his investigations and he did contact Max Cohen. Nica was also dubious about him, but we figured—why not dream a little, what did we have to lose?

Meanwhile, things were beginning to get to Thelonious and he was miserable. The club was particularly noisy, the piano was dreadful, and the atmosphere, with its constant comings and goings, was about as relaxed as the floor of the Stock Exchange. Certainly not the ideal spot for an artist like Monk.

In the second week of October a cold wave hit the city, bringing icy winds and a thin, steady rain. We had brought no warm clothing and didn't have enough money to buy any. According to Oscar, the recording session for Roulette would just cover the air fares. Meanwhile, we were flat broke and had to borrow from Marshall Allen to tide us over. It was at this point that Bernard Stollman (like J. C. Moses before him) started to get very interested in my tapes. This was to be the start of a long period of harassment which, I should say at the outset, was all in vain. Then he offered to buy the reproduction rights to a portrait I had drawn of Bud, a copy of which I had with me in New York. The drawing had been used for the program cover of a benefit concert for Bud at Salle Wagram in Paris back in March 1964.

Stollman had an idea for a record, *Bud Plays Monk*, based on a selection of my tapes, and I wrote the jacket notes for it. A few days later, I wrote an article on Monk for an obscure magazine that agreed to pay cash. I put this money to good use by immediately shipping off my tapes. The episode with J. C. Moses had taught me caution. I couldn't imagine what I would do with the mass of tapes and all the other baggage if J. C. and his cowboys were to intercept me at the airport. I had phoned Nicole and she had come up with an idea. Her boss at UNESCO had offered to receive the parcel at his office, thereby avoiding customs. I was relieved, even though the shipping by registered mail cost a good part of my earnings. J. C. and his boys could do their best (or their worst). The tapes were now safely out of their reach.

The weather got colder and colder. Ornette's place was poorly heated and we were always frozen. Worried about Bud's health, Ornette suggested we ask Nica to put us up for the rest of our stay. Naturally, she said we could come at once. Although it was far away, Ornette said he'd come and see us often until we left. I felt bad about leaving him in his cold damp cellar after all his kindness to us. I settled my last financial problems, kept a few dollars for the cab fare and without saying anything to Ornette, slipped the rest into his favorite architecture book. I was sure it would come in handy some day.

Nica and Barry, who was living at her house, were delighted to put us up, and so were the cats, who gave Bud a friendly welcome. Nica set up a bed for Bud in the big studio near the piano and a cot for me in Barry's room (the room that was later occupied by Thelonious, until the end of his life).

We waited patiently for the recording session, spending most of our time in the big studio around the piano. We'd generally start playing after dinner, around nine o'clock at night. Barry would start with a tune of Bud's or another composition in the same vein. I would take up the tune and we'd try to get Bud's ideas on it. He'd listen with an amused smile, then all at once jump up, go to the piano and show us a different version or some new modulations. Our evenings passed unhurriedly by as we fiddled with the piano under Bud's vigilant eye until all hours of the morning. Sometimes the still of the night was broken by the howl of a cat stuck in a tree, and Nica would get up and go to infinite pains to rescue the poor animal. I never met anyone who loved cats as much as she did.

Around 3 A.M. Barry would cook up a little something and, after a bite to eat, we'd go back to the piano. Often we'd watch the sun rise over Manhattan through the huge window, a fascinating spectacle. A few of the cats were allowed to come into the room. Bud never took his eyes off them and in the end they worked out a *modus vivendi*. They learned to keep their distance, padding around silently in the darkness. An old sofa served as their fortress. It had a hole in one arm through which the cats could come and go at will. One would enter, disappearing out of sight, while three more would come out from some other unexpected exit holes. The parade went on all night, as graceful as a ballet. Bud watched it all with a troubled look while the rest of us couldn't keep from giggling.

Finally one day Bud asked intensely, "What are they doing? Don't they ever sleep?"

"Not at night, Bud, you know that."

"Well, tell them to go outside. Make them go out."

"It's no use, they only listen to Nica," said Barry.

Beyond the bounds of our peaceful haven, the weather was still dreadful, and finally, so as not to see the rain, we inverted day and night, staying up all night and sleeping by day. One night, when he'd stayed downstairs after one of our late night snacks, Bud discovered Nica's wine cellar. Every year she received a shipment of Mouton Rothschild from the family vineyards in France. By the time he came upstairs to join us, I could see right away that he'd been drinking. It never failed to amaze me how quickly wine affected him. He tried to look casual, sitting down on the piano bench to contemplate the keyboard. The minutes went by as we feigned not to notice the disordered movements that began to agitate his body. All at once, he stood up and, with faltering steps, headed for the staircase. Before we knew what was happening, he had missed the first step, tumbled down the others headfirst at a frightening speed and crashed into a wooden closet at the bottom. With Barry right behind me, I rushed down the stairs, certain I would find Bud more dead than alive. He was out cold but already so comatose from the wine that it was impossible to determine how much damage had been done. Barry and I got him upstairs, undressed him and put him to bed, where he fell asleep at once (or so we thought). We talked at length about the accident, wondering if he'd sprained or fractured something. In any case, at four in the morning in New Jersey without any car it was too late to do anything. We decided to take him for X-rays the first thing in the morning. As it was, we had only three hours of sleep.

When we woke up Bud was gone. Had he overheard our conversation? Had he guessed what we intended to do? The very mention of a medical check-up or even the sight of a doctor (with whatever horrible associations it conjured up) was enough to set off a panic, making him categorically refuse any kind of medical treatment. We all set out to look for him, each taking a different direction. We were in a small town in New Jersey and it wasn't as easy to vanish as in the middle of New York. But after going over the place with a fine-tooth comb, we had once more to admit the obvious—Bud was nowhere to be found.

This third disappearance was a terrible blow. Bud seemed determined to undo all that had been done for him. All our efforts and successes, our victories and little joys were being undermined, continually and irreversibly, in these hostile surroundings. Bud would sometimes look at me so helplessly and miserably that even my fairly optimistic nature began to falter. Barry came back from his search on foot, soaked to the bone. By chance he had met someone who said he'd seen a black hitchhiker picked up by a truck heading for New York. From his description, we were sure it was Bud. So Bud was on the loose now, somewhere in the city, this time in the cold and rain, with only his summer clothes on.

Nica immediately jumped into her car and we started on a round of searches through Brooklyn, the Bronx and finally Manhattan, ending up in Harlem in the early morning. The city was waking up as we still desperately combed the streets. I suggested Nica get some rest while I went off to see Marshall.

Once again I alerted the journalists in the hope that someone would recognize him and get in touch with us. *The New York Post* published this short piece, with quotes from Bernard Stollman, who seemed very concerned and remarkably well-informed:

> Bud Powell, a pioneer figure in modern jazz, was reported missing today. The 40-year-old pianist wandered away from the home of friends in Weehawken, N.J. early Sunday in a mood of "deep depression," according to Bernard Stollman, an attorney for Powell's agent. Powell, who has been living in Paris for the last six years [*sic*], was due to fly back to France Sunday night. "He has no money, no papers," Stollman said. Friends said that when last seen Powell was wearing a gray summer suit, brown sweater, white shirt, red tie, and black shoes. He is five-foot-eight and weighs about 210 pounds. Powell recently completed a month-long stand at Birdland.

In another article, Bernard Lefkowitz wrote, under the headline "Bud Powell, Jazz Great, Missing for Third Day":

> . . . In the last few months before he left this country for voluntary exile in Paris, Powell looked more and more like a wounded bear. He had that look again this fall when he returned from Paris, weakened by mental breakdowns and recurrent bouts with tuberculosis, to play piano at Birdland. . . . During his date at Birdland, he disappeared three times. Sunday night, when he left his friends' home in Weehawken, N.J., he was a greatly troubled human being. Today he was reported missing.

Another anguish-filled day. Ornette came to keep me company and tried to console me, then Cecil Taylor showed up with Bill Dixon.

The telephone remained silent. Nica and I decided to head back to New York to search through another night.

Naturally, I phoned Oscar Goodstein, who canceled the session with Roulette. He was madder than ever and I was too worn out to answer. What could I tell him? That it was fate? The papers went on talking of Bud's disappearance, in particular Bernard Lefkowitz, who had been a close observer throughout our stay. "The Past Haunted Missing Jazzman," said the headline, and the story reported:

> Three years ago a Parisian jazz fan met and befriended a down-and-out pianist named Bud Powell. The fan's name is Francis Paudras and he let Powell share his home in Paris. . . . But all Paudras's efforts may be fruitless. Sunday morning, a few hours before he was to return to Paris, Powell disappeared. . . . He slipped out of jazz patron Baroness Nica Rothschild de Koenigswarter's home in Weehawken, N.J., and has not been seen since. "He had so many problems," Paudras remembers. "He had lost his job, he had no money and all he could remember was the old days." A lot of Powell's fans knew less about his music than about his nervous breakdowns in 1945 and 1951 and his attempt at suicide in 1953. He couldn't walk down Broadway without a pusher pulling at him. Sometimes it got so bad he'd just jump in a cab to get away. He'd tell the driver to take him to any friend he could think of, anybody who would pay the cab fare.

Once again, the newspapers dragged out the old stories of Bud's psychiatric history and his involvement with drugs and alcohol. No one seemed to remember that on his arrival in New York from Paris, Bud Powell had been a new man!

The next day was horrendous—it was cold and rainy and the traffic was unspeakably snarled. From the teeming streets rose the unbearable wail of sirens that made all my nerve endings throb. I felt like a prisoner in hell. Whatever happened, I wasn't going to leave Bud here! I would find him somehow, I told myself, and we'd get on that goddam plane together. It was beginning to feel like a curse.

I stayed up the next night with the help of some Benzedrine offered by a sympathetic friend, and Nica and I made another grand tour of the nightspots. Never in my life did I visit so many clubs and musicians' haunts in so short a time. Nica spent a fortune that night. She knew everyone and often, before leaving a place, she would leave a little money for someone in trouble. She dropped me off at Marshall's empty-handed and said she'd be back that evening.

I was no longer hungry or thirsty or sleepy. I felt a permanent nausea. Marshall rarely left his apartment in the daytime but on this day he had an appointment and left me alone in the house. Before going out he asked me to try and stay awake till early afternoon to let in a friend he was expecting, someone who was just passing through New York. I assured him it would be no problem, I was too tense to sleep anyway. He seemed upset that he had to be away and was relieved that I'd be there. He explained that the friend was an exceptional person, a sage, a guru, who had been around the world several times on foot and was nothing less than a saint. He was just returning from a long journey through India. I listened with a certain curiosity, but was in such a state that nothing could really move or surprise me. Numb and empty of feeling I waited for the "holy man."

He arrived right on schedule in the early afternoon. Compared to him, Gandhi would have looked obese. Very tall, amazingly thin, he looked as fragile as glass. A wonderful smile shone through his sparse and graying beard. He seemed to float in his clothes, light as air. When he held out his hand I shook it carefully, in fear of breaking his fingers, which were as translucent as alabaster. I offered him a seat and something to eat or drink, but all he wanted was a glass of water. There was something unreal about him. He seemed to give off a strange light and an extraordinary current of friendship was instantly established between us.

"Who are you," he asked, "aside from Marshall's friend?"

I briefly explained why I had come to New York and the state of anxiety I was in at the moment. He gave me a searching look of such pure goodness as I had never seen. Then, in a calm and solemn voice, he said, "I see you love this man very deeply. Your feeling for him is pure and beautiful."

This somewhat religious tone left me ill at ease. He went on in this vein for a while, though he could tell I was troubled by the certainty of his affirmations. On a nearby table Marshall had put a framed photo of a bearded Hindu, the quintessential guru. The holy man pointed to the photo, and asked, "What's your name?"

"Francis."

"Well, you see, Francis, this man is my spiritual master. And Marshall's as well. He is a guru, a wise man. He's your friend, too."

I listened, more and more astounded, not quite seeing where this was leading, to what perilous slope this kind man was taking me.

"You want to find Bud, don't you? Well, it's very simple."

I started squirming in my chair, more uncomfortable by the minute, cursing Marshall for leaving me in this preposterous situation. But he went on talking, as calm as could be.

"You see, when you love someone, everything is simple. You just need to know how to go about it. Will you try something that is in your power to do?"

It was all very embarrassing, but in the face of such kindness, such candor, I couldn't show my feelings. His eyes implored me and I was fascinated in spite of myself. He must have understood my accord for he stepped closer, and said gravely, "Now listen to me carefully. Think of your friend very hard with all the force of your love. Concentrate very hard and when you feel that you're with him somewhere, pronounce these words, 'Bud ramanahome . . .'"

I listened with mixed emotions, torn between the seemingly ridiculous aspects of the situation and the intensity and utter conviction of his intense look that went right through me. I let myself go to the madness of the moment and carried out the ritual exactly as he had suggested, without holding back. When I got to the last syllable, he grasped my hands with a vigor I wouldn't have suspected and burst into joyous laughter as if I had accomplished a great feat. "Wonderful! That was wonderful! You did it! Your friend will be here tonight."

I must have looked incredulous, for he added, "Yes, yes, you did it right. There's nothing more to worry about. Your friend will be here tonight, never fear! I'm sure of it!"

Not wanting to argue or contradict him, I tried to change the subject. Then Marshall came home and they fell into each other's arms. The holy man explained what had just happened, and added, his voice full of passion and admiration, that thanks to me Bud would soon be home, we had only to wait. Marshall didn't bat an eyelash. He looked at me with perfect conviction and said, "You know, this man is a guru. If he told you that, it's because he knows. He's never wrong."

It was all very mysterious. Marshall made us some sandwiches but our friend only had another glass of water. A little later, Ornette and Cecil arrived, soon followed by Nica, who was shattered to learn we still had no news. From her office Margareta had called the police and the hospitals, with no luck. Marshall ended our speculations by saying that this "saint" and I had done all that was necessary and there was no more need to worry. I didn't dare look the others in the eye. Just then the ring of the telephone broke the silence. It was a black policeman who had heard about Bud's disappearance and had immediately recognized him when he found him collapsed in a doorway in the Village. He said Bud didn't look good and told us to come get him quickly at the police station, before his superiors got back. The holy man gave me a big wink. I looked around at all the happy faces and I pulled myself out of my torpor. Nica offered to take me there. With a knowing look, she put a roll of dollar bills in my hand and we hurried down to the police station.

I relate the above story at the risk of making some readers smile and maybe even of undermining my credibility. But I want to make clear that this entire period of my life was filled with uncommon events and strange phenomena. With Bud, nothing was ever ordinary or logical. There was always something unpredictable or paranormal in the air.

When we got to the police station Bud was in a worse state than we feared. His suit was spattered with mud, and he looked like a tramp who hadn't had a bite to eat for three days, which was probably the case. The police officer was cordial and let him out at once, asking us to keep quiet about what he had done. I shook his hand warmly and slipped him Nica's money, which he pocketed hastily with a knowing wink.

Bud looked at us with anguish in his eyes. His first words were, "Please don't send me to the hospital." We reassured him instantly and Nica took us back home. Bud slept two days and two nights at a stretch, with me sitting guard by his bedside. When he emerged from his long sleep, he behaved as if nothing had happened. He took a bath, had a big meal and came out of it looking fresh and rested. His powers of recuperation were remarkable. With a more stable life he might have outlived us all.

He asked about the date of our departure. I told him we'd missed the recording session and didn't have enough for the plane fare. He didn't answer and looked devastated. We had so often talked about the baby and he knew how anxious I was to see him at last. Whenever he spoke of him, it was with his old tender smile that we saw so rarely now. He said he wanted to speak to Goodstein and Nica passed him the phone. He was so convincing that Oscar called us back a few minutes later and proposed a new record date for October 22 at the Bell Sound Studios on 54th Street. I wrote to Celia and her mother at their Brooklyn address to invite them to the session. But they were still in North Carolina and the letter came back a few days later.

Ornette came to see us one day with Margareta and I took the opportunity to interview him about his life and his music. His musical conceptions were still a mystery to me despite our close friendship. I considered him a composer of genius. He presented himself as a humble researcher, regretting only that he couldn't pursue his ideas of composition in the course of his own improvisations.

Bernard Stollman came around nearly every day. To hear him tell it, he was going to do great things for Bud, including pay all his medical debts, thanks to unpaid royalties. He, Bernard Stollman, chairman of ESP records, would make it his business to get to the bottom of the whole mixed-up situation. He spoke so fervently that Bud signed a power of attorney authorizing him to do any necessary investigation in his name. I saw nothing wrong with this, so I gave Bud my okay. Stollman composed the following letter which Bud signed on October 24, 1964:

Dear Mr. Stollman:

    You are hereby retained as my sole attorney, with an absolute and un-conditional power of attorney, and with the sole and exclusive authority to act as my professional agent and personal representative in all matters re-lating to my professional career as a composer and performing artist.

    . . . You are requested to provide reproductions of this retainer agree-ment to all individuals and firms presently engaged in the exploitation and use of my original compositions and my recorded performances.

Wasting no time, Stollman had gotten things under way to take Bud's affairs in hand. He sent letters to Maxwell T. Cohen, Oscar Goodstein, and Broadcast Music to inform them of the new arrangements. Now we had to wait for their reactions and hope it would bring results, this time the jackpot for sure!

At the same time, with speed that resembled haste, Stollman offered me a contract concerning the tapes I had made of Bud. This contract, in Bud's name, specified that I would have a thirty percent share of the percentages. That was his first mistake. He had never taken me seriously when I expressed my position (though I tried to make it extremely clear) that I neither had nor wanted to have any financial share of Bud's work.

Meanwhile, Margareta was back with Bud and they seemed happy, so I could relax a little again. I had gotten in the habit of staying up all night listening to Nica's fabulous stories and I learned the true version of a lot of famous anecdotes that have passed on to posterity with the usual distortion. I plied Nica with questions about Charlie Parker, Bud, Thelonious, Coltrane, and Art Blakey, and also about Teddy Wilson, Mary Lou Williams, Sonny Clarke, and many more. Nica had tales to tell about them, and also about many other figures of jazz. She remembered names and dates and places with astonishing accuracy and a wealth of detail. Her memory is a veritable treasure house and with her critical eye, her infallible ear, and unfailing wit, she painted for me a unique and utterly memorable fresco of the music world. Guided by her innate sense of beauty, she was for so many jazzmen, at one and the same time, their friend, patron, fan, confidant, and protector. This was confirmed by Bird, Blakey, Bud, and Thelonious, all of whom were among her closest friends.

One afternoon Thelonious showed up at Nica's in a state of excitement unusual for such a calm man. His eyes were shooting daggers and he couldn't sit still. When Nica asked what it was all about, he said he'd just heard that one of his children had brought a Beatles record into the house. He had searched the apartment and hadn't found it, but that only made him madder. Nica later told me that at the children's request, she had hidden the record at her house. Poor Thelonious! What a terrible blow for an artist like him, a musician who existed in the world of music almost as the archetype of extreme artistic integrity.

The record date finally came. Oscar got there first, accompanied by Morris Levy, manager of Roulette. They both seemed relieved to see Bud looking well. Then John Ore, the bassist hired for the session, arrived with his friends, followed by J. C. Moses wearing his perpetual sneer. As soon as he saw J. C., Bud froze and his eyes grew hard. I noticed it instantly and tried to divert his attention with some inconsequential remark. He ignored my comment, pointed his finger at J. C., and declared in no uncertain terms, "I won't play with him!"

Knowing how stubborn Bud could be, I had a vision of the complications that were about to rain down on us. Oscar saw that something was wrong and came over to inquire. It didn't seem to be the moment to launch into a long explanation of the conflict with J. C., so I eluded the question with a vague, "It's nothing, Oscar. It'll be all right."

Bud, still glaring at J. C., repeated, "I won't play with him." He sounded like he meant it.

"Listen Bud, you just played with him for weeks at Birdland. What's the matter now?" said Oscar, in consternation.

J. C. had noticed us talking and the rhythm section was already beginning to grumble. All at once, I had a brainstorm. Turning to Oscar, I said quietly, "Bud thinks J. C. plays too loud." (Which, indeed, had always been true.)

"Well, if that's all it is," he said with relief, "the engineer can fix it up with soundproof partitions so Bud won't be bothered by it."

Bud was so surprised by what I had said that he didn't answer. When Oscar had gone and I begged him to accept this solution, he looked resigned and said, without enthusiasm, "Okay, Francis, it'll be all right."

The sound engineers had already set up an opaque screen with a window at eye level. They moved the piano into position and started placing all the mikes. Morris Levy signaled me to join him in the booth. Just at that moment, I became aware that on the terrace adjoining the studio, a party was going on. I heard people laughing and the unmistakable sounds of glasses and bottles. One glance at Bud showed me he had heard it, too. But Morris had some important things to ask me.

"Francis, do you know what tunes Bud's going to be doing?"

I took out the list Bud and I had made, trying to remember the dates of the numbers previously recorded. A voice on the loudspeaker was asking the musicians for some sounds and I looked around frantically for Bud. He wasn't in the studio. I ran to the terrace and there he was, coming back into the room, wiping his mouth on the back of his hand. He took a few steps toward me and I could see that his walk was already unsteady and his eyes had lost their clarity. I felt my world cave in again. Meanwhile, J. C. was tuning up his drums and avoiding my eyes, as John Ore waited stoically for the hostilities to commence.

I prayed that Goodstein and Morris Levy wouldn't notice. The chief engineer asked for another test on the piano and Bud sat down with a casual air. He laid his head on his arm, which was resting on the edge of the piano, and tinkled a few notes with his left hand. The engineer asked again for a little more sound. Bud shook off his torpor and played, this time with greater authority. I was in a cold sweat, waiting for them to begin. Bud was looking over at J. C. with an expression of disgust on his face. Just then, a photographer came in to shoot some pictures. He asked me to sit down next to Bud on the piano bench for a few shots and Bud, like a pro, made an effort to smile. When the photos were finished I started to stand up but Bud stopped me, "No, stay there, Francis, please."

Oscar noticed the gesture and gave me a nod as he brought over a chair. The engineer called for silence and the session began. From the exposition of the first theme, I knew that at this moment Bud was far from his usual assurance. The articulation of the phrasing was hesitant and he started to perspire heavily. By the first chorus, the pulse was there, even if it was a little slow.

Whew! The machine had started up. Sitting close by, I heard clearly the muffled grunting sounds that accompanied his improvisations. He moved his lips constantly as if he was chewing gum. It was fascinating to be so close at such a moment. I was perspiring as much as he, as if I were involved in his efforts. I felt that he was summoning up his last bit of strength, fighting against the numbing effects of the alcohol he had just consumed. The masterly fingering I had always admired was still there. I knew the importance of finding the ideal fingering in classical music, and for Bud there was no doubt that he had his own down to perfection in the flawless execution of his magnificent phrases.

The session went smoothly, except for a few weak starts in the fast numbers. After the break at the end of the first chorus, when they started improvising, the music got going, even if it was a little shaky. For me, this recording proved that chaos had returned, the chaos I remembered all too well from the days when Bud had nothing to believe in and his mind was muddled by drink and Largactyl. I tried to help him out until the end, giving him encouraging looks each time his searching eyes met mine. The others seemed satisfied with the best of the takes and we left the studio with a great sense of relief. I said goodbye to Oscar, who handed over the plane tickets, while Bud, seething with impatience, waited in the doorway.

I couldn't avoid reflecting that this disappointing session, which came out under the title *The Return of Bud Powell*, would remain for posterity the only illustration of this specific moment in his musical life. Fans and critics alike would have nothing else to go on but this record, in order to judge his music of this period, at least as long as the more luminous moments, captured forever on my tapes, remained in my private domain.

Another reservation had been made for an Air France flight for the morning of October 27. I could think of nothing else. I felt as if I were coming out of a long, dark tunnel. Marshall invited us for one last evening at his house and then Nica picked us up to take us back to New Jersey. I didn't want to leave before Bud had a chance to say goodbye to Frances and Celia, so I sent a telegram notifying them of our departure.

The last four days were spent peacefully at Nica's, together with Barry Harris. Bud was relaxed and Margareta came every night. Our bags were packed, I couldn't wait to get back and finally see my son. By the last day, Frances had still not been in touch. I was getting worried when the phone rang late in the afternoon. Frances announced she was coming that evening with her sister and Celia.

I was glad things were finally working out, despite the disastrous events of recent days. Of course, I still owed Goodstein $42, despite his fit of altruism. I also owed money to Nica and Marshall, but as soon as I was back in Paris I could pay them back with no problem. We would go back penniless but glad to have gotten off no worse than that. I had made some wonderful friends and had experienced some moments of incredible intensity. I had shipped back hours and hours of tapes. These tapes, I knew, would one day benefit those who were entitled to them. Bud's rights of succession were complicated to say the least, but in 1979 I left the entire collection to his daughter Celia, in an attestation witnessed by my trusted friend Max Roach and in front of his lawyer Ed Howard, who later handled the estate of Jimi Hendrix and who has always staunchly defended the rights of blacks.

In making this legacy I think I honestly respected Bud's wishes. He recognized Celia as his daughter in 1965 (which he had been unable to do while he was hospitalized at Creedmoor). He always told me he regarded her as his only child. This was in no way a position against Buttercup's son Johnny, whom I never held responsible for his mother's actions. Today Celia is the only person who can decide what is to be done with the original tapes. I would add that all Celia's kind attempts to reach a compromise with Johnny regarding rights and royalties have come to nothing. The result of all this is to keep up a permanent conflict, so that the American government periodically collects the unpaid royalties which, after a certain time limit, fall into the public domain. And the curse goes on . . .

The eventful years I lived through with Bud enhanced my understanding of the man and his music, an understanding, however elusive or incommunicable, that continues to grow with the inexorable passage of time. This is perhaps the one, the only, privilege that makes it worthwhile growing old.

Bernard Stollman was announcing happy days ahead for Bud. He was going to see to it that Bud would be able to enjoy the use of his royalties, so that we could go back feeling like we'd accomplished something. We had taken leave of our friends, now Bud would say goodbye to Celia and Frances, and all would be in order. It seemed to me we had acted honorably and had done the best we could.

Celia, Frances, and her sister didn't arrive until ten at night, just as we were beginning to give up hope. Frances's sister hadn't seen Bud since they were teenagers and they struck up a very lively conversation. With great verve, she brought up a host of exciting memories and anecdotes, and Bud eagerly drank in her words. The stories seemed to revive the memory of the good days when he could still hope for personal happiness and a brilliant career. He was obviously very moved, spurring her to remember more and more details. Frances added her recollections too, as she got into the spirit of the thing.

"Hey Bud, do you remember so and so? And cousin what's his name? And remember how you loved those baked beans I used to make . . . ?"

As time went on and the reminiscences never seemed to end, I wondered, with some resentment, why couldn't they have taken place a little bit before, two months earlier, for example? During his whole Birdland date, with the exception of the single visit of Frances and Celia, not one family member had ever come to hear him. Now, after midnight, everyone suddenly felt like talking to him! We were due to leave early in the morning—it didn't give us much time to sleep. Margareta was silent and Nica started to yawn. Suddenly, Frances's sister, who was obviously the leader of it all, said reproachfully to Bud, as if reprimanding a child, "Hey, how come you're goin' away? Why not stay a little with us? We've hardly had the time to see each other . . . " Then, to me, "It's true, you know. Bud could stay with us for a while. After all, we're his real family."

Bud gave me a questioning look, but didn't say a word. After all we'd been through, I didn't know what I could possibly say to this woman, who was so convinced of the truth of what she said. I felt paralyzed and Bud took on his old submissive look. One thing was certain in my mind—we had to leave New York without delay, but at that moment, I was incapable of saying a word. In any case, what right did I have to oppose their suggestion? Bud himself seemed hesitant. These two women with their flood of words, the wonderful memories they recalled and the hopeful prospects they implied had completely shaken his resolve. The idea had been tossed out and now there was a heavy silence.

"Bud is free to do what he wants," I said at last, exhausted. "But I think it would be good for him to go back to France as soon as possible." Bud looked at me hard, obviously in great conflict. "Bud, you know we put off our trip several times already. Now our money's run out and I have to go home. I want to see my baby. Nicole is waiting and I have to go back to work."

"Okay Francis, but do you think I could at least spend the night with them?"

It was very late. I could see that Margareta, Nica, and Barry all looked glum. "Bud, you do what you want. Just remember that tomorrow morning you have to be on time. The plane leaves at ten o'clock sharp."

Bud seemed pleased and, with a childlike smile, said, "I'll be there, Francis. I promise, I'll be there."

So it was decided. Within minutes, they got ready to leave. The women said goodbye to everyone and I kissed Bud good night, as I did every night. But I was overcome by a sudden wave of sadness.

"See you tomorrow, brother, at the airport."

"See you tomorrow, Bud. I'll take your suitcase and your ticket and I'll see you there."

"Okay. Bonne nuit."

The night was short and full of anguish. I couldn't sleep. Nica wasn't very happy about the evening, Margareta didn't say a word, and Barry kept telling me to be patient and not give up hope. In the early hours of the morning I said my farewells to Nica, telling her she needn't worry about taking me to the airport, as Barry was going to accompany me for this last and final trial.

It was a gloomy morning. A thin cold rain was falling and our taxi crawled in the dense morning traffic on the highway. Barry and I were both silent, each of us probably thinking the same thing—how slim our chances were of finding Bud at the airport. Suddenly the infernal traffic came to a complete stop and we remained stuck for over half an hour. We had left well in advance but now as the time ticked by, I grew more and more nervous. We now saw all the signs of a major accident: ambulances going by, then a fire truck and a number of police cars, their lights flashing and sirens blaring. After an hour, the traffic started moving again and a few miles further on we saw the burned-out cars still smoking by the side of the road. This nightmarish vision added to the nausea that I was already feeling in the pit of my stomach.

I was sure I'd missed my flight and the thought was strangely comforting. This last blow would give me one last chance to find Bud. At best, I was sure he'd be late. Perhaps this accident would turn out to be a blessing in disguise. At the airport, the loudspeakers were announcing a two-hour delay because of it. I could breathe again, convinced that it hadn't been blind chance at all, but would in fact help solve all our problems.

I checked my baggage at the last minute. Barry, still calm, continued to keep an eye on all the taxis pouring in in front of the terminal building in the hope of catching sight of Bud.

The last call for boarding was announced. With a firm gesture, Barry nodded in the direction of the escalator. I looked at him in despair, then without a word, clasped him in my arms, feeling I was leaving behind a brother, my brother in the music of Bud.

I handed over Bud's suitcase and ticket and also gave him the prescriptions for the medication that Bud would have to keep taking regularly. To gain another few minutes, I repeated my instructions about Bud's health. The minutes ticked dangerously by. The escalators leading to the boarding zone were empty by now and with sinking heart and tears in my eyes, I finally forced myself to leave. The control tower had to radio the pilot and the plane returned to the gate to let me on board.

Deep down, I had always known Bud wouldn't come, but I had refused to listen to the inner voice.

The flight was endless. My heart was broken and my body crushed as well in the jam-packed plane. The homeward trip that I had so desired had turned into a nightmare and as the hours passed I sank deeper into gloom and misery.

In the arrival terminal I quickly spotted Nicole, my father, my sister, all the friends and the whole *Jazz Hot* crowd. Their faces fell when they saw I was alone. As for me, I couldn't talk and their questions went unanswered. Between the reality of the situation and my certainty that Bud should have come home with me, there was a mountain of incoherent events and inexpressible regrets.

We got back home and I had my first look at my infant son, a tiny bundle, all wrapped up and fast asleep. A wave of love and tenderness swept over me, but it was soon followed by a second wave, of pain this time, as I thought of Bud, somewhere over there . . .

TEMPUS FUGUE-IT

(Recorded in New York, May 1949 [Verve])

I went back to work at once and threw myself totally into my job, to try to block out the host of useless questions preying on my mind. I had come out of a long, dark night to find all my problems just as I'd left them, among others, the sanatorium bills, which I started paying again by installments.

The first news from New York was a letter from Bernard Stollman. It was dated October 10, and he had written in French. "Mon cher Francis," he began. He said he'd heard the bad news about Bud from Nica and was in touch with Margareta, who was planning to see Bud and bring him the medication he needed. He promised to keep me posted and added that "destiny" had now freed me from my role as Bud's protector. Then he returned to the subject of my tapes and our plans to issue a record based on them, asking for my suggestions and promising me once again a share of the profits. He said he planned to be in Paris around Christmas.

I was glad he was coming to Paris. The idea that together we would work out a strategy for Bud's future gave me renewed confidence. From the old tapes I had recorded in Paris, I tried to compile a selection of pieces by Monk. The parcel from America sent through UNESCO channels took two and a half months to arrive and by the time it came I was worried sick. I wrote to Stollman suggesting a list of tunes and explaining once again my position as far as Bud was concerned. "Mon cher Bernard: . . . There is something here that seems to escape you. My role in Bud's affairs is purely amicable. All I want is to know that Bud is in good health and that he is living in good conditions. Please try to give me some precise information, as you promised. . . ."

His answer distressed me deeply. His casual tone in describing his last visit to Bud made it quite clear to me how unaware he was (he wasn't the only one, alas!) of what was at stake. He described the two-hour visit with Mary Frances as amiable. Bud, he said, came out of the bedroom at one point to join the conversation. Stollman described Bud as healthy and having lost twenty pounds—"Slim but vigorous," he wrote. And although he reported Mary Frances saying that Bud's diet was quite good—drinking a quart of milk a day and eating a lot of meat and fruit—he mentioned that Bud was drinking half a bottle of whiskey a day at home, and that sometimes he'd walk down the street to a neighborhood bar, but he found his way home without problems.

Stollman expressed every confidence in Mary Frances's caretaking. He wrote of his desire to continue in his efforts on Bud's behalf, so sure was he of Bud's health. He even mentioned Oscar Goodstein's offer to meet him and discuss Bud's business affairs. And he closed his letter with real bonhomie toward me: "I'm happy to have a real pal in Paris."

The writer of these words was far from realizing the dangers of alcohol for someone who has had tuberculosis. I wrote to Frances and Celia but got no answer. Margareta, on the other hand, wrote immediately. Her letter showed how concerned she really was.

New York, December 7, 1964

Dear Francis,

Your letter brought tears to my eyes, I think it is the most beautiful letter I have ever received. I read it over and over again . . .

I haven't really been doing very much worth telling you since you left except seeing Bud. I try to go and see him every Sunday and have been there three times. The first time I went was a very bad experience for me. Bud looked very tired and not well at all and I must say I didn't like it at all. He didn't talk, only smoked and asked for money. He said he was in debt. But I knew why he wanted the money so I didn't give him any. The people he lives with don't seem to have much money and they cannot afford to buy him anything. But they say he eats well and they give him the medicine every day, according to your instructions.

I was so sad and upset that I called Bernard Stollman just to let him know that something had to be done. He said he was going to call you to ask you if you would take him back to Paris. But I suggested that he himself went down [sic] to Brooklyn to see Bud. I told Bernard to let Frances know he was coming.

Bernard called me a couple of days later and told me the exact opposite of what I had told him. He said Bud looked just fine, clean, he had had a haircut, he was shaved, wore a white shirt and so on. Evidently they had tried everything possible to make a good impression, I thought. But of course I was very glad to hear that Bud was well.

The next Sunday Ornette and I went down to see him. I told Ornette that I had just received your letter and he told me that he also had received one and was very happy about it. Well, that visit was different and

I must say that I was glad to see Bud looking so well. Of course he wanted to have something to drink. Frances told me that he goes to a bar around the corner once in a while to have a beer or two, so Ornette and I said OK and went there with him. . . . He didn't talk much so I tried to carry on a conversation with him. I asked him questions such as: How is everything? Are you happy? What do you do during the days? The answer to that question was: "Nothing." I felt like shaking him hard, very hard just to put some life into him. But I can't do anything for him right now. The only thing I can do is to see him as often as possible . . .

. . . I know Oscar Goodstein wants him to play there [Birdland] weekends! This is what Bernard told me! I know that Birdland is not the right place for Bud. Tell me, Francis, what do you say about that?

Another thing I must tell you is that I don't know if I trust Bernard very much. He might be a good lawyer but I'm sure he doesn't do much to help Bud. He has told me he has found quite a bit of money. Then I ask myself: "Why don't you take him to the doctor and let him go through a thorough examination?" Just to make sure Bud IS alright!

Bernard called me last week and suggested we meet. Naturally, I thought he would take me to dinner so we could talk about Bud. He and his mother picked me up outside the office. They told me they were moving their offices and wanted me to come and see them. I went there with them and after a couple of hours Bernard asked me if I was hungry. Then I was ready to leave, already. I told Bernard I wasn't very hungry but of course it would be nice to have something. So he said goodbye to his mother and we left. But first he wanted me to see his room. I thought nothing of it and went with him. It was a very small room with just a big bed. He asked me if I wanted an apple! An apple! By then I started to get a little angry but tried not to show it to him. Instead I started to ask questions about what he has been able to do regarding the Genius of Bud Powell. To me it seems he has done hardly nothing. Instead he started telling me I was attractive, tried to caress my hand and to take me into his arms. After I had refused three or four times I told him that I had better go home and asked him to take me to the subway station. He thought I was pretty strange, naturally, but I was disgusted, almost, and very angry, and very, very disappointed. . . . If he at least had bought me a dinner or a drink I would have forgiven him, but this was so very cheap, Francis. Maybe, I said, maybe he is a good lawyer, but I don't trust his interest in Bud . . .

Stollman's next letter, dated December 19, shed new light on the situation. His version and Margareta's were so contradictory that I couldn't help feeling, aside from his interest in my tapes, that his letters were merely intended to allay suspicion. He said that he had only good news to report. He expressed in upbeat terms Margareta's Sunday visits to Bud, and claimed that she said he was in good spirits, often pleading with her not to leave. Stollman also said the press had reviewed the Roulette record favorably and that sales of it were very good. After mentioning that the papers "talk a lot about Bud," he asked for tapes of *Bud Plays Monk* and demanded that I take action immediately: "Don't wait for my visit," he wrote.

In early January 1965, I got a letter from Ornette, who also tried to write in French with the help of a dictionary. His syntax would have amused me greatly if the news about Bud hadn't been so alarming. He spelled my name phonetically, just the way he used to pronounce it. "*Cher Frahn Swalz ...*" In his broken French he tried to tell me that he'd seen Bud and felt he was unhappy, though Frances did her best. He needed rest and peace of mind, a piano, some money and most of all, an honest friend. He missed us and all the Paris gang. The signature read, "God bless you, Live and Love, Ornette."

There was nothing more I could do for Bud directly. Now I tried to learn how to laugh again, taking care of the baby. I could devote a lot of time to him as I was still working at home. He was becoming aware of things around him and beginning to react to music. His peals of laughter had a way of punctuating the syncopations.

Then came the news that Birdland had closed. An important page in history had been turned. (It later reopened.)

I wrote again to Stollman, reiterating the recommendations I had made to everyone and saying that, to my mind, all his promises had put him in a position of responsibility (at least from a material point of view) since the power of attorney Bud had signed gave him both the right and the duty to act independently.

> ... I am very happy to have news of Bud, but do you think things are as good as you say they are? As you have occasion to meet Bud often, as well as the people who are taking care of him, please be kind enough to remind them of the medical conditions which will keep Bud in good health (and I say "good health" when I should really be saying "survival" considering the seriousness of his illness): he should absolutely not drink! After the things I learned from you, from Margareta and from Ornette, who just wrote to me recently, it seems that Bud is drinking way too much. So, Bernard, this is very important, as the doctors (who were the very best we could find in Europe) were very, very positive and firm about this and considered that drinking would absolutely kill him.
>
> It is a grave responsibility and I ask you to seriously consider it because of the importance of Bud as a person, and because of the results which I had personally obtained by getting him to lead a different life simply by

means of friendship and love. Ornette told me that he had seen Bud and that undeniably he is extremely unhappy. Margareta said the same thing.

. . . Bernard, I speak to you as a friend and man to man. I am sure that you will use good judgment in this serious situation. Be just. Do not hesitate, if your conscience tells you to, to cut short Bud's stay in the States. You know that Bud will always have a place here, and that we would accept him in an environment and under conditions which have proven that Bud is not yet ready to die.

Bud is one of the most important persons of our time, one who has brought a great deal to the world in which we all live, and I think that everyone who has an opportunity to help him in this grave situation ought absolutely to do everything they humanly can . . .

My dear Bernard, please excuse this long letter. I was compelled by my worries . . . Please send me an answer soon. I await your letter with impatience. I hope you have a very Merry Christmas . . .

Babs Gonzales also wrote, but his news wasn't great and despite the lack of detail I could detect a lot of bitterness and a desire to spare me the worst.

Then I received a letter from Dr. Joussaume, confirming receipt of my final check. The sanatorium bill was now paid in full. At least that part was over!

A very sweet letter came on March 12, 1965, from Toshiko Akiyoshi. She had seen Bud. "I saw Bud my first night in New York. He was very happy to see me. He was starting Birdland that night. I heard he got fired the next day, but I don't know why."

The news I got from Margareta a few days later was far from encouraging. She sounded depressed and pessimistic:

Dear, dear Francis,

. . . Bud . . . He is a BIG problem as far as his future is concerned, musically. He does not seem to want to have anything more to do with it. The only person he wants to play for is me when I am there. And I am not offering him any drinks for playing for me. They (the people he lives with) tell me that he only wants to play if somebody offers him a drink, but I have told them that it is dangerous to do so, because Bud is not allowed to drink because of his health. Somehow they have come to understand it because lately they only give him a can of beer. I know it is hard for them to look after him all the time, and especially when he is not in the apartment, and I certainly have no way of doing it now. I go to see him as often as I can but how am I going to be able to continue? . . .

It finally dawned on Stollman that I wasn't being fooled by his optimistic reports on Bud's health, for his next letter was less reassuring.

He wrote in English this time and the tone was more formal. It was no longer "Bud," it was "Mr. Powell." This was now the official attorney who was writing, describing a recalcitrant client whose "usual habits" had Stollman "greatly alarmed."

After mentioning Bud's depression and the two aborted Birdland engagements, for which Goodstein refused to pay Mary Frances, he returned to his old demand for the *Bud Plays Monk* tapes. Now he brought "Nika," as he called her, into the picture, claiming that she, too, was eager for the tapes.

Stollman "discussed with Mr. Powell at great length" his plans for the tapes, which included my retaining a 25 percent interest in the music as well my getting a "certain sum" for each master I edited. He offered me a payment of $500 as an advance against my earnings from sales, and he offered to send another $500 to the hospital to pay Bud's bills. He then asked me to send him a copy of the outstanding hospital bill, claiming that Bud wanted to see it.

Apparently, even at a distance of thousands of miles, he seemed to think I was the only one who could arrange Bud's future. We were far from the miracles he had promised four months ago. He went on to urge me to send him the unreleased music, "as you love your friend . . . help him now." He felt that if we worked quickly to issue the recordings, "Mr. Powell can live comfortably, without anxiety."

He persisted in thinking that offering me money would speed up our projects, and all of a sudden, he was greatly concerned about the sanatorium bill. I had told him the bill was paid and now he was pretending that he didn't know.

In his previous letter, Stollman had admitted that Bud had a bad cough and was incapable of playing in public. Yet he didn't hesitate to book him at Carnegie Hall a week later in a tribute to Charlie Parker. His daughter Celia told me much later that she and her mother had accompanied Bud to this concert. Bud wanted Frances to wear a tiara for the occasion and to persuade her he had said, in a fleeting moment of humor, "It's perfect. You'll look like a queen. I'm playing at Carnegie Hall and you'll be queen."

Before the concert, Bud asked the technicians to set up a chair in the wings facing the piano but invisible from the audience, so that Frances could sit and watch him play. This unusual situation intrigued the backstage crew and they kept asking who was the lady in the tiara. "Who is it? Who can she be?"

"She's the queen," said Bud, simply.

According to several observers, including Dizzy Gillespie, the *Down Beat* critics, and Don Schlitten (who that night shot the last photos of Bud ever taken in public), Bud was nothing but a shadow of himself.

The New York Times wrote: "... Mr. Powell ... was barely able to force out enough of the effort necessary to laboriously complete the three songs he had chosen. 'We would have preferred not to be here!' said a noted critic in private ..."

I could imagine it only too well. It was heartbreaking. In the past, when things were bad, I had always tried to preserve Bud's reputation by preventing him from making a spectacle of himself. But even this appalling incident didn't diminish Stollman's poise and optimism. On April 2, this time by registered letter, he gave me an upbeat account of this pathetic performance, claiming that the audience's "tumultuous ovation" and his reunions backstage with Coleman Hawkins and Dizzy Gillespie had raised his morale. Although he admitted that Bud had been depressed, he cited a performance for children and the Carnegie Hall Concert as evidence that his good humor was returning. Stollman felt the key to further improvement was Bud's maintaining a good appetite and cutting down on his smoking.

He was still trying to get my tapes. His insistence was beginning to sound more like an order than a request. He now claimed that "Earl Rudolph 'Bud' Powell," as he wrote in the letter, was asking Stollman to "get him some recompense for his contribution of music ... during these past twenty years." Stollman wrote that Bud had signed to him all rights to all of his performances that I had taped. The letter was full of legalese.

It all seemed more and more dubious. He went on tirelessly offering me financial deals on any future productions. It's unbelievable how some people, whose only goal in life is to make money, will stubbornly refuse to see that there are other things in life, other aims, other priorities. They cannot understand that some things, valuable though they may be, are simply not for sale!

I continued to receive alarming news from people who were genuinely worried about Bud. On April 5, Toshiko wrote from New York where she had just returned:

Dear Francis,

... Guess what! The day I arrived in N.Y.C. Charles had a record date. So I went to a movie with my former bassist Gene Cherico. And after the movie, we stopped over at a coffee shop and who do you think we saw?

Bud!! He opened that night at Birdland. He was very happy to see me. But I am afraid that he is having a lot of problems. I feel terribly sad about him . . .

Most of the time, Bud hung around his neighborhood in Brooklyn, going from bar to bar, trying to cadge drinks as he used to in Paris. His favorite hangout was the Melrose Lounge, right near his house, where the owner, warned by Frances, negotiated the number of beers he was allowed. The rest of the time, he sat in a park across the street, enveloped in his eternal solitude. When Celia came home from school they would go back to the apartment together. Sometimes, he looked over her schoolwork and for these few privileged moments found a part of his lucidity again. Thanks to the new family situation, Celia was able to get the financial assistance she needed to continue her studies. Now that Bud had formally recognized her, Celia, who had known the hardship of growing up without a father, could now, for the first time, benefit a little from his presence. Buttercup, who of course knew of her existence, did all she could till the end of her life to keep her out of the picture and deprive her of what was rightfully hers.

DRY SOUL

(Recorded in New York, May 28, 1958 [Blue Note])

The long stretch of bad news seemed never to end. On March 3, 1965, the ultimate tragedy struck: at the age of six months our baby died. This was the beginning of a long nightmare, an endless night in which I lost all my desire to live. Nicole and I separated, torn apart by the cruel blow and by the meddling of the in-laws. To make it even more painful, Nicole was already pregnant with another very much wanted baby. This period left a gaping hole in my life, like a savage wound.

The months of torment passed and I slowly began to emerge. Even if I couldn't heal the incurable wound, once again, just as it had done once before in Algeria during that other terrible period, music saved my life.

In the meantime, Bud was not getting any better. I wrote to Stollman for the last time on May 6, 1965.

Dear Bernard,

I was most surprised to receive your last letter, and by registered mail, to boot, which sounded to me more like a legal brief than a friendly letter. Let me remind you once again, Bernard, that all our conversations and any proposals I made concerning Bud came out of pure friendship, with no commercial designs on my part. I devoted a good part of my life to helping Bud and everything that I did was done for no other motive than defending his interests.

Throughout our correspondence, I have appealed to you again and again as the sole person now responsible for Bud's affairs in the United States. I must point out with disappointment and regret that my appeals have gone unanswered. You will note that your previous letter dates back to December 1964.

According to your last letter, you have now found a source of revenue in Bud's past works. I fail to understand, in that case, why you didn't answer me or Alan Bates or Jean Tronchot, who also wrote to you.

You can stop worrying about the Bouffemont bills, too. I have finished paying them in full, as you can see from the enclosed receipt signed by the director of the sanatorium.

By this time Art Taylor had returned to New York. I begged him to help, asking him to inquire personally about Bud's health and general situation. I knew that with his long experience, I could take his opinion seriously. His reply came in the form of two letters.

May 7, 1965

Dear Francis,

I received your letter today and was very happy to hear from you. I have not seen Bud as yet but I hear he is not doing very well. I will try to see him in the next few days and will write you when I do. Things are about the same here in New York as when I left 2 years ago only much sadder . . .

May 17, 1965

Dear Francis,

I hope this note finds you and your wife well. Things for me here in New York are as good as can be expected . . .

Well, I went to see Bud one day last week and he was drunk so I did not stay because it was impossible to talk to him. I will not go to see him again unless you wish that I do so. I don't think he knew me and has a bad cough. I wish I could give you some good news but there is not much of that at this time. Tell Johnny [Griffin] he better stay over there because it is sad here. Well, Francis, that is all I can think of now. I just tried to call Nica but got no answer. Hope to hear from you soon.

Your friend,
Art Taylor

CASKET IN THE SEA

(Recorded in New York, May 1, 1965 [unreleased])

T hough Bud was more and more exhausted, Stollman nevertheless scheduled a concert at Town Hall for May 1, 1965. According to Don Schlitten, Bud struggled desperately to remain seated
at the piano. For the last time in public, he gave the hideous image of
a man at the edge of an abyss. He had somehow found the strength
to compose a new tune, prophetically entitled "Casket in the Sea."
Stollman recorded it for his company, ESP Disk, but I heard shortly
afterward that the sound engineer had destroyed the tapes. This was
never confirmed, but in fact no recording of this concert ever came
out. Stollman, who was responsible for Bud's unfortunate appearance
at Town Hall, started harassing me again on September 29, 1965,
apologizing for not keeping me informed, and claiming he had done
what he could for Bud, though he got a mere $250 from Blue Note
Records in addition to the Town Hall concert fee. That was the extent
of his success in charge of Bud's affairs. He continued to promise
great things, through his record label ESP.

Stollman remained hopeful as well about Bud's personal situation.
But he itemized material things Bud needed, and again he stressed
how the sale of records could take care at everything. He reiterated
his desire to get Bud's sanatorium bill from me, assuring me that ESP
would pay it in full in exhange for "our understanding concerning Mr.
Powell's tapes . . ."

I had last written Stollman five months before but had heard nothing from him. Now, though he couldn't help Bud financially, he was
still talking about paying the hospital bills. The ridiculous contradic-
tion was so glaring I made up my mind once and for all that he was
untrustworthy and unreliable.

The letters now were few and far between. At last Randi Hultin
brought some fresh news. She had received a letter from Stollman,
whom she had never heard of before, who was looking for work for
Cecil Taylor:

> He told me that Bud was supposed to start at Birdland. In my reply I
> asked him to say hello to Bud for me. Then he wrote me back to tell me
> that he had been very disappointed because this was the first time he had

listened to Bud in person and he had found him so strange . . . especially the way that he moved his head. He added, "But when I closed my eyes I really heard some beauty." I was so irritated that I wrote to him right away, saying, "But why didn't you close your eyes from the very beginning?" . . .

She later read in *Down Beat* that the same lawyer had recorded Bud in a studio the past fall. Thelonious, whom she'd met when he was passing through Oslo, told her that when the session was over, they gave Bud $75 and left him alone in the street. This was confirmed by another friend, the trumpeter Dizzy Reese, who ran into Bud that day and took him home to Brooklyn.

The next thing I knew, Stollman's brother was in Paris with a letter annoucing that he was now general manager of ESP. Bernard Stollman had delegated his brother to obtain my tapes, adding that Bud had "fully authorized and empowered" him to do so. He ended the letter expressing his delight in my being on the verge of reaping financial benefits for the years I spent with Bud.

He made one last attempt—this time the emissary was his mother! You can't say he didn't try everything, but it got him nowhere. I was sorry I had ever trusted him. Letting Bud sign the power of attorney seemed to me now a great mistake.

More news came in a letter from our friend Alan Bates, who had made *Bud at Home* and *The Invisible Cage*. He was passing through New York and knowing how worried I was, he promised to look up Bud. This was the terrible blow I had always known would come one day or another:

Wednesday, Nov. 10, 1965

Dear Francis:

. . . Great news! I found Bud. He is in Kings County Hospital, Kings Park, Long Island, N.Y. This is a mental hospital to which Bud was taken about five weeks ago. At this time he "arrested" Frances for allegedly killing a rat in the apartment in Brooklyn. He told her that he did not know she could kill and that he would have to arrest her. So Bud insisted that they go to the police station. Frances went so that she could get some help with Bud. Of course they had him examined and he was sent to King's County for an indefinite period.

Kings County is a HUGE institution with 10,300 patients, many of whom have spent most of their lives there. Bud is in a ward with about thirty other men, although some of the more violent cases have their own rooms (or cells). It is like an "easy" prison. The doors are always locked and you cannot escape.

Margareta was the one who told me where Bud was. She and I went out there on Sunday and spent four hours with Bud. Frances was there too. Stollman was supposed to come but did not show up, much to Margareta's disgust, as she had reserved a place in the limousine for him. He did not even phone to say that he was not coming. What a schmuck.

Bud has lost a lot of weight—at least thirty pounds I would say. I did not know what to expect. Whether he would recognize me. The first thing he said was "Alan Bates! Where's Francis?" Isn't that fantastic! His memory is quite good and he even remembered Itla (Ben's wife) when I told him that she was dead.

He said, "Hey Alan, have you come to get me out of here?" Of course I wanted to know if he could still play and if he had still the desire to play. He has. I asked the doctor to take us to the piano and Bud played for thirty minutes. If he can play regularly he can play fantastically again. No question. He has written four new tunes. He plays twice a week in a half-assed band in the joint but I asked the doctor to let Bud have an hour every day at the piano by himself.

He is not getting much special attention, I'm afraid. The place is just too big and the doctors are too busy. His teeth are still a mess but apart from that he looks wonderful.

I had long talks with Margareta and Frances. Frances is a well-meaning woman but she still does not realize the discipline to which Bud must be subjected. She is talking about taking Bud back home and throwing all the kids out, but Margareta thinks that is no good as Bud will still go out, get drunk, and the whole thing will start again.

The doctor told me that he will be in the hospital at least another month. So now of course we have the problem of what happens when he gets out? There is only one answer and you know it as well as I do.

However someone (and I'm pretty sure it's Stollman) has started an anti-Francis campaign saying that you took advantage of Bud and so on. Completely amazing. Margareta says she doesn't know how it started and that she keeps telling everyone they are crazy. Which of course I do too . . .

Margareta and I were talking about the best thing to do. He CANNOT be allowed to stay here. We figure that he will have no work when he comes out (Stollman has done nothing) and therefore if we can fix up a concert or a club engagement over there, there will be every logical reason why he should make the trip. Once over there of course he will never come back here.

So I think we should wait to see when he is going to get out. The stay in Kings County is doing him a lot of good and Margareta and I think he should stay there as long as they feel he is deriving some benefit. Then we should immediately get him back there before the rot has time to set in.

Do you still have his air ticket??? Is it still valid? If so you had better send it to me, I think. In the meantime I'm going to try to get to know Frances better as she has to be made to realize that she has to do what is right for Bud's welfare . . .

For a long time I had been thinking about a trip to New York together with my friend Roger to try to pull Bud out of his terrible decline. My finances were not in the best shape. After paying off the sanatorium I had just managed to wipe out my debts to Nica and Marshall. Roger suggested we put off the trip for a little while.

Alan Bates went to see Bud again and wrote that he was asking for me: "Where's Francis? Where's Francis?" I was heartsick. About five months later, I heard that a journalist friend, Daniel Berger, and the filmmaker Alain Corneau were going to New York. Margareta had written that Bud had lost his passport so I gave them the letters and photos needed to get him a new one. As soon as they arrived, they went to see Bud at Frances's and on April 4, 1966, Daniel wrote:

Dear Francis,

Arrived this morning . . . and we headed immediately for Kingston Avenue to see Frances Barnes. We found Bud in bed at four o'clock in the afternoon, in a dreadful state. Frances had brought him home from the park where he'd passed out on a bench after having had too much to drink. Frances's sister and Celia were there, too, and they gave us a very warm welcome as soon as we mentioned your name.

. . . At least Bud doesn't seem to be on any kind of drugs. Frances says his health is pretty good despite everything, that he is "fruitful" and could still be productive "if someone like Francis could take care of him." . . .

Fruitful indeed! Stollman had tried to set up another recording session with Scotty Holt on bass and Rashied Ali on drums. The record never came out. I can imagine only too well why not. Daniel went on:

We saw Bud's piano, too . . . Every other key is dead and it's practically unusable.

If he wanted to go back to Paris, his family would probably not stand in his way. It's up to you to decide what has to be done. The best thing, obviously, would be if you could come yourself.

P.S. Bud refuses to go to the dentist and Frances says she's going to have to take him by force . . .

At my suggestion Daniel and Alain went to see Miles Davis in the hope of getting some financial help for Bud's return to France. Bud had given Miles his chance at the start of his career and I thought he might be willing to help out now that Bud was in need. Miles's reply was very brief and revealing: "Bud Powell? Who's that?"

A month later, another letter came from Daniel. Now my mind was made up. I had to get over there without a moment's delay:

> I've just left Bud. Margareta and Alain were with me. Since my previous visit last Wednesday, a doctor has been in to see him and prescribed some pills that are supposed to "put him back on his feet." He's not allowed to drink at all, not even a drop of wine. He has started eating again, which he hadn't been doing for over a month. We found him changed, weaker than before, but at the same time in better shape, smiling and more sociable.
>
> . . . I still have to get in touch with Marshall about Margareta's ticket. That is, if she can manage to convince Bud to go back to France, on the pretext of a tour or just a visit (which I admit I wasn't able to do), then she'll have to get on the plane with him.
>
> Bud is due to enter the hospital next Tuesday for a few days, for a drying-out cure, I suppose. I hope it won't last too long.
>
> So that's the latest news. We don't want to come home without Bud . . .

Alas, Daniel and Alain came sadly back to Paris, Budless. Their attempt had failed and they were very disheartened. They brought back a series of photos, awful to behold, that showed only too clearly the appalling state Bud was in. At last the momentous decision was made. Roger called me to say, "Okay, man. Don't worry about a thing. I took a few days off and I've got enough bread for the plane fare. We'll get our asses over there and rescue Bud from the clutches of the Yanks."

After Daniel and Alain's fruitless quest, it was our turn to try. I got hold of the papers for Bud's new passport, finished up my most pressing work obligations (luckily, early July was not such a busy period), and started to think seriously about the best way to get Bud back to France. The trip was closer to a commando raid than a pleasure jaunt. We wouldn't be able to count on the people in New York, most of whom had despaired of helping Bud and had slowly stopped taking an interest in him and his welfare. Several times I even heard rumors of his death and once during a TV news broadcast the well-known French newscaster Léon Zitrone came on with some photos showing Bud and me at home.

I wrote to Margareta to announce we were coming and at just about the same time, got a letter from Anita and Gil Evans, enclosing a press clipping dated July 10, 1966: "The pianist Bud Powell lay critically ill Saturday at Cumberland Hospital. A hospital spokesman said the famous pianist had pneumonia and was 'weakening.' . . . He became ill five days ago."

I felt the earth reel once again. The curse was relentlessly pursuing us. I called Roger to say that we had to delay our departure in the hope of better news.

I had been through hell with Bud, but at that very moment I would have gladly gone through the trials and tribulations all over again just to get him out of this ordeal. His trust, his affection, the intense musical enjoyment he gave me and the lessons of life he taught me—for the rest of my life—they made the difficulties seem minor and inconsequential.

All this time, there had been no word of Buttercup. Now she was back in the news. Without hesitation, she had gone to see Bud in the hospital and had of course taken a photographer with her. A story appeared in *Jet Magazine* (August 18) with three pictures of Buttercup: one in her Paris club with the caption, " . . . singing 'Lover Man,' dedicated to Bud"; another with her son Johnny, in front of a plaque reading Cumberland Hospital, in which she wears a great big smile; and the third, still smiling, holding Bud's skinny hand. Bud has lost a lot of weight, his face is emaciated, and he looks at the camera with despair and resignation. The caption reads, "She left her Paris club to help Bud in his affliction." Buttercup had been back in New York for a year and had never once given any sign of life. Frances and Celia, who had taken care of Bud for two years, would remain anonymous, while Buttercup, who had always maintained her image of loving wife and longtime protectress, would manage in no time to put herself back in the limelight!

When asked why she hadn't accompanied Bud to New York herself, she said that her condition made it impossible, as she was eight months pregnant at the time. This startling assertion was reported by Chris Sheridan in the jacket notes for *Bud Powell at the Golden Circle, vol. 4*. Well, there was one we hadn't thought of!

By mid-July Bud was transferred to Kings County Hospital. When he heard they were planning to give him more shock treatments and knowing the horrendous effects they had on him, he wrote to Frances in a panic. As Frances told me:

> After Bud was transferred to Kings County Hospital, they interviewed him and they decided to do some more shock treatments on him. He refused. And then he sent me a letter saying, "Please come immediately and speak to the doctors. It's about the shock treatments. Did you agree to let

them do that to me again? I'm a writer and a composer, and these treatments are destroying my brain . . . "

So I came right away and I did what he had asked. They didn't give him any shock treatments. In the hospital he wrote a little bit . . . "Casket In The Sea." This was about a dream he had had while he was there. He wanted his body to be buried at sea. And his last piece was done to a poem called "Eternity." Francis, I want you to look at this poem, because I have this feeling that it was for you . . .

(Frances told me that she had found this last poem on Bud's bed table the evening he passed away.)

It's true, of course, a large public institution can rarely take into consideration who their patients are. This anecdote, recalled by Max Cohen, is a good illustration:

> . . . When Bud was admitted to the Psychopathic Ward at Bellevue Hospital for observation in 1951, he was questioned by the psychiatrist and a social worker concerning his occupation. He stated, truthfully, that he had composed, published, or recorded over 100 songs. "Delusions of grandeur and a detatchment from reality" was the medical finding by those who had not taken the trouble to find out who the patient was . . .

The treatments inflicted on him were aimed at curing this psychiatric disorder. I shudder to think of it . . .

Walter Davis, talking about the composition of "Glass Enclosure," showed very well some of the secondary effects Bud felt after some earlier shock treatments. He had composed the piece at Creedmoor, but he worked on it again with Walter at home in Willow Grove. Walter knew the piece well because Bud would ask him to play it, just to hear how it sounded by somebody else. Bud had been out of the hospital for some time and was very worried about his persistent memory loss. When he arrived at the Blue Note studio for the session he had practically forgotten the composition. The version we know from this record (an admirable one at that) has nothing in common, according to Walter, with the original version. Also concerning this piece, Max Cohen has this to say:

> . . . Bud could not recollect his music or even identify his music when performed. One of his best known compositions, a jazz classic, is the "Glass Enclosure." When it was suggested to Bud that "Glass Enclosure" could be developed into a jazz piano concerto, to be commissioned by Dizzy Gillespie, he was noncommital because he could not remember the composition and would have to hear it played back to him . . .

This brief testimony, taken at random from among a host of similar ones, shows us a little more of the ravages caused by these brutal treatments, ill-advised and perhaps even ill-willed, on one of the most brilliant minds of our time. America is certainly not the only country guilty of such mistreatment. One need only think of the tragic lives of Van Gogh, Antonin Artaud, or Maurice Utrillo, to see that France hardly did any better. We know their stories because they are famous today. But how many other rebellious spirits or brilliant minds may have been arbitrarily crushed in this way?

I will simply add this statement by Bud's childhood friend, Freddie Jones:

> Bud had superior intelligence. He was someone who was always brilliant, active, lively, with a quick mind and always so very creative. Then one day I heard that he had been busted, and then hospitalized in one of those horrible places where people just disappear . . .
>
> When I knew Bud as we were growing up, he was a very outgoing and outspoken cat. He never bit his tongue. He said what he had to say, and after the shock treatments Bud was just not the same Bud that I knew. In fact, he wasn't the Bud Powell that I liked anymore. I can't emphasize enough the destruction that this society did to my friend Bud. . . . There are so many things that are done to stifle jazz musicians here . . .

This old friend, now a dignified middle-aged man, sobbed as he recalled this terrible memory. His pain was heartbreaking to see.

During his stay at Kings County Hospital, Bud was visited every day by Frances, Celia, Margareta, and his faithful friend, Jackie McLean. All of them expected Bud to pull through. They thought he would surprise everyone with another of his miraculous recoveries.

As for me, I looked forward to better news and drowned my anxiety in work, stopping my professional occupations only for brief and melancholy incursions at the piano, trying to communicate in some way with him. One evening, after putting the finishing touches on a drawing, I resigned myself to going to bed, my mind tormented by a raft of conflicting thoughts, and finally fell into a restless sleep. I woke with a start and a strange sensation of not having really slept. It was 3:30 A.M. and I was overcome with anguish. Finally, I got out of bed and paced mindlessly around the apartment, like a zombie, chain-smoking cigarettes and trying to calm down. The anxiety wouldn't subside. After finishing all my cigarettes and then the butts in the ashtrays, I forced myself to go back to bed. I dozed off into a troubled sleep filled with disordered, incoherent images, until finally I was awakened by a faint but distinctive sound.

My bedroom door faced the front door of the apartment where I had installed a large letter box big enough to hold the oversized envelopes sent to me by my employers. The little sound that woke me up was unmistakable: the edge of an envelope hitting the bottom of a mailbox. The lightest of sounds, just the weight of a telegram, but what a load of woe it carried! I leapt out of bed, crossed the hallway and opened the letter box. In the semi-darkness I could make out the faded blue rectangle of a telegram. I tore it open with trembling hands and read the words my mind refused to grasp:

New York, July 31, 1966:

Bud is no longer with us. He died at 9:40 this evening.

Margareta.

With the time difference, the hour of Bud's death corresponded to 3:40 A.M. in Paris, the exact time of my startled awakening. A wave of dizziness made me stumble and I felt nauseated. My soul emptied, I was numb. And all at once, closing my tear-filled eyes, I saw, like a freeze-frame in a brutally interrupted film, Bud's face, lit by a strange and enigmatic smile.

A part of myself had died with him.

ETERNITY

I never knew the joy of laughter
Even after you were gone.
I never knew a more politeful smile,
And after a while,
Your kiss!
I never knew the joy of living
After giving you my love,
You went away, didn't say goodbye to me.
What is to be will be.
Strange enough, I found someone that just filled a space,
Somewhere, somehow, "yes".
It should never have been like it was for me,
What the hell do I care now, let's face it.
I'm not the one to be belated,
I'm ill fated.
You will see,
Even if we never embrace again,
There is know* end.
So long.

Kings County Hospital July 24, 1966
Unpublished text
kindly provided by Mrs. Frances Barnes

*[sic]

CODA

There are a million things I could say. But one thing, a hell of a lot more should have been said and done for him when he was alive. He was the most comprehensive compositional talent of any jazz player I have ever heard presented on the jazz scene. He had the potential of a true jazz player. He expanded much in a legitimate, organic way. Because of his history, he never got to use that potential that much, though he did plenty. His insight and talent were unmatched in hardcore, true jazz.

Bill Evans
Tribute to Bud Powell
from *Down Beat*
September 22, 1966

Other titles of interest

Available at your bookstore

OR ORDER DIRECTLY FROM

DA CAPO PRESS

1-800-321-0050